CLINICAL-COGNITIVE PSYCHOLOGY
Models and Integrations

CHAPTERS BY

LOUIS BREGER

GEORGE S. KLEIN

JANE LOEVINGER

MICHAEL SCRIVEN

DAVID SHAKOW

PETER H. WOLFF

ROBERT W. ZASLOW

PRENTICE-HALL, INC.

CLINICAL-COGNITIVE PSYCHOLOGY

Models and Integrations

Edited by

LOUIS BREGER

Langley Porter Clinic

Englewood Cliffs, New Jersey

PRENTICE-HALL SERIES IN CLINICAL PSYCHOLOGY
Richard A. Lazarus, Editor

13–137620–9

Library of Congress Catalog Card Number 70–85956

Printed in the United States of America

Current printing (last digit):

10   9   8   7   6   5   4   3   2   1

PRENTICE-HALL INTERNATIONAL, INC., *London*
PRENTICE-HALL OF AUSTRALIA, PTY. LTD., *Sydney*
PRENTICE-HALL OF CANADA, LTD., *Toronto*
PRENTICE-HALL OF INDIA PRIVATE LTD., *New Delhi*
PRENTICE-HALL OF JAPAN, INC., *Tokyo*

THE AUTHORS

LOUIS BREGER received his B.A. from UCLA and his M.A. and Ph.D. in 1961 from the Ohio State University. He has taught psychology at the University of Oregon where he was also Director of the University Psychology Clinic. At present he is on the staff of the Langley Porter Neuropsychiatric Institute and is Associate Professor at the University of California Medical School in San Francisco.

GEORGE S. KLEIN received his Ph.D. from Columbia University in 1942 and is a graduate of the New York Psychoanalytic Institute. He has been on the staff of the Menninger Foundation and the Department of Social Relations at Harvard University. He is, at present, Professor of Psychology and Codirector of the Research Center for Mental Health of New York University. Professor Klein also holds a Research Career award from the National Institute of Mental Health.

JANE LOEVINGER took both B.A. and M.S. degrees in Psychometrics at the University of Minnesota and then a Ph. D. in Psychology from the University of California, Berkeley, receiving the latter in 1944. She has taught at the University of California in Berkeley, Stanford University, and the University of Colorado. At present she holds a Research Scientist Award from the National Institute of Mental Health and is Research Associate in the Social Science Institute and Research Associate Professor in the Graduate Institute of Education at Washington University.

MICHAEL SCRIVEN graduated from the Honors School of Mathematics in Melbourne, Australia, and then took his Ph.D. in Philosophy at Oxford University. He has taught at the Universities of Minnesota and Indiana and been a Fellow at the Center for the Advanced Study in the Behavioral Sciences. He is on the editorial board of the *International Journal of*

Psychiatry and *Contemporary Psychology*, and is currently Professor of Philosophy at the University of California, Berkeley.

DAVID SHAKOW did both undergraduate and graduate work at Harvard University, receiving his Ph.D. in Psychology in 1942. He has been Chief Psychologist and Director of Research, Worcester State Hospital; Professor of Psychology at the University of Illinois College of Medicine and the University of Chicago; and Chief, Laboratory of Psychology, National Institute of Mental Health. At present he is Senior Research Psychologist, National Institute of Mental Health.

PETER H. WOLFF graduated from the Medical School of the University of Chicago in 1950. He took his psychiatric residency training, with concommitant neurophysiological research, at the Yale University School of Medicine and the Austin Riggs Center. At present he is Assistant Professor of Psychiatry at the Harvard Medical School, Director of Psychiatric Research at the Children's Hospital Medical Center, and Research Associate at the Boston Lying-In Hospital. He is also on the staff of the Judge Baker Guidance Center, and an instructor at the Boston Psychoanalytic Institute, of which he is a graduate. Dr. Wolff holds a Career Development Award from the National Institute of Mental Health.

ROBERT W. ZASLOW did his undergraduate work at UCLA and received his M.A. and then his Ph.D. in Psychology in 1957 from the University of California, Berkeley. He has taught at Western Washington College, the University of Oregon Medical School, and is, at present, Associate Professor of Psychology at San Jose State College.

CONTENTS

Introduction   1

I. THE LEGACY OF THE PAST: A CRITICAL ANALYSIS

1. Psychology without a Paradigm   9
   Michael Scriven

2. The Ideology of Behaviorism   25
   Louis Breger

3. Psychoanalysis and American Psychology   56
   David Shakow

II. VIEWS TOWARD THE FUTURE: AN INTEGRATED CLINICAL-COGNITIVE PSYCHOLOGY

4. Theories of Ego Development   83
   Jane Loevinger

5. Freud's Two Theories of Sexuality   136
   George S. Klein

6. Dream Function: An Information Processing Model   182
   Louis Breger

7. Piaget's Sensori motor Theory of Intelligence and
   General Development Psychology   228
   Peter H. Wolff

8. A Theory and Treatment of Autism   246
   Robert W. Zaslow and *Louis Breger*

Index   293

CLINICAL-COGNITIVE PSYCHOLOGY
Models and Integrations

Introduction

I suspect that many in psychology share my feeling that the field is not quite what it should be, that it never quite turned out the way we hoped it would when we entered as students. Such a feeling of disappointment may be the inevitable disillusionment of youth following contact with the world of hard reality and, no doubt, this accounts for part of it. But more seems involved here: there is a substantial core of conflict built into the field and it is this which may lie at the root of our dissatisfaction.

This core of conflict is a complicated matter stemming from a variety of sources including the commitment of much of academic psychology to the pursuit of what it takes to be pure science—a commitment that leaves little room for the subject matter of the clinical psychologist. In addition, the most important set of observations and ideas relevant to clinical psychology—those originating with Freud and continuing in the work of the psychoanalysts, neo-Freudians, and ego-psychologists—are separated from psychology and suspect on "scientific" grounds. Psychoanalysis, for its part, suffers from fractionation into schools, isolation from the mainstream of social science, and an untenable alliance with medicine. Its most orthodox groups have developed a sort of theoretical ethnocentrism which makes communication difficult indeed.

Thus, the student drawn to clinical psychology by his interest in the subject matter finds himself caught between an academic tradition which questions the validity of this very subject matter and a set of very foreign-appearing theories and practices. These are, no doubt, only some of the forces contributing to the conflict. It is clear that conflict exists, however, and being human, workers in the field attempt to resolve it in various ways. Some abandon psychology and embrace existentialism or devote themselves purely to the practice of psychotherapy affiliated with some one or another of the various analytic, neo-analytic, or anti-analytic schools. At the other extreme are those who identify with traditional academic psychology and who would make clinical psychology over in the image of behaviorism. This is a particularly dangerous trend, in my view, because behavioristically dominated psychology seems such a grand mistake in its own right. Attempts to apply it as a model run the risk of reducing clinical subject matter to the human equivalent of rats in mazes. Both extremes seem unsatisfactory, the one because it gives up much that is valuable in psychology and the other because it abandons meaningful subject matter.

Recent developments point a way out of this dilemma. The re-emergence of cognitive psychology indicates that a meaningful integration of clinical and general psychology is now possible, an integration that preserves clinical subject matter while introducing valuable ideas, findings, models, and methods from the cognitive area. As long as behaviorism held sway, such an integration was doomed to conflict since the behaviorist paradigm declared both the methods (for example, psychotherapy) and much of the data (for example, thoughts, affects, and fantasies) of the clinical psychologist to be scientifically unacceptable. Cognitive psychology differs from behaviorism in two primary respects which point toward a meaningful integration. First, workers in this tradition have been open to a variety of methods; naturalistic observation, case and field study have been given status along with more controlled experimental work. Second, as the term cognitive implies, this is a tradition which places men's ability to symbolize in a prime position, thus allowing a central place for the data which make up such a large part of clinical subject matter.

These developments within psychology are supported by the work of Polanyi, Bronowski, Kuhn, Toulmin, and others in the history and philosophy of science. Their work shows that the positivist doctrines that academic psychology has typically assumed to characterize science do not fit the actual practices of most scientists. In addition, the view of science developed by these writers stresses its cognitive aspect, in the sense that the term is used in this volume (that is, Kuhn's concept of paradigm determined perception or Polanyi's "tacit knowing").

A synthesis of clinical and general psychology thus becomes more meaningful and likely as general psychology becomes more cognitive. Cognitive psychology refers to a loose grouping of approaches which give a central place to man's symbolic capacities, which stress adaptation, the functionality and goal-directedness of thought and action, and which emphasize human-environment interaction. Psychologists in this group would include Dewey and James; experimentalists such as Lashley, Tolman, and Hebb; neuropsychologists such as Luria; the ethologists; developmental psychologists such as Werner and Piaget; contemporary workers in cognition such as Bruner; and modern linguists like Chomsky. The kind of psychology represented by these workers has come into its own within recent years. American psychology has rediscovered the mind; it now looks more to William James than to John B. Watson. While behaviorism is by no means completely dead—its methodological strictures still exert a great influence—it is dying. Its substantive contribution amounts to little. The fervor of the radical behaviorists—of Skinner and his followers—is the clamor of a fundamentalist sect which senses that the world has passed them by in some way they cannot understand and who react by attempting to reaffirm traditional values in ever more extreme form.

It is the purpose of this book to explore the prospects for a clinical-cognitive integration. The chapters in Part II present selected attempts at applying cognitive ideas to traditionally clinical subject matter such as ego development, dreams, and the treatment of psychological disturbance. These chapters represent some of the possible substantive contributions of a clinical-cognitive synthesis, a synthesis in which seemingly settled issues are looked at afresh, old problems are redefined, and new models and methods suggested.

Because of certain features in psychology's history, the concept of integration itself may be easily misconstrued. Thus, before attempting a synthesis, it will be necessary to examine certain historical factors including the central assumptions of the behaviorist paradigm, the relationship of general psychology to Freud's contributions (which form the theoretical backbone of much of clinical psychology), and the very nature of theoretical commitments in psychology and social science. The three chapters by Scriven, Shakow and myself, which comprise Part I, attempt to do this.

While behaviorism is losing its dominant hold in psychology, there are many respects in which the assumptions of the behaviorist paradigm, embodied in what I will call the ideology of behaviorism, continue to exert a powerful and negative influence on the field. These assumptions include certain very definite ideas concerning the "application" theory. It is the misleading effects of these assumptions which must be clarified before attempting an integration. The behaviorist paradigm assumes that principles from general psychology may be applied to areas such as clinical, social or educational; that experimental psychology is the basic science which will supply the laws to these areas much as the physical sciences presumably do for engineering or the biological sciences for medicine. This is one of those background beliefs in psychology that stands largely unquestioned. It is manifested in the many textbooks which begin with a review of general principles—say, of learning—and then attempt, with quite variable success, to treat other areas in terms of such principles. It is a central assumption of those who would make clinical psychology over in the image of a behavioristic science. The problems with such assumptions are numerous. Perhaps most damaging is the minimal success of the traditional experimental psychology program itself. While success in this sense is a difficult matter to assess, it seems fair to say that those parts of experimental psychology which rely most heavily on the "basic science" argument still have a largely programmatic air about them; their achievements lie in the hoped-for future and not in the demonstrable past or present. Next, there is the attempt to support this view by drawing on analogies with other fields. While it is possible to draw parallels with the physical science-engineering model, there is also a good deal of evidence from the history of science to suggest quite a different view of the relationship between basic and technological or applied areas, a view which stresses the essential interdependence and inseparability of basic and applied pursuits, particularly during the early stages of scientific development. It is also questionable if the contemporary relationship between science and engineering or biology and medicine is in fact the way many psychologists picture it.

These issues are treated in greater detail by Scriven, who presents a rather convincing case against the search for laws or principles modeled after physical science. He further suggests that psychology give up its pretensions at being a grand paradigmatic science and, rather, let its efforts be determined by an attention to useful problems and practical advantages. His conclusion—that the restrictiveness of paradigmatic theories be abandoned—converges with the conclusion of Chapter 2, that relevant human subject matter replace methodological propriety as the criterion of valuable work in psychology. This does not mean that all theorizing be abandoned nor that we return to some form of blind empiricism. What is being suggested is that important subject matter define the focus of interest and that we approach this subject matter with whatever theory, ideas, models, common-sense notions, and methods that can be mustered.

In clinical psychology the central set of observations and theory are those which stem from Freud. But again, certain historical developments, in both psychoanalysis and psychology, must be clarified before attempting to integrate psychoanalytic ideas with cognitive psychology. Nowhere is the conflict in psychology more salient than in the collision between psychoanalysis and academic psychology. The paradigmatic restrictions of behaviorism have in large part prevented psychology from coming to grips with Freud—his observations, theories and methods. Freud's achievement was, of course, of such proportions that it flourished and grew independently, much to the detriment of academic psychology. At the same time, psychoanalysis was deprived of what could have been a useful influence from a scientifically oriented psychology. Without such an influence, psychoanalysis has remained a narrow method while undergoing tremendous elaboration as a theory. At its worst, this becomes another form of paradigmatic grandiosity, of theory building in that rarified air removed from the world of observations.

Shakow traces the complicated course of this relationship. He shows how psychology's reaction to Freud was and is a mixture of misunderstanding, rejection on methodological grounds, and large scale, surreptitious importation. Such importation was necessary, of course, because psychologists were interested in talking about meaningful human subject matter and the failure of behaviorism to address such subject matter gave them few other ways of doing so. Shakow's discussion of the role of the *Zeitgeist* in determining the reaction of psychology to Freud parallels the discussion of ideological and paradigmatic influences outlined in Chapters 1 and 2. He concludes with the important reminder that Freud's contributions belong, not to any organized group, but to mankind. It is up to psychology, as the discipline most directly involved, to make use of this rich set of observations and ideas. In a very important sense, psychoanalysis and psychology need each other. Breaking free of ideological and paradigmatic restraints on both sides allows an integration in which the best in both traditions may be brought together.

It is my hope that the issues dealt with in Part I will contribute to a feeling of freedom, a freedom for psychology in confronting its subject matter. We should now be able to accept what is valuable in the behaviorist tradition—the empirical emphasis, the concern for objectivity, and the examination of the defining characteristics of concepts—without being so constricted by these considerations that meaningful subject matter is avoided. By recognizing that a scientific approach is not synonymous with the highly controlled laboratory experiment nor with the banishment of mind, we are free to recognize the value of a variety of ideas and methods, including naturalistic observation and introspection. In addition, we may make use of the rich body of ideas contributed by Freud and his followers in a way that does them justice. We may, in short, investigate meaningful subject matter—complex human functioning in a complex environment—with a variety of appropriate methods and with adequate conceptual tools.

The Legacy of the Past: 1
A Critical Analysis

1. Psychology Without a Paradigm

Michael Scriven

1. I begin by stating some views, in prejudicial terms, about schools of thought in human psychology, and I shall then consider whether they are *mere* prejudices. The reader will thus be able to decide in short order whether he can stomach the approach at all and if so, what to skip and where to stop.

We may think of the different approaches to psychology as courses adopted by mariners attempting the difficult passage to the rumored new continent of Psychological Science. Introspectionist psychology charted a straight course and foundered on the reef of subjectivity.[1] Behaviorist psychology took a more devious course to avoid the big reef, observed some interesting new shores, but found the Sargasso Sea and there still stirs in the turgid wastes of triviality. Psychoanalysis steered between the other two, also caught glimpses of promising coasts, yet now finds itself caught in the verbal whirlpool of endless redescription. Neurophysiological psychology simply caught the wind and went off at great speed in another direction—but nonetheless made some interesting landfalls. The same is true of invertebrate psychology and most comparative psychology, excepting some primatology—interesting in their own right, but limited as approaches to the great topic of psychology: human behavior. I think a better course can be charted, one that bypasses these hazards; and though it will not guarantee arrival at the land of the legends, that is only because no such land exists. Instead, however, there is an archipelago, a cluster of islands—some small, some large—which together constitute the territory of useful psychology.

[1]However, a lifeboat was eventually lowered and has succeeded in crossing the reef and making land. It represents the valuable parts of phenomenological psychology; see, for example, Wann (1964). The contribution thereto by the present author expands on some points made here, though it presents a less radical view.

2. Neurophysiology and psychopharmacology have achieved some re-markable successes, obviously with more to come, but they are simply not molar (or macro-)[2] sciences of human behavior as psychology for the most part must be. They are physics to its chemistry, not answers to its prob-lems. The defining feature of human psychology—the greater part of it—is that the questions are stated and the answers required in the language of molar or macro-behavior. Sometimes this requirement can be proved incompatible with useful results, but in general not. Psychology's value is both intellectual and social, but if merely intellectual, it is ignoring its social obligations and someone else will have to tackle these chores. The social obligations are the primary problems of psychology, for whatever route we take to them, there will arise plenty of intellectually stimulating problems, whereas the reverse is not the case.

In general, we want to know such things as what study plans or presen-tations are best for learning or teaching various materials and skills, what tests will best predict a student pilot's performance, which small groups stand up to strong stress and how, why children plan and marriages fail and martyrs suffer and nations fight, when suicide threats are serious and what to do about them. And we usually prefer macro-answers to these questions, if we can get them. *Usually* this means a macro-theory will be the best approach. There are certainly important exceptions, however. For example, we might be able to show that certain pathologies (paresis or schizophrenia) are essentially micro-caused and the micro-cause lacks reliable macro-indicators. In such cases, the macro-hunt must be called off, and we hope that, as in this case, the micro-theory will prove practi-cally useful. Even where some micro-cause is the crucial factor, it may be that macro-precipitators are also important (for example, sexual inter-course or parental use of withdrawal of love as a punishment, in the examples given) and a hybrid approach is required and useful. Again, we may be able to show that ataractic drugs control anxiety or violence better than any environmental variables; but the great importance of such re-sults provides no grounds for supposing that *all* psychotherapy can be replaced with drug therapy. For much successful verbal therapy is simply the giving of good practical advice, or the provision of another's affective support, or the discussion of philosophical and moral issues or of per-sonal hang-ups, and no drug does that. Reduction of anxiety may make people philosophical, but it doesn't make them philosophers. They need wisdom and knowledge to make good choices, not just the capacity to

[2]The practice in psychology has been to use the terms molar and molecular for the two approaches, one of which treats the whole human as the basic indivisible entity, the other treating the human as a compound whose behavior can best be explained in terms of its components. The more usual and more easily generalizable terminology in the philosophy of science would refer to these as macro- and micro-approaches to human behavior.

endure the consequences of bad choices. The micro-approach can't do it all, though of course science requires that any macro-theory must have a micro-equivalent which explains why it works. The point here is only that the theory which does that job is typically very poorly suited for the explanation-prediction-description-control tasks we need done at the macro-level. There *is* certainly a neural account of classroom role-playing, but it is virtually certain to be totally unilluminating to the educational psychologist or practitioner. There is certainly a particle and field theory account of the changes in form of terrestrial organisms, but it takes the macro-theory of evolution to make sense of it. We must not assume that the ontological and perhaps epistemological ultimacy of the micro-entities engenders any methodological or cognitive utility for them in the macro-study.

3. The human, or the human group, constitutes a system whose gross features immediately imply important methodological conclusions. (By and large, the same is true of the non-human organisms down to the bacterium; phages and viruses are somewhat different, that is, significantly simpler.) Humans interact with their environment, including other humans, in a way that virtually precludes any simple relationships between the macro-variables of interest to us.

Remember the basic methodological fact that whereas the behavior of two point-masses in empty space can be mathematically determined, if they are affected only by each other and in that respect only by the simple inverse-square law of gravitation, the behavior of even three such idealized "bodies" is in general incalculable. Mathematical physics, despite its difficulty, its sophistication, and its successes, has *extremely limited* powers. It works quite well for the problems of planetary motion only because the planets are (1) separated by distances which are vast, compared to their diameter, from each other and the sun; (2) separated by incomparably greater distances from everything else; (3) approximately spherical; (4) approximately radially homogeneous; (5) the gravitational law is extremely simple; (6) the sun's mass is much greater than the planets; (7) the planets move in roughly the same plane; *and* because the questions we want answered are comparatively crude. Even then, Newton couldn't handle mutations (which he ascribed to angels), and no one could handle Mercury without the earthquake shock of relativity theory. Start talking about micro-masses instead of large ones and our brains have to boggle over quantum theory as well as relativity, and we have to give up any hope of exact solutions to many significant problems. Introduce typical realistic considerations such as irreversible flow or degenerative processes like elastic fatigue and corrosion, and physics loses almost all predictive utility; only engineering remains, and engineering is the art of the possible, not the science of nature.

Now consider how many independent variables have already been shown to affect human behavior in observable and important respects, and in ways which have already been shown not to obey simple laws. Now think of the unsolvable three-body problem. It is patently absurd to act as though a Newtonian synthesis is possible in the behavioral sciences or in any large sub-area of them. It is a sign of stupidity, not of heroism, to seek it.

4. Might there not be some complex concepts, each involving many of these variables, which are connected by simple laws? It is indeed *possible*, about as possible as that we will find elementary proofs of the four-color theorem or simple deterministic substitutes for quantum theory. This is exactly what everybody is feeling for when trying to develop new conceptual schemes. All you need to justify spending further time on such searches is some reason for supposing you are better equipped for such a discovery than your ten thousand predecessors, or some reason for thinking the search is a kind of lottery. It is not a lottery but a highly systematic (though not always a conscious) process, and the intellectual qualifications that would be exceptional by an appropriate order of magnitude are rarely in evidence, only a lemming-like commitment to a wildly irrelevant paradigm.

5. To a considerable extent, the preceding condemnation applies to the behaviorist movement, not because of the behaviorist doctrine itself but because it has generally accepted the ideal of an axiomatic theory of vast scope, a mathematical model, whether for learning or for perceiving or maturing. The behaviorist element varies in intensity, and correspondingly in worth, from a conceptual analysis such as (1) that psychology should be a molar not a molecular science of human behavior (as discussed above), to indefensible methodology such as (2) that interjudge reliability is (a) essential for scientific data and (b) excludes introspection, on to (3) the ontological fantasy of the empty organism. The methodological fact of the matter is that the requirement of interjudge reliability neither excludes the utility of introspection nor is essential for objectivity (think of validating REM criteria for dreams or of research on the hypnotic induction of anaesthesia). Historically, however, one may concede that the fanatical forms of behaviorism fueled some fruitful voyages of early psychology. Perhaps the fanaticism was psychologically required to get the ship moving, though it seems unfortunate that revolutionaries in psychology should have to believe falsehoods in order to make progress even if this is the usual pattern in politics, athletics, and even physics. Not only behaviorists, however, but some of the clinicians have suffered from the megalomania of monolithic theorizing. The early Freud, for example, shows signs of such hopes, at least for much of human behavior. Perhaps, that long ago, it was still appropriate to try once more. It is obviously no longer defensible.

6. The Newtonian fallacy has two bad effects, or one with two faces. The first is the general failure to aim for and achieve modest but useful theories, with all the gains they would yield. The second is the direct cost in time and resources involved in, for example, scholastic nit-picking about the behavior of rats in mazes (the fractional anticipatory goal-response debate, for example). Research is worthwhile if it has a reasonable chance of yielding results that are valuable *either* for theoretical *or* for practical reasons. The rat work stands or falls on its contribution to a theoretically important learning theory and thus has fallen, though it often acts as if it didn't know it had. Its role in this respect has been taken over by work on the mollusca, anthropods, planaria, fish, and primates, to mention the chief current areas. There is great significance in this diversity and much more promise about the work. But its effects on human psychology remain to be seen; it is highly likely it will affect human neurophysiology more directly than psychology. There is no need to repeat the excellent critical analyses of Hullian, neo-Hullian, and even statistical learning theories (Koch, 1954 and 1959; Deutsch, 1960), but perhaps we should add, in memoriam, that negative knowledge is also knowledge and in this sense we learnt something from it. At least, the psychoanalytical tradition retained its connection with therapeutic, prophylactic, and educational problems and in spite of its theoretical and evidential deficiences has probably made some contribution to these independently (that is, non-theoretically) valuable areas.

It seems possible that some psychological motive other than the desire for understanding is involved in the behaviorist theoretician's exclusive concern with what he sees as pure research and his distaste for basing one's work on data from socially useful problem areas. Perhaps he feels, possibly unconsciously, that it is best not to get involved in an area where one's non-scientific values may come to influence one's interpretations or energy outlay. It may even be that he feels the need to demonstrate his devotion to the search for Truth Untrammeled, by spurning work with any other pay-off. Whatever the reasons or causes for this behavior, it is pretty hard to avoid the impression that academic psychology would have a great deal more to show for its last fifty years, and might well have better theories to show, if it had not allowed the theoretician's work to drift so far from the practical problems. Suppose that, in learning research, work had been restricted to humans and hawks, to crows, cows and horses, each learning skills and information they normally need or which we would like them to have. What losses would psychology have suffered? It is clear where gains might have been made. Instead, the present situation appears to be that most animal trainers and many classroom teachers can out-train or out-teach most experimental psychologists: we haven't even mined the surface ore.

7. I do not think that this view is simply being wise after the event or

overweighting practical pay-off. I think that even the theory-oriented reasoning behind the move to the supposedly simpler organisms was faulty. It was thought that this move corresponded to Galileo's move from studying falling bodies to studying balls rolling down an inclined plane when he could not handle the technical problems of measuring free-fall times and distances. But Galileo had a highly plausible proof of the equivalence of the results. In general, the move to the simpler entity or situation is justifiable *only* if we can show how to get back from any results there to our original problem area *or* if we have exhausted all direct approaches. In view of what we knew and did not know about inter-taxa transferability of results, the first alternative did not apply, and the second is clearly false. There is always room for a little blue-sky exploring, on flatworms or fourfooted beasts, and this has sometimes paid off handsomely. But as the standard approach, it was and is indefensible, especially when coupled to the negligible work on great areas of immense theoretical and practical interest—for example, autoanaesthesia, rapid reading, kindergarten typing, psychotherapy, industrial psychology, empirical studies of sexual behavior which were left to an entomologist, memory training, or placebo studies. Only America could afford it, but even America can't afford it.

8. Nor is this pessimistic view of the prospect of a Newtonian theory a doctrine of despair born of temporary failure. There is the strong plausibility argument above in its favor and another from the history of science. It is often argued that psychology is a relatively young subject, and it would be unreasonable to expect the Newtonian synthesis so early in its development. But in fact, it is an extremely old subject in the sense of a serious study of human behavior, with Herodotus and Aristotle deeply involved in it. What is new is the apparatus of science—verbal and otherwise—and quantitative results. Even these refinements have not significantly altered the kinds of knowledge that typify psychology, the loose organization, the tendency statements, the wealth of idiographic detail, the explanations outshining the predictions, the low level of generality and abstraction of the successful theories. They *have* greatly increased our factual resources. In some of the physical sciences, simplicity emerged from the application of quantitative techniques, but only for a while and in certain areas.[3] In psychology, it was pretty clear this would not happen and it did not. So what do we do now?

9. It is worth looking carefully at clinical psychology because it has stuck closest to its clear task and has attracted enough good men to suggest that it has probably developed at least many of the possible useful

[3]Mathematical physics is still, of course, immensely valuable even if not simple. But its value exists only because of the frequency with which configurations recur (for example, fundamental particles) whose complete set of behaviorally relevant properties is relatively small, can be specified to a useful degree of accuracy, and is covered by relatively simple, albeit statistical, laws.

systematizations. In this volume, there are a number of essays that either suggest that clinical psychology should be a model for new approaches to psychology in general, or that embody an approach that we might consider as enshrining a model, intended or not. It has sometimes been suggested that clinical psychology provides a model for, or should model itself on, the paradigm of an *observational science*, behaviorism being the counterpart for *experimental science*. I do not think such an extreme opposition can be defended in detail, for there are behaviorists in ethology and clinicians using control groups or intuitive self-controls. Indeed, I suspect that if the distinction did exist or were insisted on, there would be too little left of clinical psychology to constitute a defensible paradigm. Certainly there would still be a practical methodology for clinical psychology; we could still teach interns how to apply the Revised Standard Nomenclature, administer TATs, and so on. But even that could not be done as well, since the use of tests is often a form of experimentation and manipulation; moreover, the original development of a good nosology is much benefited by extensive experimentation, at the very least on interjudge and test-retest reliability.

10. It is sometimes claimed, on the other hand, that psychoanalysis is itself an experimental scientific method of investigation. A milder version of this view is the kind of background *Zeitgeist* of many clinical psychologists who think of the psychotherapeutic interaction as their basic research tool, one whose product is valuable introspections or self-perceptions by the patient/client/subject. The opposition regards this approach as almost classically unscientific in its use of an instrument which cannot be independently validated. This conflict is by now a charade but so important in practice that we shall rehearse it briefly.

It is just as obvious that there are significant risks in the acceptance of introspection as that there is significant value in its use. The suggestion that the real data is the verbal behavior of the patient is the behaviorist's way of putting the latter point, but by itself it doesn't disbar inference from this data to the perceptions and feelings of the patient. The real data about the surface conditions on Venus are instrument readings at the moment, and the instruments have only been calibrated under non-Venusian conditions; but it is quite reasonable to make cautious inferences from them. Similarly, interpersonal differences do not make the use of another's introspection wholly unreliable. It is noticeable that in REM research, as in Hull's work on hypnosis, behaviorists have no hesitation about the *cautious* use of introspective reports. Hence, we must locate the real objection to its use in clinical psychology in a combination of sensitivity to its possibly low reliability there and, perhaps, some anti-psychoanalytical prejudices. We can admit the first possibility without abandoning the use of introspection, so let's admit it.

Special grounds for suspicion about *any* use of introspection include the commitment to the empty organism (which begs the question) and the methodological counterpart of the philosophical problem of other minds—the impossibility of direct check. The latter is not a crucial objection despite the existence of some monumental examples of erroneous inferences from introspection, for example, Freud's patients' fantasized traumas. On the contrary, it is just because such inferences refer to the occurrence of external events that they provide one way of checking on the reliability of introspection. For introspection about pictures of the past—that is, memory—is surely not wholly different from introspection about pictures of the present—for example, perceived hostility in peers. And as Freud pointed out, whether the believed event existed or not, that the belief did is virtually certain and may be of greater psychological significance. How can we be sure that the belief exists? By triangulation in evidential space, from baseline estimates of mendacity and self-deception drawn in territory where direct check is possible. This answer also handles the other minds problem (Scriven, 1966).

Returning from this skirmish over the legitimacy of using introspection, there is still the problem of whether to classify it as experimental or as observational. The issue is not simply semantic, since considerable ideological baggage is attached to the alternative conceptions. (At least, it's a very *deep* semantic issue and hence a perceptual and hence a cognitive one.) Now the pure experimental approach is one where the values of the independent variables are entirely under the control of the experimenter—tests on a new vaccine, for example. The pure observational approach, although it often proceeds from a background of experimental checks on the instruments, uses them to analyze a naturally or spontaneously occurring phenomenon—one thinks here of the astronomer, geologist, or ecologist. It surely follows that the diagnostic interview or typical psychotherapeutic session is hybrid in character, for the clinician manipulates some of the environmental variables (for example, by asking questions or suggesting dream recall) but often cannot or does not control certain crucial variables such as spouse hostility, workload, general affectual level, self-interpretations, and so on. It may be best to regard this not so much as a hybrid but as a third mode, the *investigatory mode*, for it has analogies in electronic trouble-shooting, chemical analysis, and other fields.

So (1) no defensible methodological rules are broken by the use of introspection, (2) the clinical interview or therapy session is properly classified as investigatory, involving some experimental and some observational features, (3) clinical psychology as a discipline does and should involve some purely experimental and some purely observational research, depending on the problem (and some problems will require extensive research of both kinds *and* of the investigatory kind), (4) none of the foregoing legitimates the typical psychoanalytic fantasies put forward as interpretations of introspected material and which have approximately the same foundation as phrenological interpretation of skullshape or naïve theistic interpretation of personal religious experiences.

11. So there is or can be an experimentally backed clinical psychology which constitutes a powerful science of behavior, although it does not accord closely with the usual conception of a paradigm. It may be misleading to argue that a good, healthy, active science must be operating on or be in the process of developing *a* paradigm. This claim is certainly misleading in Kuhn's sense of 'paradigm' and no clear alternative has been proposed, or is evident, which makes the suggestion satisfactory.

Consider an analogy. Scientists and philosophers have long debated the nature of scientific method. Various definitory suggestions have been made, for example, the hypothetico-deductive approach, the AAAS or Deweyan sequence. But many have thought it a Procrustean task to cram the many procedures of the many sciences into one formula or even one coherent sequence of steps or processes. Percy Bridgman expressed the point well by saying that the scientific method seemed to him to be simply "doing one's damndest with one's mind, no holds barred," although it might be argued this was an equally good description of a buffet dinner approach to the hallucinogenic drugs. Max Black's study of Claude Bernard led him to the conclusion that the only element worth identifying as essential to the scientific method is inveterate scepticism. Bridgman's and Black's suggestions are certainly anti-paradigmatic, partly because they are insufficiently content-specific to distinguish readily between, for example, science and Christian Science. Similarly, I believe it may be best to avoid the suggestion that there is a model or paradigm or ideal for a science or even for the scientific subdivision of clinical psychology. More is to be gained by using every kind of scientific approach that pays off, trying every paradigm on every sub-area of research (once or once in a while) but expecting that a new synthesis or alliance of several will emerge each time.

The paradigm approach itself is, in my view, often *contrary* to good scientific method unless it is modified to the point where the paradigms are treated as simply some of the repertoire of models, or perhaps meta-models. Any insistence that one of the traditional or exogenic paradigms must be generally appropriate to a topically defined area runs a high risk of being stultifying. An example of this is the idea of tics and phobias as symptoms of neurosis. This application of the medical model is so deeply ingrained that we actually see them as symptoms, in truly paradigm-dominated fashion. But the behavior therapists, driven by *their* paradigm, see these symptoms as the dysfunctional condition itself, not as symptoms at all. Whether they are right or wrong, the traditional psychotherapists' complaint that the behavior therapists are only treating the symptoms is suddenly seen as a completely contaminated judgment. The traditional data was actually an interpretation, and one needs more justification than is readily available. The paradigm had corrupted, or at least affected, our vision. We should not make demands on the *form* of knowledge structures—that is, theories and taxonomies—unless they are based on extremely well confirmed and area-validated models. It is quite otherwise with respect to *factuality*. We have now achieved considerable insight into the requirement of objectivity, and this is attainable by dream-content reports as well as PGR and EEG readings. This should be our basic demand, and from there we should develop explanatory or predictive or manipulative procedures according to our criterion task.

12. What about so-called evolutionary and ecological paradigms for psychology? People using this language are often simply stressing the need to consider the adaptiveness, the functionality of psychological phenomena such as what we usually think of as neurotic syndromes; or sometimes they are stressing the need for longitudinal study and for subject-environment interaction analysis. And they are implicitly recommending de-emphasis on behavioral genetics, neuropsychology, perhaps even depth psychology, S-R theory, and so on. Certainly it's an excellent idea to remember the possibility that a strong emphasis on environmental variables may be helpful, may regroup the elements of the phenomenon into a more readily grasped gestalt. But the same can be said, sometimes, and often simultaneously, about the opposite tendency. I think we must reject the straitjacket of thinking in terms of *the* paradigm for psychology, or for educational or learning psychology, or for psychobiology, or even just for theoretical models for schizophrenia.

13. Another picture that sometimes appeals to us in thinking about the nature of psychology is seeing it as a combination of physics and engineering. Then, learning theory corresponds to part of physics, and clinical or educational psychology becomes the domain of application of the physical principles, that is, the engineering domain. Probably this picture should not be called a paradigm, but it has been; and there is an important similarity to paradigms in the way it controls our thinking and even our perception, which makes it more than a theory as well as less than a decent theory. These conceptions of psychology are part of the ideology or metaphysics or metamethodology or *Zeitgeist* of the subject and have been extensively discussed, and often centrally located, in analyses of the determinants of scientific thinking (Burtt, 1954; Koyre, 1957; Butterfield, 1949; Boring, 1950, among others).

This particular picture, the pure-and-applied picture, has its uses but there are serious difficulties with it. If more psychologists coming in from other fields had a professional training as engineers and fewer as mathematicians or physicists, it is possible that less would be heard of this argument. Engineers are very sensitive about the popular view of, for example, space travel or artificial kidneys as contributions to progress by modern science. As they see it, science had virtually nothing to do with the matter—it was essentially an engineering feat. The pure-and-applied picture suggests that pure science is a cloud hovering above the ground from which flashes of lightning occasionally emanate, instantly illuminating and perhaps eliminating some trouble spot on the ground below. The engineer's picture has pure science as a cloud, all right, but simply the cloud that forms around the peaks of the mountain range of engineering practice. It is dull to point out that both pictures are exaggerations, but it is often necessary. As one reads book after book on educational psychology, for example, with at least some chapters devoted to applying the findings of academic psychology (for example, learning theory) to the practice of education, one discovers very little agreement as to how these findings apply, and in fact not very much as to what they are. There are plenty of difficulties about applying theoretical physics to real cases, too; it was half a century after the relativity theory emerged before there was general agreement on how to handle the clock paradox (the twin paradox). But axiomatizers and math model theorists in general tend to forget this, and it threatens their enterprise with the same kind of sterility that has affected much mathematical economics. It is, in my view, much better to move into theory exactly where and only when obliged to by the combination of data and needs that define our task. Speculation in the absence of a clarification of these parameters is too often merely idle, the kind of irresponsible gambling with society's resources that is lauded in cheap histories of science and was once a rich amateur's prerogative.

There are many areas of knowledge that, with respect to the modest but valuable role of a model or low-level theory, are paradigms for psychology—for example, the theory of differential equations, the play of contract bridge, and comparative anatomy. There are no abstract theories in these areas with the kind of range that Newton's theories of gravity and dynamics had in classical astrophysics, or that Maxwell's equations had in classical electromagnetism, *nor will there ever be such theories.* Enormous masses of data will have to be learned or stored accessibly, loose generalizations by the score will be employed extensively, but knowing their exceptions will be the distinguishing mark of the professional; and so on with the other properties of complicated fields. The opposite situation obtains in cosmology, for example, and an uncertain situation obtains in prime number theory and topology.[4]

4Much of the most interesting work on alternative methodologies for psychology has appeared in the guise of 'analytical philosophy of history,' since history is an obviously

14. Do any practical suggestions follow from this view of psychology? I have already mentioned the most important, including these: (1) the selection of problems for research should be much more closely guided by considerations of practical needs and advantages, (2) the search for theories should not be restricted by the single-paradigm demand, and (3) the tolerance for low-level approximations must be increased. But there are other parts of scientific methodology that become particularly relevant to psychology as I conceive it and that have been sadly neglected. The elaborate development of statistics and control-group methodology in psychology are examples of important and appropriate additions to the scientist's investigating tools, and the fact that they have been developed in psychology is implicitly informative about the nature of the subject. But there has not been a corresponding development in taxonomical theory, despite one or two interesting papers (for example, P. Meehl); nor in the closely related area of concept analysis and techniques of non-operational, non-formal definitions; nor in systematizing non-verbal methods of presenting and preserving data (for example, multi-phasic profiles); nor in systematizing methods of storing non-verbal data (for example, Paul Ekman's work on film records of the range of patients' expressions to which clinicians apply certain terms); nor systemization and exploitation of the many types of causal or explanatory claim that become very important in a sub-formal science, including those which are very far removed from predictions. It is certainly true that logicians and philosophers of science must share the responsibility here, since, unlike the mathematicians in the case of statistics, they have not generally seen the need for and created the prototypes for the new tools. But the blame is still largely on the paradigm fixation of the psychologists; for example, in the area of definition theory there have been for decades enough devastating criticisms of operational definition to banish it from every other field besides psychology. There it has remained, indeed flourished, in the fertile soil of positivism-behaviorism and in its shade more fruitful concepts have starved or wilted and died. There is insufficient space here to set out what has been done toward developing the alternatives needed; an excellent reference for much of the material is Abraham Kaplan (1964).

15. Why has psychology failed to explore the alternatives that did exist, in however primitive a form? Why has it failed to expel the discredited methodology of early positivism after it served its useful time? In the first place, because the lure of the Newtonian paradigm is so powerful, its promise of riches so immense. In the second place, because the alterna-

---

unformalized domain of knowledge in which well supported explanations appear to be common, though predictions and precise generalizations are extremely rare. See, for example, the anthologies edited by W. Dray (1967), S. Hook (1963), and P. Gardiner (1959).

tives were still too weak and unclear to make it worthwhile abandoning the ship for them, even if it was widely agreed that serious leaks were outgaining the pumps. Third, because of the tremendous conformism within the ideological sub-groups of academic psychology, which may be no greater than in other disciplines but might possibly be more culpable in the most self-referential science—the science for which the human activity of scientific investigation, and not merely its agent, is a proper subject. This conformism makes it very hard for one generation of grad-uate students to reject the ideology of their instructors except by moving to the shelter of a rival. The same situation makes it hard for people to believe that United States foreign policy is totally wrong, though they may migrate from a Democratic to a Republican view of it. Well, it may be a wrench, but it seems to me the time for the wrench has come; it is necessary to stay within the empirical tradition (long live mother-hood!) but radically to re-orient its thrust. The blunt weapons of early positivism-behaviorism made possible a breakthrough at one time but are now simply destructive.

Perhaps we can usefully conclude with consideration of two important contemporary positions that are well illustrated in this volume and which go beyond the long established approaches already discussed.

16. Dr. Jane Loevinger's essay on ego psychology in this volume is a characteristic, though especially good, example of what might be called the modernized concept juggling approach. With a remarkable breadth of vision, she attempts to sort out for us the competing and reinforcing strands in the history and present practice of ego psychology. I do not consider my inexpert judgment of her work to be very reliable, but I can indicate certain dangers in the approach, and I have to mention that I believe, without being certain that I am right, that she has fallen victim to them. It seems to me that there is still too much theory for the facts, too many conceptual schemes too soon. Her subtlety in discerning dis-cords within the compositions with which others have been playing is impressive, but can she demonstrate real inconsistency, or even great inconvenience in empirical applications? It is not clear to me that she can, though that may be due to my own limitations of background. But her criticisms may also be based on making conceptual vocabularies run before they can walk. It must be remembered that even in the simpler field of classical dynamics there was extraordinary difficulty in showing that the Galilean scheme was superior to the Aristotelian one. In the end, the decision was a cumulative and not a sharp one, but it is even more significant that it was based on an overall assessment of many cases in each of which the opposing formulations were rather clear—for example, the continued motion of an arrow after it left the bow, the absence of a perpetual hurricane due to the earth's rotation. I do not find this clarity

to be present in the alternative theories of ego psychology; there seems all too much room for readjustments within each theory—for example, on the relative importance of the consistency and socializability ego drives. Hence, each runs the risk of being merely a data free vocabulary and not a genuinely enlightening conceptual scheme which must have substantial empirical content. When Dr. Loevinger talks about meta-theories or ideologies of ego psychology, such as behaviorism and holism, the situation becomes even more elastic and although I should feel more at home with these philosophical concepts, I am uneasily aware of too many alternative paths through these jungles which would avoid the snares she sets. Surely, for example, she is not right in thinking that single-drive theories cannot really explain development? I think she is in business as a kind of conceptual marriage broker, pointing out incompatibilities here, suggesting reconciliation there, but relying very heavily on her own reading of the character of the concepts when it is very hard to objectify such judgments. And unless she can objectify these judgments, the marriages she arranges may be less successful than those she argues against. It is much to her credit that her own research work has been closely concerned with just this point. But I cannot help thinking we need much more like it before we can draw any definite conclusions about the superiority of any ego theory.

There are other methodological points about which I feel uneasy. For example, at one point she appears to be saying that theories using concepts of psychic energy are "in the wrong universe of discourse." Recall that the use of the concept of energy in *physics* is itself an anthropomorphic analogy which has worked as well as any scientific concept has ever worked. Why shouldn't another transposition of the concept also work?

Dr. Loevinger is clearly aware of the problems of experimental validation in her field, but I am not sure she is sufficiently sensitive to the problems of theoretical ambiguity. Certainly we disagree on one major methodological issue: "Theoretical paradigms are the essence of an abstract science and psychology is an abstract science or not a science at all"! Of course, I do not wish to support a "blind or near-sighted empiricism." I want understanding, insight, explanation, and *useful* knowledge. But I think it has to be built up from the ground with more secure framing than the theories or interpretations she takes as reasonably well founded. Let none of the preceding suggest that concept juggling can be wholly avoided or that I think she is doing it in the irresponsible way that characterizes the Joycean performances of many psychoanalytic theoreticians (for example, Rapaport 1959). I tentatively incline to think she is still a little too far from the ground.

17. Computer simulation, to take up the other innovatory article on which I wish to comment, seems to me a tremendously fertile, and already

the most significant, innovation in twentieth-century psychology. I use the term computer simulation loosely enough to include the kind of hybrid, neuro-psycho-mechanics involved in Breger's paper on dreams in this volume as well as the almost entirely mechanical theories of dreams. The exact role of software and hardware analogies is complex. They are often merely stimuli which lead us to valuable ideas about human behavior, on both the macro- and micro-levels. Sometimes they are really models, in the original sense of mechanical simulacra of human brains. In any case, it has turned out to be more fruitful to consider brain mechanisms—at least at the level of an information processing analysis—than to restrict ourselves to psychic mechanisms, and an interesting feature of Breger's essay is the attempt to combine the two. I think the evidence indicates that the introduction of software analysis into psychological theorizing will not only have more effect, quantitatively and qualitatively, than the Freudian hypothesis, but also considerably more value than the pure neurophysiological considerations of Hebbians and some of the psycho-pharmacologists.

For the information processing models are not merely reductive. To see dreaming as analogous to the clearing process of a computer or as analogous to the storing of internally generated data or as re-programming is to have a hypothesis with rich consequences at the molar level, consequences that are quite different from the hypotheses of Freud or the "sleep as bodily rehabilitation" tradition and consequences that are important for therapy as well as theory.

18. In summary, psychology is about too complex a set of questions and—a separate point—about too complicated a set of phenomena to permit a paradigm. I suspect that the same is true of physics and chemistry and that the concept of paradigm is less useful now than in the early history of science. But there might still be some local paradigms, specific to certain areas or problems. And there might still be prophylactic or therapeutic uses of paradigms to apply a preventive or remedial pressure on the subject as a whole. I have made here some suggestions for modifications to the overall approach in psychology and, to some extent, to the specific approaches of sub-areas. I see them as requiring not a synthesis but a selection from the smorgasbörd of methodologies as well as models. The misguided task of trying to blend all these together will simply make one sick.[5]

<hr>

[5]To what extent do the above remarks apply to (1) fields of psychology besides those specifically mentioned, (2) quasi-psychological areas like psycho-biology, hemo-physiology, psycho-pharmacology, and (3) the other social and behavioral sciences? In my view, they apply very forcefully. To see whether I was simply applying my anti-paradigm prejudices like another paradigm, to select favorable instances, I made a fairly systematic content analysis of the reviewers' evaluation, in a sequence of issues of *Contemporary Psychology*, and of *Annual Review of Psychology*, and in some surveys of

24   Michael Scriven

REFERENCES

Boring, E. G. *A history of experimental psychology*. New York: Appleton-Century-Crofts, 1950.

Burtt, E. A. *Metaphysical foundations of modern science*. New York: Doubleday & Co., Inc., 1954.

Butterfield, A. *The origins of modern science*. London: G. Bell & Sons Ltd., 1949.

Deutsch, J. A. *A structural basis to behavior*. Chicago: University of Chicago Press, 1960.

Dray, William. *Philosophical analysis and history*. New York: Harper and Row, Publishers, 1967.

Gardiner, P. *Theories of history*. New York: The Free Press, 1959.

Hook, S. *Philosophy and history*. New York: New York University Press, 1963.

Kaplan, Abraham. *Conduct of inquiry*. San Francisco: Chandler Publishing Co., 1964.

Koch, S. *Modern learning theories*. New York: Appleton-Century-Crofts, 1954.

Koyre, A. A. *From the closed world to the infinite universe*. Baltimore: Johns Hopkins Press, 1957.

Rapaport, D. The structure of psychoanalytic theory: a systematizing attempt. In S. Koch (ed.), *Psychology: a study of a science*, Vol. III. New York: McGraw-Hill Book Co., 1959, 55–183.

Scriven, M. *Primary philosophy*. New York: McGraw-Hill Book Co., 1967.

Wann, T., (ed.). *Behaviorism and phenomenology*. Chicago: University of Chicago Press, 1964.

---

social science, particularly *The Social Sciences Today*. Without claiming great objectivity, I would be prepared to predict that the average reader undertaking the same enterprise would be struck very hard by the extraordinarily consistent complaints of the reviewers, coming from every field of psychology. They are asking for exactly what I suggest above is possible for an untidy subject, *not* the supertheories or interfield concepts or axiomatizations or an end to introspection, reduction, holism, and so on. In short, the nearer one gets to his own area of specialization, in the role of *critic*, the more clearly conscious he becomes of the practical (including explanatory) needs there and the less swayed he is by his picture of the subject as a whole. But the latter may direct and dominate his own research, and it is this tendency to assume there is a paradigm, I have argued above, which is all too often bad ideology and not good meta-theory.

2. The Ideology of Behaviorism

Louis Breger

Psychology is a field with great promise, a field that is of intimate interest to us all as the study of ourselves—of human behavior, of thought, of man's relation to man and to society. Yet there seems to have been a betrayal of this rich promise. Students attracted by the lure of the subject matter are frequently disillusioned to find that most of academic psychology has very little to do with the sorts of things they expected. As Tolman (1952, p. 325) commented about his own first encounter with psychology at Harvard some years ago, ". . . [the course] proved a terrible letdown from the really humanly important problems which I had supposed Psychology was to be concerned with. . . ." This situation has changed little in recent years; in fact, it has in some ways intensified within the core of academic psychology.

As in Tolman's day, large numbers of students are still attracted to psychology by their interest in human concerns. As evidence of this, clinical psychology and related areas have come numerically to dominate the field. And yet the students and professionals in these sub-areas are in conflict about their work, a conflict that stems from the continuing domination of psychology by an ideology which is intrinsically hostile to the data and methods of the clinical psychologist. In some cases, they even feel guilty and must rationalize their work in terms of the beliefs of the dominant academic tradition. At its worst, this leads to a betrayal of subject matter as exemplified by the attempt to make clinical psychology a "pure research" area, or as shown by the many ways in which personality and social psychology become more methodologically respectable at the expense of social relevance (see Sanford, 1965).

Earlier drafts of this chapter were read by Les Davison, Michael Scriven, and James L. McGaugh, and I found their comments very helpful in the preparation of the present version.

A full understanding of how psychology has faltered in realizing its promise would require an extensive historical, philosophical, and factual analysis. The aim of the present essay is more modest. I wish to analyze certain of psychology's assumptions so that we may, hopefully, free ourselves from the constraints they impose. I will argue that psychology remains dominated by the ideology of behaviorism—a set of ideas bound up with our identification as a science. In anticipation, let me indicate one conclusion that this discussion will lead to: *That the study of meaningful human data not be tied down by methodological strictures—especially when these are ill-founded.*

While behaviorist ideology continues as a pervasive influence in many areas of psychology, behaviorism itself remains but one of many schools that make up the field. A second major tradition, the functional psychology which is the background of many of the chapters in Part II of this book, has existed as a perennial counter-force throughout the period of behaviorism's dominance. In addition, there has been the psychoanalytic tradition, coming from Freud and the post-Freudians. The relationships among these various psychologies will be taken up shortly and are dealt with in detail by Professor Shakow in Chapter 3. At this point, I wish to present an overall scheme within which to consider differing approaches to psychology.

An excellent way of dealing with competing approaches in science is presented by Kuhn (1962) in *The Structure of Scientific Revolutions.* Though based on an historical analysis of physical science, Kuhn's model can be used to aid our understanding of historical developments in psychology. Kuhn distinguishes three basic stages in the development of science: (1) a pre-paradigm stage in which several theories compete—each best suited to part of the data, but none completely adequate; (2) a 'normal science' stage in which a single paradigm has gained wide acceptance and provides the primary structuring of the field; and (3) a crisis stage in which an accepted paradigm appears inadequate and a new one replaces it. An example would be the progression within physics. Prior to Newton, the field was characterized by competing paradigms and a recognition of the inadequacies of existing theories. This was the pre-paradigm stage. Newton provided the structure, the paradigm that superceded all existing theories and provided the basic structure for the 'normal' work of physics for the next 200 years. Then, physics found itself in a state of crisis, which was eventually resolved by the emergence of a new paradigm, that provided by Einstein and Bohr.

It is important to specify what Kuhn means by a paradigm. A paradigm is a model which provides the basic structure to a particular scientific field. But it is not an abstract model; it stems directly from the achievements of a particular work which serves to define the legitimate problems and research methods in a field. The work of Newton in physics, of Copernicus in astronomy, of Lavoisier in chemistry are all examples. As Kuhn (1962, pp. 10–11) puts it:

> . . . these and many other works served for a time implicitly to define the legitimate problems and methods of a research field for succeeding generations of practitioners. They were able to do so because they shared two essential characteristics. Their achievement was sufficiently unprecedented to attract an enduring group of adherents away from competing modes of scientific activity. Simultaneously, it was sufficiently open-ended to leave all sorts of problems for the re-defined group of practitioners to resolve. Achievements that share these two characteristics I shall henceforth refer to as "paradigms," a term that relates closely to "normal science." By choosing it, I mean to suggest that some accepted examples of actual scientific practice—examples which include law, theory, application, and instrumentation together—provide models from which spring particular coherent traditions of scientific research. . . . Men whose research is based on shared paradigms are committed to the same rules and standards for scientific practice. That commitment and the apparent consensus it produces are prerequisites for normal science, i.e., for the genesis and continuation of a particular research tradition.

Thus, the paradigm is based on actual achievements and includes data, instrumentation, and methods all intertwined with the theory, laws, and hypotheses that we more readily associate with ideas like models or paradigms. Kuhn demonstrates how, in field after field, paradigms contain the background set of assumptions which are then inextricably intertwined with *all aspects* of the on-going work of normal science, from specific laboratory techniques to abstract theorizing. The historical evidence he cites also demonstrates that the establishment of a paradigm, or the replacement of one paradigm by another, rests on concrete scientific achievement. It is, typically, an achievement that convinces a majority of workers in the area by the force of its theory, the penetration of its methods in explicating theory, and its superiority over existing models in solving certain crucial problems and in opening up the field to new problems.

Psychology, as well as the other social sciences, has never achieved a normal science stage in the sense that the physical sciences have. Kuhn's model is nevertheless useful, for the proponents of various competing views during a pre-paradigm phase tend not to think of themselves in these terms—they are likely to be every bit as committed to their particular paradigm as the post-Newtonian physicist. This has been particularly true of the proponents of behaviorist ideology who frequently act as if they were engaged in a 'normal science' enterprise. Although there are no paradigms in psychology in exactly the sense that Kuhn applied the term to the physical sciences, there are certain broad groupings of ideas, methods, and assumptions that may be subsumed under Kuhn's model for purposes of discussion.

Figure 1 displays four such groupings or paradigms—psychoanalysis, traditional-academic psychology, and the two main off-shoots of traditional-academic psychology in this country, functionalism and behaviorism. Psychoanalysis fits the concept of a paradigm fairly well; Freud's achievements defined the paradigm, both its major theoretical structure and the methods to be used in demonstrating the theory and exploring its limits. The traditional academic psychology of Fechner and Wundt was clearly an attempt to define psychology paradigmatically (Boring, 1950). The eventual collapse of this attempt led to two reactions; the first, functionalism, is the less consciously paradigmatic. Functionalism is made up of a variety of workers who share assumptions from the Darwinian-biological-naturalistic tradition rather than from physics, who have been willing to include mental data and introspection of some form, and who have been concerned with organism-environment relationships and the problems of function and adaptation. Functionalism and psychoanalysis both share an appreciation of observation and naturalism. They both derive a great deal from Darwin, both are oriented toward data bearing on the problem of adaptation, and, finally, both are psychologies which deal with intrapsychic data. Thus, it is indeed unfortunate that these two streams have not been integrated, for such an integration would have been beneficial to both.

Some of the reasons for this lack of integration are presented by Shakow in Chapter 3, and Part II of this book may be viewed as an attempt to integrate these two streams.

Behaviorism, the other paradigm, has clearly held the dominant position in American psychology. Its central assumptions overlap so closely with those of the older psycho-physical psychology that they may almost be considered a single paradigm. In fact, when Watson proposed to rid experimental psychology of mental data and to substitute observable physical acts (later to become stimuli and responses), he was defining the field in such a way as to bring it more in line with certain of its own background assumptions. That is, by casting out introspection he brought the field closer *in appearance* to physical science which, of course, had been the goal of the psycho-physicists all along. This is probably one reason for the predominance of behaviorism—its program was compatible with the assumptions of many workers in the field. Similarly, its methods, while departing in certain important respects from its predecessors (the elimination of introspection and the trained introspectionist) are quite similar in basic form. Thus, the highly controlled laboratory experiment of part processes, whose chief characteristic is that they lend themselves to

FIGURE 1. *Political and Historical Separation of Psychoanalysis from Psychology*

PSYCHOANALYSIS
(Freud, Neo-Freudians, Ego-psychology))

1. Intrapsychic as well as interpersonal.
2. Influence from Darwin and naturalism.
3. Primarily observational rather than experimental.
4. Data selection determined by its functional significance for the individual.
5. *Goal:* thorough description and understanding of adaptive behavior.

TRADITIONAL-ACADEMIC-PSYCHOLOGY
(Fechner, Wundt, Titchner)

1. Modeled after physics, the Helmholtz program, an attempt to reduce psychology to quantifiable laws.
2. Highly controlled laboratory experiment the chief method.
3. Data consists of small units; part processes, mental elements.
4. *Goal:* very general, abstract laws; in form like the law of gravity.

Reaction

FUNCTIONALISM
(W. James, Gestalt, Lewin, Ethologists, Cognitive Psychology)

1. Concern for function, for adaptation of organism to environment.
2. Influence from biology, Darwin, and naturalism as well as physical science.
3. Observation and experiments in nature given a place along with laboratory experiments.
4. Data selection determined by concern for function and adaptation.
5. *Goal:* the thorough description and understanding of adaptive behavior units.

BEHAVIORISM
(Watson, Hull, Skinner)

1. Modeled after physics.
2. Controlled laboratory experiment the chief method.
3. Data consists of units (S and R) which lend themselves to objective measurement.
4. Attempt to rule out mental data.
5. *Goal:* very general, abstract laws of behavior or functional relationships, etc.

measurement, remain central as method. Therefore, when it became clear that the traditional academic psychology of Wundt had foundered on the rocks of sterility, behaviorism could argue, in terms of the paradigms' own assumptions, that the problem consisted of not emulating physical science closely enough. In this sense, the behaviorist reaction may be seen as an attempt to make the traditional approach true to its own assumptions by getting rid of what seemed like the last stumbling block (introspective data) in the way of a completely mechanistic, physically based science.

Examining Figure 1 we see that there are essentially three competing paradigms—the psychoanalytic, the functional-cognitive and the experimental-behavioristic—each of which defines the field of psychology in a way that, in part, excludes the definitions of the others. In academic psychology, the experimental-behavioristic paradigm has been dominant, though one might argue that the most significant substantive contributions have come from workers in the functional tradition.

Now I wish to argue that one of the central problems of academic psychology under the dominance of the behavioristic program is that it has been acting like post-paradigm normal science, when in fact, it is at a pre-paradigm stage. That is to say, the paradigm espoused by behaviorism has come to define and dominate the field in a fashion analogous to what happened in physics after Newton. Many research workers are engaged in what resembles the work of normal science, that is, they are busy solving all sorts of minor problems within the framework of an established theoretical structure. This structure defines, in no uncertain terms, the correct methodology for work in psychology and is intolerant of work based on methods which depart from this acceptable form. The great difficulty with all this, of course, is that there is so little solid scientific achievement on which to base this activity. Watson's own program was essentially unproductive both as a developmental psychology and as a psychology of learning. The later examples of the program, the attempts at large scale theory construction as typified by Hull, have also proved disappointing. Thus, we have a normal science psychology that is not based on actual achievement, either theoretical or empirical, of sufficient magnitude to warrant the shutting out of alternative paradigms. We find a restriction of acceptable research methods to a very narrow band, when these methods have not proven their superiority by actual accomplishment.

We must ask the question, "How is it that behaviorism has maintained this domination in psychology, not because of any striking achievements, but in the face of successive failures?" The answer is *that in place of actual achievement, behaviorism has substituted an identification with the achievements of physical science.* This identification is embodied in the *ideology of behaviorism*. It is, in point of fact, what makes the behaviorist program an ideological fiction rather than a scientific paradigm based on actual achievement. Before directly confronting this ideology, it will be helpful to examine how behaviorism came to its position of dominance. Of particular importance are the positive contributions made in connection with behaviorist methodology as distinct from behaviorist theory.

The attempt of behaviorism to bring the accomplishments of physical science to psychology was, perhaps, inevitable. During behaviorism's initial phase, it had a number of beneficial effects on the field, many of which we now take for granted. For example, there was the rejection of loose, vague, and anthropomorphic explanations as embodied in doctrines such as animism and animal consciousness. The emphasis on looking at the operations of measurement as crucial defining characteristics of concepts is another. While no one now should seriously contend, as behaviorism in its early enchantment with operationism did, that the *only* valid meaning of a term resides in the operations of measurement, we have become greatly sensitized to looking closely at the operations involved in any data collection effort. Many conflicts, such as occur when two studies find contradictory results with respect to anxiety, are resolved when we see that in one study anxiety is operationally defined by a true-false scale, while in another it is defined as changes in galvanic skin conductance, and that these two measures are only weakly related. These and others are ways in which behaviorism has brought a critical scientific spirit to psychology. They represent the first and most valuable phase of what Hebb (1960) has called "The American Revolution" in psychology.

The rejection of the mental was also a part of the attempt to emulate the success of physical science. Since it was carried out more or less simultaneously with the methodological revolution, the two have tended to become fused together into a single paradigm. But there is no necessary connection here; it is possible to use the methodological advances without ascribing to the input-output or S-R model.

This is essentially the position that Hebb and other contemporary workers in the behaviorist tradition (Osgood, 1953; Miller, 1961) find themselves in. Using behavioral research methods, they have shown, time and again, the inadequacy of an external input-output model which excludes what goes on in the organism to explain even simple animal learning. This problem is so central to behaviorism and yet so little appreciated that it warrants a more extended discussion here.

The main thrust of behaviorist theory was to apply the S-R formula to all aspects of behavior; to make learning the central focus of psychology. Learning was defined as the acquisition of specific responses to specific stimuli and any talk of what lay between, whether instincts, consciousness, or cognitions, was dismissed as unscientific because unobservable. Almost from the outset, however, the attempt to answer the question "What is learned?" as "specific responses to specific stimuli" ran into difficulty. First, it was easy to show, even in a Pavlovian conditioning experiment, that animals learned not only the original response but a series of related responses, and that these were made not only to the original stimulus but to a series of related stimuli. This was handled by the introduction of the concept of generalization, the idea that learning consisted of the acquisition of single S-R connections which generalized along dimensions of physical stimulus similarity so that, for example, when an animal learned to jerk its knee to the sound of a tone that had been previously paired with an electric shock, this learning generalized to different tones varying in loudness or frequency and consisted of other leg movements similar to the original knee jerk. Thus far, the extension of the S-R formula by generalization posed no serious problem, for the analysis was still within the behaviorist paradigm of observable physical events. A consideration of more complex forms of behavior soon began to strain the paradigm, however. Gestalt oriented experimenters demonstrated that animals could learn to respond to relations between two stimuli; for example, they could learn to go to the larger of two squares or the darker of two cards. Another set of experiments showed that a variety of responses could be used to achieve the same end result so that, for example, the animal who learned to jerk its knee to avoid shock would also, when turned upside down, lift its head to do the same. These and related findings put a great strain on the concept of generalization for it is difficult, if not impossible, to view the learning of relationships or the acquisition of equipotential responses as varying along dimensions of physical stimulus similarity. In attempting to accommodate to this strain, the concept of generalization underwent a transformation. It became the concept of mediated generalization—that is, it was assumed that mediators consisting of little s-r bonds that one could not quite observe were learned at the same time as the big S-R connections were established, and that these mediated phenomena such as relational learning and equipotentiality. Thus, the behaviorists arrived at "r_g," the fractional anticipatory goal response, which is not a response at all but what is inferred to go on *inside the animal's mind* between the observable S and R.

Parallel developments have occurred within traditional S-R theory with respect to other complex phenomena. Thus, the more sophisticated S-R theorists may argue that they are able to encompass such complex processes within their paradigm. The point is, that they do so by *extending the meaning of stimulus to include anything that has an effect on the organism and of response to everything that the organism does*, including thinking, fantasy or what have you.

Most of these difficulties were encountered within the simple animal experiments with which behaviorists concerned themselves. When we look at complex human phenomena such as language or the other symbolic activities that occupy so much of human life, we see that the problems that originally led to the necessity of mediation are greatly compounded. Simple observation will show that human learning in these spheres must consist, at a minimum, of the acquisition of a host of symbolically related responses to a host of symbolically related stimuli. Chomsky (1957) presents an excellent review of this issue in his discussion of the behaviorist attempt to deal with human language. Wolff (1967, p. 301), again discussing language, summarizes observations which indicate, ". . . that from the samples of speech they hear and repeat, children intuit syntactic rules consistent with the formal structure of their language; they do not learn their primary language by rote imitation, generalization and reinforcement. The capacity to intuit grammatical rules is all the more impressive when we consider that all languages have complex and unique grammatical structures (often unknown in a formal sense to the native adult speaker), yet children acquire them without formal instruction or schedules of reinforcement."

It should be clear that what is true of the language learning of the two year old child is true of a great deal of subsequent human learning. And, I would point out, it is complex human behavior akin to language that psychology is, or should be, interested in.

Returning to 'generalization,' it is clear that this concept is called on to perform a task to which it is not equal. The problems that gave rise to the introduction of mediation within S-R psychology have eventually led to a complete redefinition of what is learned. Most of the sophisticated modern forms of behaviorism are cognitive psychologies in this regard; "what is learned" are mediators—central processes which are inferred in order adequately to explain observed behavior. The traditions of behaviorism, however, dictate that these inferred processes still be cloaked in the garb of behaviorist terminology. Thus, the words stimulus and response keep getting attached to concepts that have no direct reference to external events.

An analogy might be helpful in understanding this problem. During the seventeenth century, various "fluid" theories of electricity led to attempts to capture the "fluid" in a container, the Leyden Jar eventually succeeding in doing so. After the assimilation of a different paradigm, one which saw electricity not as fluid but as "charge," it became recognized that what was essential to the Leyden Jar was not its jar shape or the fact that it was a container at all, but that it was a condenser which contained two conducting plates with a non-conductor between them.

This shift in view did not replace its predecessor overnight, however, and written discussions and pictorial representations of the Leyden Jar only gradually changed from container to condenser. (Kuhn, 1962, p. 117; Roller and Roller, 1954.)

In many ways, the situation in behaviorism with respect to the basic question of "what is learned?" is quite similar. The shift from external to inferred internal processes has, in the main, taken place. But workers from the older tradition and the textbooks they write are only gradually accommodating themselves to this shift. As in other fields, it will clarify matters if we recognize the extent of change, for this shift is a basic one that undermines the whole basis of behaviorist theory. The acceptance of an internal unit (a cognition, a plan, a mediator, a scheme) as what is learned provides an entirely new orientation to the field. The central problem of learning becomes one of understanding the acquisition, organization, modification, and utilization of these central processes. The problems that posed such difficulty for the S-R concept of generalization are circumvented by a paradigm that begins with an assumption of generality as its central concept (that is, what is learned is the mediator, so that it is specific response learning that presents the special case that requires a special explanation). As we will see shortly, the data and methods that such a cognitive paradigm entails are of greater relevance to human subject matter than are those of the typical behaviorist experiment.

This basic change in theory comes about from the influence of the second tradition, functionalism, on behaviorism. Since its accomplishments stem from a different tradition and a much broader conception of acceptable methodology, one must question these aspects of behaviorism also.

THE IDEOLOGY OF BEHAVIORISM

In its present form, behaviorist ideology consists of a set of beliefs associated with the image of psychology as a science, with the concepts of prediction and control, and with a tremendous concern for methodological propriety. Koch (1964) has analysed the history of this set of beliefs in great detail, and the reader is referred to his paper for a full picture. I would like to comment here, in a summary fashion, on several of the assumptions of behaviorist ideology. Central to the ideology has been the attempt to establish criteria which determine legitimate ways of talking about subject matter. Thus, the set of beliefs, imported largely from the logical positivist school of philosophy of science ("operational definitions," the "verifiability criterion of meaning," and so on). Then there are a host of rules, mainly informal, concerning how laboratory experiments should be done, what constitutes certain or reliable knowledge, and the like. These rules are built into the background of the field, as it were; they manifest themselves in texts on experimental psychology and research methodology and in the criteria which guide advisors in evaluating theses, editors in making journal selections, and panels in giving out research money.

It is crucial that we recognize that these aspects of behaviorism have become ideological; they consist much more of a set of beliefs, value laden terms, prescriptions for action, and catch phrases concerning how a science of psychology *should* be than they do of a well established body of scientific knowledge. In fact, it is hard to find much solid scientific knowledge of the kind that behaviorist ideology would lead one to expect. Furthermore, it is possible to show that most of the central tenets of the ideology cannot be substantiated even in its own terms. Thus, as Koch (1964) and others (Kaplan, 1964 and Scriven's chapter in this book) have shown, more sophisticated recent analyses by workers in the philosophy of science have disposed of the early doctrines of operationalism, if not of all strictures on what constitutes legitimate discourse within science. More empirically based analyses—that is, those based on the history of science, (Conant, 1953; Bronowski, 1951; Kuhn, 1962; Hanson, 1958)—point to quite a different picture of the scientific enterprise. Some of these issues are dealt with in greater detail by Scriven in Chapter 1.

Yet we still find text after text in psychology putting forth outmoded and untenable criteria as the basis for a scientific approach. This illustrates the cultural lag that characterizes psychology's attempt at gaining scientific status via identification with what it takes to be the methods of the successful physical sciences. What is emulated, however, is typically a slightly distorted version of an outmoded philosophy of science. Thus, we find textbooks in the areas of personality, abnormal psychology, and learning putting forth old positivist doctrines that even their originators no longer hold to (Bridgeman, 1959; Koch, 1959, especially pp. 733–736). These behavioristic psychologies are like the aspiring bourgeois who, in his eagerness to identify with the upper classes, flaunts exaggerated versions of last year's fashions.

The use of science to gain status has led to a state where the set of beliefs, terms, and concepts have acquired what sociologists call a legitimizing function. As such, they are relatively impervious to challenge or modification on theoretical or empirical grounds. The beliefs have become part of a ritual that must be performed before a psychological work can be considered legitimate.

Consider, as a prime example, the use of the term behavior. As originally employed by Watson and others, the term was part of an attempt to define the subject matter of psychology in terms of overt behavior, the external actions of the subject that were open to the observation of all. This was, of course, in reaction to the introspective methods and data of Tichnerian structural psychology (Boring, 1950). As Koch (1964) points out, the behaviorist program underwent considerable expansion during the 1930's and 1940's, acquiring an additional set of legitimizing beliefs imported from the philosophy of science and best exemplified by the program of Hull's learning theory (Hull, 1943). From the very beginning, however, the Watsonian definition of behavior was much too restrictive; psychologists were interested in talking about the internal states of people, about the mental that Watson attempted to rid psychology of. But, once the behaviorist terminology had acquired an ideological function, they were forced to do so in a cumbersome, round-about or even contradictory fashion. Thus, "verbal behavior" for talking; "implicate" or "sub-vocal verbal behavior" for thinking; "fractional anticipatory goal response" for the response that the animal doesn't make, but thinks about making, and so forth. The problem, with all this, aside from its silliness, is that the use of the term behavior has lost whatever distinct meaning it may have had, that is, in distinguishing observable acts from private experiences that are inferable from observations, a distinction that may be valuable to make. At the present time, the term behavior is used to talk about almost anything that the user wishes to imbue with the aura of scientific psychology, an aura that derives from the legitimizing function of the term within the behaviorist ideology. This point is developed in much greater detail by Chomsky (1957). He shows how this false sense of the scientific can become a cover for what is, in fact, a very unsystematic and frequently uninformed approach to complex psychological problems (for example, the relationship between thought and speech—they are not the same thing and calling them by the same behaviorist name does not make them so).

Two other concepts which figure prominently in behaviorist ideology are worth consideration: control and prediction. Like behavior, these terms have come to have an aura of the scientific about them that serves to obscure their loose usage. Both terms are used in both a specific or narrow sense and in a very broad sense, with a very slippery transition from one to the other. Control is used, in the narrow sense, to refer to what one does (or is supposed to do) when carrying out a laboratory experiment; that is, keep all but a few aspects of the environment constant while varying one aspect to observe its effects. In this sense, control refers to *restriction of the environment*, a characteristic of many laboratory environments like the Skinner Box that sharply distinguishes them from the complex, fluctuating environments that people and animals live in. Prediction, again in the narrow sense, refers to the immediate goal of a controlled laboratory experiment, for example, by keeping everything in the environment constant but the rate of reinforcement, the experimenter is able to predict the rate of bar-pressing. But these terms are also used in a much broader sense in the behaviorist ideology. Here, controlled experimentation is put forth as the essential step in the formulation of behavioral laws that will ultimately lead to the scientific control and prediction of human behavior. In this usage, control refers to the control that is the fruit of a well established scientific theory. Prediction is also used very broadly, in the sense in which scientific knowledge in general allows one greater prediction or understanding of the world. This differs greatly from the narrow meaning of being able to predict what will happen in a highly restricted experimental environment. Control and prediction are asserted to be the goals of a scientific psychology and the behaviorist program is, either explicitly or implicitly, viewed as the way to achieve this goal. *The ability to predict what a subject will do in a highly controlled experiment is then put forth as evidence for the success of the program's broad goals.*

But you will notice that a shift in the meaning of control and prediction from the very specific to the very general has taken place, a shift that is made possible by the loose usage of the terms within the ideology. With the terms used in these two shifting senses, the behaviorist can use the predictions of behavior in the highly controlled experiment as presumed evidence for both the scientific nature of his findings and as evidence that the behaviorist approach is on its way toward producing predictions which enable him to control human behavior. Does this claim make sense if we re-translate control as follows? "When we place a subject in a highly *restricted environment*, certain of his responses are predictable, given certain other conditions, for example, that he is hungry, and so on." I think not. It is a great leap from this re-phrased statement to the assertion that these experiments are leading to the control and prediction of human behavior. Obviously, this latter assertion is an affirmation of faith in the behaviorist ideology rather than a conclusion that follows in any direct way from the results of the typical laboratory experiment. What is most striking about such experiments is that they typically have very little to do with human behavior, as this phrase is usually understood, except in the allegorical sense where the terms used in describing the laboratory operations are loosely used in their alternate, everyday sense.

It should be made clear that the above criticisms are directed at the use of the term control in the behaviorist ideology and not at the concept *per se*. The controlled experiment has proven its value in a number of scientific fields. Furthermore, it is possible to utilize various forms of control in naturalistic and semi-naturalistic research—as with multidimensional methods—which do not entail the distortions of data characteristic of the kind of behavioristic research under discussion.

The use of terms in both a very tightly defined and a very loose fashion has long been an outstanding feature of behaviorism. It is this feature of the program that has enabled behaviorists to present their approach as objective and scientific, with terms operationally defined and rigorously related to one another, while at the same time seeming to talk about matters of very broad human concern such as reward and punishment, motivation, fear, learning, and the like. Consider, as an example, the analysis of anxiety and the motivating effects of this secondary drive in maintaining a neurosis, as put forth in the well known experiment by Miller (1948). In this experiment, rats are placed in a box with two compartments, a black and a white, separated by a barrier. They are shocked in one compartment and rapidly learn to move to the other. On subsequent trials, they flee from the compartment in which they were previously shocked, before the electricity is turned on. The strength of this habit (or of the animals' motivation) is demonstrated by its persistence on later trials, even when the rats have to engage in additional learning (for example, turning wheels to open a barrier between the compartments), all in the absence of further shocks. The model provided by this experiment is then utilized by Dollard and Miller (1950) in a rather broad analysis of anxiety, anxiety motivated learning (seen as the creation of neurotic habits), the unconscious nature of these habits, their persistence in the face of frequently unpleasant consequences and so on. Now, the specific inadequacies of Hullian drive theory, of the concept of habit, or of the difficulties with the concepts of stimulus and response generalization need not concern us here. Rather, let us direct our attention to the alternately strict and loose usage of terms that is illustrated by this example. Why, we must ask, is anxiety operationally defined in terms of electric shock and shock avoidance with rats in a box rather than, say, in terms of a human subject's report of whether he is anxious or not? The answer is to be found in the behaviorist ideology, that is, that all concepts must be defined in terms of external, measurable stimuli (shock) and responses (running to avoid shock). Further, the concepts and operations of the experiment are given meaning and a certain flavor by their connections with the total theory and with other experiments employing drives, secondary drives, experimental extinction, and the like. All of this is further embedded in the set of arguments backing up the theory that convey its objective, rigorous nature, its close relation to the successful physical sciences, and its eventual goal of achieving broadly applicable laws. Without these background beliefs, it would be hard to understand why someone would choose to study the effects of electric shock on rats in a two-compartment box if he was really interested in the problems of human neurosis and anxiety. Thus, the objective, measurable, and very narrow definitions of the terms anxiety and neurosis are central to maintaining the scientific status of the system. The behaviorist is then faced with a key problem—how to move from the experiment, where terms are defined in the narrow or tight sense, to other more broadly defined situations. Generalization from the results of such experiments must take place along several dimensions: first, across species —from rat to man (including the other species in between); second, across environments—from shock box to the most complex society; and third, across the very dimensions of stimuli and responses—from the electric shock to everything that produces pain or fear, and from the responses of running, in the absence of further shock, to a host of compulsive or persistent neurotic symptoms. How is this generalization accomplished? How is it possible for Dollard and Miller or others to bring the results of an experiment like this to bear on the phenomena of human anxiety and neurosis? The answer is simple—the gulf is bridged by the words themselves. When generalizing across species, environment, stimuli, and responses, the terms pain, fear, anxiety, escape, and neurosis are used in the loosest of senses. No bridging experiments are performed, nor is observational evidence produced to show, for example, that human neurotics have been exposed to specific pair-producing experiences in connection with their symptoms. At the same time, the initial association of the terms with the apparatus of the experiment, with learning theory, and with the whole behaviorist enterprise, has imbued them with a scientific aura which is carried over when they are later used in this much looser fashion. It is this aura, rather than any demonstrable evidence, that prompts Hall and Lindzey (1957, p. 420) to describe the S-R approach to personality in the following way:

We shall present here the personality theory that is most elegant, most economical and shows the closest link to its natural science forebears. Stimulus-response (s-r) theory, at least in its origins, can accurately be labeled a laboratory theory in contrast to the other theories with which we have dealt where the role of clinical or naturalistic observation has been much more important. Consistent with these origins is the position's explicitness, economy of formulation, and the serious efforts made to provide suitable empirical anchoring for the main terms of the theory.

In fact, what the behaviorist does is to assert: "My approach is rigorous and scientific, I define my terms in a narrow operational sense; when I say anxiety, I mean the response that the animal makes in this experimental situation." Having established his claim to scientific status in this fashion, he then allows a host of meanings associated with terms such as anxiety and neurosis—meanings which his own definitions initially ruled out—to re-emerge and to bridge the gap from narrow experiment to broad application. This leads to the embarrassing situation that Koch

(1956) has described as talking out of both sides of the mouth at the same time, as when the most minute differences in species or experimental apparatus are described and caution is expressed over generalizing beyond these, on the one hand, while the most general, broad sweeping claims are made for the theory on the other.

Let us examine a second example. Adopt, for a moment, the point of view of a naïve but intelligent observer who knows nothing of the *reasons* psychologists give to explain their experiments. An investigator tells you he is interested in "learning" and you think to yourself: "This is certainly an important area with a direct bearing on all those years I spent in school learning, not to mention the learning that took place outside the class room." You are then surprised to see that the investigator is not studying children at all but white rats. "All right," you think to yourself, "animals have to learn also, perhaps something of value can come from studying their simpler learning processes for, after all, biology has profited from the comparative study of animals." You are then again surprised to see that your investigator has no particular comparative interest and has, in fact, restricted his attention to the speed with which the rats can get through a maze and how this relates to sips of water or pellets of food or electric shocks that are given to them. You begin to wonder what possible relevance this enterprise can have for the learning that you experienced as a child. If you ask the investigator what his laboratory experiments have to do with school learning, he will give you a ready answer; you will, in fact, be treated to a brief lecture drawn from behaviorist ideology having to do with the place of rigorous experimentation in the development of scientific laws (or functional relationships) which, because of their objective character and extreme generality (like the law of gravity) have the most important relevance for the learning of almost anything by any organism in any situation. You will, in other words, be treated to a great deal of *argumentation* which attempts to prove that what is found out about how the sips of water or electric shocks affect the maze running performance of the rat does have relevance for the learning that human beings undergo. Without such a rationale, the work of such an investigator skirts the edge of triviality.

This example reveals several important things. First, the investigator is, in fact, interested in learning as it is commonly understood. He is not likely to respond to your question by stating that he has no interest in what happens with human children, or that he cares only about what rats do in mazes. Quite the contrary, behaviorism is noteworthy in the extreme generality, one is tempted to say grandiosity, of its claims. And, in fact, textbooks dealing with a variety of complex human learning situations, from the classroom to psychotherapy to socialization, freely use the "principles" drawn from controlled laboratory studies. What the reply of our hypothetical investigator indicates, above all, is his faith that the behaviorist program will lead to general principles of the sort found in classical physics.

The repetitiveness and vehemence with which these arguments are made indicates their importance to the behaviorist approach. Without them, much controlled laboratory work becomes virtually meaningless. Thus, when Koch (1959) points to the flaws in behaviorist ideology and the failure of what he terms "The Age of Theory Code" to deliver on its grand promises, he is posing a threat of the most serious kind to established experimental psychology.

When one examines the actual evidence on which the behaviorist position is based, it becomes clear just how little foundation there is for the type of generalization illustrated by our examples. Just to cite a few examples, minute species differences have proven to be extremely important (Bitterman, 1965); the centrality of both species, age or developmental stage, and interaction with the environment is illustrated by a variety of studies (Scott, 1962; Harlow, 1952; Hebb and Thompson, 1954, for some of the many possible examples). Space prevents going into the very interesting comparative literature, but what is clearly indicated is that the sort of generalization illustrated by the Miller experiment is on the shakiest of grounds. It would probably be tenuous to generalize from an experiment such as this to other, closely related animals or even other rats (Richter, 1958), much less to the remote analogy of human neurosis. Thus, it seems clear that the application of these laboratory findings is based on faith in the behaviorist ideology, a faith that remains unshaken by the extremely limited generality of such experiments demonstrated by research evidence.

Lest I appear to be belaboring this particular form of animal research or creating the impression that these considerations are applicable only to this particular brand of neo-Hullian learning theory, let me ask the reader to try the analysis on other examples or other theories. I think he will find that the general point holds up; Scientific status is gained in the context of tightly controlled laboratory experiments on very remote data, with subsequent application to complex human phenomena accomplished by the loose use of terms which have very broad meanings. For further examples, see the analysis of aggression by Berkowitz (1962), or of socialization by Bandura and Walters (1963).

It is worth stressing that the experimental or laboratory approach has been of value in some areas of psychology, much more so than in those I have been discussing. Sensory psychology and physiological psychology are areas where more highly controlled laboratory work has proven valuable because the *subject matter under study, that is, the sensory apparatus, the brain and central nervous system, is the subject matter the inves-*

tigator is interested in eventually applying his findings to. Thus, though experimentation is employed, the primary data are still available to bridge the gap from experiment to application.

These areas have been more amenable to an approach derived from physical science because their basic data can be easily specified in physical terms. The variables in other areas of psychology, such as learning or personality, are largely arbitrary, the result of historical accident, and lacking in any unambiguous physical referrant. Yet problems remain even in areas whose subject matter lends itself more easily to physical measurement. These are exemplified by physiological psychology's concern with behavioral data. It must deal with such data if it wants to be physiological psychology rather than physiology, and once such data are encountered, one is faced with many of the same problems that confront areas such as learning and personality.

DATA AND METHODOLOGY

We would be foolish if we did not learn from this experience, for a number of lessons are to be gleaned from the failure of the behaviorist program. Perhaps the most important concerns the very data that we, as psychologists, study. The traditional ideology has placed concern for method first and for data or subject matter second. Thus, research journals tend to be filled with studies of the utmost methodological elegance, in the service of trivial problems. The operations in such experiments are then named with terms having sufficient surplus meaning to allow for speculation to non-trivial subject matter. Reading a number of widely used textbooks as well as review articles of important areas in the field reveals the application of the criterion of method in action. Findings based on "good" experimental methodology tend to be accepted, even when the data they deal with is quite remote, while findings based on "bad" methodology (for example, observation, case history, and the like), tend to be ignored even though they may deal directly with the subject matter. For example, the belief that punishment could not eliminate responses (and was thus ineffective as a controller of behavior) was put forth and accepted as applicable to humans on the basis of a small number of animal experiments (Estes, 1944). Skinner even makes this "principle" the backbone of his version of utopia. And all this in spite of the fact that a host of common observations, including our own experiences, our experiences with our children, our pets, and so on, reveal this principle to be utter nonsense. It remained for an experimentally oriented review (Solomon, 1964) to dispose of this belief.

The lesson to be learned from these examples is simple: *Methodologi-*

cal restrictions should not obstruct the study of meaningful human data. The investigator interested in the effects of punishment on human beings should study the effects of punishment on human beings, in the home, in the classroom, on the job, and in the laboratory. Within the confines and demands imposed by the subject matter (and certainly he will not be able to study as intense punishment in a laboratory situation as he might by observation in a prison or a Marine Corps training center), various methods may be utilized.

Perhaps the most pervasive characteristic of behaviorism has been its concern for methodological respectability. What constitutes respectable methodology, of course, has been a central part of the guiding ideology of the movement as seen in the concern for operational definition—objective measurement, the controlled laboratory experiment, the formulation of theories from which hypothesis could be deduced and tested under laboratory conditions, and the like. It is by reliance on such beliefs that the behaviorist typically rationalizes the relevance of his work and its application to life situations. *But,* if the ideology is wrong, as it now certainly appears to be, then a tremendous amount of work carried out under its guidance may prove to have been a waste of time. Contrast this with investigations guided by a concern for content or data. Here, for example, we might find the counterpart of our earlier investigator observing the effects of different teaching techniques, and attempting to formulate some generalizations from these experiences (Bruner, 1960). He might, of course, come up with very little; live children in a school environment present such a number of complexities that it is difficult to perceive general principles or the effects of different techniques. Thus, there is the danger in data oriented work of not finding out anything or of findings being unreliable due to difficulties in observation. But there is little danger of complete irrelevance as there is with a methodology oriented approach. That is to say, what emerges from a study of classroom learning may be wrong or unreliable, but it will almost certainly bear on the problem of how children learn in school. The problem of reliability can always be dealt with in a subsequent investigation. The methodologically respectable laboratory study, on the other hand, may be more reliable, but it runs the danger of being totally irrelevant to classroom learning. What is worse, there is no way to correct this irrelevance, except by abandoning the whole approach.

Later I will develop the closely related issue of the role of these two sorts of data in discovery and hypothesis creation. Let me emphasize here a conclusion suggested by the above considerations. Behaviorist ideology has made methodological respectability the central criterion of meaningful work in psychology. I would propose that we recognize the bankruptcy of this position and adopt in its place a criterion of *relevance.*

Thus, rather than asking of any piece of research, "Does it meet the methodological criteria? Is it a well-controlled study? Is the data of such a form as to lend itself to objective measurement?" we should ask, "What is the ultimate aim of the work and how does the particular research relate to that aim?" If the aim is an understanding of how children learn in school, then we must ask, "How can this research bear on school learning, not necessarily immediately, but at all?" Unless there is a great deal of overlap between the data under study and the data one is ultimately interested in, then generalization from one to the other is likely to rest on the loose, analogical use of terms. It is, after all, the data or subject matter itself that must carry the ultimate burden of relevance, of relationship from laboratory to complex human environment.

In short, there exists no substitute for coming directly to grips with the data that are the ultimate aim of study. Formulating hypotheses and devising relevant experiments within the confines of subject matter requires openness and invention. There are no rules in this sort of science, hypotheses do not fall from a theory like fruit from a tree, nor are meaningful experiments, ones which capture in their operations an essence of the subject matter, easy to invent. Psychology's rapture with a particular brand of 'science of science' has obscured these facts. Our over-evaluation of a particular kind of methodology has blinded us to the greater value of the insightful observation, the creative idea, and the truly inventive experiment.

A closer examination of these issues branches off in a number of directions. There is the relationship between observation and experiment, between the place of naturalistic description and the ordering of data, that in other sciences has characteristically preceded the emergence of a later stage of broad generalizations (Kuhn, 1962). There is the consideration of the uniqueness of psychology. While there are things to be learned from a study of other fields, the history of science and psychology's own history show that each field has its own particular problems. A part of the bankruptcy of behaviorist ideology stems from the belief that a 'correct' methodology may be imported from other fields to solve the problems imposed on psychology by its subject matter. The experience of behaviorism should teach us that these problems cannot be avoided by attempting to emulate other sciences; they have a way of coming back to haunt us. These issues are developed in greater detail in Chapters 1 and 3 of this book.

PROOF VERSUS DISCOVERY

At this point, I would like to explore several further problems that result from the constraints imposed by behaviorist ideology. Consider the problem of discovery. Without attempting anything like a complete analysis, I think certain general things can be said about the conditions fostering discovery in science as well as in other areas. First, the investigator is typically driven by curiosity, by a desire to find an answer, to seek a way through the unknown, to impose order on disorder, or, in Kuhn's terms, to solve a puzzle. But such drive is always with reference to some specific subject matter. Thus, for the sixteenth and seventeenth century scientists, it involved the questions of astronomy, of the motions of the stars and planets, and of their relation to the earth. In the nineteenth century, concern centered on the age of the earth and the descent of man. In each instance, there was a vital involvement with the subject matter central to these concerns, a preoccupation with both the logical questions and arguments (geocentric vs. heliocentric; man's unique nature vs. his evolution as a species) and the empirical observations bearing on them. The context of discovery was one of intense involvement with the subject matter and a preoccupation with questions and their existing answers, as well as an openness to the discovery of new solutions. Central, of course, is asking questions in a particular way and looking at data closely enough so that something new may be noted. And, of course, being free enough of old conventions to see this something when it appears.

To phrase it another way, one gathers data or makes observations with a certain aim in mind, and this aim determines what one observes and does not observe and how one interprets these observations. Discovery and the creation of new hypotheses involves moving beyond these original aims. Now I wish to suggest that there are a number of characteristics of contemporary psychological research which seriously interfere with this process. To put it briefly, much research seems oriented toward *proving* something rather than toward *finding something out*. Lip service may be paid to the philosophy of science distinction between the context of discovery and the context of verification, but too much research seems to be in the service of the latter.[1] What is even worse, the criteria for evaluating the worth of research are almost entirely based on considerations of proof and correct methodology.

These problems stem from psychology's premature identification of itself as a normal science like physics. The work of proof—particularly the testing of very specifiic hypotheses within a theoretical framework whose major paradigmatic achievements are presumed to be established

[1]More recent work in the philosophy of science (Hanson, 1958) suggests that this distinction between discovery and validation does not exist the way many writers in psychology suppose it to. Rather, discovery and verification are intertwined in an all but inseparable way throughout the scientific process. Kuhn's analysis likewise points to an inseparable interdependence of discovery, method, and theory acceptance within the framework of a paradigm.

—is antithetical to the search for adequate paradigms, the orientation toward discovery that would be more appropriate to psychology's actual state. Similarly, casting research in a highly restrictive methodology is also more appropriate to normal science than to a pre-paradigm stage. Let us examine briefly the ways in which this over-evaluation of proof and method at the expense of discovery have operated in psychology.

First, there have been a number of research efforts characterized by the formulation of theory, the deduction of hypotheses from this theory, and the testing of these hypotheses in experiments. Hull's learning theory (1943) is perhaps the best known example of this hypothetical-deductive approach, Festinger's theory of cognitive dissonance (1957) is a more recent example, as is the work on achievement motivation (Atkinson, 1958). The attempt is made to justify this work by resorting to a number of the canons of behaviorist ideology already discussed, and by the additional claim that the criterion of a good theory is to be found in the research that it stimulates. This research, of course, is evaluated in terms of the usual methodological strictures. While this assertion may be relevant to work in normal science, as it is employed in psychology it reveals the problems that arise from the premature solidification of the field around the behaviorist paradigm. Research does get stimulated by the theory; in fact, that is the problem with it. It tends to relate primarily to theory to the exclusion of much relevant human subject matter. The function of such research becomes one of proving whether the theory, typically as a whole, is right or wrong. If wrong (that is, if a particular experiment is inconclusive), then the whole enterprise produces nothing. But even where it is right (that is, even when experiments yield predicted results), there may remain a good deal of ambiguity since these results are defined within the system of the theory, are primarily in contact with it, and may not easily be extrapolated to other data of human relevance. It is a striking characteristic of such theories that they are turned in on themselves in this fashion. Their concepts and findings are meaningful primarily to the in-group; the theories demand acceptance of a host of assumptions about the world, about idiosyncratic ways of defining certain concepts, and of the meaningfulness of certain operations. The preoccupation of those working within the structure of such theories becomes one of gathering evidence to support this structure, which stands or falls as a whole and is typically unresponsive to outside findings or developments, even though these may be in the same field. As an example of this last point, the developments within Hullian learning theory and its contemporary neo-neo-Hullian descendants seem totally unresponsive to, and certainly make no adjustments in theory to deal with, evidence in the broader field of learning such as Harlow's work with learning sets (1949), Piaget's discoveries, or the evidence on imprinting and other critical period phenomena (Scott, 1962).

It should be stressed that theories that are turned in on themselves (that is, those that essentially ignore phenomena that fall outside their scope) are not necessarily bad. They are quite appropriate to the normal science stage of progress within a closed paradigm. But such a paradigm must be based on real achievement. One should hesitate to close the door to observations, which in a sense is what normal science does, until a paradigm has established its value. Again, we see that paradigmatic theories in psychology lack this established achievement. Thus, their pose as normal science is premature and interferes with the discovery oriented activities of a pre-paradigm phase.

In fact, the most interesting things to be discovered are typically taken for granted in the assumptions, hypotheses, and operations of measurement embodied in such theories. Consider just two examples. Would Fleming have discovered the effect of mold on bacteria, leading to the development of antibiotic drugs, if he was engaged in a hypothesis testing experiment of the sort so common in psychology? Or, to take an example closer to home, Aserinsky discovered the phenomena of rapid eye movements during sleep and their relation to dreaming in the course of an investigation of infant sleep patterns. Would he have done so if he was working within the framework of a highly controlled experiment where attempts were made to control all but a few quantifiable variables? While it is impossible to give clear-cut answers to these questions, the fact that these sorts of discoveries were not made in the context of controlled theory testing is certainly suggestive. Also, we can point to the lack of such discoveries coming from work in the hypothetico-deductive framework. What does seem required for discoveries such as these is intimate contact with the primary data, a close questioning approach to observation, and an openness to discovery. This last, while perhaps most crucial, can only be defined as an attitude on the part of the investigator. Workers within a theory testing framework really cannot afford an open attitude of this sort; they have too much invested in the grand structure of their theory. Incidental findings such as Fleming's or Aserinsky's get ignored or, what is more common, experiments are arranged in such a way that few incidental observations of this sort are possible.

Let us turn our attention now to the way methodological restrictions may interfere with discovery. The work of Skinner and his followers makes a good illustration here, since Skinner ostensibly does not engage in theory building or theory testing of the sort just discussed. Here, the research typically takes the form of imposing tremendous environmental restrictions so that all that can be observed is the rate of a single response. Frequently, these responses are not directly observed but are automatically recorded so that what serves as primary data to the investigator is a cumulative record, that is, an ascending line on graph paper which represents the number of responses per unit time. There is very little that can be observed in so restrictive an environment as the Skinner Box. Taken together with the disdain that Skinner and his followers have for speculation and the place of ideas in science, this approach is hard to surpass for sterility. It is almost as if it were deliberately arranged to forestall the careful observation and involvement with meaningful data that have characterized scientific discovery. What this work does yield are so-called functional relationships, that is, relationships between the rate of a single response to the rate and/or ratio of food pellets, which are then extended, in the grandest manner, to human conflict situations (Lundin, 1960), human language (Skinner, 1957), psychotherapy (Krasner, 1962), and so forth, which overlap in almost no way with the data from which the functional relationships were drawn.

In sum, the belief in abstract theory building and hypothesis testing, the emphasis on control and methodology at the expense of meaningful data, and the restriction of environmental complexity in the name of control all seriously interfere with the process of deep involvement and careful observation of relevant data from which creative hypotheses are likely to be formed.

As Bronowski (1951, pp. 52–53) puts it with respect to a similar situation in the early history of medicine:

It was these large reckless theories which made a caricature of medicine and turned the doctor into a quack. . . . The great advances in medicine from the end of the eighteenth century were of quite different kind. They were scrupulous observations of the complex of symptoms which characterises one disease and not another. . . . It was typical of the best work of the century, a patient work of observation and order *which was not to be diverted by the triumphs of astronomy.* (Italics added.)

The parallel is obvious. Behaviorist psychology has indeed let itself be diverted by the triumphs of physical science, to the detriment of the sort of patient observations that should have preceded such an entrancement with grand theorizing. Now it is time to recognize that the larger theories, lacking the base of observation, have proven a failure and to return our work to a more fruitful, pre-paradigm phase.

One final consideration concerns the relationship between theory, hypothesis formation, and empirical data. Psychology has had its period of blind empiricism which has, in its own way, proven just as barren as the period of grand theorizing. I hope that the foregoing discussion is not taken to mean that we should return to an atheoretical empiricism of the sort once advocated by Frances Bacon. What I would argue for, and what I think the history of science substantiates as most fruitful, is an approach in which both theory and methodology are continuously intertwined with meaningful questions put to relevant subject matter. It is impossible to pose such questions without exhibiting certain theoretical inclinations, certain presuppositions and assumptions. This is not to be avoided; indeed, it cannot be. Furthermore, there is a host of observations and hypotheses—from psychoanalysis, functional psychology, comparative psychology, and from common sense—which are based on insightful observations and experiments and which constitute our best knowledge about many areas at the present time. New work must begin with these observations and theories. But theory at this level is not at all the same thing as the sort of large theory (what Mills calls "Grand Theory" in an analysis of sociology that parallels the present discussion in some respects, 1959) discussed above. Rather, it is possible to strike a balance in which what is known about a particular area (that is, the best existing set of hypotheses) is utilized in putting research questions to data.

THE DATA OF PSYCHOLOGY

In what has gone before, I have spoken a great deal about the importance of data being kept *relevant*, of working with meaningful as opposed to trivial subject matter, and the like. Much of this is based on the assumption that if the ultimate aim of psychological work is directed toward complex human behavior, then this complex behavior must be a substantial part of the data that are initially worked with. Thus, good or relevant data in the area of human learning are illustrated by the recent work of Bruner (1966) as contrasted with much of traditional work on human learning which has never proven of much relevance. In the area of child psychology, relevant work is illustrated by the studies of Piaget and his students (see Flavel, 1963, for an overview) as contrasted with experimentally oriented work as illustrated by Bijou and Baer (1961). In the area of personality, of course, we might contrast Freud, Erikson, and the work of Rogers and his students, all of whom have worked with relevant data, with the work of Eysenck (1953) or Cattell (1950), whose work is characterized by elaborate methodological manipulation of data that are, at base, rather trivial. (It is interesting to note that this work typically imports "meaning" back into the data when assigning names to the end products of the methodological manipulations, for instance, when factors are labeled introversion and extroversion. The meaning comes, of course, from theory based on very different sort of data.) In each of these examples, those working with relevant data have been guided by a concern for a particular problem (for example, what is it possible to teach children in the classroom, how does intelligence develop, what constitutes a neurosis, or how does psychotherapy work?) which has dictated what the data shall be. In the contrasting examples, the concern for method has provided the initial structuring of the field, with data and problems typically limited to whatever can be dealt with by the particular methods (for example, nonsense syllables that will fit on a memory drum, behavior which is limited to a single response system or whose rate changes can be easily measured, or test responses which led themselves to correlational analysis).

At this point, let us direct our attention to a prominent rationale put forth in support of experimental or controlled research of the sort described above. It is frequently argued that while such research does not lend itself to any immediate application, it will in the long run lead to general principles of great predictive power. Thus, what I have been criticizing as the irrelevant, highly remote, or abstract quality of such work is put forth as its primary virtue—it is just this remoteness that constitutes the basic or pure characteristics of the work. I want to discuss several ways in which this is misleading, if not completely wrong.

First, as I have attempted to show earlier, a great deal of the argument for highly controlled research is based on an appeal to traditional behaviorist ideology. Thus, the terms basic and applied have very definite values within the system, the former is good and tends to be equated with control by environmental restriction and primary concern for methodology, while the latter is seen as superficial, lacking in methodological precision, bad and so forth. Once the labels basic and applied have been attached in this fashion, all arguments are settled in advance. But, as we have seen earlier, this sort of appeal rests on ideological rather than factual grounds. It is quite possible to interpret scientific progress as moving from the applied, practical, observational levels to abstract or more general levels. In fact, the history of scientific progress indicates just such a progression (Conant, 1953, Brownowski, 1951). Further, history provides many examples of the close intermingling of applied or technological concerns with so-called basic research (Pasteur and the silkworm industry, Watt, and Faraday, for example).

Thus, the separation of basic from applied research exists more in the fairyland of behaviorist ideology than it does in the reality of scientific history.

In addition, methods, subject matter, and theory are almost always intertwined in such a way that they exert a variety of influences one upon the other. Commitment to a particular kind of methodology is in part determined by the theory about subject matter (about how best to achieve scientific understanding) that one holds. The methods used, in turn, determine what sort of data will be observed. Thus, the methods of traditional experimental psychology from Fechner and Wundt to Hull and Skinner are based on the ideas I have been calling the ideology of behaviorism. These ideas, in turn, prescribe the methods (that is, the highly controlled laboratory experiment, the quantifiable single response) which, in their turn, prescribe the data that are worked with.

Next, let us consider the problem from a slightly different vantage point, one suggested by the complexity of psychological data. What I have been calling relevant data have, in almost every instance, consisted of very complex interactive systems. Thus, the child with his existing knowledge, predispositions, and personality, interacting with other pupils, teacher, and instructional materials in the classroom environment. Or the psychotherapy patient with his difficulties, his particular character structure, defense mechanisms, readiness to form transferences, all interacting with the therapist, with his personality, training, orientation, experience, and readiness to form counter-transferences. It is these complex interactive systems that comprise the most meaningful data for psychology.

This point of view has a history in psychology; it is an essential part of any psychology that concerns itself with adaptive behavior.

There are two points here. First, there is the issue of the level of the data. If we are interested in understanding the anxiety that is experienced by a disturbed human being, then the response of a lower organism to electric shock won't do because it is too remote. It connects with human anxiety only if we attach the same term to each, but the levels of data, the actual facts that are observed in the two instances, are very dissimilar. Thus, the experience of anxiety by a human being comprises a complex system the components of which include his dispositions based on past experiences (these determining his interpretation and response to present input), plus the present input situation.

Second, complex interactive systems exhibit characteristics which cannot be predicted *even if we had a knowledge of the laws governing the actions of the parts comprising the system* which, in psychology, we typically do not have. I think some of the best illustrations for this come from the physical sciences, and I will cite these at the risk of being tainted with the ignoble behaviorist tactic of attempting to gain status by identification with a more prestigious field.

We tend to think of the laws and principles governing the motions of physical bodies as being among the best established predictive scientific principles. In fact, the triumph of Newton's principles had much to do with shaping the whole age of scientific thinking which it ushered in. Yet, it is worth noting that principles such as the law of gravity or Bernoilli's principles of aerodynamics apply in the ideal case—the case of the body falling through empty space or of the perfectly smooth airfoil moving through the uniform airstream. When it comes to the world of objects as they actually exist, these ideal states do not obtain. We are faced, rather, with very complex systems whose parts exert a number of constraints on each other. General principles are sometimes helpful in understanding such complex systems, but they are rarely sufficient in making a prediction. Thus, knowledge of the principles of physics does not enable a geologist to predict when a landslide will occur, or once the landslide is begun, what the position of all the rocks will be at the bottom of the mountain, even though there is "nothing more" involved in a landslide than well known principles governing the motion of physical bodies. The argument that such a prediction is possible in principle is of the same form as Laplace's famous dictum that if one knew the position and speed of every atom in the universe at a particular instant, then one might forecast the fate of the entire universe, including men, nations and heavenly bodies, from that instant until eternity. Not even an approximation to this goal is to be found in science. Laplace's dictum is, rather, a logical extension of the faith in a completely deterministic science that prevailed in the eighteenth and nineteenth centuries. The facts are, that predictions of complex interactive events such as landslides (or the weather, or of the effects of teaching methods, or of psychotherapy) cannot be made from general principles because there are too many variables, all interacting one with the other, more than even the most sophisticated computer could handle if it was constrained to working from principles like the law of gravity. Further, much of the data needed for such a prediction are difficult or impossible to obtain. Does this mean that nothing can be predicted about such events? No, a geologist can probably make a fairly good prediction about the behavior of a landslide, just as meteorologists are able to predict, within certain limits that we are all aware of, the weather. But these predictions are based on direct work with the subject matter; predictions of landslides stem from the study of landslides and not from the laws of physics. Similarly, there is much more to predicting, say, the behavior of an airplane in the air than can be done from principles of physics. Thus, engineers and scientists interested in such predictions work directly with the data; they build mock-ups and put them in wind tunnels, or even better, they send actual airplanes up in the air to see what happens. Our subject matter bears many more similarities to these complex systems than to the highly abstracted data of the theoretical physicist. There is good reason to suppose that the predictive aspirations of psychology are more likely to be met by research that deals directly with complex data treated as a system. The further explication of these issues has been presented by Professor Scriven in the preceding chapter.

Let us hope that these considerations will prove helpful in liberating psychology from the constraints imposed by behaviorist ideology. The argument that this traditional approach will lead to the big pay-off in the long run appears less and less persuasive. The beginnings of experimental psychology date back to Fechner's work over a century ago and the fruits of this tradition have been meager indeed. Is it not time to recognize the limitations of this approach and abandon it in favor of another?

REFERENCES

Atkinson, J. W. *Motives in fantasy, action and society.* Princeton: D. Van Nostrand Co., Inc., 1958.

Bandura, A., and Walters, R. H. *Social learning and personality development.* New York: Holt, Rinehart & Winston, Inc., 1963.

Berkowitz, L. *Aggression: A social psychological analysis.* New York: McGraw-Hill Book Co., 1962.

Bijou, S. W. and Baer, D. M. *Child Development: Vol. I. A systematic and empirical theory.* New York: Appleton-Century-Crofts, 1961.

Bitterman, M. E. Phyletic differences in learning. *American Psychologist,* 1965, *20,* 396–410.

Boring, E. G. *History of experimental psychology.* New York: Appleton-Century-Crofts, 1950.

Bridgeman, P. W. *The way things are.* Cambridge: Harvard University Press, 1959.

Bronowski, J. *The common sense of science.* London: William Heinemann Inc., 1951.

Bruner, J. S. *Studies of cognitive growth.* New York: John Wiley & Sons, Inc., 1966.

Cattell, R. B. *Personality: a systematic, theoretical and factual study.* New York: McGraw-Hill Book Co., 1950.

Chomsky, N. Review of B. F. Skinner, *Verbal behavior,* in *Language,* 1959, *35,* 26–58.

Conant, J. B. *Modern science and modern man.* New York: Doubleday & Co., Inc., 1953.

Dollard, J., and Miller, N. E. *Personality and psychotherapy.* New York: McGraw-Hill Book Co., 1950.

Estes, W. K. An experimental study of punishment. *Psychological Monographs,* 1944, *57,* (No. 263).

Eysenck, H. J. *The structure of human personality.* New York: John Wiley & Sons, Inc., 1953.

Festinger, L. *A theory of cognitive dissonance.* New York: Harper & Row, Publishers, 1957.

Flavell, J. H. *The developmental psychology of Jean Piaget.* Princeton: D. Van Nostrand Co., Inc., 1963.

Hall, C., and Lindzey, G. *Theories of personality.* New York: John Wiley & Sons, Inc., 1957.

Hanson, N. R. *Patterns of discovery*. Cambridge: Harvard University Press, 1958.

Harlow, H. F. The formation of learning sets. *Psychological Review*, 1949, *56*, 51–65.

Harlow, H. F. Mice, monkeys, men and motives. *Psychological Review*, 1953, *60*, 23–32.

Hebb, D. O. *The organization of behavior: a neuropsychological theory*. New York: John Wiley & Sons, Inc., 1949.

Hebb, D. O. The American revolution. *American Psychologist*, 1960, *15*, 735–45.

Hebb, D. O., and Thompson, W. R. The social significance of animal studies. In G. Lindzey (ed.), *Handbook of social psychology*. Cambridge: Addison Wesley Publishing Co., Inc., 1954, 532–62.

Hess, E. H. Ethology: An approach towards the complete analysis of behavior. In *New directions in psychology*. New York: Holt, Rinehart and Winston, Inc., 1962, 157–266.

Hull, C. L. *Principles of behavior*. New York: Appleton-Century-Crofts, 1943.

Kaplan, A. *The conduct of inquiry*. San Francisco: Chandler Publishing Co., 1964.

Koch, S. Behavior as "intrinsically" regulated: work notes towards a pre-theory of phenomena called "motivational." In M. R. Jones (ed.), *Nebraska symposium on motivation*, 1956, *4*, 42–86.

Koch, S. Epilogue. In S. Koch (ed.), *Psychology: A study of a science*. Vol. III. New York: McGraw-Hill Book Co., 1959, 729–88.

Koch, S. Psychology and emerging conceptions of knowledge as unitary. In C. W. Wann (ed.), *Behaviorism and Phenomenology*. Chicago: University of Chicago Press, 1964, 1–41.

Krasner, L. The therapist as a social reinforcement machine. In *Research in Psychotherapy*. Vol. II. Washington, D.C.: American Psychological Association, 1962, 61–94.

Kuhn, T. S. *The structure of scientific revolutions*. Chicago: University of Chicago Press, 1962.

Lorenz, K. Z. *On aggression*. New York: Harcourt, Brace & World, Inc., 1966.

Lundin, A. *Personality*. New York: The Macmillan Co., 1960.

Mills, C. W. *The sociological imagination*. New York: Grove Press, 1959.

Miller, N. E. Theory and experiment relating psychoanalytic displacement to stimulus response generalization. *Journal of Abnormal and Social Psychology*, 1948, *43*, 155–78.

Miller, N. E. Liberalization of basic S-R concepts: Extension to conflict behavior, motivation and social learning. In S. Koch (ed.), *Psychology: a study of a science*. Vol. II. New York: McGraw-Hill Book Co., 1959, 196–292.

Osgood, C. E. *Method and theory in experimental psychology*. New York: Oxford University Press, 1953.

Richter, C. P. Rats, man and the welfare state. *American Psychologist*, 1959, *14*, 18–28.

Roller, D., and Roller, D. H. *The development of the concept of electrical charge*. Cambridge: Harvard University Press, 1954.

Sanford, R. N. Will psychologists study human problems? *American Psychologist*, 1965, *20*, 192–202.

Skinner, B. F. *Verbal Behavior*. New York: Appleton-Century-Crofts, 1957.

Scott, J. P. Critical periods in behavioral development. *Science*, 1962, *138*, 949–58.

Soloman, R. L. Punishment. *American Psychologist*, 1964, *19*, 239–53.

Tolman, E. C. Edward Chance Tolman. In E. G. Boring, H. S. Langfeld, H. Werner, and R. M. Yerkes (eds.), *A history of psychology in autobiography*. Vol. IV. Worcester: Clark University Press, 1952, 323–39.

Wolff, P. H. Cognitive considerations for a psychoanalytic theory of language acquisition. In R. R. Holt (ed.), Motives and thought: psychoanalytic essays in honor of David Rapaport. *Psychological Issues*, 1967, *5*, No. 2–3 (Monograph No. 18–19), 300–343.

3. Psychoanalysis
and American Psychology

David Shakow

"Psycho-analysis is not a specialized branch of medicine. I cannot see how it is possible to dispute this. Psycho-analysis is a part of psychology; not of medical psychology in the old sense, not of the psychology of morbid processes, but simply of psychology."

Thus spoke Freud in 1927 (p. 252). And yet, despite his belief, psychoanalysis and psychology can hardly be said to be united. While other schools of psychology have tended, with time, to become absorbed into the mainstream, the relationship between psychoanalysis and psychology has run a different course. This is due mainly to two factors. Whereas the other schools have grown up in the tradition of academic psychology and within its fold, psychoanalysis has developed almost entirely outside this environment, both spiritually and physically. Psychoanalysis also differs because it is not only a school of psychology offering a theoretical system; it is several other things besides. Thus, psychoanalysis may be thought of as (1) a therapeutic method, (2) a method of investigation, (3) a body of observations, (4) a body of theory about human behavior, and (5) a movement going far beyond its scholarly aspects.

This chapter will concentrate on the theoretical system growing out of the body of observations of psychoanalysis and on the influence of this set of ideas on American psychology. I shall, however, have to consider several other aspects of psychoanalysis as well. The study of the complicated relationship between psychoanalysis and American psychology will necessitate an exploration of the various processes which compose the totality called the *Zeitgeist*. In assessing the impact that Freud has had on American psychology, I shall begin by drawing the distinction between the pervasiveness of Freudian conceptions and the misunderstanding of Freud's concepts. This will be followed by an examination of the nineteenth century milieu in which both Freud and psychology developed.

Next, I shall attempt to trace both the direct and indirect influences of Freud in the first half of the present century. To complement the general survey, two specific areas—the unconscious and motivation—will be examined in greater detail because of their particular importance.

The history of psychology (and philosophy) shows many ideas which bear a resemblance to Freud's theories. Some of them, for instance the earlier theories of the unconscious of Herbart, von Hartmann, and Carpenter, appear to have had little direct effect on the development of Freudian concepts. Freud was probably familiar with a few of them from his youth and was very likely influenced by them, as he was by Nietzsche and Schopenhauer, but only in a general way. What seems certain, however, is that they helped to shape that vague complex of forces called the *Zeitgeist*, and their influence made the *Zeitgeist* ultimately receptive to Freud's influence.

The ideas of Freud's immediate forebears, including Meynert, Brücke, Charcot, Breuer, Bernheim, Brentano, Fechner, Hering, and Lipps, seem to have had considerable influence on Freud, although they were not predecessors of his central ideas. They contributed to the intellectual development of the period, a development which came to a culmination with the impact of Freud's theories.

The ideas of Freud's early American contemporaries, such as the functionalists (James, Dewey, Angell), while they do not seem to have influenced Freud directly, were precursors of some of his central ideas, and they helped to pave the way for the acceptance of Freud's conceptions. James played an especially important role by his anticipation of some of Freud's particular insights and by his influence on the thinking of his students (Holt, Woodworth, Thorndike, and others).

The various concepts of the subconscious held by Freud's later contemporaries (Janet, Prince, and Sidis, for example) affected Freud's thinking little if at all, yet contributed a great deal to the receptivity in psychological circles to Freud's conception of the unconscious.

I have used the two terms 'conception' and 'concept' and shall be making the distinction between them repeatedly. By conception I mean the broad matrix from which theories and concepts crystallize. Concepts have definitions; conceptions make ready use of any term and apply concepts in a common sense way in disregard, or even in ignorance, of their definitions. Theories, by and large, use only terms which have a conceptual status. When terms (for instance, relativity, libido, survival of the fittest) are used outside of the theory, they become conceptions, as they may have been before the theory gave them definition as concepts.

Thus, these predecessors and early contemporaries are not truly genetic antecedents of Freud. They are, instead, representatives of numerous parallel developments.

Those who followed Freud present no less complex a situation. On the one hand, many trends in psychology appeared after Freud's publications which seem to represent direct effects of his influence but are said to derive from independent sources. On the other hand, many theorists who claim that their views are derived directly from Freud seem to have utilized only certain of Freud's ideas in combination with other theories.

In the course of my presentation, I may appear to be suggesting a steady growth of Freudian influence. That such a semblance of continuity is illusory, however, should not surprise anyone who is accustomed to genetic observations and who has learned to think in terms of 'epigenesis' rather than 'preformation,' in terms of saltatory rather than uninterrupted development, in terms of advance by developmental crises rather than along smooth growth curves.

Forewarned against the simplistic assumption, we notice not only the obvious, increasing respect which finally reaches a crescendo of homage to Freud, the man, and his conception of man, but also some of the other attitudes which color whatever acceptance his work has gained:

(1) What is accepted is Freud's new view of man and his pioneering in new areas for psychological study. There has been a slow realization that Freud awakened interest in human nature, in infancy and childhood, in the irrational in man; that he is the fountainhead of dynamic psychology in general, and of psychology's present-day conceptions of motivation and of the unconscious in particular.

(2) Although there are many striking exceptions, it is for the most part his *conceptions* of these fields of study and his *observations* in them, not his *concepts* and *theories* about them, which have been accepted.[1]

(3) When the theory itself is referred to, it is usually transformed into some 'common sense' version or is taken at the level of its clinical referents. In either case, it is likely to be criticized. It can even be said that until relatively recently no serious efforts were made to study thoroughly or to define Freud's concepts before either testing them experimentally or rejecting them.

(4) The methods by which Freud arrived at his theories have not been used. Only recently has there been some effort made to examine the psychoanalytic method as a tool for research.

Thus, along with the non-linear growth of influence, we find that at almost every step the increase of Freud's influence is accompanied by

[1]To these considerations may be added the state of psychoanalytic theory itself. The exact meaning of key concepts such as cathexis (see Holt, 1962) and libido (Holt, 1965) is not always clear. Thus, in psychoanalytic writings, and particularly in post-Freud writings, there is frequently the same blurring of concepts and conceptions found in the popular literature. Klein (Chapter 5) analyzes Freud's concept of sexuality with reference to just this sort of problem. Similarly, Loevinger (Chapter 4) deals with the related problems of the psychoanalytic theory of ego development, and I (Chapter 6) attempt to do the same for the theory of dreams. (Editor)

opposing or confounding trends. What has occurred has been increasing verbal acceptance without proportionate growth of true conversance, acceptance of Freud's conception of man but not of the means by which he derived it. In fact, it has been an influence that was not accompanied by true understanding.

In the case of psychoanalytic theory, barriers in the way of ideal understanding were numerous and weighty among psychologists. Generally speaking, the scientist, because of the limited working time available to him, tries to learn more and more about his area of specialization and inevitably attends less and less to everything outside it. In his specialty, he may try to be completely rational and objective. But outside of it—and for a long while psychoanalysis was outside to most psychologists—where he lacks tested knowledge, he will act, not like a scientist, but like any other person. Common experience indicates that when tested knowledge is not available, implicit regulations of various sorts, whether ideologies, commitments, biases, predilections, or aversions, will select and shape the understandings he gains and mold the influences which impinge upon him. It is easy to see why many psychologists, involved in their specialized concerns and protected by their ideologies (see Chapter 2), were immune to the influence of this new theory.

The historical influence of a theory cannot be measured by the degree of familiarity with and acceptance of it or its precise parts. Rather, Freud's influence on psychology must be gauged by the reactions of psychologists to any idea which demonstrably originated in Freud's observations and theories, regardless of whether the idea came from original sources, secondary sources, popularizations, or hearsay. (Compare Hoffmann, 1957.)

Our task is to trace the details of this influence and to establish how closely the accepted ideas resemble the original theory. This calls for an examination of the ideological commitment of Freud and the channels through which his theory was presented, and the specific ideological commitments of psychology which determined its reaction to the impingements of Freud's theory, as well as some aspects of the broader ideological situation in the United States at the time of the first impact of Freud's theory. For, while such factors are irrelevant to the appraisal of the theory itself, they nevertheless helped determine the character of Freud's influence.

NINETEENTH AND EARLY TWENTIETH-CENTURY BACKGROUND

The nineteenth century appears to have been a period in which mechanism, naturalism, and positivism were dominant, although represented in a narrower and more materialistic way than they had been during the eighteenth century Enlightenment. An appreciation of the factors which imposed limitations on Freud's influence, including the differing commitments of academic psychology and psychoanalysis, requires reaching back into the nineteenth century philosophical matrix out of which psychology grew.

A partial explanation of the separation between psychoanalysis and psychology is probably to be found in the bifurcation of philosophy into natural philosophy and moral philosophy. Out of natural philosophy grew present-day epistemology and science. In this context, arose the key topics of early psychology—perceiving and knowing. Out of moral philosophy grew present-day ethics, with its relevant psychological problems of willing, wishing, feeling—topics central to psychoanalysis.

Of more immediate relevance for an appreciation of the influence of psychoanalysis on psychology, however, is the nature of their respective commitments to an important scientific outgrowth of nineteenth century philosophy, to what has come to be known as 'the Helmholtz program.' In part, it was psychology's commitment to the Helmholtz program which separated it, and even now keeps it somewhat apart, from those roots which gave rise to moral philosophy.

The Helmholtz program was a reflection of the philosophy embodied in a statement made in an 1842 letter to Eduard Hallman by du Bois-Reymond:

Brücke and I pledged a solemn oath to put into power this truth, no other forces than the common physical-chemical ones are active within the organism; that, in those cases which cannot at the time be explained by these forces one has either to find the specific way or form of their action by means of the physical-mathematical method, or to assume new forces equal in dignity to the chemical-physical forces inherent in matter, reducible to the force of attraction and repulsion [du Bois-Reymond, 1918, p. 108].

This statement was accepted in principle by the group which shortly came to include Helmholtz and Ludwig, known later as the Helmholtz school of medicine.

Cranefield (1957, 1959) points out that the '1847 program,' as he calls the program of the Helmholtz school, had three goals: (1) to establish an anti-vitalist position with the accompanying idea of intelligible causality, (2) to provide argument for the use of observation and experiment, and (3) to attempt to reduce physiology to physics and chemistry. Following a searching review of this topic, Cranefield concludes that the program had more or less success in achieving the first two goals. However, with the molar methods then available, the achievement of a truly physicalistic physiology was impossible. Not until present-day molecular biophysics and chemistry was this reduction possible. Thus, even the Helmholtz group turned to the assumption of the "new forces equal in dignity" part of the oath and to an attack upon the multiple problems of physiology by experimental methods using as tools physics and chemistry.

With this clearer understanding of what was actually represented by the Helmholtz program, we are ready to examine the different ways in which psychology and psychoanalysis reacted to and interpreted the philosophy of the program, and how these respective interpretations affected both the course of Freud's thinking and psychology's receptiveness to Freudian theory. If psychology or psychoanalysis were to try to carry out the Helmholtz program, they could not reasonably be expected to do more than physiology itself was then able to achieve. At most, they could adopt a mechanistic-deterministic point of view, apply experimental and observational methods to their phenomena, use physical and chemical techniques, and deal with their phenomena in terms of forces which were of "equal dignity."

Psychology was at first committed by Helmholtz, a physicist, to becoming an exact science in the same sense that physics was an exact science. But, like physiology, psychology had to compromise and settle for an experimental rather than a physicalist approach. Psychology, in the attempt to be exact, restricted itself to the use of the experimental method and consequently to the study of phenomena about which it *could* be exact. What came to be known as sensory psychology and psychophysics appeared to be the general areas to which these methods were applicable.[2]

As we shall see below, it was not the theoretical commitment alone, but rather this commitment in combination with the choice of the experimental method and of the subject matter for the application of the method, which was fateful for psychology. Psychology, in aiming to establish itself experimentally, came increasingly to focus upon introspective reports. This led to an intense preoccupation with the mental elements constituting subjective experience. Finally, in the hands of such structuralists as Titchener, the description of these mental structures seemed to become the very goal. When introspective data proved to be unreliable, the shortcomings of the subjects were held to be at fault. The resultant use of trained 'introspectors' led to still another problem: increasing dependence of experimental results upon the research center in which the subjects were trained with the likelihood of nonreplicable results. A crisis in experimental psychology developed.

The resolution of this crisis split psychology into two camps, one of them rather accessible and the other much less accessible, to Freud's

2Chapter 2 "The Ideology of Behaviorism" attempts to spell out in somewhat more detail the implications of these methodological restrictions for psychology. (Editor)

oncoming influence. The first group to rebel against the sterility of the structuralist program were the functionalists (James, and Dewey, J. R. Angell, and the Chicago school). They believed the experimental program had miscarried because of the quest for fixed mental elements (structures).

We can call on William James to illustrate the more general roots of the functionalists' dissatisfaction. James (1890, Vol. 1, pp. 548–549) characterized the exactitude of Fechner's law (and of psychophysics) as pseudo-exactitude, and asserted that whatever validity it had was in physiology, rather than in psychology. He commented as follows: ". . . it would be terrible if even a dear old man as this could saddle our Science forever with his patient whimsies, and, in a world so full of more nutritious objects of attention, compel all future students to plough through . . . his . . . works. . . ."[3]

By raising the question of the use and purpose of psychological structures and processes, the functionalists became involved in issues of adaptation, development, and the relationship between organism and environment. Accordingly, they contributed to the growth of naturalistic observation and developmental theorizing. The functionalists' program thus shared with Freud's program allegiances to both the Helmholtz school and to Darwinism and initiated a trend which augured favorably for Freud's influence.

Somewhat later than the functionalists, the behaviorists (Watson and others), the representatives of the second trend, rebelled against the structuralists' miscarriage of the experimental program. This group turned against the introspectionist aspect of the structuralist program, restating and reinforcing the exact science program in a form even more rigorous (or should we say more rigid?) than the original. They saw the fruitless, deceptive shadowboxing of the structuralists' introspections as the cause of the sterility of their experimental program and concluded that consciousness was an epiphenomenon. It was as if they had deliberately agreed that consciousness was not reducible to the forces of "attraction and repulsion" and therefore not of the character demanded by even a modified form of the original Helmholtz program. The behaviorists declared observable behavior to be the only proper subject matter of

3James' rebellion against the Helmholtz program and his criticism of Fechner's psychophysics reflects his personality, showing his freedom as a psychologist to look at and think about an amazingly broad range of human phenomena. Through his opposition to the limiting requirements of the 'exact science' commitment he was able to face 'life in the raw' and to consider all facts of life proper subject matter for psychology. Evidence for the similarities between the functionalist and Freudian trends are especially clear in James, who in many respects appears to have anticipated Freud's ideas. Examples of James' anticipation are so abundant that their neglect by both psychologists and psychoanalysts is not only puzzling but embarrassing. Note particularly his discussion of the vague and the fleeting (1890, Vol. 1, pp. 254–255).

an exact science of psychology, thus ruling out both consciousness as a subject matter, and the use of introspection as a method. In this way, they reaffirmed the constriction of the field imposed by the exact science interpretation of the original program and exacerbated this constriction by an accompanying blindness to the possibility of "new forces equal in dignity." Once consciousness and introspection were declared illegitimate, the source of the data on which psychoanalysis was built was, of course, excluded from the behaviorist's scientific psychology.

The general result seems to have been that the functionalists, who were directing their attention to more meaningful areas, made only little progress toward exactitude and unified theory, whereas those who remained faithful to the earlier program made equally little progress in extending their exactitude beyond the confines of limited laboratory problems. While functionalism, through its emphasis on use and adaptation, gave rise to applied psychology and the psychology of individual differences, the mainstream of American psychology came to adhere to the new and extreme form of what was essentially the original exact science program as interpreted by the behaviorists.

Thus, Darwinian influence and functionalism, especially Jamesian open-mindedness and genius, led to psychological thinking akin in many respects to Freud's. It seems reasonable to assume that these account for part of whatever subsequent receptiveness there was to Freud. But functionalism was itself isolated from the mainstream of American psychology, a circumstance which partially explains the reluctant acceptance of Freud in most Western psychological circles.

It is important to recognize that although psychology's particular interpretation of and commitment to the Helmholtz program was an obstacle to Freud's influence, it nevertheless also served as a link between psychology and psychoanalysis. Freud, too, was committed to the Helmholtz program, and a consideration of this commitment will help to explain this paradoxical situation.

During his years at the University of Vienna, Freud was strongly influenced by Brücke, the "Far Eastern" representative of the Helmholtz group. He worked on neurophysiological problems in Brücke's laboratory and described Brücke as the person who "carried more weight with me than anyone else in my whole life . . ." (Freud, 1927, p. 253). Freud's early speculations concerning the neuroses bear the stamp of this influence, an influence clearly revealed in the "Project for a Scientific Psychology" (1895). In the "Project," Freud made a valiant attempt to develop a neurological theory of psychopathology and psychology, but when he failed in this, he turned to what amounted to a search for forces "equal in dignity" in the psychological sphere. This was not, however, the sphere of academic psychology, for the problems Freud settled on—those of affectivity—were more consonant with the subject matter of moral philosophy.

From about 1900 on, Freud's theories essentially emphasize the psychological—the *motivational* psychological—though there are occasional backward glances at physiology (as in *Three Essays on the Theory of Sexuality*, 1905). Freud's early commitment and his difficulty in giving up this physicalistic background led to certain theoretical difficulties that are only recently being clarified (Holt, 1965, 1967, Klein, 1967, and Chapter 5 of this book). Despite these problems, it seems clear, as Loevinger points up in Chapter 4 and as the rest of Part II of the present volume illustrates, that Freud's theories are primarily *psychological*, that they deal with meanings and ideas (conscious and unconscious), symbolic transformations, feelings, human relationships, and the like.

If we re-examine the Helmholtz program in the context of the oath taken by duBois-Reymond and Brücke, we see that the spirit of the program could be fulfilled wholly or in part in three ways: (1) by a true physicalist physiology (which was not attained during the whole Helmholtz period), (2) by an objective experimental physiology (Ludwig, Helmholtz, Brücke, duBois-Reymond, *et al.*) or an objective experimental psychology (Wundt, G. E. Muller, Ebbinghaus, *et al.*) which used physics and chemistry as *tools*, or (3) by a consulting-room psychology which used objective observational methods (Freud). The inclusion of the last naturally raises a question, for a consulting room psychology utilizes neither instrumental controls nor the controls usually associated with experiment, coming closer to the naturalistic situation with which biology proper was occupying itself at the time.[4]

In point of fact, the area of psychology Freud chose did not lend itself readily to experiment or to the application of physical and chemical techniques, whereas the area of the experimental psychologists in part did, and that was the part which was most impressive to the scientific public. For the period in which Freud worked, the nature of the material, and the stage of development of the field appeared to call for an acceptance of the kind of observational technique and the kind of theory that he developed. To Freud and others, his endeavor was an indirect but essential step toward the realization of a program which was to include obviously significant and even apparently trivial facets of ordered and disordered human behavior.

The experimental psychologists were so imbued with the narrower interpretation of the Helmholtz philosophy and their interpretation of its methodological restrictions that they limited themselves to areas of

[4]In Chapter 1, Scriven argues that it was probably a mistake all along for psychology to have attempted to model itself after physics. He outlines some interesting alternatives that are more consistent with recent thinking in the philosophy of science. (Editor)

psychology in which the method was applicable, that is, to sensation and perception, the fields closest to physiology. This meant that they worked in the laboratory where they could choose their problems and consequently could apply the method without much difficulty. Freud, on the other hand, working in the consulting room, had to deal with the problems which came to him. Careful analysis convinced him that these were affective ones. To these he tried to apply the Helmholtz philosophy as far as possible, but obviously he could not do so as rigorously as could the experimental psychologists with their more limited segmental problems. Nevertheless, he held strongly to the anti-vitalist position of the Helmholtz school and to the use of observation, if not experiment. The essence of the program, common to all its parts, was an exceptionless determinism. For Freud, the "equal in dignity" part of the program took the form of the postulate of thoroughgoing *psychic* determinism. It is true that in a number of places (for example, 1913, p. 182; 1925, pp. 25–26) Freud indicated the hope for an eventual physicalist explanation. It is nevertheless clear from other statements (for example, 1913, p. 166) that he was not willing to accept superficial and easy biological hypotheses—for instance, Jung's simplistic theory of a toxic cause for dementia praecox—when he felt that psychological ones were much more relevant and meaningful.

The "new forces" which Freud postulated were not "reducible to the forces of attraction and repulsion" by the means he had at his disposal. His methods did serve, however, to encompass in the scope of the scientific program a broad range of phenomena which exact academic psychology could not at that time, nor even now, deal with adequately. It was, then, the equivalent of a psychological extension of the "equal in dignity" part of the Helmholtz program that Freud pursued for the rest of his life. In the present context, it suffices to say that by assuming the existence of such forces, he made *psychological reality* a subject matter of psychological study having for many psychologists the same dignity as did the *impingements of external reality* for psychophysicists and behaviorists.

FREUD AND DYNAMIC PSYCHOLOGY

The course Freud followed was in some respects similar to that of the functionalists who rebelled against the narrower interpretation of the Helmholtz program and concentrated on areas foreign to the dominant behavioristic group, areas such as instinctual drives and emotions. As we have seen, functionalism helped to prepare the ground for Freud's influence on psychology and became the area of psychology most open to his influence. Together, Freudism and functionalism came to serve as the main sources of nourishment for dynamic psychology. In the long run, however, Freud, not functionalism, was decisive for the survival and growth of dynamic psychology, so much so that, at present, dynamic psychology and Freud are often considered synonymous.

It is true that one trend in clinical psychology, that represented by Witmer, can be said to derive from Wundt and the structuralist point of view. However, this was not the trend which prevailed. Rather, it was the trend initiated by Healy, largely influenced by Freudian psychology, which became the dominant one (Shakow, 1948).

All in all, it is understandable that Boring should conclude: "The principal source of dynamic psychology is, of course, Freud" (1950, p. 693).

The dynamic trend was alien to and combatted by the mainstream of development in psychology. For a very long while, the commitment of the mainstream to "exact science" and the skipping by academic psychology of the naturalistic phase which had been so well represented in biology did not encourage interest in naturalistic observation, let alone in the rough and ready observations and theorizing characteristic of psychoanalysis.

Woodworth clearly saw the intrinsic contrast between Freudism and the main trend in psychology: "As a movement within psychiatry, psychoanalysis was a revolt against the dominant 'somatic' tendency of the nineteenth century, and a springing into new life of the 'psychic' tendency. Just when psychology was becoming more somatic, psychiatry started in earnest to be psychic" (1931, p. 126).

It is obvious that the choice of subject matter and explanatory level, which Woodworth stresses, was important. But there is perhaps something even more crucial in the contrasting methods used in psychology and psychoanalysis. Freud resorted to methods which we still do not know how to describe precisely. The "exact science" of psychology, on the other hand, adhered to exact methods which were not easily, if at all, applied to the subject matter on which Freud developed his theories. Psychology did not have the means to prove or disprove Freud's theories.

While James' commitment was to face unflinchingly life in the raw and Freud's was to carry out, implicitly if not explicitly, the Helmholtz program as well as clinical reality permitted, the mainstream of psychology uncompromisingly stuck to the narrower aspects of the Helmholtz program, which the originators of the program had not been able to carry out even in physiology (Cranefield, 1957). I once speculated how much further developed and more widely applicable our exact scientific methods might now be if all of psychology had initially committed itself to carrying out the Helmholtz program on the subject matter of and within the limitations of clinical reality (Shakow, 1953). If nothing else, the question does identify this problem as the age-old one of the difference between working inductively from the material of naturalistic observation and working inductively from narrow premises. It would seem that major scientific advances arise from the interplay of these two quite separate approaches, and it was precisely this interplay that was prevented for a long time by the differing commitments of the main-streams of psychology and psychoanalysis. In such interplay, methods develop which increasingly fulfill both the demands of the material and the demands of the criteria for relevant levels of rigorous proof. It seems that the different commitments of academic psychology and psychoanalysis not only interfered with their taking note of each other's methods, but also resulted in their focusing on different subject matters. Because of these events, the development of rigorous methods applicable to the data of psychoanalysis was prevented.

I have surveyed the differing commitments of psychology and psychoanalysis and some causes of psychology's reluctance to recognize Freud. Later, we shall consider some of psychology's ambivalent feelings further, but at the moment we are faced with another problem. Assuming the accuracy of this description of the relationship between academic psychology and psychoanalysis, it would not be surprising if a stalemate prohibiting any interaction had resulted, with little or no Freudian influence on psychology. The fact that there *has* been a profound Freudian influence calls for an explanation.

GENERAL ASPECTS OF TWENTIETH-CENTURY DEVELOPMENTS—INFLUENCE AND OBSTACLES TO INFLUENCE

In analyzing the way in which psychoanalysis came to affect psychology, two mutually supporting lines of influence, one indirect and one direct, seem to emerge. Although they cannot be completely separated, the indirect influence seems to be that which came predominantly from the surrounding culture, from that part of the *Zeitgeist* which was itself greatly shaped by Freudism. The direct influence appears to be that which came along natural professional lines, from sources more immediately related to psychology and psychoanalysis. Let us first examine the various streams of *indirect* influence.

The American atmosphere of the first decades of the 1900's was a peculiarly favorable one for Freudian ideas. The muckrakers (Tarbell, Norris, Sinclair, Steffens) and early realists (Crane, Dreiser, London) of the last decades of the nineteenth century had already laid the foundations for breaking down the genteel traditions of a primarily Puritan and Victorian culture. This trend was markedly accelerated by the social protesters (Eastman, Goldman, Dell, Debs), the feminists (Schreiner), and the Bohemians (Dodge), all of whom were influential in the period immediately before and after World War I. Freudian ideas were welcomed with open arms by these rebellious forces, and relationships developed among them in which the Freudian influence became paramount. In fact, Freudian ideas became so integral a part of the *Zeitgeist* that this *Zeitgeist* became an indirect but major channel for Freud's influence on professional psychology. The impact of the new ideology led to the development of a simplified and distorting popular and semi-popular literature dealing with Freud which continues even to the present. This, in turn, contributed to the public consciousness of psychoanalysis which led students and members of other disciplines to expect psychologists to deal with dynamic aspects of human behavior. By the nature of the ideas it dealt with, Freudism re-aroused dormant guilts among psychologists for not having met a reasonable obligation—the greater understanding and control of the forces of human nature.

Concurrent with these indirect factors which played varying roles in Freud's influence, more *direct* professional influences were at work. But in spite of the combined pressures of public consciousness, impatient colleagues (such as Tansley, 1920, and Wheeler, 1921), students, and professional influences, psychoanalysis did not immediately become a part of American psychology. It had first to overcome many difficulties, some of which were actually created by the very vehicles that carried it.

There were, of course, many general professional factors which no doubt worked against psychology's receptiveness to psychoanalysis. Freud was a stranger and an outsider, one whose unconventional methods were suspect, whose air of condescension to academic psychology was repugnant, and whose use of the doubtfully defensible resistance argument was particularly antagonizing.[5] A further obstacle was probably the pro-

[5]This is the argument that opposition to psychoanalysis is motivated by unconscious resistance on the part of the opponent, that, for example, one cannot accept the idea of the Oedipus complex because it arouses anxiety to think of one's own. In a related argument, it is asserted that only he who has engaged in psychoanalytic therapy can fully understand psychoanalytic theory. There are insidious aspects to these positions and, when carried to their extremes as they sometimes are, they place the theory in the position of a religious dogma that is impervious to all questioning. At the higher levels of theoretical abstraction, the connection between theory and therapy is frequently not clear, making the resistance argument of little relevance.

Nevertheless, the insidiousness with which the argument is sometimes used should not blind us to certain elements of truth in it. For one thing, certain phenomena can best be understood from first-hand experience which is, after all, what distinguishes science from arm-chair speculation. Hence, it is quite reasonable to demand such a first-hand acquaintance with psychoanalytic therapy, either as patient or therapist, as a necessary prerequisite for an informed discussion of it.

The resistance argument itself touches on a somewhat more complicated issue stemming from the peculiar problems that arise from introspective methods. Bakan (1967) points out how Külpe and the others of the Würzburg school around the turn of the century, in using the method of introspection on the problem of "imageless thought,"

fessional medical orientation of psychoanalysis, whose students were trained in independent and non-academic settings, in contrast to the conventional academic setting of the psychologist.

But such factors were, in the end, probably only accessory to the major obstacles. Most of the difficulties grew out of particular qualities of the material provided by psychoanalysis, material which is the usual means of transmitting new theories and ideas. The language barrier, confounded by the circuitous course of psychoanalytic development, made it difficult for the psychologist to be sure what psychoanalysis really was. The subtlety of Freud's writing made understanding of the original German difficult, even for those who knew German fairly well, and it was a rare psychologist who could do better than this. Those who went to whatever translations were available were hindered by their general inadequacy. Further, psychologists seemed preponderantly to prefer secondary sources. But it was difficult to find a reliable secondary source which covered even a portion of psychoanalytic theory. Until fairly recently, the secondary sources made no pretense of providing any systematic presentation of psychoanalysis. At the very best, they presented only parts of the theory, frequently emphasizing the clinical rather than the general theory; at the worst, they were misleading. To the general lack of familiarity with psychoanalysis was added the misinformation provided by the oversimplifications and distortions of the more popular sources.

The opinions of outstanding psychologists from James and Hall through Dewey, Watson, Woodworth, McDougall, Thurstone, and Terman, and historians such as Boring and Murphy provide a glimpse of the academic reaction to Freud. Whether the responses were made as a man in the street or as a psychologist, whether they were the result of dormant professional guilt or of the particular quality of the written sources, they ranged from the violently negative, through the indifferent, to the generally positive. At all these levels, however, reactions were characterized by conflict and hesitancy.

Thus, while Freud's influence was being inescapably forced upon psy-

---

began using free associative methods very much like Freud's. Their work led them ever closer to psychoanalytic data and methods. For example, Messer posits unconscious processes. Ach stresses the role of motivation in guiding thought and uses hypnosis, and Bühler stresses the importance of empathy with the subjects in such research (Bakan, 1967, pp. 96–97). Suddenly, the work is dropped and Külpe's subsequent publications contain no mention of it, nor of the entire topic of thought! It seems reasonable to assume with hindsight that their methods led the Würzburg group to the same place that they led Freud, that their probing of each others' minds produced unconscious material, generated anxiety or other forms of discomfort and defensiveness or resistance, which in turn led to an abandonment of the whole enterprise.

Resistance, as the above historical example illustrates, is an important psychological phenomenon; it does occur in relation to the data generated by introspective methods, a fact that is extremely important in understanding the historical development of psychology as well as certain reactions to Freud and psychoanalytic theory. (Editor) chology by various public and professional pressures in a period of great social and moral upheaval in the United States, particularly during the years just before and after World War I, concrete and practical factors joined cultural and social trends to complicate and obstruct the course of this influence. Clashing philosophical and professional commitments, language and methodological barriers, and mutual defensiveness and misunderstanding prevented any semblance of continuous integration of psychoanalysis into American psychology, leading instead to complex interactions that resulted nevertheless in a fitful, though steadily increasing, growth.

THE UNCONSCIOUS AND MOTIVATION

Of the many major contributions of Freud to psychological theory, we might deal briefly with two of especial importance—the unconscious and motivation. These are selected because they are areas central to the interests of psychologists and lend themselves more readily to examination than do other areas to which Freud contributed, such as dynamic psychology and the understanding of human nature.

The long history of the conception of the unconscious, represented by both Freud's precursors and contemporaries mentioned earlier, laid the foundations for receptiveness to the idea of an unconscious when this was proposed by Freud. On the other hand, it made true appreciation of his concept of the unconscious, which included two different kinds of unconscious, one unrepressed and the other repressed (Gill, 1963), much more difficult.[6] In fact, psychologists often acted as if they were not aware of this distinction.

In the case of motivation, Freud's theory was caught up in the controversies related to various polarities—determinism-teleology, mechanism-vitalism, pro- and anti-hedonism, and nature-nurture. These controversies served as obstacles to the penetration of Freud's concepts but nevertheless helped to spread his general conception of motivation. The very involvement of his theory on both sides of the controversies clearly demonstrates the misunderstandings of it which were prevalent.

When we examine the specific course of Freud's theory of motivation, we see its relationships with certain aspects of the association and act psychology of his predecessors Herbart and Brentano (active ideas and intentionalism) and its similarities to such sibling theories as those of Thorndike, Claparède, and Ach. Definite likenesses can also be seen between Freud and the theories which derived from these latter three

---

[6]See the discussion by Klein (in press) and Loevinger (1966) of the two principles of the dynamic unconscious (or repression) and the "reversal of voice" principle. What Klein and Loevinger present are essentially cognitive formulations of the two forms of the unconscious referred to here. (Editor)

psychologists—those of Piaget, Lewin, and the adopters of Thorndike's law of effect, most particularly of Hull and the Yale group.

Piaget's theories show parallels to Freud's theories in their union of nature and nurture, in the pervasive role they give to motivation, and in their hierarchic conception of motivation.[7] Lewin's theories of tension systems and his concern with emotions are also parallels to Freud. The attempt made by Hull and the Yale group to reconcile psychoanalysis with conditioned reflex theory generally resulted in an invasion of the literature by Freudian terms but at the price of turning Freud's concepts into conceptions only barely related and sometimes contradictory to the original concepts. There can be no doubt, however, that Hull's drive concept and the concepts of Dollard, Miller, and Mowrer, all of which differed from the psychoanalytic one, did a great deal to make Freudian ideas familiar and of great interest to psychologists.

If we follow Freud's concepts along another line of development, along the line of instinct, we see a somewhat similar result. The comparison of the instinct conception with Freud's concept of instinctual drive reveals developments which were both an aid in a general way to keeping the instinct idea alive and a hindrance in a specific way to Freudian influence. We see this both in those who rebelled against the instinct idea (Bernard, Watson, and Kuo) and in those who, like Tolman and Woodworth, needed some kind of nativist conception for the completion of their psychological systems. In the case of McDougall, who was particularly concerned with a nativist basis for his psychology, Freud's emphasis on the drive concept appears to have reinforced his persistence in his own hormic psychology.

It is difficult to summarize the meandering course of Freud's influence on the birth and development of motivation theories in psychology. One can only be amazed by the intricate intertwining of influence and by the unpredictable channels through which influences are effected. What appears highly probable, however, is that the passage through a stage of acceptance, which amounts mainly to taking the specificity out of concepts and turning them into vague conceptions, is unavoidable in the historical process.

PROBLEMS AND PROSPECTS FOR THE FUTURE

Having looked at some aspects of the historical background of the present position of psychoanalysis, it remains for us to examine briefly some of the problems and prospects for the future, as psychoanalysis takes

---

[7]Some of the relations between the theories of Freud and Piaget are considered by Wolff in Chapter 7. In a sense, much of Part II of the present volume is concerned with bringing together Freud and cognitive psychology, of which Piaget is perhaps the leading figure. (Editor)

its place as part of psychology. Rapaport, in attempting a systematization of psychoanalytic theory, has presented the main lines of the problems that lie ahead (Rapaport, 1959, pp. 155–167).

The obstacles to the integration of psychoanalysis with psychology are of two types: practical obstacles that lie in both psychology and psychoanalysis, and certain theoretical obstacles that arise from the nature of their common field of study.

The practical obstacles lying within psychology are various. We have already noted some of the problems arising from psychology's self-consciousness, a self-consciousness which is reflected in a preoccupation with *the* scientific method and with experimental design at the cost of substantive concern. There has been, too, a tendency in psychology toward addiction to a single theory or to a single method, a trend closely associated to the prevalence of schools. Another obstacle is the extension to problems in psychology of what Adelson (1956) has called the notion of "perfectibility," the natural American propensity to be optimistic (Shakow, 1960). Although this attitude of optimism has become most obviously involved in problems of therapy, it can also be seen in theories about the basic nature of man (Maslow, 1962). These theories have developed largely in reaction to an exaggerated concern with the pathological but tend to neglect the negative forces with which individuals must contend. Psychoanalytic ego psychology, especially Erikson, appears to have dealt with this area in a much more realistic fashion.

Psychoanalysis, too, has its practical obstacles. The first of these is a problem which was considered earlier: the lack of systematic theoretical literature, especially on the general psychoanalytic theory. Although this situation is to some extent being alleviated by the work of persons like Rapaport (1959) and Gill (1963), it still remains an obstacle to theoretical progress.[8] Another handicap is the training offered by psychoanalytic institutes. Its almost exclusive limitation to physicians, its essentially night school character, and its emphasis on private practice which does not foster theoretical interest and development and results in a limited number and kind of patient are all handicaps to theoretical progress. It is not surprising, therefore, that some demand has grown up in recent years for relatively independent institutes to be associated with both medical schools and with graduate departments of psychology (Shakow, 1962).

In addition to the two kinds of practical problems just considered, there are a number of theoretical obstacles arising from the very nature of the subject matter and the field which psychoanalysis and psychology have in common. Regard for the individual's legal and moral rights is a

[8]Several of the chapters in Part II may be seen as formulations on the general theoretical level, though the type of theory that emerges is much further from the orthodox psychoanalytic view than that of Rapaport and Gill. See especially Klein and Loevinger. (Editor)

major empirical barrier to the observation and manipulation of behavior inside and outside the laboratory. This problem also has important theoretical aspects: the effects of such trespass upon the subject, the observer, and the observation. There is, too, the hierarchy problem. Much experimentation lies ahead before laws of hierarchic transformation are developed which will permit adequate handling of field problems taken into the laboratory. Still another problem grows out of the fact that a large proportion of psychological phenomena occur only in the contact of one person with one or more others. The method of participant observation has been developed to deal with this problem, but the implications of the method have not yet been theoretically formulated, and the lack of such systematization has in turn retarded the theory's development. A final obstacle is that of mathematization, including quantification.

Some progress has been made in the attempt to deal with these various problems. First efforts are being made toward handling the difficulties created by participant observation through the development of alternative techniques. Knowledge of dyadic and other social situations is being advanced by the use of techniques for studying organized complexity and modern computational devices (Weaver, 1948). The hierarchy problem has offered more difficulties because the theoretical aspects of hierarchic transformation have not been developed. This difficulty is, of course, somewhat alleviated by the fact that not all problems need to be taken to the laboratory. Although as many problems as possible need to be brought under laboratory control, efforts to deal rigorously with field situations should be continued and increased.

Over a decade ago, I was afforded an opportunity to take stock of mid-century trends in what was broadly defined as the area of experimental psychology (Shakow, 1953). At that time, a number of trends appeared conspicuous. One of these was the growing awareness by psychology of its own overconcern with its formal disciplinary aspects and the resultant ego orientation rather than task orientation. Together with this awareness were early signs of revolt against this preoccupation with our neighbors' presumed interest in our affairs. Another important trend was the growing interest in Jamesian "more nutritious objects of attention," reflected in increasing attention to molar studies, accompanied by a diligent search for methods to handle the organized complexity involved.

Rapaport (1959) has made some important complementary points. More recently, Koch (1959, pp. 729–788) has presented a more systematic statement of a similar point of view. In his concluding perspective, based on his review of the formulations made by the thirty-four contributors to the first three volumes of his work, Koch (1959, pp. 783–785) says:

"It can in summary be said that the results of Study I set up a vast attrition against virtually all elements of the Age of Theory [approximately the 1930–1955

period] *code*. . . . [None of the contributors] is prepared to retreat one jot from the objectives and disciplines of scientific inquiry, but most are inclined to re-examine reigning stereotypes about the *character* of such objectives and disciplines. There is a longing, bred on perception of the limits of recent history and nourished by boredom, for psychology to embrace . . . problems over which it is possible to feel intellectual passion. . . .

"For the first time in its history, psychology seems ready—or almost ready—to assess its goals and instrumentalities with primary reference to its own indigenous problems. . . .

"This preparedness to face the indigenous must be seen as no trivial deflection in the line of history. . . .

". . . at the time of *its* inception, *psychology was unique in the extent to which its institutionalization preceded its content and its methods preceded its problems.* If there are keys to history, this statement is surely a key to the brief history of our science. . . . Never had inquiring men been so harried by social need, cultural optimism, extrinsic prescription, the advance scheduling of ways and means, the shining success story of the older sciences."

Why do I make so much of these developments? Because they have direct reference to a central aspect of Freud's influence—the long delay in integration of his ideas and the many vicissitudes hindering the achievement of their appropriate place in psychology. But in making these points about the past, am I not, as Koch says, "decrying the inevitable"? Am I not trying to hurry history, questioning the relentless march of historical forces, the forces of the dominant aspects of the *Zeitgeist*, which nothing could have changed? Those of us who have wished that the integration of Freud into psychology had been more rapid recognize that it would have required psychologists who were objective and task oriented, who saw their central concern as the understanding of human nature, who reacted to Freud as a colleague (rather than as an outsider) equally interested in achieving this understanding, who accepted Freud as bringing to the field an insight into areas of crucial importance for psychology, who did their utmost to understand the theories and the methods which were being proposed, who marshalled the forces necessary for developing topics in these areas further, expanding the methods to make them more searching. In fact, earlier integration of psychoanalysis into psychology would have demanded that the psychologists of the period disregard both internal and social pressures, would have demanded that they disregard both their own values and prejudices and those facets of the scientific *Zeitgeist* that impinged on them most closely.

It may be, of course, that just as the attainment of hybrid vigor requires different combinations of periods of inbreeding and outbreeding, so the optimal development of a science requires different concentrations of attitudes at different periods in its development. If this is so, then psychology has certainly gone through its period of inbreeding. We have been through a period which has been weighted heavily with the strongly held narrownesses and limited commitments previously described, as well as with the negatives which Boring discusses with such tolerance (Boring, 1942, p. 613). Perhaps these were inevitable for the period.

Can it be, however, that an atmosphere favorable for the outbreeding which some wished for in this earlier period, but which the mainstream of the *Zeitgeist* was not ready to support, is now in the process of developing? Can it be that our judgment is correct in holding that now the main force of the scientific *Zeitgeist* is changing and asserting itself in an emphasis on meaningfulness, even though the new atmosphere is still permeated with the smog of tradition, the heritage of an irreversible history?

As the effects of its early negative characteristics—which I, however, cannot help believing any science needs, in at least some degree, during all phases of its growth—subside, psychology seems to be developing more positive qualities. These include a readiness to face substantive aspects of problems, with insistence on only the degree of rigor necessary to protect the substance; an appreciation of the psychologist's personal motivations for entering the field (Roe, 1953); an appreciation of the stage of psychology's scientific development (Adrian, 1946; Tolman, 1947); a readiness to participate in a group commitment to a field where tolerance for tentativeness needs to be great; above all, an ability to recognize the value of a variety of approaches to psychology, even if one's personal commitment is to one particular approach. These are the qualities of mature psychologists who have to work with an inevitably adolescent psychology.

Freud has at times been compared with various great idea men—Jesus, Leonardo, Newton, Kant, Darwin, Pasteur, Einstein; with great conquistadors—Moses, Columbus, Magellan; and with great methods men such as Socrates. It is actually not surprising to find this number and range, and even exaltedness, of the comparisons. Besides the difficulty of categorizing great men simply by finding their counterparts, there is the difficulty of keeping individual emotions out of the situation. From one point of view, Freud *was*, despite his own denials, a great idea man, whose ideas revolutionized not only psychology but a large part of twentieth century thought. From another point of view, Freud *was* a conquistador, a great discoverer who opened up and explored hitherto unprobed areas in man. And again, Freud *was* a great methods man (Bernfeld, 1949, pp. 183–184), as the free association method attests.

But one thing characterized Freud above all—the constantly changing, developing nature of his theoretical system. He continually checked his hypotheses and theories against his observations, always ready to adjust them in reply to demands of new facts. (There was, of course, an element of natural reluctance about revising his views, particularly in cases where new data originated outside of his own experience.) In all his correcting and revising, he was constantly building, basing new ideas on new or old theories and hypotheses, even going back to long abandoned ideas if the new data warranted.

Should we not try to emulate him by avoiding the extremes of either accepting his theories as dogma merely because they are his, or rejecting these same theories merely to indicate our independence from him? Can we not follow his own essential concern for congruence between fact and theory, building in part on what he has already given us, examining his views and testing them to the fullest, and developing new theories as needed?

Freud, after a period of intensive work in various fields of medicine and physiology, turned his attention to problems more directly related to the understanding of human nature. He saw psychological phenomena differently from both his predecessors and contemporaries. When he reported what he saw, he was generally greeted with skepticism. Thereafter, through his long, active and markedly productive life, he developed his ideas in isolation, assisted only by a group who identified strongly with him. In such circumstances, how did his vast influence on the psychology of which he had never been a part come about?

Using a broad definition of influence as a guide in my attempt to answer this question, I found that ideas which demonstrably originated in the Freudian body of theory and observation have indeed permeated virtually the whole range of psychology. In fact, with the cumulative growth of this influence, Freud has become the most prominent name in the history of psychology. Nevertheless, this growth in influence has not, at least so far as psychology is concerned, been continuous; it has had its ebbs and flows, its enhancements and abatements, its leaps and halts.

A separation existed between psychoanalysis and psychology in spite of their common heritage from the Helmholtz tradition, a tradition which permeated the biological and physiological sciences when Freud started his work. It would seem that this gulf actually arose out of the different way in which each viewed its commitment to the Helmholtz program. Psychology did not recognize Freud's serious commitment to the "forces equal in dignity" part of the tradition as parallel to their own concern with the first part of this oath, the part which called for a "reduction to physical-chemical forces." Its own early focus on the "rigor" demanded by the latter led psychology to skip almost entirely the naturalistic stage usual in the development of a science and to identify itself with the "exact" of a hypothetical science, rather than with the "meaningful" that psychoanalysis had chosen. Since psychology had not come to terms with defining the proper place and time for exact measurement and quantification, there arose confusion in the use and meaning of the terms good and bad science—bad science being taken to be that which characterized psychoanalysis. The naturalistic method which fitted psychoanalysis so well was derogated as being unscientific.

What use are *psychologists*—all those professionally involved with human nature—to make of Freudian thinking? The answer lies essentially in the recognition that Freudian thinking is part of man's conquest of nature, the understanding of human nature. Psychoanalysis, like psychology of which it is a part, is not the possession of any group, not the property of the members of any organized association; it belongs to man. Being an early Freudian or a trained Freudian (or even a convinced anti-Freudian!) may carry certain rewards and certain claims in other settings but has no relevance here, for psychoanalysis is part of the heritage which great men provide. As the discipline most directly involved, it is up to psychology to understand, develop, and build on this heritage, making the changes that imagination, coupled with careful observation and experiment, indicates.

REFERENCES

Adelson, J. Freud in America: some observations. *American Psychologist*, 1956, *11*, 467–70.

Adrian, E. D. The mental and the physical origins of behavior. *International Journal of Psycho-Analysis*, 1946, *27*, 1–6.

Bakan, D. *On method.* San Francisco: Jossey-Bass, Inc., Publishers, 1967.

Bernfeld, S. Freud's scientific beginnings. *American Imago*, 1949, *6*, 163–96.

Boring, E. G. *Sensation and perception in the history of experimental psychology.* New York: Appleton-Century-Crofts, 1942.

Boring, E. G. *History of experimental psychology*, 2nd ed. New York: Appleton-Century-Crofts, 1950.

Cranefield, P. F. The organic physics of 1847 and the biophysics of today. *Journal of the History of Medicine and Allied Sciences*, 1957, *12*, 407–23.

Cranefield, P. F. The nineteenth century prelude to modern biophysics. *Proceedings*, First National Biophysics Conference, 1959, New Haven.

duBois-Reymond, E. H. *Jugendbriefe von Emil duBois-Reymond an Eduard Hallmann.* Berlin: Reimer, 1918.

Freud, S. The project for a scientific psychology. In M. Bonaparte, A. Freud, and E. Kris (eds.), *The origins of psychoanalysis: letters to Wilhelm Fliess, drafts and notes, 1887–1902.* New York: Basic Books Inc., Publishers, 1954, 352–445.

Freud, S. The claims of psycho-analysis to scientific interest. *Standard Edition*, *13*, 163–90. London: The Hogarth Press, Ltd., 1955. (First printed in 1913.)

Freud, S. An autobiographical study. *Standard Edition, 20*, 1–74. London: The Hogarth Press, Ltd., 1959. (First printed in 1924.)

Freud, S. Postcript to the question of lay analysis. *Standard Edition, 20*, 251–58. London: The Hogarth Press, Ltd., 1959. (First printed in 1927.)

Gill, M. M. Topography and systems in psychoanalytic theory. *Psychological Issues*, 1963, *3* (2, Whole No. 10).

Hoffman, F. J. *Freudianism and the literary mind*, 2nd ed. New York: Grove Press (Evergreen Books), 1959.

Holt, R. R. A critical examination of Freud's concept of bound vs. free cathexis. *Journal of the American Psychoanalytic Association*, 1962, *10*, 475–525.

Holt, R. R. A review of some of Freud's biological assumptions and their influence on his theories. In N. S. Greenfield and W. C. Lewis (eds.), *Psychoanalysis and current biological thought*. Madison: University of Wisconsin Press, 1965, 93–124.

Holt, R. R. The development of primary process: a structural view. In R. R. Holt (ed.), Motives and thought, psychoanalytic essays in memory of David Rapaport. *Psychological Issues*, 1967, *5*, No. 2–3 (Monograph No. 18–19), 345–83.

James, W. *The principles of psychology*, 2 vols. New York: Henry Holt & Co., 1890.

Klein, G. S. Peremptory ideation: structure and force in motivated ideas. In R. R. Holt (ed.), Motives and thought, psychoanalytic essays in memory of David Rapaport. *Psychological Issues*, 1967, *5*, No. 2–3 (Monograph No. 18–19), 80–130.

Koch, S. Epilogue. In S. Koch (ed.), *Psychology: a study of a science*. Vol. III. New York: McGraw-Hill Book Co., 1959, 729–88.

Loevinger, J. Three principles for a psychoanalytic psychology. *Journal of Abnormal Psychology*, 1966, *71*, 432–43.

Maslow, A. H. *Toward a psychology of being*. Princeton: D. Van Nostrand Co., Inc., 1962.

Rapaport, D. The structure of psychoanalytic theory: a systematizing attempt. In S. Koch (ed.), *Psychology: a study of a science*. Vol. III. New York: McGraw-Hill Book Co., 1959, 55–183. Also in *Psychological Issues*, 1960, *2*, No. 2.

Roe, A. A psychological study of eminent psychologists and anthropologists, and a comparison with biological and physical scientists. *Psychological Monographs*, 1953 (67 (2)), Whole No. 352.

Shakow, D. Clinical psychology: an evaluation. In L. G. Lowry and V. Sloane (eds.), *Orthopsychiatry, 1923–1948: retrospect and prospect*. New York: American Orthopsychiatric Association, 1948, 231–47.

Shakow, D. Some aspects of mid-century psychiatry: experimental psychology. In R. R. Grinker (ed.), *Mid-century psychiatry*. Springfield, Ill.: Chas. C. Thomas, Publisher, 1953, 76–103.

Shakow, D. Psicopatologia y psicologia: nota sobre tendencias. *Revista de Psicologia General Aplicado* (Madrid) 1960, *15*, 835–37.

Shakow, D. Psychoanalytic education of behavioral and social scientists for research. In J. H. Masserman (ed.), *Science and Psychoanalysis*. Vol. V. New York: Grune and Stratton, Inc., 1962, 146–61.

Shakow, D., and Rapaport D. The influence of Freud on American psychology. *Psychological Issues*, 1964, *4*, No. 1, 243. Also published as Meridian Book (paperback), Cleveland: The World Publishing Co., 1968.

Tansley, A. G. *The new psychology and its relation to life*. London: George Allen and Unwin Ltd., 1920.

Tolman, R. C. A survey of the sciences. *Science*, 1947, *106*, 135–40.

Weaver, W. Science and complexity. *American Scientist*, 1948, *36*, 536–44.

Wheeler, W. M. On instincts. *Journal of Abnormal Psychology*, 1921, *15*, 295–315.

Woodworth, R. S. *Contemporary schools of psychology*. New York: The Ronald Press Co., 1931.

Views Toward the Future: An Integrated Clinical-Cognitive Psychology

11

4. Theories of Ego Development

Jane Loevinger[1]

Unless it can be asserted that mankind did not know anything until logicians taught it to them . . . it must be allowed, that even the originality which can, and the courage which dares, think for itself, is not a more necessary part of the philosophical character than a thoughtful regard for previous thinkers, and for the collective mind of the human race. What has been the opinion of mankind, has been the opinion of persons of all tempers and dispositions, of all partialities and prepossessions, of all varieties in position, in education, in opportunities of observation and inquiry. No one inquirer is all this; every inquirer is either young or old, rich or poor, sickly or healthy, married or unmarried, meditative or active, a poet or a logician, an ancient or a modern, a man or a woman; and if a thinking person, has, in addition, the accidental peculiarities of his individual modes of thought. Every circumstance which gives a character to the life of a human being, carries with it its peculiar biasses; its peculiar facilities for perceiving some things, and for missing or forgetting others. But, from points of view different from his, different things are perceptible; and none are more likely to have seen what he does not see, than those who do not see what he sees.

—JOHN STUART MILL, Bentham.

Interest in the self or ego and its development extends back over 2000 years to the time of the Hebrew prophets, the Greek philosophers, and corresponding figures in other cultures (Jaspers, 1948). All the same, ego development is not a well recognized field of study with authoritative texts. The purpose of the present review of conceptions and theories of ego development is to bring into relation with each other materials from

[1]Preparation of this paper was supported by a research grant from the National Institute of Mental Health, United States Public Health Service. I am indebted to Augusto Blasi, Alden Fisher, John W. Higgins, Hans W. Loewald, M. Brewster Smith, and Louis Breger for critical comments.

diverse sources and to encourage recognition of ego development as a major field for systematic study. Since relevant theories are to be found in the fields of psychiatry and philosophy, including ethics, epistemology, and political theory, a prodigy of scholarship would be required to know all the important theories and who first proposed them, though one can be sure that it is hard to say anything truly new. All one writer can do is to make a beginning and to let others point out the omissions. Relevant present-day sources are as likely to be couched in terms of moral judgment, interpersonal relations, and conceptual complexity as in terms of ego development.

Although the topic has a modern ring, the greatest interest was probably around the turn of the century. In the enthusiasm for evolutionary theory, the developmental point of view invaded all fields, including ethics and psychology. Both the reductionistic and non-reductionistic views of the ego were strengthened by Darwinian theory. Man was shown to be truly one with lower animals in his origins; hence, it was no mere fantasy that his motivations were at bottom the same. And yet birds truly fly as their primordial ancestors did not; so man may live by purposes and meanings that his ancestors did not know.

In the dark middle age of this century, terms such as ego and self fell under a ban in academic psychology (Allport, 1943; Hilgard, 1949; Hebb, 1960); strict behaviorists allowed for no such construct. Psychoanalysts preserved the term ego but denigrated its functions. Meanwhile, the wives and children of psychologists and psychoanalysts continued to live their lives in terms of conscious purposes and meanings, which a few maverick psychologists also acknowledged. (Similarly, Freud noted that nursemaids were familiar with the facts of childhood sexuality that his learned colleagues denied.) The pendulum has now swung. Ego development is the *dernier cri* among psychoanalysts. Increased interest among academic psychologists may reflect less a shift in attitude than a shift in head count. There are more clinical students who want a psychology germane to their profession.

Before the discussion is launched, some clarification of ground rules is in order. A central theme of the discourse is coherence, which enters via two terms of the title. Coherence is taken as definitive of ego, and coherence is also the hallmark of theory (Polanyi, 1968). To take the latter point first, wisdom about man's ego is a long slow growth and will not change greatly in one generation. A novel theory, however, can come to one overnight. A theory must be a more or less formalized set of notions. Erikson, for example, is widely and justly regarded as one of the foremost contemporary authorities on ego development; yet he plays a comparatively small part in this chapter. The explanation lies in the informal, poetic character of his views. It is unlikely that there is anything about ego development in the present chapter not known to Erikson and demonstrably present in his writings. But there is a difference between knowing something, even knowing it in a way clearly conveyed to one's readers, and incorporating it in a formal theoretical structure. Similar remarks apply to the well known writings on ego theory of Hartmann, Kris, and Loewenstein. Valuable clinical contributions can fail as theoretical ones. We shall look at the work of every author as with an X-ray, seeking the bare bones of the theoretical skeleton with no implied evaluation of the man's wisdom about our topic.

The central term of the present chapter, ego, is its most difficult one. Fine distinctions between ego and self, between the I and the me, or between ego as knower and as known, are not germane, much less is a transcendental entity. Thus, most of the philosophical discussions are not pertinent. The outlines of the ego are not given by a definition but by life.

To define the ego is perhaps not possible, but one can think about it. One device is that of the author of a book on probability who, in place of defining probability, assured the reader that after doing all the problems in the book, he would know what probability is. Defining the ego is difficult in the same way that defining life is. Air and water are not living beings. When one drinks water or breathes air, at what point does it become part of a living object? (This illustration is borrowed from a lecture by James Franck, who used the question to show how misguided are attempts to define life rigorously.) If we think of life as being a process of interchange with the environment, the question loses point. There is no problem. Similarly, the ego is above all a process, not a thing. The ego is in a way like a gyroscope, whose upright position is maintained by its rotation. To use another metaphor, the ego resembles an arch; there is an architectural saying that "the arch never sleeps." That means that the thrusts and counterthrusts of the arch maintain its shape as well as support the building. Piaget (1967) uses the term "mobile equilibrium"— the more mobile, the more stable. The striving to master, to integrate, to make sense of experience is not one ego function among many but the essence of the ego.

Many persons consider ego development to be in the domain of psychoanalytic theory. The discussion must therefore be aligned with respect to major positions of that school of thought. Freud originally used the concept of the ego (das Ich) as a term taken from the common domain. His elaboration of consciousness (more correctly, the pre-conscious) as a system distinct from the unconscious as a system took the place of the ego at the time of The Interpretation of Dreams (1900). The major difficulty that led to return to the concept of the ego and replacement of unconsciousness as a system by the concept of the id was the question of where repression took place. If the repressing force is in the unconscious, then the notion of psychic systems, proposed as a means of portraying inner conflict, loses point, for both parties to the conflict, the repressed idea and the repressing force, are in the same system. If it is consciousness that represses unconscious ideas, why are we not conscious of repression? Must there be a repression of the fact of repression, and so on in infinite regress? Use of the term ego permits a kind of solution of the problem by definition. To say that there is an unconscious part of the ego is less awkward than to say that there is an unconscious part of consciousness.

Waelder's summary of Freud's position on the ego in his last years outlines a view that many ego psychologists outside the psychoanalytic group proper will find acceptable:

The boundary [between ego and id] is the boundary between instinctual and purposive processes, between blind propulsion on the one hand and the choice of suitable means for particular purposes on the other hand. . . . Psychoanalysis includes in the id everything by which man appears to be impelled to function, all the inner tendencies which influence him, each *vis a tergo*. The ego, on the other hand, represents the considered direction of man, all purposeful activity. . . . Psychoanalysis, in so viewing the id and the ego, thus perceives man's being both impulsively driven and his being purposefully directed. . . . The scheme of processes in the id would then be, in short: instinct—instinctual expression; those of the ego, however, are: task—task-solving, or attempted solution (Waelder, 1960, p. 177).[2]

Before leaving these general considerations, one may at least ask whether a thoroughgoing process conception of the ego would obviate the necessity for assuming an unconscious part of the ego. Repression, as Freud pointed out, is something that occurs between systems. Is not the question of whether repression is in the ego analogous to the question of whether air in the lungs and water in the stomach are part of the living body? Or, to put the matter another way, will it not suffice to say that non-inclusion in the ego is what repression is? We must drop the question, for a full answer would lead to technical questions beyond the scope of the present chapter.

The first section of this review will be concerned with seven theoretical issues that arise in conceptions of the ego and of ego development. A comparison of psychoanalytic with other conceptions will be made under several headings. The second section will be concerned with theories of developmental stability and change, that is, the dynamics of ego development. Again, psychoanalytic formulations will be compared with others opposed to or derivative from psychoanalysis.

[2]These passages were first published in 1928 and 1930.

THEORETICAL ISSUES

Theories of the ego and of ego development can be characterized in terms of seven issues.

The Ego Functions Holistically

Most contemporary theories of the ego are holistic, as opposed to dualistic or elementaristic. The primary datum is the person. While his ideas and sensations (in another era) or his traits or sensorimotor functions may be studied, he is the unit of study. Moreover, the ego is not a spirit animating a machine or a pilot in a ship; the Cartesian dichotomy of mind and body is currently rejected.

In a witty essay, Jung (1933) argued that scientific reductionism, expressing mind in terms of body, is logically no different from the creed of an earlier, theological era that believed that the physical world was no more than a manifestation of the spiritual one. Mind is no more reducible to body than body to mind. Although not incompatible with Jung's thesis, modern arguments have a different ring. Strawson (1958) and Polanyi (1958) maintain that person is a primitive notion; Strawson asserts there are no disembodied minds known to us. Ryle (1949) and Chein (1962) argue that there are not two series of events, say, in playing chess or taking a test, one that of the bodily movements, the other of the mind that tells the body what movements to make. The person is not thus divisible. "Neural processes cannot produce ideas, and thoughts cannot make the muscles contract, but the total organism, the person, can do both" (Angyal, 1965, p. 31).

These arguments are, in part at least, ontological. Ego development is an empirical and theoretical topic of psychology, rather than an ontology. As such, it is concerned with functioning persons, not with mind as opposed to body. The holistic view permeates writings of many psychologists and psychiatrists, for example, William Stern, Adolf Meyer, Kurt Goldstein, Gordon Allport, and Donald O. Hebb. If there are still opponents of the holistic view, they are presumably the psychologists for whom development of the ego, of moral judgment, and of capacity for interpersonal relations are not clear and present concerns.

Whether psychoanalysis is compatible with a holistic view of ego functioning is not a trivial question. Adler regarded separable drives or instincts as contrary to the holistic assumption; this was one of his reasons for disaffiliation from Freud's group. At the time, however, many members of the psychoanalytic group, perhaps a majority, thought that Freud's and Adler's views could be reconciled, according to Ansbacher (Adler, 1956, p. 72ff.). The same objection, that it violates an assumption of holistic psychic functioning, has at times been raised against the later tripartite structural view of ego, superego, and id. Indeed, Freud tended always to divide psychic structure into two's and three's, pitting one psychic structure against another, or having antagonistic instincts or groups of instincts. He did this in so many ways, some incompatible with others, some partially redundant, that one can hardly suppose that any one of them is an essential psychoanalytic tenet, and all of them have been challenged by one or another psychoanalyst. What would seem to be beyond dispute is that any truly psychoanalytic view must allow for inner conflict, because inner conflict alone occasions neurosis in Freud's formulation.

The question of whether ego functioning (or should one say psychic functioning?) is best conceived holistically remains a major unresolved issue in contemporary psychoanalytic theory. The school of thought associated with Hartmann and Rapaport, often referred to as the "new psychoanalytic ego psychology," treats the ego as an omnibus of functions, or, as they sometimes say, apparatuses, some autonomous with respect to drives and (hence?) conflict free, others derived from neutralized drive energies. Presumably, in this view, the "synthetic function" is one more task for the ego. This view seems to be incompatible with a holistic assumption. At the same time, however, Rapaport (1959, p. 42) asserted, "All behavior is that of the integral and indivisible personality." Psychoanalysts such as Erikson and Loewald unquestionably present a holistic view.

If psychoanalysis is to be integrated with other contemporary ego psychologies, it must reconcile the view that the person functions as a unity with the possibility of inner conflict. One possible resolution of the difficulty is that while the ego in general acts as a whole, some memories or experiences are retained outside this frame of reference. Freud utilized the notions of repression and the unconscious, while Sullivan and Merleau-Ponty spoke of dissociation. In either case, the juxtaposition provides one way of describing inner conflict without hypostatizing any of the variety of additional entities whose nature and functions are disputed in current psychoanalytic literature. This solution is Merleau-Ponty's (1942) description of psychic pathology. Freud's notion of the dynamic unconscious does seem to constitute a modification of the holistic assumption but one which most ego theorists today accept in some version. It is, however, a modification and not an abrogation of the holistic assumption, as Merleau-Ponty has shown. For it is the person as a whole that refuses to recognize or assume responsibility for the repressed complex of ideas. If it were not so, if the person as a whole were not involved, how would one account for the force of resistance (Vergote, 1957)?

Ego Development Is Dialectical

Most of the theories see development as more than mere growth, that is, there are definite turning points. Thus, development is dialectical. No one denies that development in the sense of growth does take place. What is called ego development, by contrast with most aspects of physical growth and at least some kinds of growth in abilities, postulates more than two stages. If there are only two stages, a low one and a high one, with smooth transition between them, one can speak of growth. There must be at least one intermediate stage for the theory to qualify as dialectically developmental in the present sense, one set of characteristics that increase up to some point in the growth process and then tend to decrease or to be replaced. Ausubel's (1952) stage of satellization (see below) is an example. One should not dismiss the Hegelian implications of the term dialectics. Each stage in a sense opposes, in a sense incorporates, and above all transmutes the previous one. This notion of development is indeed that of Hegel, though we may be more inclined to credit a recent source such as Piaget. Such a developmental process has been called a milestone sequence (Loevinger, 1965, 1966a), as opposed to a polar aspect of development. Polar aspects of ego development include, for example, the shift from primary process thinking to predominance of secondary process thinking and the shift from autocentric perception to allocentric perception (Schachtel, 1959).

Clear and still pertinent conceptions of ego development in terms of a milestone sequence can be found in the writings of Baldwin (1897), McDougall (1908), Sullivan (1953), and in a spate of recent writers all more or less influenced by the earlier versions, to wit, C. Sullivan, Grant, and Grant (1957), Isaacs (1956), Kohlberg (1964), Peck and Havighurst (1960), Harvey, Hunt, and Schroder (1961), Loevinger (1966a), and no doubt others. All of these accounts postulate several stages. There is not perfect agreement on the order or number of stages, but there is enough agreement to insure that all are talking about the same pervasive aspect of personality, which has many and varied manifestations. The study of the authoritarian personality by Adorno, Frenkel-Brunswik, Levinson, and Sanford (1950) is an example of a study of the same aspects of personality that specifically denies that they constitute a developmental sequence. (Sanford, at least, might take a different view now.)

A special interest attaches to Sullivan's (1953) formulation as the first major innovative voice. (Although the best version was published posthumously in 1953, his ideas were well known much earlier.) Sullivan avoided using the term ego, since he wanted to disclaim certain surplus meanings built into the ego-id-superego topography of psychoanalysis. He used the term self-system for what the present chapter calls ego. According to Sullivan, the earliest sanction and one of continuing, though not exclusive, importance is that of anxiety. The self-system arises in the earliest stage, infancy, as a defense against anxiety. The infant moves toward whatever decreases anxiety and away from whatever increases anxiety. The earliest self-concept is split into three elements: the *good me* is whatever leads to or is associated with reward; the *bad me* is whatever leads to or is associated with mild or moderate anxiety; and the *not me* is associated with sudden access of overwhelming anxiety, which cannot be integrated by the infant as a learning experience. The single significant other at this stage is also split into *good mother* and *bad mother*. At first mother and mother surrogates are not distinguished; all good ones are the same, all bad ones are the same. The anxious mother is Sullivan's foremost example of the bad mother. He sees anxiety as aroused in the child by a kind of empathy with an anxious mother, though this is an admittedly obscure link in Sullivan's system.

By means of experiences such as thumb-sucking, the infant integrates the good me and the bad me into *my body*, as opposed to the environment. Language helps fuse the personifications of the good mother and the bad mother into *my mother*, no longer interchangeable with surrogates. The constructs my body and my mother characterize childhood, the second period. The interpersonal modes are *acting like* and *acting as if one were*; a malignant version is *acting as if*. The transition from childhood to the juvenile era is marked by increasingly clear distinction between reality and fantasy.

The juvenile era is characterized by formation of social stereotypes, particularly those differentiated according to gender. Mother declines as a significant other in favor of compeers. Sanctions are ostracism, popularity, approval. Interpersonal modes are social subordination and social accommodation, competition, cooperation, and compromise, but the child shows insensitivity to feelings of personal worth in others.

In the relation of the pre-adolescent child to a chum of the same sex, Sullivan saw a unique opportunity to advance from the egocentric state of the juvenile stage to a truly social state. In an exclusive relation with a chum, the pre-adolescent learns for the first time to value another as he values himself. The need for intimacy propels a youngster into such a relation; loneliness is the corresponding sanction. True collaboration originates in this period. A favorable outcome of this developmental period is achievement of an orientation in living, long-term goals and aspirations. But these achievements of the pre-adolescent era are not inevitable. Many persons remain at the juvenile level of personality organization. Such a person, at maturation of the lust dynamism (Sullivan's expression for sexual maturity), may become a Don Juan or a teaser. Development tends to become arrested if the child clings to *as if* performances, dramatizations, and obsessional preoccupations to ward off anxiety and punishment, or if he undergoes a malevolent transformation, that is, adopts the attitude of living among enemies as a result of being made fun of, anxious, or hurt when manifesting a need for tenderness.

Sullivan saw the needs of early adolescence as security, intimacy, and lust. The significant other shifts from chum to a member of the other sex. Early adolescence ends with achievement of a pattern of preferred genital activity; late adolescence extends to the establishment of a mature repertory of interpersonal relations, to the extent opportunity permits. Sullivan discussed at length the fate of those arrested at various earlier levels as they face the problems of adolescence and maturity.

On the whole, Sullivan's discussion of the problems of development in adolescence and early adult life are less rewarding than the better known expositions of Erikson (1950), but Sullivan's discussion of the early phases reveals more clearly than does that of Erikson how the solution to the problem of one period generates the problem of the next period. The intimate interrelations of self-conception, conception of significant others, and mode of interpersonal relations are more patent in Sullivan's exposition. Erikson is like other psychoanalytic writers in that the course of psychosexual development is at times seen as quite distinct and somewhat independently variable of ego development, while at other times the two courses of development are merged, not to say confused.[3] Sullivan did not ignore the phenomena of psychosexual development, but he was meticulous to conceive of them as distinct from development of the self-system. Observation does not yield such distinctions; it is, rather, the concepts which inform observation. Sullivan deserves credit for being the first to conceive of ego development if not in its entirety at least in its full richness, for having separated it conceptually from psychosexual development without sterilizing his picture of man or slighting the many possible relations between these aspects of development, and for having discerned much of the inner logic of its dialectics.

Ego Theories May Be Typological

Most theories of ego development are typological, not as opposed to the notion of continuous variation but as opposed to the notion of unidimensionality or univocality. To be typological in the present sense, a theory must postulate more than two types, since the existence of only two types

[3]A closely related point is made in Chapter 8. Here it is argued that Erikson, while presenting what is essentially a social or interpersonal scheme of ego development, still clings to the biologically reductionistic view of orality, anality, and so on, thus underemphasizing the total sensorimotor, affective, and cognitive nature of the mother-infant interaction. A related point is made by Klein in Chapter 5. (Editor)

reduces the variation to a single dimension, or is formally equivalent to existence of a single dimension. Thus, the differences in ego development are qualitative, not completely reducible to quantitative differences even though they may be graded continuously. Although the authors of *The Authoritarian Personality* probably did not take a stand on this point, their methodology was such as to emphasize only two types, the highs and the lows. Where they recognized sub-types, they were subdivisions of the highs and lows rather than extensions of the original typology to include more than two possibilities. Tomkins (1965) has shown that many kinds of ideology can be cast as two extremes of a single continuum. Since ideology is an important aspect and index of ego functioning, his evidence weighs against the typological view in our sense. It is not clear, however, that his methods would allow a more complex typology to emerge.

Distinctive of a group of current conceptions of ego development and related variables is the postulation of the stages as types, that is, as descriptive of persons who do not advance beyond that stage with increasing age. Probably Sullivan (1953) was the first to make this point clearly; current advocates of the view include Ausubel (1952), C. Sullivan, Grant, and Grant (1957), Isaacs (1956), Kohlberg (1964), Peck and Havighurst (1960), and Loevinger (1966a).

That the stages of ego development also constitute a typology can hardly be called a received opinion, since the best known ego theorists do not make this point. Allport (1961) sees stages of ego development similar to those sketched by psychologists of the foregoing group, but when he talks of typologies, he refers to humoral and other typologies which appear to have no connection with ego development. His emphasis on an idiographic approach is also somewhat antagonistic to the idea of a typology. Erikson (1950) formulates ego development in terms of a series of antinomies, each of which results in some characteristic balance for that individual; he does not usually allow for the possibility, and certainly does not emphasize in his more formal theoretical presentations, that development may stop below the highest level for many persons, thus generating a corresponding typology. Maslow (1954) accounts for motivation in terms of a developmental sequence of instinctoid needs. They constitute a series that can be set in correspondence with stages of ego development, but again he does not emphasize the possibility that there may be a corresponding typology of men in whom the successive needs are uppermost. On the other hand, Rogers (1961) has described a "process conception of psychotherapy," a sequence of stages similar to those here called ego development (Loevinger, 1966a). Rogers uses the same sequence more or less as a typology, finding, for example, that clients at a low point of the scale on entering therapy are not good therapeutic prospects.

Ego Development Is an Abstraction

All of the conceptions that see ego development both as a typology and as a developmental sequence recognize thereby that it is an abstraction. It cannot be reduced to concrete, observable performances of average children, as is done in some child psychology texts. Ego development is related to and based on observation, but it is not directly observable. Thus, it is simply unavailable or non-existent to a simplistic behavioristic approach.

One of the best expositions of development as an abstraction is that of Werner (1940), who was, however, primarily concerned with cognitive development. One must not expect identity among children and primitive peoples and pathological cases but simply certain parallels, Werner wrote, since the circumstances are entirely different for primitive man living in a society where he is master and well adjusted, the sick person living in a society to which he is maladjusted, and the child living in a world of culturally advanced adults who do not operate as primitive man does. What is common is the concept of development, which is an abstraction. Werner's statement (Werner, 1940, p. 41) of the orthogenetic law of development applies as well to ego as to cognitive development: "The development of biological forms is expressed in an *increasing differentiation* of parts and an *increasing subordination*, or *hierarchization*. Such a process of hierarchization means for any organic structure the organization of the differentiated parts for a closed totality, an ordering and grouping of parts in terms of the whole organism."

Piaget and Inhelder (Flavell, 1963; Tanner and Inhelder, 1956, 1960) also stress development as having its own inner logic. As in Werner's case, they are primarily concerned with cognitive rather than with ego development, but the principles are intentionally presented in abstract form so as to apply more generally. Piaget and Inhelder see the inner logic of development as a coordinate determinant of behavior, along with heredity, past experiences, and current circumstances. Kohlberg (1964) stresses that, as a consequence, a given stage of development is not brought about by simple rewards and punishments of the relevant behaviors. Conformity or conscientiousness cannot simply be stamped in, and much less can autonomous behavior. Thus, Kohlberg opposes the behavioristic, reward-punishment approach to personality development. It would seem that a parallel objection could be made to an overemphasis in some psychoanalytic accounts on dynamic factors leading to character constellations, to the neglect of factors intrinsic to the developmental process *per se* (cf. White, 1963, Chap. 5).

Probably the exposition of ego development that most strongly emphasizes its character as an abstraction is my own (Loevinger, 1966a). In this schema, avowedly drawn wholesale from those of others, the successive stages are labelled autistic, symbiotic, impulsive, opportunistic, conformist, conscientious, autonomous, and integrated. Between the conformist and the conscientious stages there is a transitional period that could be called self-conscious; between the conscientious and autonomous stages there is a similar transition that could be called individualistic. All the terms and the corresponding descriptions are explicitly chosen so as to emphasize what is common between those persons passing through the stage in normal developmental time and those adult or adolescent types arrested at that stage. Age-specific aspects are excluded from the definitive descriptions, in contrast to the expositions of Erikson, of child psychology texts, and to a lesser extent, of Sullivan. A precedent for that kind of abstraction exists in the concept of mental age. The advantage of the abstract exposition is that it reveals and differentiates such questions as: What is the typical age for a given transition? The optimal age? The earliest possible age? The latest possible age? These are not trivial questions. They must contain the solution to the puzzling differences found between authors. For example, Erikson has the crisis of intimacy as a late adolescent problem, while Sullivan locates it in the pre-adolescent era. Abstract formulation also encourages distinguishing the inner logic of ego development from the matrix of physical development, intellectual development, psychosexual development, and social expectations in which it is embedded and from which it gains some of its impetus and form.

The Ego Is Structural

Most ego theories are structural, that is, the ego is seen as striving (or as the striving) for self-consistency and meaning. (Obviously this is not Titchener's kind of structural psychology; in fact, it is close to what was then called functional psychology.) Although this notion appeared earlier in some philosophers, it is especially characteristic of Adler, who spoke of "style of life," which he at various times equated with self or ego, the unity of personality, individuality, the method of facing problems, opinion about oneself and the problems of life, and the whole attitude toward life (Adler, 1956, p. 174). Adler saw his belief in the coherence of personality as a major point of difference between himself and Freud. Freud also spoke of the ego as being or having organization, but he assigned the ego a smaller place in life and behavior. What Nunberg (1931) called the "synthetic function of the ego" is a related idea.

For Sullivan, the organization and functioning of the self-system tends to preserve, and is in part motivated by the desire to preserve, self-consistency, by means of selective inattention to facts inconsistent with the current level of development. The notion of core function in C. Sullivan, Grant, and Grant (1957) is much influenced by Sullivan's conception. Allport (1943 and elsewhere) has always stressed the organization of the ego, which accounts for or is at least related to the functional autonomy of motives. Lecky (1945) was chiefly preoccupied with the striving for self-consistency, much as Festinger has been preoccupied with the other side of the coin, cognitive dissonance. Isaacs also has a structural point of view. Structure was the essence of the conception of Merleau-Ponty (1942), whose views on selective inattention as resulting from and preserving ego structure are similar to those of Sullivan. Kohlberg emphasizes a structural view strongly, drawing on Piaget's notion of structure in the cognitive realm.

A radical version of the structural conception of the ego is that of Fingarette (1963). He begins by accepting the observations and the essential theory underlying psychoanalysis as therapy. He points out, however, that Freud's visual metaphor, which depicts the task of psychoanalysis as uncovering hidden realities, has become an implicit ontology for many psychoanalysts, at times including Freud. The same observations and the same theories are compatible with an alternative ontology that depicts the major task of psychoanalysis as helping the patient to see new meanings in events already known to him. Successful therapy is not so much a matter of finding a rabbit hidden in the bushes as discerning the shape of a rabbit in a cloud, according to the meaning-reorganization view. The striving to make experience meaningful is for Fingarette not something that a thing called ego does; the striving for meaning, or "synthetic function," is what the ego is. Meaning is not an afterthought to behavior and experience; meaning is constitutive of experience (cf. Mead's theory, below). Fingarette defines anxiety also in structural terms. He recognizes that there is an affect called anxiety but declares this not the usage of central theoretical importance. If one thinks of anxiety as an affect, then unconscious anxiety and the substitution of symptom for anxiety become anomalies. If anxiety is interpreted as primarily a hypothetical concept, differentiated from the specific affect, these difficulties do not exist. Fingarette's structural definition of anxiety is that failure of the striving for meaning is itself what constitutes anxiety. Thus, just as meaning is not so much what the ego seeks as what it is, so anxiety is not what the ego experiences but is the opposite of ego. Anxiety may be thought of as ego disorganization, or, in short, as meaninglessness. The term neurotic anxiety is a misnomer. What is neurotic is not the anxiety (that is, ego disorganization), but how the ego responds to it, whether creatively and reparatively or by restricting itself and making its own fragmentation into a permanent structure. Fingarette mentions the similarity of some of his notions to those of Sullivan but does not refer to Merleau-Ponty. (The meaning-reorganization view of psychoanalytic therapy can also be found in Ricoeur, 1965, and Loewald, 1960.)

On the other side, the striving for consistency seems to be absent from the Peck and Havighurst (1960) conception of moral development, and Maslow also does not emphasize this aspect. Erikson's notion of the search for identity has some relevance, but it is a stage of ego development, rather than a characteristic of all stages. Gergen (1968) believes that the tendency toward personal consistency has been exaggerated in psychological theory.

Here we are close to one crucial aspect of the long opposition to the concept of ego. For years the predominant strain in American psychology was a doctrine of specificity. In part, this view served a salutary function, for example, in Paterson's (1930) demonstration that intelligence was minimally related to height, weight, head size, head dimensions, and other bodily indices. But the opposition to generalization did not stop there. Thorndike (1927) so objected to the degree of generality of function implied in the term intelligence that he called his test "Intellect CAVD," referring to the four kinds of tasks included—completion, arithmetic problems, vocabulary, and following directions. One of the most popular versions of the doctrine of specificity in the cognitive realm asserts that although a factor of general intelligence may appear in some studies, it is only an artifact due to averaging or sampling a large number of specific elements. The nature of the elements is usually left vague, perhaps genes, perhaps neural bonds, perhaps sub-abilities. They are usually hypothetically palpable things, like "neural bonds," of course never witnessed but in principle physically demonstrable. According to a naive philosophy of science, these elements are therefore more real and more scientific than constructs such as intelligence, less palpable but more clearly manifest in the data at hand.

Coming closer to the field of ego development, Hartshorne and May (1928) endeavored to show that there was no such general trait as honesty in children, that their tendency to be dishonest was specific to the situation. Lecky (1945) argued that the methods and concepts of Hartshorne and May were responsible for their conclusions, that in fact every personality is an organization, and the striving for self-consistency is the predominant motive in everyone. Others have also disputed Hartshorne and May's interpretation of their data, but this topic leads afield.

The use of the term structure in the received version of psychoanalysis seems to represent a different usage. The structural view has come to stand for the division of the personality; or person, into ego, id, and superego. These are the structures. Freud spoke of the ego as an organization, and the point has been generally recognized in psychoanalysis. The id and the superego, on the other hand, to the extent that they are unconscious, cannot be said to be organized, for the unconscious admits of no contradiction. If contradiction is meaningless, so is consistency. (This point does not exclude the possibility that there are organized ideas within the superego or the id; the notion is that the superego and the id are not self-consistent or organized wholes. Similarly, the ego may contain inconsistencies, even though as a whole it represents the striving for consistency.) Of course, the word structure is not uniquely attached to the sense of striving for consistency in which it is used in the above paragraphs. One psychoanalytic usage has the term connote degree of organization. Following this usage, Gill (1963) concludes that ego and id are two extremes of a continuum. In a more common usage, structure seems to connote stability or semi-permanence rather than organization. For while the ego is organized in some important sense in which the superego and id are not, all are relatively stable or semi-permanent. What is remarkable is that the reason for stability of the id and superego is more or less opposite to the reason for stability of the ego. Accounting for the stability of the ego is a substantive theoretical problem, as we shall see in the latter half of this chapter, and the striving for coherence is an essential element of the solution, as the gyroscope and arch metaphors are meant to suggest. The id and the unconscious component of the superego, on the other hand, owe their stability to being unconscious, hence impervious to the influence of experience as well as to the requirement of consistency. This is the principle of the dynamic unconscious, Freud's first great discovery. In accord with the tendency to interpret the term structure as primarily connoting stability, some psychoanalytic theorists (for example, Rapaport and Hartmann) seem to define the ego as a congeries of functions or apparatuses, of which the synthetic function is just another one. Other psychoanalysts, for example, Hendrick, Erikson, and Loewald, appear to have a notion of the ego consistent with that of the present chapter.

The Ego Is Social

Most theories of ego development see the ego as intrinsically social in character, that is, man is by nature a social animal, a view as old as Aristotle. Sullivan made central to his psychiatry the view that man is constituted in and by his interpersonal relations. (He might, in place of interpersonal, have said human or social relations, but that testifies to the truth of the view.) Baldwin (1897), also an extremist on this issue, argued that there is hardly anything in ego other than what is in one's alter or socius. G. H. Mead (1934) argued that while a man might maintain his ego in isolation, the ego would never come into being for a person raised in isolation.

The issue is one of the oldest ones in philosophy. Socrates, Plato, and Aristotle expressed in various ways that man is by nature a social animal, that he achieves his true estate in and through the community. The Sophists, the Cynics, and other post-Socratic philosophers expressed in various ways and with varying emphasis that man is by nature selfish and a creature of impulse, that society must be imposed on him against his will. Sartre is a contemporary advocate of this position, but few psychologists today hold exclusively to either view. At any rate, the initial thrust of psychoanalysis strengthened the view of socialization as forcibly thrust on the selfish, instinctual child, but there was not necessarily any disagreement between Freud and J. B. Watson on the point. On the other hand, the practice of psychoanalysis was interpersonal from the beginning. With the increasing importance of concepts such as transference and identification, the theory became increasingly interpersonal.

Allport (1943) somewhat straddles this issue, with his insistence that personality be defined entirely within the integument. Chein (1962), on the other hand, insists that even traits cannot be defined without invoking the social and physical environment. Mead's similar views are quoted below.

The Ego Is Purposive; Meanings Are Determinative

Finally, most ego theories are purposive, not in the sense of declaring a purpose in the universe but in the sense of being concerned with purposes as phenomena of human life. One might speak alternatively of behavior as meaningful or of meanings as determinative of behavior. The opposite view, programmatically mechanistic, but as Allport and others have noted, never more than quasi-mechanistic or naturalistic in practice, sees the causes of behavior as lying entirely in the past. But ego phenomena can hardly be formulated in such terms.

McDougall's (1908) purposive behaviorism postulated instincts as the prime movers, yet made purpose central. McDougall maintained, and Tolman (1922) agreed, that the kind of instincts postulated by the opponents of instinct theory, that is, compounds of reflex arcs, not only did not exist in man, they did not occur in other animals either.

The reconciliation of a mechanistic and deterministic view with the view that the ego acts in terms of purposes and meanings is accomplished in terms of levels of organization in Merleau-Ponty's philosophy (1942).

Psychoanalysis remains a special case. Freud avowed an allegiance to physiological reductionism from his earliest to his latest period, and his writings on psychic energy are hard to construe as anything but reductionism, even though psychic energy is not usually equated with physical energy. On the other hand, much of Freud's best writing and all of psychoanalysis as therapy are phrased in terms of meanings, purposes, intentions, wishes, and so on. Indeed, Flew (1956) has pointed out that the essence of the psychoanalytic contribution is to extend the meaning of such terms to phenomena such as dreams, symptoms, and mistakes that had previously seemed meaningless. A similar point has been made by three other philosophers, Fisher (1961), Fingarette (1963), and Holt (1915), and by Home (1966), a psychoanalyst.

Defective as cathexis theory may be, if it were nothing more than a mistake, one would be hard put to account for its long tenure. Ricoeur (1965) has accounted for it more satisfactorily than other philosophers. The ground of psychoanalysis, he writes, is precisely the juncture of an energetics and a hermeneutics. Many of the key concepts of psychoanalysis bear witness to that mixture of discourses, the discourse of force and that of meaning. Examples are resistance, repression, displacement, condensation, and dream work. All have connotations of force and of meaning. The force is displayed only in alteration of meaning, and the meanings are altered only at the behest of psychic forces. The psychic forces involved are knowable only through their effects on meanings and meaningful discourse. While recognizing the validity of the energy metaphor, Ricoeur is as unsympathetic to the bizarre algebra of cathexis, counter-cathexis, hypercathexis, and so forth, as is Flew.

There is a cleavage between those psychologists who see man as he sees himself, as searching for meaning and carrying out purposes, even if sometimes unconscious ones, and those who see his behavior as determined by meaningless forces outside his ken. Despite the assertions of some critics, this cleavage does not separate psychoanalysis from humanistic approaches to psychology. On the contrary, the cleavage goes right down the middle of psychoanalysis and indeed, down the middle of Freud's writings. On the whole, psychoanalysis must be ranked among the psychologies concerned with meanings, for without interpretation there is no psychoanalysis.

In sum, there is a group of current concepts of the development of the ego or related variables (self-system, interpersonal integration, relatability, moralization of judgment, conceptual complexity, and so on) that can be characterized as holistic, dialectically developmental, typological, abstract, structural, social, and purposive. The group includes the conceptions of Sullivan (1953), C. Sullivan, Grant, and Grant (1957), Isaacs (1956), Kohlberg (1964), Loevinger (1966a), and possibly Rogers (1961), Harvey, Hunt, and Schroder (1961), and Ausubel (1952). Other ego theories are either mute on certain points or take an opposed stand. These are some of the theoretical issues in terms of which the ego and ego development have been discussed. The foregoing group of conceptions differs from many earlier conceptions of the ego not so much on specific doctrinal points as on the unspoken assumption that the nature of the ego is most clearly revealed in terms of the dialectics of its developmental course.

THEORIES OF CHANGE AND STABILITY

There are three major theoretical issues to be handled by a theory of the dynamics of ego development. How does the ego function? How does it remain stable? How does it change? The problem of ego functioning seems to be assimilated either to stability or to change, and no author has given a major contribution to both problems. As a first approximation, one may state as the formal requirements for a theory of ego development that the postulated sequence of events be connected by an inner logic and that the successive events of the sequence not all be formally identical.

Baldwin's Dialectic of Personal Growth

Baldwin (1897) made central to his theory of ego development the dialectic of personal growth. The infant first learns to distinguish persons from other objects; then he learns to see himself as a person among persons but possessed of special feelings that he cannot observe in others. Then he learns to think of others as having those feelings he can discern in himself. By a continuation of this process, seeing himself in the light of what he can observe of others and inferring in others what he can feel within himself, his ego development proceeds. As a result, the contents of the ego and of the alter are almost identical. One thinks of oneself very much as one thinks of others (cf. Hebb, 1960).

The young child's behavior exhibits a kind of polarity: he imitates those more powerful and practices on those less powerful. Toward those in authority, he appears altruistic but toward younger sibs, aggressive and selfish. Gradually, however, he builds within himself an ego ideal, at first modeled after persons in the environment, especially parents, but gradually, through operation of intelligence, generalized into principles which even his models are required to adhere to. Imitation, a kind of instinct, is the moving force in development.

Since he leaned so heavily on imitation as the moving principle, one can guess that Baldwin would have greater difficulty dealing with stages of ego development beyond the conformist stage than in discussing earlier stages, and so it is. He did acknowledge the possibility that an individual may evolve an ethical sentiment that conflicts with the actual opinion of his society, but in principle, conscience remains an internalized version of a social judgment.

McDougall's Hormic Psychology

McDougall (1908) considered instincts to be the prime movers of behavior, but his use of the term instinct can easily be misunderstood by an American reader today. He considered instincts in both animals and men to be examples of purposive behavior; each instinct includes a propensity for a certain perception, a characteristic emotion, and a pattern of reaction. The emotion and the goal are relatively fixed, but other elements are plastic in the service of the goal. Many explicit tissue needs, such as hunger and need for sleep, were omitted from his list of instincts (why is not clear), while gregariousness and construction were included as being species-specific goal-directed behaviors. Why do men do such things? Because it is their nature to do them. There is thus a circularity in invoking instincts as explanation of behavior but perhaps no more circularity than in more popular hedonic explanations.

McDougall criticized Baldwin's explanation in terms of an instinct of imitation: actions being imitated can be almost anything; hence imitation, having no specific goal, cannot be an instinct. Imitation is a general propensity in McDougall's system. McDougall approved of Freud for making instincts the prime movers in his psychoanalytic system but complained that Freud confused the sex instinct with the sentiment of love. McDougall regarded sentiments as distinct from instincts. He defined a sentiment, following Shand, as "an organised system of emotional tendencies centered about some object" (1908, p. 122). The pathological counterpart is what is called a complex.

McDougall's notion of the self-regarding sentiment (that is, pride, self-esteem, and self-respect) as the master sentiment in higher stages of character development encompasses the phenomena of those stages, particularly that of a conscience at least partly independent of social approval, more satisfactorily than did Baldwin's idea of imitation and the near-identity of ego and alter. Beyond that, however, the account of character development is a patchwork of insights, some wise indeed, but no coherent theory.

Mead's Social Behaviorism

Although influenced by Baldwin, particularly in regarding the genesis of the self as the central problem of social psychology, Mead (1934) took exception to explanation in terms of an instinct of imitation. It is absurd to suppose that we have a ready-made response to act the way other people act, with each such response triggered by sight of exactly the same behavior in the other person. Mead rejected the view of the central nervous system as analogous to a telephone switchboard. He was a colleague of Dewey's and undoubtedly sympathized with Dewey's (1896) article opposing the resolution of behavior in terms of stimulus and response. The nervous system acts as a unity, even though we do not know where the integration lies. Moreover, the organism to a considerable extent selects its own environment or stimuli by virtue of its sensitivities. The chief thrust of Mead's exposition was to oppose the view of each man as imprisoned in the cell of his own consciousness, tapping on the walls to communicate with other such prisoners.

Mead's explanation of imitative behavior essentially anticipated the notion of circular reaction worked out in detail later by Piaget (1936). Social behavior is antecedent to mind, self, or consciousness. The social act can be analyzed into a gesture on the part of one person (or animal), an accommodation on the part of another, all relevant to some outcome which gives the meaning of the act. A gesture is a significant symbol when the sender responds to it, at least implicitly, the same way the receiver does. Vocal gestures are uniquely suited to become significant symbols because we hear our own voice much as others do, whereas we do not see ourselves as others do. Imitation is particularly characteristic of vocal gestures, which are naturally suited to circular reactions.

Mind and consciousness arise when we learn to represent ourselves to ourselves by taking the view of others. Thus behavior, the social act, is both logically and temporally prior to consciousness. Meaning is not an idea or state of consciousness separate from the social act but is constituted in the experience. Symbolization constitutes objects; language does not simply represent things already there. A most important outcome of symbolization is the self, which arises just at the point where one becomes self-conscious.

One can watch the evolution of the self in children. In play, the young child at times takes several roles alternately; some children have imaginary playmates. In either case, the child is carrying on a conversation of gestures with himself. In an organized game, characteristic of a later stage, the child must implicitly take the attitude of everyone in it. The different roles must have a definite relation to one another. Rules are part of the enjoyment of the game. Thus, in the evolution of self, one first takes the view of particular others, later that of the generalized other. The social process or community enters behavior as a controlling factor in the form of the generalized other. "What goes on in the game goes on in the life of the child all the time. He is continually taking the attitudes of those about him, especially the roles of those who in some sense control him and on whom he depends" (Mead, 1934, p. 160).

The child, of course, cannot incorporate the whole personality of the parent. He assumes only the corresponding role, for the personality of the parent has become more complex, having evolved on the basis of just such play, as well as later social interactions, so that it incorporates the various roles within itself. The young child as yet has no such complexity in himself, nor does he understand its existence in his parent. When a child behaves in a parental fashion, say, towards dolls, his own nascent and incipient parental attitudes are being stimulated by his own dependent needs, just as his parents' responses are stimulated by his needs. Thus, what is called imitation is in this and at least some other instances, rather, self-stimulation. (Here Mead seems to have overextended his argument. That the child should have spontaneous parental behavior, independently of a parental model, seems more difficult to believe than that he imitates his parents.)

Mead used the term "me" to stand for the conventional, habitual self embodying the view of the generalized other and hence largely similar to the selves of other members of the near community. The "I" or ego always remains somewhat unpredictable and spontaneous. For this reason, and also because each person formulates the generalized other from his own standpoint, Mead allowed for individual differences more effectively than did Baldwin.

It is inconceivable from Mead's view that there be a self prior to social experience, since selfhood arises in taking the view of others to oneself.

In defending a social theory of mind we are defending a functional, as opposed to any form of substantive or entitive, view. . . . We are opposing all intra-cranial or intra-epidermal views as to its character and locus. For it follows from our social theory of mind that the field of mind must be co-extensive with . . . the matrix of social relations and interactions among individuals, which is pre-supposed by it, and out of which it arises or comes into being. If mind is socially constituted, then the field or locus of any given individual mind must extend as far as the social activity or apparatus of social relations which constitutes it extends; and hence that field cannot be bounded by the skin of the individual organism to which it belongs" (Mead, 1934, p. 223).

Mead has supplied a theory of ego development grounded on philoso-phy more than on observation. The fully fleshed person, with aggression, anxiety, and unconscious conflicts, is not to be found in his writing. His philosophic stance was adopted essentially by Sullivan, who, as a psychia-trist, dealt with people in their untidy, irrational complexity. Sullivan named his system an "interpersonal theory of psychiatry," thus expressing allegiance to the interpersonal origin of the self. Freud's early psychology stressed instinctual drives and unconscious motives and could be con-strued as a psychology-within-the-skin rather than as an interpersonal theory. But was not his ego psychology just as interpersonal as Sullivan's?

Psychoanalysis

In the period 1900 to 1920 psychology included at least four schools of thought relevant to the present topic; self theory, instinct theory, reflexology, and learning theory based on pleasure or reward. Baldwin, Dewey, and Mead represented self theory. The *Ethics* of Dewey and

Tufts (1908) presented ethics in terms of both development of societies and individual development. Ultimately, the ethical problem is the problem of the growth of the self, they said; self-realization is the goal of the highest ethical stage. McDougall represented instinct theory. Tolman and Woodworth also made instinct a central concept, but they omitted emotions from the definition of instinct, and hence brought instincts within the realm of behaviorism. Tolman (1922) took the purpose or the goal as the defining aspect; later the term drive came to replace instinct, in American usage at least. Reflexology was represented by Pavlov and Watson, among others. Kuo (1921), one of their partisans, argued that the concept of instinct was superfluous because instincts are merely concatenations of reflexes. Thorndike, with his law of effect, was the representative of associationistic learning theory based on pleasure-pain and reward-punishment. Hedonistic associationism and reflexology were elementaristic and reductionistic, while both self theory and instinct theory were emphatically non-reductionistic. By comparison, instinct theory today is usually considered as reductionistic, validly if instincts are considered as tissue needs but not if they are considered as purposive behavior.

Each of the foregoing schools of thought was concerned to differentiate itself from the others, although McDougall discussed character development, as did the self theorists, and Baldwin assumed one instinct, imitation. McDougall, for example, criticized Kuo, saying that instincts as concatenations of reflexes do not exist even in lower animals. Instincts are always purposive behavior. The rigidity of behavior in lower animals results from their lack of intelligence, not their domination by instincts. McDougall criticized Freud for assuming the existence of instincts and also postulating a pleasure principle. If there are instincts, their satisfaction naturally produces pleasure, which need not then be postulated as an additional principle. Differences between explanation of learning by conditioned reflexes and by the law of effect need not be reviewed here.

Early psychoanalysis: the drive-derivative view. What shall we think of a school of thought that starts with the assumption that the reflex arc is the basic unit of behavior, adds a pleasure principle, says that all behavior is motivated by instincts, and says that the ego governs access to motility? It would be presumptuous to say that these thoughts cannot be made into a coherent system, but although they are all to be found in Freud's writings, he never seriously tried to weave them into a coherent account. Rapaport (1959) tried to construct a system using all those elements, but neither he nor anyone else was satisfied. The inconsistencies in Freud's thinking have proved an embarrassment to psychoanalysis ever since and a major stumbling block to further development of psychoanalytic theory. Freud himself often publicly changed his mind and disavowed a line of thinking, but some of his followers have been loath to abandon any of his major positions. Rather than try the apparently impossible task of construing psychoanalytic thought as a single coherent system, I shall herein select a sub-set of ideas from Freud's later writings that seem to provide a coherent, internally consistent theory of ego development. Other relevant aspects of psychoanalytic thinking provide some historical perspective.

Unlike American behaviorists, Freud and his colleagues never passed through a period when terms such as ego and self were taboo, when there was no such concept. The initial thrust of psychoanalysis, however, was to dethrone the ego and give new emphasis to instincts and the unconscious as determinants of behavior. At the time of the split with Adler, Freud declared that Adler was just an ego psychologist, that to return to that view would be to give up the hard won gains of the psychology of the unconscious. Later, Freud gave greater emphasis to the ego and propounded an original theory of ego functioning and ego growth, but his followers were slow to accommodate themselves to the change in emphasis and many of them have never given his theory of ego development full recognition. There were always divergent strands in Freud's thought and hence sanction for alternative views.

The classic essay on the psychoanalytic drive-derivative account of ego development is that of Ferenczi (1913): The essence of ego development is the replacement of childhood megalomania by a recognition of the power of natural forces. The reality sense develops through a series of repressions, to which one is compelled not by spontaneous striving toward development (probably a reference to Adler) but through adjustment to renunciations demanded by experience. In *The Ego and the Id* (1923), Freud presented the familiar picture of the ego as a minor outcropping of the id, stimulated by contact with reality; this represents a new conception or a new vocabulary, but not a new emphasis, as compared to Ferenczi's account.

Freud's ego psychology. There is also a different theory of ego functioning to be found in Freud's writings, more important and more neglected. The pleasure principle, wrote Freud (1920), cannot account for certain observations: the play of children, the dreams of those suffering from traumatic neuroses, transference in psychoanalytic therapy, and character neuroses where the same unhappy fate is repeatedly brought about in the person's life. In such cases, the persons seem to be repeating just what was most painful to them. The explanation of this repetition compulsion is that one masters experience by actively repeating what one has passively undergone. (Freud, in fact, says a number of other things as well, but this is the aspect germane to the present discussion.)

That one must do what one has suffered seems to be a (or the) basic principle of ego functioning. Freud proceeded to apply the same principle in his explanation of the signal function of anxiety in *Inhibitions, Symptoms and Anxiety* (1926). Helplessness in the face of overwhelming tension due to need is the original traumatic situation, during which the infant experiences anxiety. Since mother is the agent of gratification, her absence is experienced as a threat of such a situation. Anxiety recurs in her absence as a danger signal, partly as an appeal for help, partly as an attempt on the part of the ego to master the situation by repeating it on its own impetus. Major sources of later anxiety, such as loss of mother's love, castration fear, and fear of the superego are explained in similar terms.

Later, Freud used essentially the same line of reasoning to account for how the child learns to control his own impulses as his father has controlled him, that is, for at least one aspect of the origin of the superego. Anna Freud (1936) used the same principle to account for identification with the aggressor and for altruism. In the latter cases, another principle has also been invoked, one which Freud first mentioned in "Mourning and Melancholia" (1917), namely, that a frustrating or unsatisfactory interpersonal relation can be mastered by reproducing both parts within oneself. We may say, though Freud did not, that interpersonal schemas become intrapersonal schemas, for which they provide both impetus and model. In "Mourning and Melancholia," the principle is used to explain how one masters loss of an object-person. In *Civilization and Its Discontents* (1930), it accounts for how one masters subjection to one's parents and, in doing so, accomplishes certain aspects of ego development (cf. Loevinger, 1966b).

Both of Freud's principles were anticipated earlier. Authors as far back as Plato have drawn an analogy between interpersonal relations and intrapersonal relations, comparing self-control to government, for instance. Baldwin came close to the principle of mastering what one has passively experienced by actively repeating it when he wrote of the child's polar nature, submitting to those in authority and practicing on those smaller. Mead's account of the child's conversation of gestures within himself as the origin of the self also presents intrapersonal differentiation as a direct resultant of interpersonal relations, probably even more clearly than did Freud's account. Yet in addition to being too rational, Mead's account lacks something of the force of Freud's. Freud added the crucial *because*, thus transforming observations and points of view into theory. The child plays dentist *because* he must master the experience of submitting to the dentist; he creates the agency of control within himself *because* he must master the experience of being controlled by parents.

Another uniquely psychoanalytic principle of ego development originating in Freud's writings is the principle of progression through regression. In his essay on narcissism, Freud (1914) showed the narcissistic, hence regressive, origins of the ego ideal, itself progressive. This was a pivotal discovery, coming out of psychoanalytic instinct theory yet leading to and assuming new significance in psychoanalytic ego psychology, as discussion of Ricoeur and Loewald will show.

"New psychoanalytic ego psychology." The received school of contemporary psychoanalytic ego psychology puts little emphasis on the foregoing aspects of Freud's writings. Instead, writers such as Rapaport and Hartmann and his collaborators, while acknowledging that there are some conflict-free ego functions (certainly not the ego functions that Freud was writing about in the passages referred to above), put major emphasis on derivation of ego and superego from instinctual drives. In the latter view, the moving force is drive energy, or cathexis, modified in some not explicit way so as to become countercathexis, that is, its own control. Freud had different proposals at different times for what the basic drives are, but there is currently general agreement among analysts that the two basic drives (implied: that are relevant to psychoanalysis) are sex and aggression. To derive ego phenomena from them, one must have additional postulates (for example, drive energy can be neutralized and deneutralized, and sexual and aggressive drives can be fused and defused). However, in one of the clearest expositions of development in terms of cathexis theory, Rapaport (1960) excluded ego development. What happens in most of the writings of Freud and of Hartmann and his collaborators is that observations in other terms are interwoven to such an extent that the bare bones of the cathexis argument are not discernible.

While the definitive counterargument to all versions of ego development based on cathexis theory is that of White (1963), there is an additional formal argument. Cathexis theory differs from all other ego theories discussed so far in not being phrased in terms of meanings; it is not only more abstract, but abstract in a different sense. While contemporary psychoanalytic theorists disclaim any literal connotations of physical energy, so that the theory is not necessarily reductionistic in that sense, they also disclaim any phenomenologically identifiable connotations of cathexis. It must therefore be an abstraction, one not directly tied to immediate observables. To build such models is an important and currently popular brand of theorizing. The method and virtue of such models is that they make a parallel or analogy between obscure or unreachable phenomena and some available, simple, well understood phenomena. The available relations between the simpler things are then inferred to hold for the more cryptic objects at issue. As a model of that sort, cathexis theory is a total failure. Not even its most enthusiastic advocates will say any longer that cathexis is something simple or well understood. At least in the area of ego development, cathexis theory runs a deficit. The concept of cathexis, together with such auxiliary concepts as countercathexis and neutralization of energy, require more explaining than they furnish.

Although I do not discern, as someone else might, a coherent theory of ego development in the writings of Rapaport or of Hartmann and his collaborators, it would be an injustice to leave matters at that. Hartmann in particular has been enormously influential in persuading psychoanalysts that the phenomena of ego functioning and ego development are as much their concern as instinctual gratification and psychosexual development. In a sense, the success of his work has deprived it of some of its point. In 1939 most psychoanalysts and other adherents to their views apparently espoused a drive-derivative view of ego development. Hartmann's (1939) modification of this view, his insistence that some ego functions are autonomous from the start and others become autonomous secondarily, was revolutionary. He never asserted that these were more than fragmentary insights. What has changed is that one no longer feels compelled to start with a drive-derivative view.

The writings of Hartmann's school are a gold mine of insights into aspects of ego processes. Among the best known of these insights are Hartmann's (1939) formulation that ego and id are differentiated out of a primal matrix and Kris's (1934) formulation of artistic creation as "regression in the service of the ego." Kris made frequent use of the principle that experience is mastered by active repetition of what has been passively undergone; however, it is hard to reconcile explanation in terms of change from passive to active with the equally frequent and even simultaneous explanatory formula of a saving in expenditure of energy.

Let us take our bearings. Freud promulgated a metapsychological theory in terms of a psychic apparatus whose function is to keep tension at a minimum. At the same time, he invented and practiced a psychotherapeutic technique entirely played out in terms of interpersonal relations, which have no direct representation in the early versions of the metapsychology. In his last years, Freud turned from viewing behavior as predominantly the playing out of instincts and their derivatives in an isolated psychic apparatus to primary concern with problems such as ego growth and identification, problems deeply rooted in the social matrix. The ego psychology of Hartmann and Rapaport continued and even laid greater emphasis on ego phenomena but attempted at the same time to assimilate the new focus of attention to the old metapsychology, to the picture of a psychic apparatus describable in terms of cathexis and its variants. They paid comparatively less attention to the two great contributions to ego theory that Freud made in his later years, the principle of mastery and the principle of internal differentiation through mastery of interpersonal relations, though both principles are universally known among analysts. Rapaport (1967) devoted a monograph to the problem of activity-passivity; it was presented as a paper in 1953 and was well-known to students of psychoanalysis prior to its posthumous publication. Yet neither of the two principles is mentioned in Rapaport's (1959) most extensive treatment of psychoanalysis as a system of psychology.

In the next sections, we shall follow somewhat separately the fate in recent writings of the mastery problem and the problem of identification. Following that, we shall discuss some contributions from authors who see themselves as independent of or more or less in opposition to psychoanalysis and conclude with consideration of Ricoeur's argument with Freud and Loewald's view of ego development. Freud's principles of ego development will be seen to come together again in the latter two writers in an expanded and deepened version.

Mastery and independent ego motives: Hendrick and White. The notion that the child finds joy in being a cause, in seeing the effects of his own actions on things, is often attributed to Groos but was clearly stated in 1881 by Preyer (quoted in Kessen, 1965).

Although Freud used such terms as the instinct to master, he did not do so systematically. Hendrick (1942) took up the term and related it specifically to the problem of ego development. According to Hendrick, "Psychoanalysis has neglected the overwhelming evidence that the need to learn how to do things, manifested in the infant's practice of its sensory, motor, and intellectual means for mastering its environment, is at least as important as pleasure seeking mechanisms in determining its behavior and development during the first two years of life [p. 34]." The aim of sexual instincts or libido is always, in psychoanalysis, sensual pleasure or its derivatives, whereas the aim of the instinct to master is the pleasure of successful functioning, regardless of sensual value, Hendrick continues. Manifestations of the instinct to master include sensori-motor skills, manipulation, locomotion, comprehension, and reasoning, all of which serve to mediate adjustment to environment. Those functions are ultimately all integrated as the ego.

Mature behavior is a synthesis of capabilities developed in fragmentary fashion. Each fragment develops according to a common plan. First there is emergence of a physiological ability to perform a reflex pattern, stereotyped and closely related to specific stimuli. The second or learning phase is characterized by repetitive practice, independence of a particular stimulus, and increasing ability to modify the pattern in useful ways. Maturity of the partial function is marked by proficiency without further practice, increasing integration with other partial functions, and subordination to purposes of the total personality rather than exercise for its own sake. The compulsive repetition that is a normal aspect of the second or learning phase is comparable to the compulsiveness of neurotic traits and symptoms. This sequence is the foundation of ego development. The more mature the ego, the more integrated the partial functions; this permits adequate discharge of instinctual energies without activation of a repetition compulsion. Libidinal aims are as much channeled by the development of ego functions as the other way round: thus Hendrick.

There have been repeated attempts, outside psychoanalysis as well as within, to salvage the drive-derivative view of ego development by labelling ego functions as instincts—"mastery" among psychoanalysts, "curiosity," "gregariousness," and so on among others. Hendrick can be read that way, provided that we remember that including mastery as an instinct involves a decisive broadening of psychoanalytic theory. White (1963) prefers to codify essentially the same observations so as to break with the drive-derivative view. The issue that Hendrick frames in terms of whether there is an instinct to master, independent of the drive for sensual pleasure, White formulates as follows: Does the moving force of ego development reside in the ego itself, or is it in drives or drive energies extrinsic to the ego? White argues forcefully that from the earliest time onward mastery of ego functions is its own reward. No extrinsic drives or rewards are needed to account for the broad outlines of ego development. Ego functioning is neither necessarily nor optimally triggered by sexual and aggressive drives, though it is often in their service. Indeed, ego functioning is seen most clearly when drives are quiescent, and some area of freedom from drive pressure is optimal for ego development. From his earliest coordinated movements the child shows joy in being a cause, in seeing his effects on the environment. This motive White calls effectance. The cumulative result of his exercise of functions is competence, reflected in his long range sense of competence.

The chief data to support White's thesis are the usual data of child psychology, also invoked by Hendrick, in part available prior to Freud's time but largely overlooked by psychoanalysts in the first flush of their discoveries concerning the unconscious. Goldstein's (1939) view of the organism as striving for self-actualization, based in large part on experimental studies of patients with brain injuries, also supports the view that the fundamental motive force of the ego is intrinsic to it rather than in drives arising outside the ego. There is a large overlap between what Goldstein calls self-actualization and what White calls sense of competence. A big difference is that Goldstein considered self-actualization the only drive, with all other motives subordinate to it, while White acknowledges psychosexual motives in addition to ego motives. The monolithic assumption may be interpreted as contradictory to the basic psychoanalytic view, for inner conflict accounts for neurosis in psychoanalysis. Even if the account of inner conflict does not rest on separable drives, there is no precedent in psychoanalytic thinking for postulation of a single, monolithic drive or motive. White's view remains in the psychoanalytic tradition, while Goldstein's did not.

Support for the notion of independent ego motives comes from another source that White does not acknowledge (perhaps because he does not want to sanction some misrepresentations of psychoanalysis to be found in the same writings), namely, the experiences of Carl Rogers and his school of non-directive psychotherapy. Rogers (1964) argues that he depends entirely on the strivings toward growth and self-actualization of his clients in place of any manipulation of their motives. Although the technique of orthodox psychoanalysis differs from that of non-directive counseling, the same motives for self-directed growth are ultimately depended on. Unfortunately, Rogers misses this point and cites as representative of psychoanalytic theory a minority opinion sanctioning a manipulative approach. Rogers, like Goldstein, stakes everything on the single motive of self-actualization, hence this theory is by no means a psychoanalytic one, even though his experiences support White's views.

For whatever reason, neither Hendrick nor White stresses the specifically psychoanalytic version of the mastery principle, that the ego masters experience by actively repeating what it has passively undergone. This principle has been used and extended by Erikson (1950), particularly in writings on the use of play for diagnosis and therapy, where he leans heavily and explicitly on the principle that one must do what one has suffered. Erikson distinguishes the micro-sphere of toys, the macrosphere of play with other children, and the autocosmic sphere of one's own body. Experiences in one sphere can be re-enacted in the others. He suggests that play is the child's form of dealing with experience by creating model situations and of mastering by experiment and planning.

Identification and identity: Erikson. The second of Freud's major contributions to theory of ego development, that intrapersonal schemas are modelled after and stimulated by interpersonal schemas, is represented in psychoanalytic literature by the more conventional language of identification. Neither the nature of identification nor its relation to ego development is beyond dispute. At one extreme one finds, for example, Sanford (1955), who sees in identification and its precursor, introjection, a pathological process or a response to an emergency situation, without long term significance for character building. At the other extreme is White (1963), who reduces identification to a kind of apprenticeship in acquisition of social competence and hence a chief source of ego development. Without attempting to ascertain whether it is the received opinion, we shall follow a line of thought between those extremes. In this view, identification is a major factor in ego development, but it is not shorn of its unconscious dynamics nor of its pathological potential.

Erikson (1956) envisages identification as the middle term in a sequence that begins with introjection and ends with identity formation. These are not stages of ego development but rather modalities of ego formation and transformation. In reference to identification proper, he speaks of the child identifying himself with "overvalued and ill-understood body parts, capacities, and role appearances" (p. 112) favored by the child's fantasies about parents. "None of the identifications of childhood . . . could, if merely added up, result in a functioning personality" (p. 112). The final process, characteristic of adolescence, although anticipated earlier, is identity formation. "It arises from selective repudiation and mutual assimilation of childhood identifications, and their absorption in a new configuration, which in turn, is dependent on the process by which a society (often through subsocieties) identifies the young individual" (p. 113).

In calling attention to the sequence introjection, identification, identity, Erikson has underlined the transformation of the process of transformation, a complexity but a necessary one. He seems to assume that these central terms, however, are self-explanatory. Sanford (1955) shows that the terms are used variously by different authorities. In the absence of any agreed on definition, I shall venture to guess something of what is meant to be conveyed by the terms, probably by Erikson and certainly by at least some others. White (1963) and Ricoeur (1965) point to Freud's inconsistency in using the term identification both in the sense of wanting to be like and wanting to have or to devour. The term introjection, I believe, usually connotes the fantasy of early childhood that one becomes like what one eats, a fantasy that may give an unconscious coloring to later identifications when it is no longer the whole story or even the chief plot.

Identification, I believe, means invoking the power of a loved or feared person by means of its accompanying gesture. That is its magical aspect. Identification also has other connotations, some of which are carried by the term *indwelling*, which Polanyi (1968) uses in slightly different context. Polanyi, writing about the tacit component in perception, points out that when using a tool or probe, one is not conscious of the pattern of stimulation on the hand holding it; it is rather as if one's sensory boundary were extended out to the end of the tool or probe. One feels what the probe is touching. This is what Polanyi calls internalizing the tool; alternatively, the person is indwelling his tool. There is a similar connotation in the term identification both in common speech and in psychoanalysis. One, so to speak, internalizes other people by indwelling them, perceiving what one supposes they perceive and reacting implicitly as one supposes they react. Loewald (unpublished MS.) uses the term *participation* and stresses its importance in early childhood and in primitive people. We will return to the topic of identification in the contributions of Ricoeur and Loewald after considering some ideas arising outside psychoanalysis.

Sullivan's Anxiety-Gating Theory

The most important if not the only theory of ego stability is that of Sullivan (1953). Sullivan began his theory of ego development or, as he called it, development of the self-system, with a different conception of the genesis of anxiety from Freud's. Whereas Freud saw anxiety as arising from helplessness in the face of overwhelming tension of unsatisfied physical needs, Sullivan virtually excluded that possibility as a source of anxiety in early infancy. The worst that is likely to happen in such instances, he said, is delay of gratification. Much more insidious for the infant is to be ministered to by an anxious mother (or mother surrogate). Apparently from birth onward the infant experiences anxiety by a kind of empathy when the mother is anxious. Anxiety is the worst experience an infant normally has; it is the other extreme from euphoria. Moreover, it prevents gratification of other needs, even in the presence of appropriate objects, such as the milk-giving nipple. The anxious infant cannot feed. The crying, non-feeding infant creates additional anxiety in the mother, and so it goes until the infant cries itself into exhaustion or withdraws in somnolent detachment. Termination of crying may relieve the mother's anxiety and break the cycle.

The self-system is formed in the infant and develops from then on to insure satisfaction of needs with minimum cost in anxiety. While clearly recognizing other kinds of learning, Sullivan stressed as the earliest form, and one of continuing importance, learning through the anxiety gradient. The child learns to steer his behavior in the direction of decreasing anxiety, both for mother and for himself, and does so by means of minimal cues.

With increasing age, the individual's mode of operation changes from the prototaxic (primitive, immediate) mode of experiencing to the parataxic (approximately, pre-operational) mode and then in part to the syntaxic (approximately, concrete operational and logical operational) mode. The limitations in one's conception of self and others are part of the self-system, and the self-system functions so as to minimize anxiety. This is accomplished by selective inattention to observations discordant with current, however erroneous or limited, conceptions of self and others. Opening of the self-system to new and corrective observations is unusual. Normally, it occurs to some extent at each developmental threshold, in response to newly maturing needs, for example, the combination of the needs of lust and for intimacy in adolescence. Otherwise, it occurs only in rare and fortunate circumstances, of which prolonged psychiatric treatment can be one.

Some recent ego psychologists influenced by Sullivan, such as C. Sullivan, Grant, and Grant (1957) and Loevinger (1966a) have stressed a direct, specifiable relation between the stage of ego development and the nature of self-conception and of conception of others. This point, not clearly made by Sullivan, strengthens and extends his argument.

Merleau-Ponty: the structure of behavior. Although apparently neither knew of the other's work, Merleau-Ponty (1942) had some ideas remarkably similar to those of Sullivan. According to Merleau-Ponty, development is a progressive and discontinuous structuration of behavior. Structures tend to be preserved. Normally, development occurs so as to re-structure conduct in depth, so that infantile attitudes no longer have place or meaning in it. When what Freud calls repression occurs, integration appears to have been achieved but at the expense of dissociating a stereotyped attitude, a rigid and stable sub-structure, resulting from an anguishing and disorganizing experience that the subject could not master at the time it occurred. The dissociated experience is not, as some of Freud's metaphors might lead one to believe, a causative agent on its own which rises to the surface periodically. Rather, it is a permanent or semi-permanent way of experiencing; hence, it is contemporary and self-perpetuating. Thus, as he said, Merleau-Ponty replaced Freud's energic metaphor with a structural metaphor.[4] This, then, is Merleau-Ponty's formulation: The ego is a structure self-perpetuating by virtue of non-inclusion of too-discordant observations. Repression is that non-inclusion in the ego organization. In this connection, we may raise again a question dropped at the beginning of the chapter: Is it necessary to postulate a force that represses? Or to ask whether repression occurs in the ego or outside of it? The force that represses is precisely the striving of the ego for coherence.

Lecky: self-consistency. Premonitions of the Sullivan and Merleau-Ponty theory can be found in many places, for instance, the writings of Prescott Lecky. Lecky (1945) rejected both the stimulus-response view of behavior, which construes it analogously to a telephone switchboard, and the (early) psychoanalytic version, that of a hydraulic system with instincts or repressed motives as pressures seeking outlet or release. The one overemphasizes random outer stimuli, while the other overemphasizes internal forces. Mechanistic analogies do not account for the observable facts of behavior. (As with many other authors quoted, Lecky's views on

[4]This is essentially the same point made in Chapter 6. It is pointed out there how the energy model of motivation is an anachronistic carry-over from Freud's nineteenth century neurological training. A structural or information processing model is consonant with modern thinking about the brain and nervous system and, in addition, provides a superior fit with clinical data and ego theory. (Editor)

stimulus-response psychology and psychoanalysis are quoted to reveal the trend of his own thinking, not as faithful expositions of the other schools.) Given a learning theory that accounts for the ingraining of habits by repetition, how could one account for the fact that most children spontaneously give up the habit of thumb-sucking? Habits in the sense of action patterns do not exist except under rare conditions, such as some laboratory experiments provide. Stability of behavior occurs with respect to goals and results, rather than with respect to specific movements.

Personality, according to Lecky, is an organized dynamic system, not completely determined by heredity or environment but tending toward self-determination. The individual has two sets of problems, maintaining harmony with himself and with his environment. In order to maintain harmony with the environment, his interpretations must be consistent with experience. To maintain his individuality, he must organize his interpretations to form an internally consistent system. At the center of one's view of the world is one's self-conception. The child gives up thumb-sucking when it no longer accords with his view of himself. Lecky recognized the similarity of his views to those of Adler. In construing symptoms as a purposeful and organized striving for superiority, however, Adler was denying conflict and disorganization, which Lecky felt provided the explanation of feelings of inferiority.

Learning is essentially a matter of resolving conflicts, that is, of assimilating discordant stimuli. Hence, conflicts are necessary for personality development to occur. Learning is something a child must accomplish for himself, though one can assist by protecting him from problems too difficult for his current repertory. The child tends to choose those situations in accord with his estimate of his own abilities, preferring problems he can solve and thus strengthening his organization. (Here Lecky anticipated recent work in motivation. See page 117).

While everyone strives always for self-consistent personality organization, the attempt is not guaranteed to be a success. Moreover, the consistency is so in the eyes of the person himself, not necessarily in anyone else's eyes. Lecky, anticipating Erikson's thinking on the dangers of consolidation of a negative identity, noted that a self-conception of being incompetent or delinquent will be maintained and will govern behavior even at the cost of much pain to the person.

Lecky's therapeutic technique rested on pointing out inconsistencies in the patient's sets of values, in an atmosphere of acceptance and self-determination and in such manner as to encourage a sounder integration. Resistance is the person's, or patient's, effort to maintain his individuality intact. Of itself it is not an unhealthy thing, as Lecky assumed psychoanalysts to believe. Resistance is the opposite of assimilation and learning and represents refusal to reorganize values, especially ego values. The aim of therapy is not so much to root out false ideas as to encourage a reorganization of the patient's total set of values.

While Lecky clearly had a superficial view of psychoanalysis and an incomplete catalogue of human motives, he had a firm grasp of ego stability. His free use of technical psychoanalytic terms such as resistance is a potential source of confusion. Perhaps the weakest point in his theory is the notion of conflict, which he used to cover assimilation of discordant stimuli. As he used the term, it seems to mean what Piaget calls accommodation. Lecky showed no grasp of Freud's idea that only inner conflict can give rise to neurosis, for Lecky did not clearly differentiate inner conflict from the necessity for outer accommodation.

Ausubel's Theory of Satellization

A recent theorist who has drawn on Freud, Ferenczi, and Sullivan but has added a flavor of his own is Ausubel (1952). Ausubel follows Ferenczi in believing that the infant, seeing his wants gratified by his parents, fantasies himself as omnipotent, though Ausubel objects to pushing the feeling of omnipotence back to the period immediately post-natal, prior to the emergence of any distinctive sense of self, as Ferenczi did. As the child develops perceptually, he sees first that the gratification of his needs is not his doing but his parents' (executive dependence). Later, with the initiation of training, he perceives that his parents do not actually have to supply him with everything but do so of their own good will (volitional dependence). At this point, his knowledge of his own smallness and helplessness threatens a precipitous loss in self-esteem. Three courses are open to him: to continue to believe in his own omnipotence, despite objective evidence to deflate his pretensions; to accept the great loss of self-esteem that corresponds to his true abilities as a small child; or to become a satellite of his parents, that is, to transfer his omnipotence to them and shine in glory reflected from their magnificence. The latter is the normal and benign course of events, prevented, however, if parents reject the child or value him for extrinsic reasons rather than simply because he is their child. Toward the end of childhood and beginning of adolescence there normally occurs de-satellization. The child's loyalties and values become transferred first to other adults and then to peer group. Ultimately, he learns to depend on his own powers for his sense of personal worth.

This schema leaves open the possibility of tracing many deviant patterns, their origin in parental mistakes or other circumstances, and their consequences in behavioral deviations and pathology. Ausubel has, in effect, described the ego developmental aspects of the era and partly of the same sequence of events that Freud had described in terms of the

Oedipus complex. In his discourse, Ausubel takes account of many social and biological factors, but his main theoretical argument rests heavily on a single motive, maximizing self-esteem or minimizing its loss, in conjunction with changing capacities in the child and changing expectations in his social surround.

Monolithic Ego Theories

There is a group of theories that account for ego development in terms of a single striving, say, for competence or self-actualization. Adler (1956) wrote of striving for superiority, White (1963) of competence. Self-actualization and self-realization have been the terms of Dewey and Tufts (1908), Goldstein (1939), Maslow (1954), and Rogers (1961).

While a great deal of wisdom and information about ego development can be found in the writings of these authors, what they present is something less than a theory, in the sense that the term theory is being used here. What they do in effect is to take the motivation of one high stage of ego development and make of it an explanation of all previous stages and of the transition from stage to stage. A similar objection, that the motivation most prominent in one ego stage is taken as the real motivation of all people, applies to many theories of learning and motivation that do not even have words for ego development.

This is the ontological fallacy. It asserts something like the following: People only *seem* to differ in their motivations; at bottom, really and truly, what everyone wants is the same, namely, _____. The blank is then filled by pleasure, reward, self-esteem, competence, self-actualization, or some such. The ontological fallacy thus denies the very transformation of motivation that theories of ego development are called on to explain.

Monolithic theories, depending for explanation on a single type of motivation, thus do not meet the formal requirement of a theory of development: That there be a sequence of events not all formally identical and that this sequence be connected by an inner logic. No matter how true it is that individuals strive all through life for competence and for self-actualization, that fact alone does not account for the cumulative transformations that constitute ego development.

Pacers

Dember (1965) has summarized and interpreted the import of some recent experimental work in motivation, work on many species of laboratory animals but especially on humans. These studies have proved incompatible with viewing motivation in terms of reduction of physiological need states. Indeed, they resist being conceived in terms of responses. Rather, animals and especially people are motivated, at least in part, by the novelty and complexity of stimulus objects. As objects vary in their complexity, so do people vary in their ability to cope with complexity. For each person there is some ideal level, neither too simple nor too complex. When a person can choose, he chooses stimulus objects of a level of complexity that matches his own. He selects such objects, seeks them out, works for them, and learns what he must do to obtain them. Those activities are classic indicators of rewarding objects. While his own capacity determines the level of complexity he seeks, a person tends to sample stimulus objects above and below his own ideal level. Indeed, the modal amount of time goes to stimuli just a little more complex than the person's ideal. These objects are called pacers. As the person maintains contact with and thus masters a pacer, his own level of complexity grows and he is ready for a new, more complex pacer.

These laboratory studies of cognition do not, of course, prove anything about how ego development takes place. What they do is to supply a valuable model for one aspect of the dynamics of development and to give plausibility to it.

Starting from a point as far from the laboratory as possible, Brewster Smith (in press) has arrived at a notion that in abstract terms is related to Dember's concept of pacers. Smith's topic is the legitimation of evil, and his instances are Nazism, the war in Vietnam, and similar events. His method is to seek mutual illumination from the currents of social events and individual development, a method that Dewey and Tufts (1908) once made popular but that has been out of style in recent years. While the great social evils of modern times are as morally revolting as those of older history, Smith asserts, the fact of widespread moral revulsion on the part of some of the perpetrators and presumed beneficiaries is new. In this fact, there is some evidence of progress in moral development, a progress not discernible in the actual propensities of men for evil. Implied in this argument is the notion of conscience as a built-in pacer for ego development, a notion at first novel but on second thought obvious or at least inevitable. One's goals and aspirations and standards must be the harbingers of future development, a development not always realized, to be sure. The view of superego as pacer is elaborated by Loewald (1962).

Ricoeur: The Archaeology and Teleology of the Subject

Paul Ricoeur (1965), a French philosopher, has presented his views as an argument with Freud, not with psychoanalysis as practiced or as developed by disciples. He points out that psychoanalysis as method and the theory it generates are uniquely suited to revealing the archaic origins of our conduct and our nature; he calls that the archaeology of the subject. Creative development, including artistic creation and also ego development, cannot in principle be reduced to archaic causes; such achievements constitute the teleology of the subject. Freud recognized that infantile sources fail to explain precisely what is valuable in artistic achievement. In Ricoeur's terms, the archaeology of the subject does not exhaustively explain the teleology of the subject. How then are they related? Let us attempt to follow his argument.

When we speak of interpretation, hence hermeneutics, in relation to psychoanalysis, we refer only to language that has double or multiple meanings. Interpretation in Freud, as in Marx and Nietzsche, is a decoding or de-mystification, contrasting with the religious or esthetic vision, which is an encoding, a restoration or enrichment of meaning. Freud saw desire, or instinct, manifest everywhere. At first, he deciphered symptoms, dreams, and failed or distorted acts, but almost from the beginning he included works of art, witticisms, myths, and religion. Symbols in psychoanalysis are distortions, but in religion or poetry they are revelations. To what extent are these different hermeneutics in opposition? Is the revealing-hiding of double meaning always dissimulation of what is desired, or can it sometimes be revelation? And is the alternative itself real or illusory?

Freud's *Project for a Scientific Psychology* (1966), written in 1895, was his most mechanistic picture of the psychic apparatus. Successive revisions moved away from the physical model to one that is a scene of the debate of roles and masks, a place of coding and decoding. The *Project* bears the mark of Freud's erroneous belief at that time that neurosis originates in infantile trauma. Hence, there was emphasis on place for storage of memories, rather than for elaboration of fantasies, which later experience proved to be more pathogenic than memories *per se*. The metapsychology of Chapter 7 of *The Interpretation of Dreams* (1900) still bears traces of the false belief in the traumatic character of mnemonic traces of real perceptions. The Oedipus complex became important in the etiology of the neuroses as soon as Freud discovered it in his own analysis, since it replaced an hypothesis of which it was the reverse, that of seduction of children by adults. Neither the Oedipus complex nor the transference of psychoanalytic psychotherapy can be represented in terms of an isolated psychic apparatus regulated by energy seeking discharge. The Freudian wish is not a tension that can be discharged; it is insatiable.

Freud's analysis of the origins of religion and of culture in terms of murder of the primal father and the totemic feast is his fantasy, a bit of circular reasoning. It shows again how strong was the hold on Freud that a real crime had been committed, precisely the assumption that had proved false in relation to individual neurosis. For Freud, all history is subordinated to desire in its great debate with authority.

The interpretation of dreams is the paradigm of all interpretation because the dream is the paradigm of all the artifices of desire. The desire represented in the dream is always infantile; thus the interpretation is not only a decoding but a revelation of the archaisms of our nature. The dream permits us to elaborate the language of desire, that is, the architectonic of the symbolic function, to the extent it is typical or universal. Sexuality is the fundamental stuff of that symbolism.

A work of art is both the symptom and the cure, as Freud showed in his essay on Leonardo (1910). In interpreting the works of Michelangelo and Leonardo like dreams, Freud was comparing a durable creation of the day with a fugitive and sterile product of the night. Psychoanalysis calls the difference sublimation, but that only names the problem. A work of art is esteemed as a creation in proportion as it is not simply a projection of the conflicts of the artist but a sketch of their solution. If psychoanalysis is limited to understanding culture in terms of an economics of desire and of resistances, that firmness and rigor is preferable to the essays of Jung, where everything is in danger of being mixed up: the psychic, the soul, the archetypes, the sacred.

In *On Narcissism: An Introduction* Freud (1914) proposed one path to superego formation that has not been absorbed or replaced by later formulations. The formation of the ego ideal, to which all goodness is attributed, is a way to retain infantile narcissism at the same time as displacing it. Formation of ideals changes the object of the drive but not the aim; sublimation, which changes the aim, is something else. Moreover, formation of the ego ideal reinforces repression, while sublimation is an alternative to repression. Perhaps it is the narcissistic basis of the ideal self that provides a base for identification and explains how what is borrowed from others, particularly the parents, can become oneself. Perhaps it is necessary that the fragments of other people that form the ideal ego collect about an ego ideal rooted in narcissism in order that identification succeed.

Superego development is sublimation as to aim, introjection as to method, but regression to narcissism from the economic point of view. How is the regressive character of narcissistic identification brought into accord with the structural (hence progressive) effect of identification that sets up the superego?

The foundation of the superego in the Oedipus complex shows its close relation to the id, farther from consciousness than the ego. The superego is the inheritor of the Oedipus complex in the double sense that it is derived from it and it represses it. The Oedipus complex must decline because its aims are unattainable, and also because the phallic stage, to which it corresponds, is ended by threat of castration, which receives quasi-empirical support from the knowledge of sex differences. These facts explain how the turning away from the Oedipus complex saves narcissism, and they show also that the superego is the expression of the most powerful drives. The decline of the Oedipus complex is both a sublimation, because a de-sexualization, and indistinguishable from a repression, though sublimation and repression are concepts ordinarily opposed.

The daily bread of psychoanalysis is the lost or absent or substitute object. The Oedipal drama would not be possible unless the child wished for too much, for what he could not obtain. Wish fulfillment is basic to theory of primary process, and it is essential to wish fulfillment that the fantasy be a substitute for a lost object of desire. There are no derivatives, derivatives cannot be displaced or distorted, without a meaningful relation to something lost. The dream, all symbols, all works of art are representations of lost or absent objects. Reality testing is the comparison of a mental representation, always the reproduction of an absent object, with the outside world. There is here a common element underlying the disappearing-reappearing Freud noted in children's play; the disavowing-surmounting of fantasy in artistic creation, as analyzed in Freud's essay on Leonardo; and the loss and finding again involved in perceptual judgment. Freud stated that the ego is the precipitate of abandoned objects. Thus, the idea of absence is introduced into the constitution of the ego. Reality is the correlate of that internalized absence. The psychoanalytic conception of the ego, and particularly its structural autonomy, is inseparable from the lost or absent object.

The problem of the ego is domination. The original of non-mastery is danger. The ego is what is menaced—by reality, by instincts, and by conscience—and it must dominate the situation to defend itself. Like Spinoza, Freud approached the ego in terms of its initial situation of enslavement, that is, non-mastery.

The interior instance of morality is an exterior menace internalized. Moral man is at first *aliéné*, submitting to the law of a foreign master as he submits to that of desire and as he submits to the law of reality. The theme of the three masters in *The Ego and the Id* (1923) is instructive. Because the superego remains my alter in myself, it must be deciphered; foreigner, it remains foreign. Interpretation, in exploring hidden desires that disguise themselves in dreams and the like, unmasks all sources not original or primitive, all sources foreign and properly alien to the self. In passing from the oneiric to the sublime, interpretation changes its object but not its sense.

The superego is a construction, not an observation, though it is based on such discoveries as unconscious guilt observed as obstacle to cure. It includes three functions: the ego ideal, self-observation, and conscience. Self-observation denotes the doubling of self, an idea derived from Hegel. Psychoanalysis is always concerned with a doubling of consciousness, beginning with the pre-Oedipal desire to be like the father. This is never adequately represented in the metapsychology, which sees it only in its regressive aspect. Since desire is from the beginning interpersonal, identification is not something added on from outside; it is the dialectic of desire itself: Desire is always a desire that another desire. The profound and constructive significance of the Oedipus complex is not captured in the economic version, where it is spoken of as abandoned or as libidinal investment renounced.

Freud never explained the mechanism of sublimation or its epigenesis. Economically it is regression to narcissism, hence progression by means of regression. The innovation of meaning in sublimation requires another hermeneutics than that of libido. The task that where id was, there shall ego be cannot in principle be reduced to the economics of desire.

Freud explicitly created an analysis, not a synthesis. But, writes Ricoeur, in reading Freud, I do not understand myself except by forming the notion of an archaeology of the subject, and I do not understand the notion of an archaeology except in relation to a teleology. Returning to Freud, I find this dialectic in his work.

There are many points in common between Ricoeur's philosophic exposition and Loewald's psychoanalytic one, to which we turn next. To provide continuity, let us anticipate some of them. Freud's early version of psychoanalysis is contrasted with his later theory, and a stand is taken for the later version. The tension reduction model is disavowed; psychic functioning is interpersonal from its beginnings. Ricoeur's complex discussion of the death instinct, omitted here for brevity, includes the points made by Loewald. The constructive significance of the Oedipus complex and the relation of superego to ego development are stressed; the terms ego ideal and ideal ego are revived to designate stages in the development of the superego, though with reversed meanings. Progression through regression is a common theme; both emphasize Freud's saying that "where id was, there ego shall be." Loewald (1960, p. 11), like Ricoeur, sees interpretation as not only revealing but also creating meaning. The problem of ego mastery in Ricoeur is related to the topic of active and passive repetition in Loewald. Doubling of consciousness in Ricoeur becomes the topic of internal differentiation in Loewald. Although less obvious, there is a link between parts of Loewald's treatment of transference and Ricoeur's discussion of the lost or absent object.

Loewald's Psychoanalytic Ego Psychology

In a series of papers, not all published as yet, Loewald (1951, 1960, 1962a, 1962b)[5] has formulated a psychoanalytic theory, or version, of

[5]This summary is based also on manuscripts entitled "Some Considerations on Repetition and Repetition Compulsion," "On Internationalization," and "Activity-Passivity," which Dr. Loewald kindly made available to me.

ego development that is compatible with many of the insights originating outside the psychoanalytic group. The following is a condensed version of those of his ideas most germane to the present chapter.

Psychoanalytic ego theory, as developed in Freud's later writings, is not simply an addendum to the older theory of instincts and the unconscious, not simply an elaboration of the functions of yet another psychic institution, but rather a new way of looking at all of psychic functioning. There is even a question whether one should speak of ego development or of development of psychic functioning or apparatus. The way instincts are conceived of in psychoanalysis changed with the development of ego psychology. The out-of-date reflex arc model did not dominate Freud's later writings; instincts became strivings for objects rather than strivings for a contentless satisfaction. Thus instincts, in Freud's later writings, imply a relation to the environment as much as does the ego, but the relation is integrated on a more primitive level. Freud did not fully or consistently carry through the implications of the ego-theoretic orientation of his later years, and psychoanalytic theory has tended to remain under the sway of the older version of instinct theory. Some deviation from the text of Freud's writings is necessary to carry out the spirit of the new approach.

To see the child as born into a reality-world from which he is separate and with which he then establishes relations is not to see from the point of view of the child or even the mother. Rather, the infant and mother are originally a unity, at first biologically and increasingly psychologically.[6] Each step of the increasing differentiation between them leads to and is accompanied by a corresponding integration. Reality is necessarily psychologically constituted for the child in the same stages as his ego develops, for they are differentiated out of a common matrix. Differentiation of mother and child gives rise to the striving for reunification characteristic of all later stages. This urge is the origin of the child's libidinal tie to the mother as well as the origin of the synthetic function of the ego.

The primal unity between mother and child is gratifying, but the strong early tie to mother, and particularly regression to it from later stages, is also threatening, since it implies return also to an earlier, less differentiated stage of ego development. To the young child, father serves as an identification figure needed as a defense against ego regression, as well as being a rival for mother's affection. The Oedipus complex is thus given an extended meaning, including both positive and negative feelings toward both parents and occurring over an extended period

[6] A closely related view of mother-infant attachment as beginning in total sensorimotor contact as well as a view stressing the centrality of separation in the genesis of anxiety is presented in Chapter 8. (Editor)

rather than a single or a few traumatic events. Indeed, ambivalence toward both parents (or parental roles) plays an essential part in growth of the ego. Freud overstressed the aspect of the castrating father as representative of external reality opposing and interfering with the libidinal tie of mother and child. But in the pre-ego of primary narcissism, reality is not something outside. Genetically, reality and ego are one. Since instinct and environment are mutually structured, just as at later stages reality and ego are mutually structured, instinct is no longer conceived as something inside and hostile to the ego, nor is reality something outside and hostile to the ego.

The regressive phenomena of neurosis and particularly of psychosis are understood differently in these terms. The schizophrenic does not so much withdraw from reality as lose the boundaries between ego and reality. For the infant and for the regressed psychotic, magical qualities are experienced as both in the ego and in the outer world, hence as threatening and overpowering.

The process of ego development takes place by means of progressive restructuring of the child's relation to his environment and by a correlative internal restructuring of the child. It is not, however, a matter of a changing relation to fixed objects; the reality to which the child adjusts, the love objects to which he is attached, are also changing for him as he becomes different. In the pre-Oedipal period, the predominant aspect of ego formation is establishing externality and internality as such; introjection and projection are not so much different processes as different directions of the same process. This stage precedes true attachment to external objects, which presupposes a clear external and internal sense, and first takes place in the Oedipal period. The optimal outcome of the Oedipal period is formation of the superego, that is, internal differentiation of the psychic structure, or ego. This is not sufficiently described in terms of internalization of parents or of images of the parents. Rather, the *relation* is re-established internally to the child's psychic structure. But that implies that the old relation is destroyed, not repressed, and the elements are reintegrated into something new, making the child different and thus giving him a different view of his parents. Repression must be sharply differentiated from the formation of psychic structure; repression precludes development by making the constituents unavailable for a new integration.

An important aspect of the internalized image of the mother is the mother's attitude to, perception of, and relation with the child. Ideally, mother perceives the child not only as he is but as he will be at later stages; this is conveyed to the child and internalized by him, helping to establish his feeling of identity. There is a tension set up between the stage of the child's present level of psychic functioning and the more mature stage represented by the mother and by the mother's hopes for his future. There is a similar tension between the level of the patient's ego functioning and that of the analyst, as he appears in the therapeutic hour, and of the analyst's appreciation of the patient's potential growth. The tension between what one might be at best, in the future, and what one is at present exists not only between parent and child, between analyst and patient, but also between superego and ego. Thus, the condition for psychic growth and development is itself internalized.

Internalization means the process by which relations between the person and his environment become transformed into intrapsychic relations. The inner world thus constituted establishes new and more complex relations with the environment. Terms such as introjection and identification are aspects of internalization. The psychoanalytic terms neutralization and de-sexualization refer to the destructive aspects of internalization; identification and sublimation refer to constructive aspects. Identification involves some confusion or merging of subject and object; but ultimately internalization leads to differentiation between subject and object. Thus, internalization goes beyond identification as well as beyond the libidinal and aggressive elements of the child's relations to others.

The death instinct, the tendency to abolish stimulation, reduce tension, seek rest, is not what is "beyond the pleasure principle," for it turns out to be another version of Freud's earliest assumption of the constancy or pleasure principle, based on nineteenth century mechanistic physics. What is truly beyond the constancy principle is Eros, the life instinct, the tendency to integrate or to create structure. Satisfaction for Eros is not reduction of stimulation leading back to a previous level of equilibrium but absorbing and integrating stimuli, leading to a higher level of equilibrium. Only the latter is compatible with Freud's formula for psychoanalysis, that where id was, there shall ego be.

The term transference has three usages in Freud. It refers to the transfer of libido to objects, as when one speaks of transference neuroses; this sense is virtually synonymous with object cathexis. The second meaning is that of transferring relations with infantile objects onto later objects, especially the analyst during psychoanalysis. This is the currently predominant usage. The third meaning is the transferring of intensity from an unconscious idea to a preconscious one. Only in seeing the connections between these three meanings does one fully perceive the nature of psychoanalytic therapy and of normal growth. The mechanisms of neurosis are, after all, distortions of normal processes. The transfer of libido to objects and of infantile object relations to contemporary figures are normal processes; life draws its vitality from them. Only by means of such transference does the ego integrate the instinctual life with current reality and thus achieve maturity. The difference between the conscious-preconscious psychic system and the unconscious is another version of the differential between more maturely organized and more primitive psychic apparatus that is the condition for psychic development.

The id is the past as represented in the present. The superego is the future as anticipated and aimed for in the present. The ego as an organizing agent integrates and presents them in the present moment. Ideal ego and ego ideal can be taken as precursors of the superego. In this sense, ideal ego refers to the recapturing of the primary narcissistic, omnipotent perfection of infancy by identifying oneself with parents seen as omnipotent. The term ego ideal indicates a later realization that perfection is something to strive for. In these notions, the parents' idealization of the child is involved as well as the child's idealization of the parents. Some disillusionments and modifications in the direction of more realistic understanding of potentialities foster growth of the superego. The superego is a "differentiating grade in the ego," recognizable when there is a clearly internal authority, differentiated from external authorities and from ideal images.

Elements of the superego can be thought of as at varying distance from the ego core, this constituting degrees of internalization. Although the superego endures as a structure, its constituent elements change, for example, toilet rules cease to be experienced as aspirations or demands and become automatic. Normally, superego elements become assimilated as ego elements when an aspiration becomes an actuality, but the process can be reversed in ego disorganization, growth crises, or psychotherapy.

Repetition is basic to psychic life. All psychic functioning is in some way repetition; yet in being repeated, it becomes different. Repetitive behavior which is a re-enacting of repressed, unconscious experiences has a compulsive, unchanging character and does not contribute to development; this is passive repetition. The person is not conscious of its repetitive aspect. To become conscious of experience as repetitive of one's past is to assume an active role. In doing so, one lifts the experience to a new plane and puts it within the scope of the ego as integrating agent. In active repetition, the old is mastered, not eliminated or abolished, but dissolved and reconstructed. Where id was, there ego shall be means a change from passive to active repetition. It is not only the formula of psychoanalytic therapy but an aspect of all of ego development.

Comment: Loewald's use of terms like Oedipus complex and castration complex generalizes them somewhat. The sexual connotations remain, but ego related connotations are added. The situations referred to are complex and take place over extended periods of time. One assumes that his reason is the same as his reason for extending the term transference beyond its accepted usage. Only in the extended meaning is the more usual psychoanalytic meaning fully understood, and only in the specific psychoanalytic meaning is the broader situation fully understood. Concepts are not arbitrary; their limits are set by the way things are.

If internalization is a solution to the riddle of ego development, it is also a riddle itself. We must ask about internalization (or identification or introjection): Exactly what process does the term signify? How does the process come about? It is a never-ending path, yet every step is progress. Loewald has gone further along that path than anyone else.

DISCUSSION

While there have been many cogent insights into the process of ego development, there is nowhere one can go for a single persuasive account that integrates all of them. The integration has been stymied not so much by the intrinsic incompatibility of the several contributions as by a tendency in current psychological and psychiatric thinking toward cultism, in particular, toward accepting or rejecting as a whole the views of Freud, Sullivan, or occasionally some other major thinker. If there are psychoanalysts who think, to paraphrase Mill, mankind did not know anything until psychoanalysts taught it to them, there are psychologists who think mankind should not believe anything until it is demonstrated in a laboratory. We ignore the accumulated wisdom of mankind at our loss.

Freud made trouble for unquestioning followers by endorsing the basic premises of several opposed schools of thought, schools that have persistently and not without logical consistency opposed psychoanalysis as therapy. Despite all logical difficulties, some followers of Freud continue to reiterate that psychoanalysis declares that the reflex arc is the basic unit of behavior and that man strives always for pleasure and tension reduction. Neither reflexology nor hedonistic-associationistic behaviorism has entered the present discussion, since neither school of thought has made major contributions to the theory of ego development, if, indeed, they even have words for it.

Ausubel is an example of a writer whose central theoretical network depends heavily on the single motive of self-esteem but whose exposition is embroidered with passages giving due recognition to many other motives. The richness of his exposition lends a greater plausibility to the theory than it would have if stripped to its systematic essentials, though his concept of satellization is a brilliant and permanent contribution. Freud is at the other extreme. Where other writers embellish their central themas so as to create a spurious plausibility, Freud embellished his theories with assumptions of other schools which lend a spurious implausibility to the central themas of psychoanalysis. Some of the most portentous of later theorists have laid special stress on the irrelevant psychological postulates, long past the time when those postulates have been discredited in the eyes of academic psychologists by new experimental findings as well as by reconsideration of long known facts. That the facts of ego and character development are incompatible with theories based on psychological hedonism (currently, reinforcement theory) was effectively demonstrated by Mill (1838) in his discussion of Bentham, for example, and Dewey (1896) criticized the reflex arc concept in psychology before Freud published *The Interpretation of Dreams.*

Theoretical paradigms are the essence of an abstract science, and psychology is an abstract science or no science at all. A mélange of theory, bizarre theoretical constructs, empirical observations, and wise advice does not constitute or contribute to science, however much it may enlighten, guide, comfort, heal, or confuse. The belief that animates the present essay is that the raw materials of a theoretical science of ego development can be discerned in classic writings already at hand, far more than in the blind or near-sighted empiricism of much current research in child psychology. But the theories do not sort themselves from the homilies of their own accord. A major effort is required to see what is theory, what is observation, what is common-sense advice, what is fantasy, and which of all these go together in some coherent, logical fashion. One cannot assume that because two ideas occur in a single essay of Freud's (as the principle of mastery through reversal of voice and the postulation of a death instinct occur in *Beyond the Pleasure Principle*), they form a logical entity to be accepted or rejected in toto. Someone else may discern theoretical constructs in psychoanalysis or other branches of psychological literature different from those presented here, but they will have to make a similar reconstructive effort. The task is to find those coherent theoretical networks obscured by the wise sayings and the gullibility of its great creative geniuses; to do this it has been necessary to schematize and to oversimplify the life work of many authors.

Baldwin's dialectic of personal growth remains as a viable format for further insights. Mead supplied a philosophical foundation for a theory of ego development, though his own account made no attempt to deal with aggression, anxiety, or inner conflict, topics essential to a full understanding of the psychic process. The process that some psychoanalytic accounts set apart as introjection, implying something special and possibly pathological in outcome if not in origin, Mead saw as the essence of early social experience and constitutive of the self, a view more radical and yet less bizarre than some psychoanalytic accounts. There is probably something more in the psychoanalytic concept of introjection than in Mead's view of the genesis of the self; that should be clarified. Sullivan deliberately adopted Mead's philosophic view, which Freud presumably was not familiar with; yet the structure of Freud's theory is similar to that of Mead.

Sullivan's delineation of the successive stages in the development of the self-system, barely sketched above, contains by implication the notion that the course of development is governed in part by its own dialectic or inner logic. Most psychoanalytic accounts neglect or understress this possibility. The question of whether what guides the course of ego development is intrinsic to the ego or lies in the environment is separate from the question of whether the moving force lies within the ego or in drives extrinsic to it. Werner and Piaget have discussed the dialectics of development in relation to development in general and cognitive development in particular. In Piaget, the inner logic of development is related to the notions of structure and equilibrium, a set of ideas that has eluded some of his followers and critics. Sullivan's intuitive appreciation and application of this set of ideas help establish his place as the greatest of ego theorists or at least as second only to Freud.

The nature and origin of anxiety is a topic on which Freud and Sullivan clearly differed; other theories, not reviewed here, also have been expressed in this controversial area. What is not clear, in either Freud's or Sullivan's case, is the connection between the theory of anxiety and the major contribution to ego development, theory of stability in Sullivan's case and of change in Freud's case. Sullivan's anxiety-gating theory of ego stability and Freud's theory of mastery through reversal of voice and of conversion of interpersonal schemas to intra-personal schemas remain the major theoretical insights. These theories are not incompatible, and they do not seem to have been seriously challenged, but they have often been ignored, most remarkably by the "new psychoanalytic ego psychology."

It is also remarkable that many of the leading issues of ego theory split psychoanalysis down the middle. High authorities, including Freud himself, can be cited for putting the weight of psychoanalysis on either side of many issues. Sometimes it is early Freud *vs.* late Freud, but often the incompatible trends were concurrent. These contradictions will serve a good purpose if they force the day when being certified as authentically Freudian neither validates nor discredits a theory. For psychoanalysis to take its place among scholarly disciplines it must devalue authority and recognize the same standards of verification as other discourses, standards such as closeness to experience, conceptual consistency, and elegance, not to mention the often difficult standard of empirical verification. Ego theory, more than other realms of psychology, provides both opportunity and need for an intellectual openness, an assimilation of insights whatever their origin into a new discipline.

The foundation of that new discipline has been sought in this essay at a particular level of abstraction and generality that has led to neglect of some of the best known and most highly esteemed contributions to ego theory. Erikson's chronicle of the successive crises of normal development may be assimilated as a modification of the very concept of development, but the developmental concept itself is not yet clear enough for Erikson's modification to find its proper place. Theories stated in terms of energy concepts have been ruled out, in part because they are in the wrong universe of discourse. Calling attention to importance of work and competence is valuable but less than theory. The proper scope and generality of a scientific theory appear when a common principle is shown to underlie phenomena as different as the intransigence of symptoms, the possibility of therapy, and the gratifications of achievement. Such a principle is Freud's theory that one masters experience by actively repeating what one has passively undergone. Only a Freud can discover such a principle, but any competent scholar can follow his reasoning. The mystery is why so many of Freud's disciples have not discerned its central importance in ego functioning.

Much of Freud's later writing was based on the principle of mastery through reversal of voice. Since every attempt to master one experience through active repetition must precipitate one into new situations and experiences that in turn require to be mastered, this principle leads to a view of life as a never ending, ever widening search. That view is the one that has inspired major ego theorists of all eras. Though Freud continued to advocate the contradictory view of life based on tension reduction postulates, his own life remains a splendid example of the unending, purposeful quest.

If we put aside our philosophical and methodological scruples, we can read *Beyond the Pleasure Principle* asking: What in nature was Freud grappling with, however unsatisfactorily? To what phenomena was he drawing our attention? The answer lies somewhere in the dialectic of quest and rest, the striving for improvement versus the seeking of peace. The several dichotomies that Freud proposed elsewhere were in part attempts to conceptualize inner conflict as the core of neurosis. But the life and death instincts looked rather to an inevitable dialectic in normal life. Although Freud's postulation of life and death instincts has not been widely accepted, especially among psychoanalysts, the contradictory currents remain. There are people dominated primarily by one or the other, those who seek the Lost Paradise and those who seek the New Utopia. There are psychological theories built on one model, tension reduction, or its contrary, striving for competence and self-realization. But normal life is built on both models; indeed, their alternation provides the rhythm of the day. The present essay, being concerned with ego development, has emphasized one side, but theories of ego development cannot stand alone. They must be integrated into general psychology, including psychopathology and other aspects of life. The most profound recent contributions, those of Ricoeur and Loewald, although different, appear largely compatible with each other as well as with contributions from outside psychoanalysis and with the theory of psychoanalytic therapy. Both of them have raised theory to this plane, that of the dialectic of progression and regression, of the origins of creative development in the archaisms of our nature.

REFERENCES

Adler, A. *The individual psychology of Alfred Adler.* H. L. Ansbacher & R. R. Ansbacher (eds.). New York: Basic Books, Inc., 1956.

Adorno, T. W., Frenkel-Brunswik, E., Levinson, D. J., and Sanford, R. N. *The authoritarian personality.* New York: Harper & Row, Publishers, 1950.

Allport, G. W. The ego in contemporary psychology. *Psychological Review,* 1943, *50,* 451–78.

Allport, G. W. *Pattern and growth in personality.* New York: Holt, Rinehart & Winston, Inc., 1961.

Angyal, A. *Neurosis and treatment: A holistic theory.* New York: John Wiley & Sons, Inc., 1965.

Ausubel, D. P. *Ego development and the personality disorders.* New York: Grune & Stratton, Inc., 1952.

Baldwin, J. M. *Social and ethical interpretations in mental development.* New York: The Macmillan Co., 1902. (First printed in 1897.)

Chein, I. The image of man. *Journal of Social Issues,* 1962, *18,* 1–35.

Dember, W. N. The new look in motivation. *American Scientist,* 1965, *53,* 409–27.

Dewey, J. The reflex arc concept in psychology. *Psychological Review,* 1896, *3,* 357–70.

Dewey, J., and Tufts, J. H. *Ethics.* New York: Henry Holt & Co., 1908.

Erikson, E. H. *Childhood and society.* New York: W. W. Norton & Co., Inc., 1950.

Erikson, E. H. The problem of ego identity. In E. H. Erikson, Identity and the life cycle. *Psychological Issues,* 1959, *1* (1, Whole No. 1). Pp. 101–64. (First printed in 1956.)

Ferenczi, S. Stages in the development of the sense of reality. In S. Ferenczi, *Sex in psychoanalysis.* New York: Dover Publications, Inc., 1956, 181–203. (First printed in 1913.)

Fingarette, H. *The self in transformation.* New York: Basic Books, Inc., 1963.

Fisher, A. L. Freud and the image of man. *Proceedings,* American Catholic Philosophical Association, 1961, *35,* 45–77.

132   Jane Loevinger

Flavell, J. H. *The developmental psychology of Jean Piaget.* Princeton: D. Van Nostrand Co., Inc., 1963.

Flew, A. Motives and the unconscious. In H. Feigl and M. Scriven (eds.), *Minnesota studies in the philosophy of science.* Vol. I. Minneapolis: University of Minnesota Press, 1956, 155–73.

Freud, A. *The ego and the mechanisms of defense.* New York: International Universities Press, 1946. (First printed in 1936.)

Freud, S. *The project for a scientific psychology,* Vol. I. (Standard edition.) London: The Hogarth Press Ltd., 1966, 283–397.

Freud, S. *The interpretation of dreams.* Vols. IV and V. (Standard edition.) London: The Hogarth Press Ltd., 1958. (First printed in 1900.)

Freud, S. *Leonardo da Vinci and a memory of his childhood.* Vol. XI. (Standard edition.) London: The Hogarth Press Ltd., 1957, 59–137. (First printed in 1910.)

Freud, S. On narcissism: an introduction. Vol. XIV. (Standard edition.) London: The Hogarth Press Ltd., 1957, 67–102. (First printed in 1914).

Freud, S. Mourning and melancholia. Vol. XIV. (Standard edition.) London: The Hogarth Press Ltd., 1957, 237–60. (First printed in 1917.)

Freud, S. *Beyond the pleasure principle.* Vol. XVIII. (Standard edition.) London: The Hogarth Press Ltd., 1955, 7–64. (First printed in 1920.)

Freud, S. *The ego and the id.* Vol. XIX. (Standard edition.) London: The Hogarth Press Ltd., 1961, 3–66. (First printed in 1923.)

Freud, S. *Inhibitions, symptoms and anxiety.* Vol. XX. (Standard edition.) London: The Hogarth Press Ltd., 1959, 75–174. (First printed in 1926.)

Freud, S. *Civilization and its discontents.* Vol. XXI. (Standard edition.) London: The Hogarth Press Ltd., 1961, 64–145. (First printed in 1930.)

Gergen, K. Personal consistency and the presentation of self. In C. Gordon and K. Gergen (eds.), *The self in social interaction.* Vol. I. New York: John Wiley & Sons, Inc., 1968, 299–308.

Gill, M. M. Topography and systems in psychoanalytic theory. *Psychological Issues,* 1963, *3,* (2, Whole No. 10).

Goldstein, K. *The organism.* New York: American Book Company, 1939.

Hartmann, H. *Ego psychology and the problem of adaptation.* New York: International Universities Press, 1958. (First printed in 1939.)

Hartshorne, H., and May, M. A. *Studies in deceit.* New York: The Macmillan Co., 1928.

Harvey, O. J., Hunt, D. E., and Schroder, H. M. *Conceptual systems and personality organization.* New York: John Wiley & Sons, Inc., 1961.

Hebb, D. O. The American revolution. *American Psychologist,* 1960, *15,* 735–45.

Hendrick, I. Instinct and the ego during infancy. *Psychoanalytic Quarterly,* 1942, *11,* 33–58.

Hilgard, E. R. Human motives and the concept of the self. *American Psychologist,* 1949, *4,* 374–82.

Holt, E. B. *The Freudian wish and its place in ethics.* New York: Henry Holt & Co., 1915.

Home, H. J. The concept of mind. *International Journal of Psycho-Analysis,* 1966, *47,* 42–49.

Isaacs, K. S. Relatability, a proposed construct and an approach to its validation. Unpublished doctoral dissertation, University of Chicago, 1956.

Jaspars, K. The axial age of human history. In M. R. Stein, A. J. Vidich, and O. M. White (eds.), *Identity and anxiety.* New York: The Free Press, 1960, 597–605. (First printed in 1948.)

Jung, C. G. The basic postulates of analytic psychology. In H. M. Ruitenbeek (ed.), *Varieties of personality theory.* New York: E. P. Dutton & Co., Inc., 1964, 46–64. (First printed in 1933.)

Kessen, W. *The child.* New York: John Wiley & Sons, Inc., 1965.

Kohlberg, L. Development of moral character and moral ideology. In M. Hoffman and L. W. Hoffman (eds.), *Review of child development research.* Vol. I. New York: Russell Sage Foundation, 1964, 383–431.

Kris, E. The psychology of caricature. In E. Kris, *Psychoanalytic explorations in art.* New York: International Universities Press, 1952, 173–88. (First printed in 1934.)

Kuo, Z. Y. Giving up instincts in psychology. *Journal of Philosophy,* 1921, *18,* 645–64.

Lecky, P. *Self-consistency: a theory of personality.* New York: Island Press, 1945.

Loevinger, J. Measurement in clinical research. In B. B. Wolman (ed.), *Handbook of clinical psychology.* New York: McGraw-Hill Book Co., 1965, 78–94.

Loevinger, J. The meaning and measurement of ego development. *American Psychologist,* 1966, *21,* 195–206. (a)

Loevinger, J. Three principles for a psychoanalytic psychology. *Journal of Abnormal Psychology,* 1966, *71,* 432–43. (b)

Loewald, H. W. Ego and reality. *International Journal of Psycho-Analysis.* 1951, *32,* 10–18.

Loewald, H. W. On the therapeutic action of psycho-analysis. *International Journal of Psycho-Analysis,* 1960, *41,* 1–18.

Loewald, H. W. Internalization, separation, mourning, and the superego. *Psychoanalytic Quarterly,* 1962, *31,* 483–504. (a)

Loewald, H. W. The superego and the ego-ideal. *International Journal of Psychoanalysis,* 1962, *43,* 264–68. (b)

Maslow, A. H. *Motivation and personality.* New York: Harper & Row, Publishers, 1954.

McDougall, W. *An introduction to social psychology.* London: Methuen & Co., Ltd., 1908.

Mead, G. H. *Mind, self and society.* Chicago: University of Chicago Press, 1934.

Merleau-Ponty, M. *The structure of behavior.* Boston: Beacon Press, 1963. (First printed in 1942.)

Mill, J. S. Bentham. In J. S. Mill, *On Bentham and Coleridge.* New York: Harper & Row, Publishers, 1962, 39–98. (First printed in 1838.)

Nunberg, H. The synthetic function of the ego. In H. Nunberg, *Practice and theory of psychoanalysis.* New York: International Universities Press, 1948. (First printed in 1931.)

Paterson, D. G. *Physique and intellect.* New York: Century, 1930.

Peck, R. F., and Havighurst, R. J. *The psychology of character development.* New York: John Wiley & Sons, Inc., 1960.

Piaget, J. *The origins of intelligence in children.* New York: International Universities Press, 1952. (First printed in 1936.)

Piaget, J. *Six psychological studies.* New York: Random House, Inc., 1967.

Polanyi, M. *Personal knowledge.* Chicago: University of Chicago Press, 1958.

Polanyi, M. Logic and psychology. *American Psychologist,* 1968, *23,* 27–43.

Rapaport, W. The structure of psychoanalytic theory. *Psychological Issues,* 1960, *2* (2, Whole No. 6). (First printed in 1959.)

Rapaport, D. Psychoanalysis as a developmental psychology. In B. Kaplan and S. Wapner (eds.), *Perspectives in psychological theory.* New York: International Universities Press, 1960, 209–55.

Rapaport, D. Some metapsychological considerations concerning activity and passivity. In M. M. Gill (ed.), *Collected papers of David Rapaport.* New York: Basic Books, Inc., 1967, 530–68.

Ricoeur, P. *De l'interpretation: essai sur Freud.* Paris: Le Seuil, 1965.

Rogers, C. R. *On becoming a person.* Boston: Houghton Mifflin Co., 1961.

Rogers, C. R. Significant aspects of client-centered therapy. In H. M. Ruitenbeek (ed.), *Varieties of personality theory.* New York: E. P. Dutton & Co., Inc., 1964, 168–83.

Ryle, G. *The concept of mind.* New York: Barnes & Noble, Inc., 1964. (First printed in 1949.)

Sanford, N. The dynamics of identification. *Psychological Review,* 1955, *62,* 106–18.

Schachtel, E. G. *Metamorphosis.* New York: Basic Books, Inc., 1959.

Smith, M. B. Some thoughts on "the legitimation of evil." In M. Rokeach and R. K. White (eds.), *The legitimation of evil.* In press.

Strawson, P. F. Persons. In H. Feigl, M. Scriven, and G. Maxwell (eds.), *Minnesota studies in the philosophy of science.* Vol. II. Minneapolis: University of Minnesota Press, 1958, 330–53.

Sullivan, C., Grant, M. Q., and Grant, J. D. The development of interpersonal maturity: applications to delinquency. *Psychiatry,* 1957, *20,* 373–85.

Sullivan, H. S. *The interpersonal theory of psychiatry.* New York: W. W. Norton & Co., Inc., 1953.

Tanner, J. M., and Inhelder, B. (eds.), *Discussions on child development.* Vol. I. New York: International Universities Press, 1956.

Tanner, J. M., and Inhelder, B. (eds.) *Discussions on child development*. Vol. IV. New York: International Universities Press, 1960.

Thorndike, E. L. *The measurement of intelligence*. New York: Bureau of Publications, Teachers College, Columbia University, 1927.

Tolman, E. C. Can instincts be given up in psychology? *Journal of Abnormal and Social Psychology*, 1922, *17*, 139–52.

Tomkins, S. S. Affect and the psychology of knowledge. In S. S. Tomkins and C. E. Izard (eds.), *Affect, cognition, and personality: empirical studies*. New York: Springer Publishing Co., Inc., 1965, 72–97.

Vergote, A. Psychanalyse et phénoménology. *Recherche et Débats*, 1957, *21*, 125–44.

Waelder, R. *Basic theory of psychoanalysis*. New York: International Universities Press, 1960.

Werner, H. *Comparative psychology of mental development*. New York: International Universities Press, 1964. (First printed in 1940.)

White, R. W. Ego and reality in psychoanalytic theory. *Psychological Issues*, 1963, *3*, (3, Whole No. 11).

5. Freud's Two Theories of Sexuality

George S. Klein

Many years I have wandered through the land of man, and have not yet reached an end of studying the varieties of the 'erotic man.' . . . There a lover stamps around and is in love only with his passion. There one is wearing his differentiated feelings like medal ribbons. There one is enjoying the adventures of his own fascinating effect. There one is gazing enraptured at the spectacle of his own supposed surrender. There one is collecting excitement. There one is displaying his 'power.' There one is preening himself with borrowed vitality. There one is delighting to exist simultaneously as himself and as an idol very unlike himself. There one is warming himself at the blaze of what had fallen to his lot. There one is experimenting. And so on and on—all the maniford mono- logists with their mirrors, in the apartment of the most intimate dialogue! (M. Buber, Between man and man, trans. R. G. Smith [London: Routledge and Kegan Paul Ltd., 1947]).

Recently an analyst whom I hold in great esteem wrote to me: "Now you want to eliminate the concept of drives. . . . Did Rapaport try it?" Staring at these words, I felt strong emotions, anxiety prominent among them, accompanied by images of heretics consumed in fiery pyres. This was natural. I was brought up in the value system of classical psycho- analysis, which has come to recognize the challenge, "Aha, you are deny- ing drives!", as indictment, not invitation to inquiry; a basic violation of sacrament is at issue. And in the offing is a gentleman's equivalent of the pyre, perhaps intellectual isolation in the community. So my reflex was a somewhat testy defensiveness, an impulse to cry "No, no, you misunder- stand"—a not untypical plea of the guilty.

But as I calmed down a bit, my mind drifted to Freud's remark that conceptions of instinct are the mythology of psychoanalysis. What did he mean by saying that conceptions of instinct are a "mythology"? Surely, sexuality and aggression are not. It would seem, on the face of it, that holding lightly a theory of sexuality and aggression which distinguishes its propositions from the phenomena of sexuality and aggression is a not inconceivable position. This reassuring reminder brought home to me that my acquaintance's statement had about it something of the question "Have you stopped beating your wife?" For indeed, to say "Yes" (I *do* want to eliminate the concept of drive) would carry the meaning that I am giving up the importance of sexuality in neurosis and in the shaping of motivation, and surely I have *not* given that up. And to say "No" (I do *not* want to eliminate the concept of drive) would mean that I have reaffirmed the theoretical model which views sexuality in the image of a *vis-a-tergo* force of stimulus on the mind, capable of building up a demand for discharge and the reduction of tension, and indeed, I do have great doubts about that.

There is reason to believe that the psychoanalytic conception of sexuality occurs in two versions. The first I will call the clinical theory because it is the one that tacitly guides actual clinical work. It centers on the distinctive properties of human sexual experience, on the values and meanings associated with sensual experience in the motivational history of the person from birth and in adulthood, on how non-sexual motives and activities are altered when they acquire a sensual aspect, and vice versa. The second version translates this psychological conception to the quasi-physiological terms of a model of an energic force that "seeks" discharge. This energic conception is connected with Freud's fundamental belief on which his entire metapsychology was constructed: That the source of all activity in the organism, perhaps even characterizing it as "living," is its tendency to deal with the energic influxes of "stimuli," to discharge them, and to reduce the tensions of their quantity. This was the all-embracing precept, the umbrella that included the special theory of sexuality. It was designed to serve Freud's conception of his own scientific objectives of explanation which have become the conventions of psychoanalytic metapsychological theorizing. Through the concepts of metapsychology developed from this basic precept he sought to create interfaces with other disciplines, particularly with physiology, and to coordinate his conceptions of human psychology to evolutionary issues.

It is my aim to make the two versions explicit by contrasting them, to show that the two theories are on different logical planes, are not reducible one to the other, and require different data for confirmation; they are in critical ways even inconsistent with each other. Because it is the clinical theory that was Freud's revolutionary contribution, and since its researchable potential with the actual data of clinical psychoanalysis seems to me superior to that of the drive theory, and because the clinical version of sexuality has received since Freud's time relatively less emphasis than the drive discharge model in theoretical writings, I would hope that this paper has at least the virtue of freshening attention to it.

Despite the distinctions between them, the two theories have become confounded in psychoanalyic discussion. It is highly unlikely that Freud himself thought of the two theories as distinct; there is no evidence that he did. Indeed, the drive discharge version of the clinical theory of sexuality has acquired the status of being THE theory of sexuality. It is assumed almost without exception and dispute among psychoanalytic writers that the drive conception is only a higher, more general version of the theory of infantile sexuality, an attempt to frame the latter, in the words of my analytic correspondent, within the framework of a "pure psychology." Within the tradition that has prided itself on its continuity with Freud's teachings there exists, then, the curious state of affairs in which the clinical propositions remain more or less inarticulated *as theory* even while guiding the actual ways in which psychoanalysts work in the treatment situation. In theoretical reflections upon clinical work, it is the drive-cathexis-discharge model that prevails. "Squeezed-through-the-eyelet of the drive-discharge model" is perhaps a more appropriate expression, for I hope to show that the drive theory is quite inadequate to the task of encompassing the propositions of the clinical theory.

So ingrained and unquestioned is the assumed identity of drive theory with the clinical theory of sexuality that, to cite a recent example, Waelder (1966) could entitle a paper "Adaptational Theory Ignores Drive," meaning, as we discover in the body of the paper, that the theory he is questioning ignores sexuality. I hold no brief for the adaptational theory Waelder was criticizing; I point only to the assumption of identity expressed by the title. Were sexuality and drive not identical in Waelder's mind, why should it matter that a theory ignores the concept of drive, if it does not ignore sexuality?

The drive-discharge model of sexuality has been for so long a part of the climate of psychology that it retains its hold even on those who reject it. For instance, giving up the drive-discharge conception has been taken by friends and foes alike as tantamount to denying the motivational primacy of sexuality. Neo-Freudians have agreed on making this equation; expressing dissatisfaction with the drive model, they usually conclude by disputing the importance of sexuality in the structuring of personality. On the other hand so insistent is the assumption of interchangeability that when some theorists have referred to drive *without* giving specificity to sexuality, it has gone unnoticed. For instance David Rapaport (1967b) held just such a notion of a generalized drive in which sexuality loses its distinctive position among the drives and is relegated to a lesser status than it had for Freud.

Perhaps the failure of traditionalists to distinguish the two theories comes from the tendency to regard the clinical propositions not as theory at all but as confirmed fact and its concepts simply as descriptive tools. Analysts seem particularly averse to the idea that it is not downgrading the conception of infantile sexuality to regard it as *a theory*, a viable conception to be regarded in a spirit of benevolent skepticism for investigation and test against rival assertions, and subject to revision. As a result, the propositions of the clinical theory have remained oddly static; the received systematic knowledge of sexuality from psychoanalytic sources since Freud's time has been precious little. At the same time, applications of the drive model have been long on words in "explaining" clinical data but short on actual tests with clinical data. Indeed, being removed from observation and from the clinical concepts by indeterminately long steps, they are immune to modification by clinical data. Being constantly invoked to "explain" clinical observation, they distract from the job of exploring, enlarging, and pruning the clinical theory which *is* closer to clinical observations.

To appreciate Freud's revolutionary views on sexuality, we must separate the clinical propositions from the drive model that he borrowed to state them, and to this task we turn first.

THE SENSUAL DIMENSION OF HUMAN SEXUALITY

Capacity for Sensual Experience

The crux of the clinical propositions is a radically novel view of the essential nature of human sexuality which enabled Freud to see human relationships in a fresh light.

The observations that led Freud to re-conceptualize sexuality have been reviewed many times. Since the aim here is to highlight the principles that emerged, only sketchy reference will be made to these observations: (1) Indications of sexual intent in hysterical symptomatology. (For instance, in 1905, Freud wrote: "By a rule that I have found confirmed over and over again, but which I had not the courage to formulate into a general law, a symptom signifies the realization of a fantasy with a sexual content, hence a sexual situation.") (2) Indications that the traumatic nature of non-sexual experience was traceable to sexual encounters in early childhood. (3) Pathological and perverse sexuality, where sexuality has no connection with reproduction, as in people in whom sexuality is directed exclusively toward the same sex and in other people who seek sexual satisfaction and find it without any assistance from the genital organs or their normal functioning, as, for instance, in sexual fetishism. (4) Evidence that a number of children, a much greater number than one would imagine, seem to show an interest at an early age in sexual matters and to find pleasure in them. (5) Finally, perhaps most importantly, Freud's insight into the universality of the incest taboo, a fact which made him ponder the power of impulses that would create such a universal taboo.

Some of these observations seemed to suggest that sexual conflict can occur much earlier in life than anyone had imagined before. They brought into question, too, whether sexuality was essentially dependent on the matured capacity for reproductive behavior. They all seemed to converge upon the conclusion—strange to the mind even now—that sexuality must have a much earlier origin than in puberty, *and have a bearing upon how sexuality would appear in puberty.* A paradox confronted Freud that called for solution: There seemed to be a sexual capacity common to children and adults which would justify the idea of developmental continuity in sexuality yet would be independent of procreative sexuality. It became critical to identify such a property of sexuality which manifests itself long before puberty and is at the same time not synonymous with a particular shape of sexual behavior. Freud's solution was a conception of what it is that is *common to sexuality in all its adult and infantile behavioral manifestations.* He proposed an invariant of sexual development across different forms and manifestations of sexuality allowing us to postulate its presence even in children.

This invariant—the shared factor of infantile and adult sexuality—is a capacity for *a primary, distinctively poignant, pleasure experience* capable of manifesting itself from early infancy on (when it first occurs exactly is an empirical issue). It is a primary pleasure in that it is evocable from direct stimulation of the dermal surface of the body. It has its own requirements of stimulation, its own thresholds, and its own qualities compared with other forms of cognitive, knowledge seeking, and sensory experiences that may also be associated with activities of the same modalities. Sensual experience is not simply an *outcome of the removal of unpleasure* or of "tension"; it is much more directly tied to conditions of arousal specific to itself. Sensual experience is a positive aspect of a distinctive excitatory process of a body zone, and it is different from the pleasurable experiences of satisfaction or of reward. That is why it deserves the special designation of *sensual.*

It is unfortunate that, except for passing references to sensual sucking, Freud did not refine his terminology to bring into sharper focus this critical feature of his reinterpretation of sexuality—the distinction between the sensual experience itself and the behavioral modes and regions in and through which it is obtained. He kept on using the term sexuality to refer both to the experience of pleasure which even infants can have and to the behaviors of genital sexuality, which mature only in puberty. As a result the word sexual, burdened by the older limited meaning, tended to obscure the experiential aspect he was pointing to. Sensuality would have been a natural way to refer to the crucial pleasure component of sexuality. Moreover, reference to sensual pleasure distinguishes it from other forms of pleasurable affects, a distinction also important in the theory. The term libido as noun and adjective has been used to convey this distinction, but the absorption of the libido concept into the drive-discharge model makes it difficult to employ the term in this purely classificatory aim, so I prefer the term *sensual pleasure*.

The sensual experience in Freud's proposal is one of pleasure, but it is not identical with other forms of pleasurable experience. For example, here is how Freud describes the sensual aspect of sucking distinguished from sucking in eating:

The baby's obstinate persistence in sucking gives evidence at an early age of a need for satisfaction which though it originates from and is instigated by the taking of nourishment, nevertheless strives to obtain pleasure independently of nourishment and for that reason may and should be termed sexual.

Sensual sucking involves:

. . . A complete absorption of the attention and leads either to sleep or even to a motor reaction in the nature of an orgasm. It is not infrequently combined with rubbing some sensitive part of the body such as the breast or external genitalia. Many proceed by this path from sucking to masturbation. (See foot-note description, Freud, 1905b, p. 181; also p. 168.)

It must be added that Freud's assumption that this experience is in a category of affect unto itself was dimmed by his later metapsychological theory which identified *all* pleasures as libidinal. This lost for the theory a certain power for, as we shall see, the assumption of distinctiveness is important for another critical proposition of the theory, namely, that sensual pleasure can serve various functions that are not in themselves specifically or primarily sexual. For instance, the search for sensual pleasure can come to be a means of eliminating unpleasure of non-sexual origin, as for instance, when sensual pleasure is a means of reducing the pain of experienced failure.

The distinction between sensuality and sexual behavior was a fundamental point on which Freud separated himself from his contemporaries, and it is the one that still separates the psychoanalytic from other conceptions of sexuality. While sensual pleasure is elicitable throughout human development from infancy on, its arousal is characterized by behavioral manifestations that vary in dominance and in systematic and orderly progression; this was the justification for speaking of sexual development. Before (and even in most theories today), sexuality was synonymous with genital behavior viewed exclusively in relation to the reproductive function and the phylogenetic requirement of procreation. In proposing a distinction between sensual experience and the modes of behavior through which it is elicited and expressed (the genital modality being but one), Freud raised the possibility for the first time of non-genital but nonetheless sexual stages of development.

The distinction Freud drew was revolutionary in asserting that sensual experience is not locked, as in lower species, in the behavior pattern that makes for reproduction. Freud was proposing something that may well be characteristic only of human sexuality—that in man there is an extended period of time in which the sensual pleasure experience is separable from reproductive sexuality. The two aspects of sexuality, the sensual pleasure experience and the modes of its evocation, eventually converge on the genital pattern, but even here this is by no means inevitable in man; it is a guided process—one in which societal sanctions, values, and encouragement are vital.

From the premise that the capacity for and means of sensual pleasure undergo systematic development, Freud evolved a conception of how this development is affected by the symbolic record of interpersonal encounters at each stage through which sensual arousal is actualized. The theory includes assumptions of how relationships evolve in respect to their sensual significance, and of how the meanings that have accrued to sensuality are also expressed in the form of symptoms. The assumption of continuity also made it possible to understand phenomena in terms of their indications of fixation to particular modes of sensual gratification and of sexual regression.

Sensual Arousal

It is assumed that sensual arousal develops from appropriate patterned stimulation of different areas of the body (erogenous zones). With the proper stimulating movements, these areas are capable not only of sensation but of producing feelings of poignant pleasure. Thus, a hard swipe on the buttocks produces pain, but it can also produce twinges of sensual pleasure. The adequate stimulation for sensual pleasure as compared with sensation has been neglected in psychophysical laboratories and still awaits study.

In Freud's view, given the proper patterning of stimulation, the capabilities and possibilities of arousing sensual pleasure are multiple. Although particular dermal areas are especially favorable to eliciting sensual pleasure, the experience is not confined to skin stimulation alone. Aerial movements and muscular exertions in play, seem to be capable of eliciting sexual excitement. Fathers have excited their sons by flinging them into the air and catching them, by rocking, by sitting their youngsters astride their knees, with pleasures to both not fully acknowledgeable by either.

The nature of the somatic mobilization required for the sensual pleasure experience and its stimulation is still unclear and is hardly advanced from Freud's first formulations. A psychophysics of sensuality does not exist, although the faint beginning of one is suggested by Pfaffman's solitary paper on the "pleasures" of sensation (1960). Freud offers many leads for such a psychophysics, for example, his statement that different zones have different thresholds of sensual arousal. The significance of such differences for development and motivation are unknown. No one really knows, for example, how the configuration of stimulation which is presumably necessary for sensual arousal in the oral region compares with requirements in the anal region. Nor have the pleasures of bowel retention and expulsion been subjected to systematic study. It also seems reasonable that there are genetic differences among children in the potential of different zones for arousing sensual experiences.

Sensual Arousal Through Nonspecifically Sensual Modalities

Although all body zones have in common the capability of eliciting sensual experience, some of these zones are not specifically sexual in function (Erikson, 1950). Moreover, the stimulation required for erotic arousal in one zone is different from that of another; it is quite specific to and dependent upon the forms of the responsiveness of the zone, that is, its modes, as for instance, the sucking and biting capabilities of the mouth. Thus, in this view, a zone is a perceptual and behavioral system, and sensual arousal is manifested through the behavioral activity of its modes. Gibson (1967), for example, writes of the mouth:

For the infant it is an opportunity for sucking as distinguished from eating. Hence, it is originally a means of feeling the mother's nipple and causing the mother to feel the infant's mouth—a means of mutual stimulation. This is perhaps the earliest kind of social interaction in animals of our sort. In man, the mouth remains an organ of sexual-social contact throughout life as the act of kissing demonstrates. The mouth is also an organ for haptic exploration in the infant, often with the cooperation of the hand. It is much used for autostimulation in the sense of information-getting, and the baby appears to practice something—to be interested in the regularities and possibilities of it. He drools and blows bubbles and sucks his thumb and learns how the mouth feels and what noises can be made with it. In short, the mouth is a versatile apparatus of information seeking and getting. It is a perceptual system.

Now the intimate conjoining of the informational potential of a perceptual system and the sensual pleasure derived from contacts obtained through it is an important aspect of the psychoanalytic theory of sexuality: Sensual pleasure gained in the act of receiving *and* information about that which is received are both served in the actions of receiving. Presumably such modal activity is differently patterned when it is mani-festing erotic arousal rather than nonsexual experience, though this is again a largely unexplored issue. Recent studies suggest that differently patterned sucking movements of the mouth serve different aims; there may be a difference, for instance, between the sucking patterns that have to do with searching and attending and those of eating (Bruner, 1968). Freud's propositions regarding sensual sucking suggests that still another pattern may exist which is specific to sensual experience.

This conjunction of sensual and nonsensual functions, fulfilled through the same behavioral modes, is of profound importance for the development of motivation. The fact that sensuality does not have its own organs but is elicitable only through modalities of knowledge acquisition and adaptation insures the interlocking of sensual experience and non-sensual aims in development. Not only is sensual pleasure arousal through behavioral systems required for adaptive aims, but the pursuit of such nonsexual ends may itself get complicated by connota-tions that come to surround sensual experiences. Thus, affects and frus-trations associated with its pleasure giving capacity can reverberate to the use of the mouth generally as a system of control. Erikson (1950) speaks of *social* modalities, for example, general attitudes of trust or distrust, being rooted in the configuration of manipulation and pleasure experiences that evolves in the history of modal experiences. In short, the negative and positive valuations associated with the control of sen-suality in a mode become aspects also of the structural record of experi-ences obtained through a zonal behavioral system.

In Freud's words:

. . . We are led to the suspicion that all the connecting pathways that lead from other functions to sexuality must also be traversable in the reverse direction. If, for instance, the common possession of the labial zone by the two functions is the reason why sexual satisfaction arises during the taking of nourishment, then the same factor also enables us to understand why there should be disorders of nutrition if the erotogenic functions of the common zone are disturbed . . . good portion of the symptomatology of the neuroses, which I have traced to disturb-ances of the sexual processes, is expressed in disturbances of other common non-sexual somatic functions; and this circumstance, which has hitherto been unintel-ligible, becomes less puzzling if it is only the counterpart of the influences which bring about the production of sexual excitation. . . . We must end with a con-fession that very little is as yet known with certainty of these pathways, though they certainly exist and can probably be traversed in both directions. (1905b, 205–206)

One may recognize in this assumption of the two-way traversability of connections between processes of sensual arousal and of nonsexual informational functions the more familiar version of the drive-discharge theory which holds that all motivations are circumspect forms of sexual "discharge." Critics of Freud's sexual theories have made this a target of particularly vigorous attack. But the clinical proposition makes no assumption about the primacy of discharge—that the pathways of connection between erotic sensibility and nonsexual functions are discharge opportunities for the former. Freud is affirming the ready ties of sensual experience and the instrumental processes serving nonsexual functions; he is simply proposing that the means of pleasurable sensual manipulation are also the means of manipulating and regulating things and that values accruing to the sensual potential of a mode's activity can affect the mode's functioning generally. In the system of regulation he is picturing, sensual experience acquires affective-cognitive meanings from the context of actions and relationships in which it occurs; and, conversely, the relational activities of a mode may acquire erotic meanings. Eating is in theory capable of stimulating sensual pleasure. The reverse can happen as well; sensual arousal may evoke auxiliary desires for food. Disturbances in sensual experience may reverberate to the normal nonsexual uses of a mode—a factor that loomed large in Freud's understanding of hysteria. For example, Freud suggests this possibility: "If we know that concentration of attention may give rise to sexual excitation, it seems possible to assume that by making use of the same factor the condition of sexual excitation may influence the possibility of directing the attention." (Freud, 1905b, p. 206)

The Record of Sensual
Experience as a Basis of Sensual Craving

A critical proposition is that the nature of sensual pleasure is such that once experienced it continues to be savored; the record of its occurrence is hard to relinquish. It is proposed that sensual experience is distinctively etched in memory and concept. The occasions of sensual experience in modal activities and the positive and negative values which such experiences acquire are recorded in a cognitive structure or *schema* whose activation ever after helps to shape sensual experience.

The schema includes memories of the context of past sensual arousals and also an affective record of the successes or failures that attended them. The sensual pleasure of the breast is recorded in the context of the mother's responsiveness to the feeding process itself. The mother who gives signs of disapproval of the smearing of feces is associated in her disapproval with the sensual pleasure in the smearing. It is this cognitive matrix that carries the symbolic meaning of sexuality for each person.

The evolving cognitive record of sensual experience is thus both a product of sensual experience and itself a framework which shapes the content of current sensual experience; through it the latter gathers qualities of meaning beyond simply the affective sensual tone. Freud assumed that early in infancy the capacity for sensual pleasure already has some degree of internal representation. That sensual pleasure can be autogenically evoked is discovered early by the child; before long, he reaches down searchingly and finds the genitalia. Presumably the cognitive schema of sensuality shortly after birth has affective and motor components but is almost completely lacking in a conceptual component; there is simply the zone and its mode. As development occurs, the conceptual scope of sensual experience comes to include representations of the actions and relationships through which the pleasure is won or thwarted, of restraint and controls, and of self-related meanings. Thus, the meaning of "taking in" by mouth and lips becomes a conceptual aspect which colors sensual experience when the latter is aroused by stimulation in the oral zone. "Holding back," "retaining," "expulsion," and the like become conceptual affiliates of sensual experience through the anal zone. These developments occur in complimentary response to developmental changes in the dominant zone of sensual capability for, according to Freud's clinical theory, sensual experience not only has a place of dominant focus but a time of dominant origin.

The meanings that can envelop sensual pleasure can be illustrated in respect to anal sensuality. The sensations of a full rectum as well as the physical manifestations of emptying the bowel can be primary sources of sensual pleasure, said Freud. Associated with these can be the satisfaction of performing a function desired by the parents. But they can also accrue meanings of defying authority, or refusing to do one's job at the pot, and therefore of postponing the opposite pleasure of emptying the bowel. In such fashion, through its embeddedness in a cognitive schema, the poignantly pleasurable sensual experience comes to acquire both high potential as an experience to be revived and sought, as well as connotations of one also to be afraid of, ashamed of, held in check, or even quashed in its arousal.

The importance of the cognitive framework in structuring sensual experience is illustrated by a phenomenon to which Freud first drew attention: That a zonal experience which at its occurrence had relatively sparse conceptual meanings as sexual (that is, was not understood as such by the child) can retroactively acquire such a meaning at a later time when an enlarged cognitive capacity and increased sensual capability of the zone have raised the latter to prominence. Thus, a recorded early genital experience may at puberty become coded with a significance it did not previously have and acquire influence in the current life situation.

The cognitive matrix of sensual arousal has much to do with what is commonly thought of as the driving force of sexuality. Actually, it is closer to the clinical meaning to say that sensual experience is not in itself driving, but an experience that is sought after because of meanings that have become associated with it over a person's developmental history. Signs of urgency, for example the excitement of expectation, anticipation, and fantasy, commonly regarded as the peremptory drive aspect of sexuality, are, in the clinical theory, manifestations of the cognitive schema in a state of continued or repetitive activation. We will have more to say about the nature of the intensity and force of sexual motivation.

Development

It is as an evolving cognitive structure, not as a disembodied blind energic force, that sensual experience takes on importance in the clinical theory. Sensual pleasure elicited by sucking at one period may later be elicited by biting as well as by sucking. The area of the anus and particularly of the junction of the skin and anal-rectal mucous membrane become prominent loci of the arousal of sensual pleasure. Although zones and modes of sensual arousal are not fixed at any one period, there is a relationship of dominant to recessive pattern which characterizes each period and which varies from one period to another. In time, the cognitive aspects of sensual experience of one stage are subordinated to those of the next and are carried over to affect the next developments.

Normally, the arousal of sensual experience comes to be dominantly linked to the genital, reproductive aspects of sexuality, but these two aspects—the genital and the sensual—never do become identical. To insure this development, restraints must be internalized (that is, learned) and connected with the arousal of the sensual experience itself. Thus, part of the cognitive record of the arousal and expression of sensuality includes guiding rules and reinforcing affective associations. It is part of this guidance that early forms of sensual experience come to be couched in shame, disgust, and other affects, negative as well as positive.

Early preferences for sensual pleasure are carried forward to affect later ones. What a mother means, as facilitator or inhibitor of sensual pleasure experienced by a child, may affect the child's subsequent aims and objects of sensual experience. Preferred modes of sensual pleasure may remain fixated and in times of stress, regressively emphasized. Freud quotes the case of a girl who continued thumb-sucking right into puberty and for whom kissing never reached the capabilities of sensual satisfaction to be obtained from sucking.

Conversely, the maturing of sensual potential in a new dominant zone, the learning and internalizing of societal sanctions associated with the various zones and modes, and a person's own traumatic and other impressive experiences may have a retroactively organizing affect on already recorded experiences. Earlier experiences recorded for the zone and mode, when these experiences were recessive and had little or no conceptual significance at the time of their occurrence, may acquire fresh sensual significance in the wake of the newly matured erogenous capabilities of the zone and the child's maturing cognitive capabilities. A memory that previously was relatively benign in its sensual aspect may be given ominous importance by a traumatic sensual encounter that subjectively resembles the earlier occurrence. In short, continuity in sensual development includes not only the changes in the zone-mode media of sensual pleasure but a matrix of cognitive and affective values which affect all phases of sensuous mobilization and their inhibition.

Plasticity

The aspects of erotic sensibility and behavior described thus far indicate a general property best described as plasticity. This plasticity is evidenced by the varied forms of sensual arousal, as in the fact that at all stages of development a sufficient sensual stimulus may be autoerotic, heterosexual, and homoerotic. It is evidenced in the phasic changes in sensual capability of different bodily zones and in the variations, in each stage of development, in respect to what is sensually stimulating and gratifying. Another aspect of this plasticity is the potential for disjunctions to occur between meanings associated with sensual experience, on the one hand, and those of specifically modal behaviors, including genital sexual behavior, on the other. For example, sexual activity unaccompanied by sensual pleasure is by no means a rare phenomenon, as in hysterical frigidity and in certain sexually promiscuous persons.

But these qualities of plasticity are a source of danger in which society has a profound stake. The attention Freud gave to this societal investment makes his interpretation of sexuality a profoundly bio-social one. Plasticity poses a problem in control; the organism must be guided to the goals of procreation and heterosexuality, and in this general direction, it is mandatory that choice be governed away from societally destructive commitments. Freud's great insight was in pointing to the paradox that the biologically plastic potentialities of sensual arousal and gratification include no built-in protection against societally destructive incestuousness. For a long time the easiest, most accessible, perhaps even the most satisfying, agents are those closest at hand, the very ones upon which society must impose unequivocally inhibiting sanctions at phallic maturity. Thus, the very nature of sensual pleasure as a poignantly desirable experience not thereafter easily foregone and the fact that the record of its first arousal becomes thereafter a potential basis of motivational direction which is hard to relinquish and hard to forget all add up to the requirement that the eligible means of gratification be efficiently regulated, that regulated choice and sanctions be internalized as operational rules and become part of the developmental record, the cognitive schema, of sensuality.

As Laing (1965) has pointed out: "A good deal of effort in all societies is given to deciding which bodies may be joined with which on which occasion and at what age. Persons in all cultures are governed in their actions by an intricate web of injunctions about whose bodies of what sex their own bodies should come into contact with." This is a learning experience that begins at an extremely early age and is one of the most difficult in view of the inherent desirability of sensual experience itself and of the fact that the most natural directive principle of its satisfaction is propinquity. Very young children may respond sensually in situations that appear perverse in our moral belief, simply because they have not yet learned to avoid certain stimuli that are taboo, "or may never have learned to respond positively and exclusively to certain approved sexual stimuli."[1] It was this recognition of the social consequences of plasticity that opened the way to Freud's showing "how many impairments of individual and group life . . . stem from the meaningless management of sensuality. He found that neurotics and perverts are not only infantile in their attitudes toward their fellow man, but also regularly impaired in their genital sexuality, and given to overt or covert gratifications and comforts from other than genital bodily zones . . . moreover, their sexual impairment and their social infantility are all systematically related to their early childhood and particularly to clashes between the impulses of their infantile bodies and the inexplicable training methods of their parents." (Erikson, 1968)

Inevitability of Conflict

The key element in the social regulation of sensuality and in the shaping of erotic behavior consists of the internalized values that configure sensual experience, governing its arousal, instrumentalities, and

[1]Ford and Beach (1951) make an interesting point in this connection: "Men and women who are totally lacking in any conscious homosexual leanings are as much a product of cultural conditions as are the exclusive homosexual who finds heterosexual relations distasteful and unsatisfactory. Both extremes represent movement away from the original intermediate condition which includes capacity for both forms of sexual experience. In a society such as our own a large proportion of the population learns not to respond to or even to recognize homosexual stimulation, and may eventually become in fact unable to do so." This may be regarded as an illustration of what is an inevitable inference from the assumption of plasticity in respect to sensual development in the psychoanalytic clinical theory.

objects. One might say that Freud's is not simply a theory of a biological appetite but, in the most profound sense, a "superego" theory concerned with the developmental structuring of the meanings, affects, and motives associated with this plastic organismic phenomenon.

The plasticity of sensuality creates a potential for conflict that distinguishes sexuality from all other psychosomatic cravings. Since every society requires operational rules to cope with the many options of sensual arousal and gratification, sexual conflict is inevitable, as are developmental crises created by the necessity of resolving incompatibilities between the practiced configurations of gratification of one stage and the potentialities of an emerging one; successes in accommodating the new hinge on making obsolete the old. The resolutions of these conflicts and crises become part of the internalized value structure of sensual experience and sexual behavior—their cognitive meanings—and are carried forward to affect sexual development. The predisposition for conflict is perhaps one of the most distinguishing characteristics of human sexuality compared to animal sexuality and compared to all sensory and affective dispositions within man.

Since its arousal as well as the instrumentalities of its satisfaction are subject to control and socialization, all aspects of sensual experience and behavior are potentially subject to conflict. In this respect, we see an important difference between sexuality and such "primary drives" as hunger and thirst with which sexuality is often compared. Most sexual rules have to do with admonitions and foretastes of consequences, hence the very arousal of sensual experience can be hedged by conflict. With hunger and thirst, the internalized rules have much more to do with choice than with arousal. When you become hungry, there are alternatives with respect to what you should do or eat. Where sensuality is involved, social rules govern not only choice, but equally important, arousal itself: What you must not do, *lest* you become sensually aroused, is also part of the rules, as well as how to control and direct your sensuality, once it is aroused. There are, of course, taboos connected with eating and drinking, but the fantasies connected with such taboos are not a problem. On the other hand, the taboos against sensuality are such as to produce a necessity for anticipatory control of arousal, a means for its suppression and for its redirection—a possibility allowed for by the very plasticity which necessitates the controls!

But by far the most important factor which raises the conflict potential of sensuality is the previously mentioned point that tabooed pleasures are so often associated with persons who are both the easiest and the most convenient means of sensual gratification, and who are sources of other important types of pleasure as well, for example, agents of reward and of the relief of distress and tensions. Heterosexual choice within the family would be the easiest and most congruent alternative for most individuals, because, as Lindzey (1967) expresses it, the organism seems to be "wired for sexual choice along dimensions of proximity and similarity." However, the child encounters a society necessarily programmed for the destruction and inhibition of these tendencies. It is precisely against such choices that one of the most powerful taboos and inhibitive incentives is directed—the incest prohibition.[2] The child must learn to isolate and control the sensual pleasure mutually elicitable with mother, father, and siblings, internalizing tacit canons of acceptable conduct. The child encounters this opposition at a time when he is poorly equipped to devise compromising patterns of response. "An immature individual, endowed with only limited capacity for diverse and integrated adaptive acts, is faced with the imperative that he must reorganize and channel in new directions his sexual impulses—one of the most powerful of human motives." (Lindzey, 1967)

Complicating the learning problem is the fact that the mother is a source of both sensual and of permissible non-sensual pleasures (for example, rewards and satisfactions), and these have early to be distinguished by the child. A mother gratifies in all sorts of ways, but the linking of sensual experience to her person as a specific source is not acknowledgeable as such beyond a certain age. Other pleasures, as for instance what White (1963) calls "effectance" pleasure, are likely never brought under so severe a rule of severance. These distinctions pose an uncommonly difficult task, one that is often complicated by the mother's own conflicts and her emotional stake in blurring these distinctions. It will happen, therefore, that the child's feelings on the subject of his relationship with his parents and their attitudes toward his body and person are destined to become deeply divided.

Nevertheless, preparations for the required, eventual heterosexual separation long precedes the actual maturing of genital sexuality in the child. Admittedly, the matter deserves more study than it has had but there is good reason to suppose that a mother's handling of the infant boy is different than that for a girl, guided by a subtly inbred, culture supported premonition of the inescapable sensual estrangement that is to come.

Given, then, the plasticity of sensuality, in which a natural direction of erotic arousal and culmination toward tabooed objects is an ever present potentiality, "the operation of negative sanctions against an equally strong counter-tendency constitutes a psychological dilemma of enormous consequence." (Lindzey, 1967) Bringing this dilemma to light

[2]The requirement against inbreeding transcends cultures, and Lindzey gives persuasive arguments for believing that the taboo is the product of strong evolutionary reinforcement, a biological necessity for the survival of a hardy human species.

for the first time was one of Freud's monumentally great contributions. It is at the center of his clinical theory of sexuality and is a point which separates psychoanalysis from other theories of sexuality. From it lead conceptions of the types of conflicts originating in this basic and ineradicable dilemma and of the various forms of their resolution; and these lead in turn to a discovery of a range of motivations, unknown to other theories. The conception of the Oedipus complex, of course, and many propositions concerning sexual conflict in pathology are linked to these assumptions. As Lindzey (1967) puts it:

If psychoanalysis could boast of no other achievement than the discovery of the repressed Oedipus Complex, that alone would give it a claim to be included among the precious new acquisitions of mankind.

It is often said that the importance that Freud gave to sexuality was simply a reaction to the Victorian inhibitions of his time and that in today's climate of sexual freedom, his theory loses importance. That sex is so freely discussed and its various forms openly tolerated does not minimize the profundity and relevance of the main point of Freud's theory. The dilemmas created by the plastic organismic phenomenon of sensuality are as insistent now as in Freud's time. Although the requirement for control is differently resolved by different societies and the range and nature of tolerances vary from period to period and from society to society, the requirement for control itself remains invariant, secured by the universal incest taboo and by the necessity of guiding and insuring the joining of sensuality to appropriate heterosexual expression. The plasticity of sensual arousal in a context of inevitable social guidance will always make the problem of sexuality a primary one in motivational development and, through the inevitability of oedipal stresses, an inevitable participant in the drama of the generations.

SEXUALITY IN MOTIVATION

Motive refers to the directional aspect of action, the objective for the sake of which movements and choices are made. In this view of motive, to understand the motivational aspects of sexuality is to assess the functions of sensual pleasure, the reasons for its being sought or avoided. The clinical theory distinguishes the appetitive aspect of sexuality from the aims involved in the seeking of sensual experience and behavior. Sensual pleasure may have multiple functions; sexual gratification *per se* may be an immediate but not a primary aim of sexual activity; the requirement for gratification may be the instrumental expression of a variety of motives. I may be adient to sensual pleasure and the conditions that arouse it because they give comfort, help in blotting out reality, make me feel more manly, or even perhaps because they connote or promise covert repressed incestuous meanings.

In the drive-discharge theory, the issue of aim is strictly limited to the process of discharge; whatever contributes to discharge is construed as the aim of sexuality. Therefore, on the level of the economic point of view which speaks of sexuality as the vicissitudes of the libido quantity, the distinction between drive and motive is blurred. But this is not the case in the clinical theory which emphasizes the cognitive matrix—the meaning—of sexuality. The clinical theory, indeed, assumes that the symbol and its appetitive-motor aspects, learned in a psychosocial process, are more important than the purely instinctual aspect of sexual capacity. It is the symbolization it acquires at critical periods that is crucial in shaping sexual responsiveness and even in the arousal of sexual need and that accounts for sensuality being both a source of conflict as well as a means of resolving conflict.

Being a pleasure experience that is inherently desirable, sensuality is apt to be sought. In this sense, there is a point in saying, as Koch (1956) does, that sexual activity is its own reward, that the pleasure in sexual behavior is also the reason for it. It would be foolish to raise the question whether the existence of a house is separated from or identical with its bricks and the fitting of its windows. So Koch argues in speaking about the inherent "value properties" of sexuality as "intrinsically motivating" and requiring no reference to "extrinsic" motivating conditions. It is true that pleasure is like an end in being a reason for action. However, it is unlike an end in that it does not itself terminate action since it cannot be identified separately from the activity of pleasurable experience.

Sexuality is therefore not only regula*tive* but regula*ted*. It is a major point of the clinical theory that sexuality is responsive to different motivations. One of the significant features of sensuality is that people will often go through hell for the sake of it but this feature cannot be set in its true light merely by the fact that people will *say* they are doing it for the sake of the pleasure. Although sensual pleasure is experienced without a sense of ulterior motive, the experience can be an instrumentality of, the route to, other sought-for-experiences—of the sort Buber describes in the quotation with which this chapter opened. Saying that pleasure is one's motive and being motivated by pleasure are confused in most popular accounts. For the clinician, being motivated by pleasure is itself to be distinguished from still other motives for the sake of which pleasure is sought and for which no such concept or aim may be explicit in the subject's mind. People will be able to acknowledge doing things for the sake of pleasure, but, simultaneously, through the pleasure, they may reach for aims they often cannot (even must not) acknowledge, lest to do so impair the quest.

A variety of motives involving sexuality originate as resolutions of conflict. Either sensual pleasure itself, the mode of sexual behavior, or both may be caught up in conflict and the structural consequences may be manifested in defensive, substitutive, and exaggerated actions, pointed either to the pleasure experience itself or to the modes in which it is elicited. The solutions may call, in different circumstances, for intensification of certain avenues of sensual pleasure, deflection or inhibition of sensual arousal and choice; they may involve fixation (that is, stasis in respect to modes and aims of sensual arousal), and regression to early forms of sensual gratification.

Another class of motives arises from the serviceability of sensuality as a means of getting rid of unpleasurable experiences and in assisting the achievement of essentially non-sexual aims. In these roles, sexuality is not defended against but is itself enlisted as a defense, as part of the self's repertoire of reparative and self-renewing devices when under threat. We might more aptly speak of the motives in such cases as sexual*ized* rather than as specifically sexual to convey this idea that the immediate sexual experience or action is ancillary to other aims achieved through it.

The fact that sensual pleasure is directly and even autogenously stimulable makes resort to it useful at all ages in circumstances in which the organism seeks to rescue itself from unpleasure, pain, denigration, and humiliation. To give one example: There is accumulating evidence that in early life the reaction to separation is a powerful organizing motive centering on the unpleasurable experience induced by the absence of the familiar. In relation to this aim, sensual pleasure is a valuable option of action in two respects. It is a pleasure which counters the unpleasure of experienced isolation and separation; second, it is itself an experience of intimacy. Given the sensual pleasure potential, it could be expected that its arousal and intensification would be greater under conditions of experienced isolation and separation.[3] Segal (1963) writes that "sexually impulsive behavior, precipitated by imagined or real object-loss is a desperate restitutional measure. . . . Continuing contact with such patients (reveals) that they manifest extreme sensitivity to imagined or actual separation or loss of a currently needed person." Greenacre (1955) reports that the sexual behavior of promiscuous women included bodily contact, caressing, and kissing, but that coitus was rare and provoked disgust. These activities serve, she says, as a screen for a more basic desire to "be closely fused with the mother in a symbiotic relationship."

[3]This view is congruent with the role assigned to separation in the genesis of autism in Chapter 8. See particularly the discussion of the substitution of self-directed actions as replacement for the missing mother-infant positive affective bond. (Editor)

Thus, from the standpoint of the clinical theory, assessing the motivational importance of sensual experience is not a matter simply of measuring appetitive virulence; the appetitive aspect has to be viewed in its functional significance, that is, in relation to how sensuality is internally represented for the person—its cognitive values, positive and negative. These value aspects are the crux of its motivational importance. The psychoanalytic clinical view is not to be confused with the reductionist position of the drive-discharge theory that sees the structural consequences of sensual arousal as alternative discharge channels of libido energy, nor is it a version of the pan-sexual generalization which views all motives as transformations of libido. Put in broad terms: The clinical theory of sexuality does not reduce motivations to a sexual history; rather, it locates sexual and non-sexual processes and their motivations in the one history that they both express, which is that of the social existence of a developing self.

Relationship to Personal Identity

An essential point of the clinical theory, then, is that sensual pleasure is not an autonomous experience sought after simply for its own sake. Sensual mobilization is an organismic event whose motivational importance arises from the requirements of a developing self that seeks always to perpetuate and preserve its unity, integrity, and coherence. Encounters and relationships that have linked sensual activity to self-esteem and self-conception are retained as part of the cognitive record of sensual pleasure and are, therefore, very much part of the stimulation of sexual activity. Consequently, the stimulations and gratifications in every sensual experience reverberate to affect self-esteem, self-conception, and self-identity; conversely, crises in these very respects affect the search for, the choices, and the circumstances of sensual pleasure.

It is in relation to issues of preserving self-coherence, integrity, and continuity that sensual pleasure and its arousal may become a means of confronting situations of stress, strain, and anxiety generally, and hence itself a kind of defense. It is not necessary to assume that in such instances the anxiety is necessarily associated with erotic wishes *per se* but that the latter are responses to the state of anxiety. The responsiveness of sensuality to experiences of danger is not unknown to clinical observation. Moreover, occasions of profound loss (not specifically sexual deprivation) can become occasions for seeking sensual pleasure (as well as being occasions of aggression). The complimentarity of experience of loss and erotic pleasure is an often reported clinical phenomenon. In a child, the discovery of sensual pleasure is couched by a variety of meanings connected to different needs and requirements. It can be a compensatory comfort to social failure and deprivation. In such a case, it can itself become a special kind of need to a developing selfhood but a need aroused not necessarily by a specific requirement for sexual release but by an interpersonal deprivation to which an erotic value has become attached.

Sensuality is, thus, never released from the claims and crises of self-identity and has different meanings in different contexts of self-conception. That pubertal development involves an accentuated association of sensual experience with the genitals is, of course, a biological fact. But its meanings are entwined with what one's self-identity is at that point of development. The boy's sexual orientation is focused on the phallus, and his feelings of pride and growth and locomotion can be affected by a feeling of genital inferiority. Erikson describes the modality that is specific to the phallic stage as "making" in the sense of enjoyment of competition, insistence on goals, and pleasures of conquest. The boy attaches his first genital affection on the mother and develops his first sexual rivalry with the owner of that person, so that the rival with whom he is competing is usually his father. Sensual and aggressive fantasies about the parents may contribute to a disproportionate sense of guilt which affects the meanings that accompany sensual arousal.

This relation to selfhood and relational attitudes to other people. as objects distinguishes sexuality in man from that in animals. Indeed, the more sexuality in man is divorced from this centeredness in self-development, the more it has the appearance of the mechanical, non-symbolic aspect of animal sexuality. As Merleau-Ponty (1962) expressed the matter:

. . . the significance of psychoanalysis is less to make psychology biological than to discover a dialectical process in functions thought of as "purely bodily," and to reintegrate sexuality into the human being. . . . Insofar as a man's sexual history provides a key to his life, it is because in his sexuality is projected his manner of being toward the world, that is, toward time and other men. There are sexual symptoms at the root of all neuroses, but these symptoms, correctly interpreted, must symbolize a whole attitude, whether, for example, one of conquest or of flight."

THE FORCE OF SEXUALITY

The compelling hold that sexual craving can have on thinking and behavior has been the main justification for viewing sexual behavior in the language of drive and for explaining it in terms of drive-discharge. Not active only periodically as in animals, sexual desires in man can engross a great part of his activity, not uncommonly at the expense of constructive forms of human activity with which they can be in conflict. Certainly, the feeling that accompanies such cravings is as if one is implacably steered toward objects that are satisfying sexually, as if an alien pressure were developing from within.

All theories of drive direct themselves to this experienced peremptoriness of sexual need. The solution of the drive-discharge model is to postulate an actual impulsion, taking the phenomenological fact as a model of the mechanism of sensual craving itself. It is part of the craving that one feels helpless to the desire; it is natural, then, to think of it as outside the self, because what one calls self are body-connected functions and experiences under one's control. The drive model re-defined this state of feeling possessed to possession, literally, by forces independent of the ego and operating outside of consciousness. In the drive model, the force is outside in the sense of coming from the soma without control from above (the brain), which is the locus of the self. The drive is regarded as a stimulus upon the central nervous system, creating an effective state (tension) that "stimulates" a "wish," the consummation of which is pleasure and the reduction of the tension. Drive motivation refers to a condition of dammed up libido; the force of motivation is a direct function of the quantity of libido to be discharged. All sexual behavior is, in this view, an expression of this impulsion.

The clinical theory makes less drastic assumptions about the unobservable impulsion. Although the organized appearance of a sensual appetite lends itself to metaphoric description as the reflection of an implacable force, it is misleading from the clinical standpoint to take the experience of forcefulness as the process of sexual arousal *per se*. The clinical theory is under no obligation to make any assumption that the appetite is itself the consequence of a peripheral condition (a drive) independent of itself. Its focus of inquiry is the motivational context. In the clinical theory, sexuality is viewed as appetitive activity within a reticulum of motivational meanings rather than the manifestation of a linear force impelling itself against a barrier. The structural nature of sensual craving, in the clinical theory, is not that of a flow of something but of an activated schema—a cognitive structure in action. Fairbairn captures the essence of this idea: "Impulse is not, so to speak, a kick in the pants administered out of the blue to a surprised and somewhat pained ego, but a psychical structure—doing something to something to somebody" (Guntrip, 1961, p. 281). Thus, whereas the drive-discharge model has Newtonian metaphors of the motion of particles, the clinical theory implies a system whose tendencies of activity lend themselves to description in value terms, for example, actions that are permissible or not in relation to self, that have meanings of must, must not, ought not and the like, of comfort, of power, of self-aggrandizement, and so on. Sensual experience is always hedged by such reverberations of significance or value meaning to self.

Thus, in the terms of the clinical theory, the language of force is

replaced by the language of activity and relationships. From this perspective, need has a special meaning. A need is a state of thwarted
tendency. It is misleading to picture such an active but interrupted
tendency as a region of impersonal energic concentration separated from
the sphere of the ego; the need is an ego-world relationship in a state
of active but aborted actualization. When the tendency is lived out, so
to speak, when it is smoothly and unimpededly realized, we do not speak
of it as a need. Only when any such relationship is blocked in its course
do we have a need. Gratification of a need amounts to finding ways of
circumventing such an obstacle. How many and complex are a person's
needs reflects the complexity of relationships he is able to entertain with
the world and whether these relationships are capable of being actualized. Since needs are personalized projects or tasks, need satisfaction ends
not only in pleasure or discomfort but also in ego-involved failure or
success.

When a need involves a requirement for sensual experience and sexual
behavior—especially when the sensual craving is pre-emptive and nag-
ging—the clinician suspects the active presence of such a self-world value
and that the immediate sexual aim speaks for some more encompassing
need in which self-conception and self-status are at issue. In such instances, what hurts and disturbs is not the tension of unreleased sexual
energy but the failure to actualize the self-value which has come to be
symbolized through sexual accomplishment. As we have seen, the plastic
nature of sensual capacity makes it uniquely serviceable to various motivational aims; sensual and/or sexual gratification can become subsidiary
objectives within different motivational settings. Of course, the self-
enhancing and self-aggrandizing needs involved may vary, but they share
the property of evidencing themselves through the sexual craving. It is
these rather than the specifically sexual requirement that are in the therapist's focus.

In the clinical theory, then, felt intensity is regarded as the symptomatic expression of a motive or motives to which sexual arousal and
gratification have been recruited. From this standpoint, desire for sensual gratification—the purely appetitive aspect of sexuality—is not the
whole or even the main point of motivated sexuality. Analytic clinical
experience with even the most flagrant cases of compulsive sexuality
views the seemingly quantitative aspect of intensity as involving sup-
portive stimulations of the sensual system by symbolic meanings. Therapy is conducted on the premise that if such meanings are brought to
light, the intensity can often be reduced. The clinician is not misled by
the patient's experience of peremptoriness to ignore its embeddedness
in tissues of self-identity, controls, and values. In the system language
used earlier, compulsive sexual acting out presents the clinician with

the problem of identifying the motivational matrices that are governing the appetitive experience. The pertinent questions are: How easily is sensuality aroused in relation to what motivational requirements? and, What are the corollary effects of sensual experience? In short, the problem is that of determining the functional requirements (meanings) that are making for persistent and repetitive sensual arousal.

Viewing erotization and erotic activity in its cognitive aspect makes it easier to understand that there will be circumstances when the seeking of sensual pleasure becomes especially insistent because of its relation to an insistent issue of self-identity. Take the phenomenon of sexual craving aroused in a state of grief. Here arousal of the need *per se* and the efforts at gratifying it are by no means the whole or even the crucial story but rather what Kubie (1952) calls an effort to "close a circuit." The sequence of meanings encompassing sexuality under conditions of grief would be explained not as the workings of a sexual drive which builds up to intolerable intensity but rather as a cognitive configuration in which grief leads to a loss of security, to impotence, and in turn to renewal via sexual gratification. A series of interlocked purposes are involved here. As long as the grief persists, so does the sexuality. Thus, the explanation of persistence would be not in the tension produced by arousal of the sexual drive but the cognitive structure of grief. The motive of sexual behavior is described by the clinical statement but not by the drive-discharge model, for it is vapid simply to assert that the aim of a drive is to achieve its own satisfaction.

To illustrate in detail the difference in emphasis, let us take an example developed by Erikson (1950) to illustrate this point. Peter has retained his bowel movements for a whole week. Erikson writes:

He looked miserable, and when he thought nobody watched him he leaned his bloated abdomen against a wall for support. He has reveries in which, 'I wish I had a little elephant right here in my house. But then it would grow and grow and burst the house.' A bad dream in which monkeys are after him 'trying to get into me' and bees who are trying 'to get at the sugar in his stomach.'

A number of other indicators converged on several themes involving erotic sensibility. "I no longer doubted," continues Erikson, "that this little boy had a fantasy that he was filled with something precious and alive; that if he kept it, it would burst him and that if he released it, it might come out hurt or dead. In other words, he was pregnant." Sexuality is undoubtedly involved in the above example but not in the sense that drive-reduction theory would have us believe. The terms of this fantasy express what Alexander (1935) aptly called an "emotional syllogism"—a rule or premise, expressing the logic of affective values, which guides behavior and thought.

From the therapeutic standpoint, the conscious and unconscious accessibility of the syllogism must be taken into account. Since the eroticism involved in this example is not simply a specific sexual wish, it is not clinically helpful to refer to the tension experienced in this instance as an anonymous drive energy that is clamoring for discharge. Rather, for alleviating the erotic intensity of the fantasy, the meanings of the eroticized fantasy must be unravelled, as in Erikson's interpretation: "There is no doubt that once having bloated his abdomen with retained fecal matter, this boy thought he might be pregnant and was afraid to let go lest he hurt himself or the baby." Thus, Erikson told the child, "This, I said, some children do not know. They think that the bowel movements and babies come out of the same opening in animals and in women."

Of course, there was more to the unravelling of the syllogism. Why the retention? It turned out that an abrupt separation and loss of his nurse was crucially involved. Sensual experience was doubtless part of the tie the boy felt. The relationship had included innocent sensual approaches that were dealt with playfully, perhaps enjoyed, by the nurse. That it was a conflicted tie for the boy, however, is suggested by the fact that the approaches were noticed with clear expressions of unease and even disapproval by the mother. In this context, during a period of budding, provoked, and disapproved masculinity, the nurse's leaving was disturbing. Further, the nurse subsequently wrote to the boy that she had to leave the household because it was her custom to stay only as long as the child was a baby, "because she liked best to tend babies." Subsequently, he became babyish and dependent; it is better to be a baby; and in desperation, lest you lose more, you hold on. Part of the configuration of thought evolved in the effort at repairing the loss was that "the boy identified with both partners to the lost relationship; he is the nurse who is now with child and *he* is the baby whom he likes to tend."

In this instance, conflicted values associated with a source of sensual contact received expression in the symptoms described. The erotic components could not easily be described as consisting only of specifically sexual wishes nor the symptoms classified simply as efforts to reduce "libidinal tension." It seems more faithful to the events described to say that sensual experiences were configured in a complex of positive and negative meanings of which the fantasy construction of a baby held on to was a symptomatic by-product.

DIVERGING PATHS OF THE TWO THEORIES

It is often heard that the drive-discharge model is only a general, more parsimonious version of the clinical theory given in terms that intersect with other fields of data, particularly physiology. It is useful, therefore, to bring the two into closer juxtaposition to see just how faithfully drive theory mirrors the clinical propositions, where the theories are difficult to reconcile, or where they are even at odds with each other. I will not retrace the ground covered by others (Holt, 1965)[4] who have convincingly described the deficiencies of the drive-discharge model as a general paradigm for motivation but will confine myself to the problems presented by the drive model in dealing with the clinical assumptions regarding sexuality. We would particularly want to see whether the drive theory does in fact encompass the range of phenomena to which the clinical concepts are explicitly tailored and in what respects therapeutic prescriptions are affected by the two ways of looking at sexuality.

Let us first review the essentials of the drive-discharge model.

Drive is conceived as energy generated from within the body. Being energy, it is in movement; being limited in its amount and varying in respect to the locus and the amount of its accumulation, it exerts different intensities of force which create a momentum for discharge when a threshold of tolerable intensity is exceeded. Since the discharge is controlled cortically, the energic build-up constitutes a "stimulus on the mind." In this model, the essence of sexuality is not an experience but a contentless physiological event, one might even say the radiated energy of a source, extrinsic to the psychical event produced by its cortical impact. The psychological aspect of this stimulus, expressing the momentum for discharge, is the "wish." A motive is simply drive energy that has acquired much structure. To the extent they involve drive energy, motives are pressures for discharge.

One aspect of the above account should be made more explicit. There is a distinction between the concept of libido and the drive-discharge model just described. The notion of libido is not by itself a theory of sexual motivation; it was a term Freud early employed to set apart the experiences and behaviors of sexuality from other kinds of activity, and he did this by assigning special properties to the energy involved in sexual activity. "We distinguish this libido in respect to its special origin, from the energy which must be supposed to underline mental processes in general, thus also attribute a qualitative character to it" (Freud, 1905b, p. 217). In this strictly classificatory meaning, the term libido refers to an anonymous physiological substrate of all sensual experiences. The fact that it is seen as energy could simply have been an early stage of referring to physiological processes yet to be discovered.

Freud made other assumptions about libidinal energy. It is generated within the soma, but its action is like that of an external stimulus in that its movement—its stimulus impingement—is outside the realm of voluntary action and thought. Like an external impingement, control must be brought to bear upon it, to dampen it, deflect it, reduce its impact. But being actually generated from within the organism, such stimulation is particularly difficult to control compared with external stimuli; for example, escape is impossible. The direction of its flow requires an especially strong counter force—a drain, therefore, on the organism's total energic supply. A good deal of structural growth comes from this effort and from the attempts to conserve the energic supply available for adaptive effort. For this reason, Freud said instinctual (libidinal) drives are the most important bases of psychological growth. (Rapaport made this proposition the foundation of his theory of learning, though it was a general drive, rather than libido, which Rapaport proposed.)

But Freud went beyond this to the next step of postulating a model whereby this energy is converted to sexual motivation. The model of drive discharge is not specific only to sexuality but refers to a more general regulative process having to do with what Freud considered to be the basic aim of the nervous system, namely, the discharge of excessive energic accumulation. Since libido is a *"quantitatively* variable force which can serve as a measure of processes and transformations occurring in the field of sexual excitation" (Freud, 1905b, p. 217), it seemed readily adaptable to the drive model. Although sexual energy is a particular kind of stimulation to be discharged, it shares with other types of energy the properties required by the drive-discharge model—it is in fixed quantity at any given time, it presses for discharge, the vicissitudes of its deployment and discharge lead to motivation. Thus, the drive-discharge model purports to explain how libido energy leads to motivation, but the drive model describes the workings not simply of sex but of any drive and is in this sense a graft on the theory of sexuality. In short, the drive model was part of a theoretical strategy of linking psychological activity to the body through the conception of a process of discharge— the return to an optimum quantitative level in a region where energic pressure had risen.

The distinction is important to note because just below the surface compatibility there is a serious incompatibility between the libido concept and the drive model as to what is construed to be the central event of sexual activity. Libido gives distinction to the specifically sexual aim; it implies that the primary event is a distinctive pleasure. This is not by any means necessarily the same as a reduction of tension—the central event in the discharge model. The pursuit of it may indeed involve tolerating a high degree of tension. As far as the drive-discharge notion is concerned, sexual motivation is synonymous with one aim alone— that of modulating the energic level that is felt as unpleasurable. There is even an implied difference as to what the essential pleasure of sexuality is. Insofar as one can read a phenomenological principle into the drive-discharge model, pleasure experience is to be construed as the subjective correlate of the discharge of excessive stimulation, and this pleasure is in direct proportion to the degree of unpleasure that the excessive stimulation had provoked. The pleasure in the drive-discharge model is certainly not a directly elicitable, specifically sexual pleasure. The model has no room for the idea that libidinal activation involves in its very nature a distinctive pleasurable experience. Thus, while the quantitative aspect of the libido contains no problem for the drive model, the qualitative assumption of the libido concept of a distinctive pleasure is in an uneasy and rather anomalous fit with the discharge notion, which implies another origin of the pleasure experience.

Another terminological point: Drive and instinct are quite different concepts. Instinct can refer simply to capacity, to potential activity; a drive definitely implies a quantitative force. Thus, within the clinical conception, we may speak of sexuality as an instinct, without implying the drive model.

Admittedly, these distinctions are less and less evident in the psychoanalytic literature and have been merged into the by-now almost reflex tendency to describe the clinical events of sexuality in the metapsychological terms of energy, tension reduction, drive, and discharge.

Some general differences in orientation between the clinical and drive conceptions of sexuality are immediately apparent. One conception views sexuality as a force determined by energic pressure, the other as an appetitive system whose configuration of activity in relation to concurrent motivations is far more crucial than the quantities of energy involved. The conceptions of the biological substrate differ notably. In the clinical view, this substrate is a propensity for a distinctive kind of pleasure experience, directly elicitable, having different modes, loci, and developmental phases of arousal—these constituting a pleasure system. The events that affect the mobilization of this pleasure experience or its inhibition are its central concern—the motivational aims to which the appetitive experience lends itself and the ways in which the experience and its modal expressions are disjunctively or synchronously responsive to these aims. Since the drive model regards the essential event of sexual activity to be the relief of a somatically instigated pressure, it has no easy means, or even need, of regarding the values associated with sensual pleasure or its self-related meanings to be factors which affect its arousal and color the experience.

The fundamental difference in orientation can be plainly stated: In the drive-discharge model, sexuality, conceived as drive, is something to be disposed of—by consummation or sublimation. In the clinical viewpoint, sexuality is a pleasure experience to be elicited or pursued, with variations of aim. Pleasure, in the drive model, is not something gotten from its being elicited, either passively or through active pursuit, but from being rid of a pressure felt as unpleasurable.

We now turn to some specific points of divergence of the two conceptions.

Intensity Interpreted as Experience or as Energic Pressure

We have already seen how the issue of force or peremptoriness is dealt with in the clinical theory. We will draw upon these points in reviewing how the two theories consider the intensity of sexual motivation. The drive model is biased in favor of quantitative interpretation; drive strength is viewed as the concentration of energy at a point of potential discharge. Persistent sexual preoccupation is seen as the subjective counterpart of unrelieved pressure of the quantitative increment of drive energy upon a channel of discharge.

As we have seen, clinicians have long ago given up this orientation as a principle guiding interpretation in actual clinical work. Clinically, it is far more often the case that such phenomena as repetitive and impulsive sexual behaviors, sexual obsessions, and the like are more productively dealt with in terms of symbolized sexuality, for example, its meanings in respect to relationships that are conflicted, dangerous, and feared, with which erotic and aggressive components are associated, or its meaning in relation to repressed, but active, sensual wishes manifesting themselves repetitively in forms which mask the true aim. In dealing with conflicted or even addictive sexual involvements, there inevitably appear in the clinical data echoes of past, conflicted sensual encounters and wishes or of repetitively enacted motives which have before recruited sensual activation—all now part of the cognitive record of sensual experience.

One perceives demands in the external environment; we do not say that the external environment *is* demanding. Henry Murray (1938) used the term "press" to underscore this cognitive reaction to the environment —the environment perceived as pressureful. This is helpful in thinking of sexuality. Sensual wishes can be experienced as unrelenting or implacable, but it is misleading to infer an internal environment which is demanding. The clinician's perspective is to account for such sensual wishes in terms of the functions served by sensual arousal, the latter's meaning *vis-à-vis* the self's aspirations and efforts of coping and defense, since sexual experience always has reverberations to this frame of reference. In accordance with the conception of need previously stated, the experience of feeling impelled or driven reflects a directional tendency (motive) enacted abortively but repetitively via the sensual pleasure system.

In encapsulating sexuality to properties of a peripheral force, the drive-discharge model obscures the clear implication of the clinical view that sensual arousal and mobilization is as much an activity of so-called higher centers as of lower ones. From a physiological standpoint, central events are involved in intense arousal itself; the arousal is not a one-way peripheral intrusion from the gut upon higher centers. This is embodied in the premise of the clinical theory that the nature of the record laid down by sensual experience has much to do with sensual arousal and inhibition and the intense appetitive expression of sexuality. Sensual pleasure being an exceptional, if not one of the most exceptional, of all experiences, it is to be expected that it will leave behind a record that will occupy an equally exceptional role in the controlled arousal and regulation of the sensual system. Its activation includes associated affects of guilt, shame, and other superego connotations. Why a sexual motivation becomes a peremptory, not-to-be-denied impulse is thus to be answered by specifying the meanings (cognitive schema) actively associated with the sensual system. So ingrained is the habit of speaking of sexuality as a force or a push that it comes as something of a novelty to assert that, in the clinical theory, the language of force does not suitably capture this idea of an affective experience with which are associated values and memories that participate in its arousal, inhibition, persistence, and pre-emptive hold on consciousness.

The clinical view of motivational intensity reflects a general perspective to psychologically intense experiences of all kinds, as for instance, to slight versus violent anger, strong versus weak fears, a twinge of jealousy versus its obsessional extremes, and so on. If we look for criteria of intensity that cover all these instances and also those of sexual cravings, two stand out, not always consistent with each other: (1) the extent and violence of bodily changes—physiological arousals—of general or specific variety, and (2) the persisting influence of a feeling or emotion on voluntary action over a comparatively long period of time. By this second criterion, how powerful an emotion is depends on how much of a man's conscious, volitional behavior can be explained by reference to it.

The first criterion is the one which theorists implicitly use when they explain motives on the basis of the energetics of drive; the second is the perspective which guides the clinical viewpoint.

These criteria are not merely different sides of the same coin, for they may yield contradictory conclusions about intensity. As Kenney (1963) points out, if we measure a man's fear of heights by the number of times he has such a feeling, we may get a different result than if we get a measure of strength by the pervasiveness of the effect of his fear on his behavior. A repetitive sexual craving that is relegated to the background by requirements of duty and obligation, only to be preoccupying when realistically achievable, is, by the first criterion, no less intense than a more intermittent craving which when it occurs, however, blots out all other motives; but it is less intense by the second criterion. Essentially, the second criterion is a qualitative view of intensity. Even if precisely measurable, the bodily phenomena of sexuality are not identical with the phenomenon of intensity captured by the second criterion. From the clinical standpoint, a motive is strong if it governs prolonged and varied sequences of a man's behavior; its intensity is measured by the frequency and importance of actions done out of it and blotting out all else. From here, the clinical theory looks to the aborted motive tendencies that are sustaining this arousal in accounting for the experience of craving; the physiological vehicles of sexuality are not themselves these motives of sexual arousal. The clinical theory recognizes a self-related connection between sexual arousal and its object, whereas the quantitative physiological criterion of the drive-discharge model lacks this element of intentionality.

Distinction Between Sensual Experience and Sexual Behavior

Being focused on the presumed end state of discharge alone, the drive-discharge model not only has little to say about sensual experience but assigns no importance to it. This lack renders it insensitive to many clinical phenomena.

Indeed, the only link of the drive-discharge model to the phenomenology of sexuality is through the proposition that discharge—the reduction of drive tension—is felt as pleasure. But this is in conflict with the clinical theory's assertion that sensual pleasure is not an outcome of or an accompaniment of some balancing or equilibrating process but is directly elicitable. It does not deny that equilibrating or tension-modulatory events can be pleasurable. But sensual pleasure is unlike other affects, even other pleasurable ones, in that it is directly invoked by patterns of stimulation appropriate to the receptive potentialities of a zone; it is not a derivative or consequent of other forms of experience. That relief of tension—not only sexual—is pleasurable is certainly backed up by many findings, but that sensual pleasure and tension relief always coincide or that the pleasure involved is the same is questionable.

Freud himself was troubled by the incapacity of the drive-discharge model to provide for the pleasure aspect of sexuality. The notion of a distinctive kind of energy, libido, was meant to carry this meaning and that is why he spoke of libidinal drive and not simply of drive. But accommodating the phenomenology of sensual feeling to the drive model through the conception of libidinal tension was no easy feat, and the strain did not escape Freud's notice. In one place, he wonders "how it can come about that an experience of pleasure can give rise to a need for greater pleasure. If an erotogenic zone in a person who is not sexually excited is stimulated by touch, the contact produces a pleasurable feeling; but it is at the same time better calculated than anything to arouse the sexual excitation that demands an increase of pleasure" (Freud, 1905b, p. 210).

The above considerations point to a useful distinction that the clinical theory makes possible but that the drive-discharge model obscures. This has to do with the difference between the pursuit of sensual pleasure and the *pleasure principle*. The latter refers to the tenet that avoiding unpleasurable tension and the pleasure thereby gained is a basic regulative principle of the organism. The clinical theory clearly implies that the pleasure motivations of the pleasure principle are not synonymous with the seeking of sexual pleasure. At the same time, sexuality, as a systemic organization, is itself responsive to motives arising from the pleasure as well as other regulative principles. It becomes possible to interpret some sexual behaviors as in the service of the pleasure principle, as when a particular unpleasurable state such as grief might lead to sexual appetitive behavior. At one time, Freud took pains to underscore this distinction, referring to the independent sexual instinct as the weak link in the development of the pleasure principle into the reality principle. But he obscured this distinction in his later dual instinct theory of libido and aggression; he then tended to speak of the energies involved in all motivations governed by the pleasure principle as themselves libidinal and aggressive.

Of course, the assumption that sensual pleasure is distinct from the pleasure of tension reduction and from other pleasurable affects such as accompany experiences of rewards and satisfactions has barely advanced beyond its first formulation by Freud. It is by no means clear, for instance, how sensual pleasure is distinguished from these other forms of pleasure, or how infantile sensual experience differs from that of adult sexuality, or how people differ in erogenous and other forms of pleasurable excitability. One of the unfortunate byproducts of the libido drive reduction theory has been to deflect interest away from these experiential properties of sexuality itself.

One other aspect of the quantitative emphasis of the drive model deserves notice. In coupling sexual hunger with food hunger and thirst under the seeming parsimony of a single conception of drive, the differences which were vital in accounting for why sexuality was so prominent in Freud's theories are obscured. A critical difference lies in the paradoxical quality of sexuality that it is a valued and poignant source of pleasure the deprivation of which can nevertheless be suffered, if not indefinitely, yet with tolerances far exceeding anything ever demonstrated for hunger and thirst. Moreover, unlike hunger and thirst, the arousal and consummation of sexuality can be accomplished autogenously. Leading out of these differences in plasticity is the most crucial difference: That in neither hunger nor thirst do we see the magnitude of associated values of guilt, sin, license, and superego valuations generally that are characteristic of sexuality. Experiences that elicit such valuations tell the clinician he is in a realm of phenomena easily caught up in conflict. It is its potential for conflict, as distinguished from frustration, that distinguishes sexuality as an appetite from appetites serving bodily survival.

The clinical theory prepares the analyst for possible disjunctions between sensual experience and sexual behavior. The distinction is clinically helpful; for example, sexual behavior and sexual intent without accompanying pleasure is symptomatic of repressed ideas. Thus, sensual experience may be subject to repression because of negative connotations of fear and anxiety which stimulate its inhibition. Or again, the arousal of sensual pleasure may be the occasion of nausea expressing a repressed sensual involvement hemmed in by humiliation or guilt or shame. The theory is prepared for a phenomenon such as promiscuous sexual behavior unaccompanied by sensual pleasure, as if the patient were following a syllogism of action whereby sexual indulgence is permissible provided the pleasure not be experienced. The point here emphasized by the clinical theory is that sensual experience itself is symbolized in a cognitive matrix.

The clinical propositions also provide for the expectation that the symbolic elaboration of sexual experience (as, for example, that of orgasm) will be different in men and women. The cognitive context of sensual encounter is framed by the presence of a penis in a boy and its absence in a girl, the presence in a girl of a cavity that, in Erikson's words is destined to be filled, and its absence in a boy. The detection of these anatomical differences is a vital aspect of the different developmental tasks of each sex, and the successes and failures in respect to them will color the sensual experiences closely bound up with them.

Phenomenology of Infantile Sexuality

Freud's reinterpretation of the psychological meaning of sexuality, the separation of sensual experience from the modes of its expression and behavior, and the proposition of continuity from infancy all contradicted the traditional view of a sexual instinct linked to procreation as the only inherent aim of the sexual drive. But in adopting the model of discharge and equilibrium to portray the motivational processes of sexuality, Freud came curiously close again to the traditional view.

The main tenet of Freud's revolutionary reinterpretations of sexuality was that the bond of sensual pleasure and genital orgasm specifies a developmental stage, but is not itself the prototype of sexuality. But in construing sexuality as a discharge phenomenon at all ages, Freud was on the edge, in the libido drive theory, of reverting to the traditional view which identified sexuality with the mode of genital orgasm; he was simply pushing the matter back by speaking of earlier stages with different discharge aims.

By now it is evident that the drive discharge conception is a dubious one for encompassing even the phenomenology of adult sexuality, let alone the observations of infantile sexuality.

Viewing genital sexuality in others may arouse sexual feelings, and there are such phenomena as sensual play, sensual handling, sensual rhythms, and movements. These seem more in the nature of excitatory events that evoke a distinctive experience than spontaneous build-ups and discharge of sexual energy. As for discharge, it would seem to be most easily imaged for the genital mode. It is, at any rate, exceedingly more difficult to tailor the concept of discharge to fit the phenomena regarded in the clinical theory as pre-pubertal sexuality. Particularly in young children, sensual pleasure is variable in its forms, in the manner of its arousal, and in the aims for which it is sought, with the genital aim and modes more recessive at these stages. Cases of actual pre-pubertal coitus are not unknown, but they are not like those of full maturity. Again, these phenomena seem more in keeping with a system conception of sexuality through whose arousal sensual experience can be brought about by means of body movements and tactual contact in particular zones—indeed, by appropriate manipulations of any excitatory mode of the sensory systems, for example, by being touched or touching, being manipulated and manipulating, smelling and being smelled, listening and being heard, seeing and being seen.

Although the forms of experience of childhood sexuality are not equivalent to the sexual feelings of adults, that the two are continuous was Freud's main point. At all stages of development, sensual experience has properties that stamp it as uniquely different from other forms of experience. This assumption of a class of experience, sensual pleasure, which is invariant over the course of development under variations in the shape of sexual desire made it possible to account for transfers forward and regressions backward in sexual development.

Conception of Conflict

In the drive model, an enforced delay in the flow of drive energy intensifies the pressure for discharge. Since the model represents only impediments to discharge which create a condition of mounting drive tension, it does not distinguish conflict from frustration. In the clinical theory, however, it is important whether an obstacle to sensual gratification is of the nature of a frustration or is symptomatic of a conflict. The latter involves simultaneously active but contradictory tendencies which are innervating the sensual system; identifying these tendencies is the critical therapeutic objective. Thus, in the clinical theory the focus of effort is not the tension resulting from a conflict but the incompatible meanings which simultaneously prescribe and proscibe sensual experience and behavior. These are of key importance in the clinical conception because the theory tells us that the valuations attached to sensual experience, including internalized parental convictions which act as a demand structure, become extremely important factors in arousal itself, in shaping the aims of arousal, the choice of objects and modes of gratification, and inhibitions in all these respects. Since such values owe their origins in part to conflicts, therapy requires a probe of this history. Such considerations of value or superego components of the system of sensual arousal and its genesis are very difficult to capture with the purely quantitative terminology of the drive model.

Why sexuality is universally a focus of conflict is thus brought into the foreground by the clinical theory but is virtually irrelevant to the drive-discharge model. As we saw earlier, the clinical conception tries to tell why the plasticity of the sensual pleasure system makes inevitable a societal structure which is programmed for deflecting and inhibiting tendencies of sensual arousal and choice and, therefore, for an equally inevitable conflictual confrontation which is guaranteed by their interaction.

Equation of Sexual Activity with Primary Motivational Aim

The drive model equates discharge with motivational aim. Since erotic manifestations are viewed solely as the release of libidinal energy, the relief of sexual tension is apt to be taken as the primary motivational objective of all instances of sexual activity.

The import of the clinical propositions is that much more is at stake and is sought in sexual activity than simply sexual release; associated value properties of sensual experience color its arousal and expression. These possibilities stem from a conception of sexual motive that is tacit in the clinical theory: Sexual motives are based on learned expectations regarding the consequences of experienced sensuality; to bring about this experience again is a sexual motivation, but the aims of seeking it can extend beyond the relief simply of sexual tension, and most of the time do. Anticipation of sensual pleasure stimulates behavior, but this anticipatory excitement can be a response *by-product* of other aims. The motivational significance of an erotic need is revealed by the role sensuality may play in the aims of coping and mastery at the moment—an interpretive guideline which directs attention not so much upon the immediate actuality of sexual arousal but upon those aims which have recruited sensual experience in their behalf.

For example, a specific sexual need expressed via oral gratification may itself have a variety of meanings in which the experience of sexual tension and its relief, *per se*, are of far less importance (at least for therapeutic understanding) than the reparative means they afford of healing a wound of self-esteem having a variety of expressions, the sensual desire being just one. As a functional system, sexual arousal is possible in situations of boredom, of emotional stress and frustration, as a means of replacing an unpleasure experience with one more desirable and less damaging to one's sense of self-coherence and identity where these are being threatened.

Correspondingly, the clinical theory does not have to assume that the motivations provoked by repressed ideas are necessarily primarily sexual in objective. The example of Erikson's young patient whose bowel was distended illustrated this point. There was no sexual appetite or specific wish clamoring for discharge; the bowel retention reflected a complex emotional syllogism originating in eroticized relationships which accounted for the specific erotization of the bowel. Effective therapeutic aid required the unravelling of this syllogism, not the satisfaction of a sexual wish or intent.

The Issue of Sublimation and Displacement

Both the clinical theory and the drive model provide for circumspect sexual activity through substituted aims and choices which do not have a primarily sexual intent. In the libido drive theory, the sexual tendency is a potential of so much energy; an unsatisfied tendency of this much energy remains active until its release, and this release can be effected through activities of an utterly different nature. This is the essence of its notion of displaced sexuality. Sublimation is a special form of displacement which refers to the diversion of sexual energy and its discharge through higher, more socially acceptable activities that, in their adaptive aspect, are non-sexual.

The clinical conception also provides for alternative activities originating in enforced deflections of sexual aim and choice. However, an important point of difference has to do with a distinction implicit in the clinical conception that is not deducible from the drive model, namely, the difference between substitutes *for* sensual pleasure and alternative means *of* sensual arousal.

From the assumptions regarding plasticity it is evident that erotic pleasure is potentially achievable in a variety of ways. The mouth, anus, genitals are in large measure interchangeable as sources of excitation, while potentially satisfying objects may range from auto- to homo- to hetero-erotic, including even inanimate objects (fetishes). However, the clinical conception also recognizes that there are other sources of pleasure besides sensuality, and, therefore, that pleasure aims are substitutable. A deflection in aim from that of sensual pleasure can occur in the form of reinforcement of another pleasure aim. A critical point of difference between this and the drive model is that it is not necessary to assume that it is specifically sexual pleasure that is experienced in substitutive activity that had been generated by the thwarting of a sensual aim. It is thus within the bounds of the clinical conception that erotic sensibility may stimulate interest in subject matters in which a sensual experience is no longer an immediate objective. In the framework of the clinical theory, the nature of the pleasure aim in the substitution is an all important consideration in analyzing substitutive behavior.

There are, indeed, activities not socially identified as sexual that do actually evoke sensual pleasure, and these may be emphasized alternatively to specifically tagged sexual outlets, for example, picking one's nose, as a masturbatory equivalent. Although not socially labeled as sexual, the sensual pleasure aroused is the main point of engaging in such activities. But it is wrong to say that they are what is ordinarily meant by sublimation. Actually, one finds that such permissible, available means of sensual stimulation lead to intensification of the activity in question, as when nose-picking becomes compulsive to the point of bleeding. If the substitutive activity is actually sexually stimulating, the appetite for it may increase, and the problem of control will be worsened, not alleviated. Such activities do not fall into the category of what is usually called sublimation.

But there are other activities which may indeed result from the frustration of sexuality but which in themselves are truly non-sensual, that is, they neither enhance nor relieve the sexual appetite. Thus, satisfaction in another area may be great enough in a variety of ways to lessen the need for sensual gratification, not because "sexual energy" is "discharged" in an alternative channel, but simply because the role of sexuality in the motivational economy has been rendered relatively less insistent by another class of pleasurable satisfaction. Work, esthetic gratifications, and the like may have this function. This is not to rule out the possible phenomenon of erotization of work itself; we find indeed that when this occurs it interferes with work generally. I am suggesting only that the mere conjoining of reduced sexual need and heightened non-sexual activities is no evidence whatsoever that the alternative activity is a surrogate sexuality—an avenue of libidinal discharge as drive theory holds.

We may remind ourselves here of Freud's proposition regarding the two-way traversibility of the sexual and non-sexual systems and of the proposition that just as the sexual system is capable of serving non-sensual needs, other pleasure systems may be invoked in lieu of sexuality, perhaps even to participate in inhibiting sexuality's activity. We earlier discussed instances where sexual activity is indulged in substitutively upon the frustration of other aims. Sublimation is the other side of the coin; other pleasure systems may serve in lieu of sexual pleasure. Admitting this possibility, however, is not to slight the difficulties in the way of achieving such true sublimations, since the clinical theory also tells us that the promise of sensual pleasure is not easily deflected by other aims and other forms of pleasure, certainly not easily stilled, owing to the cognitive record of its unique poignancy which is unmatched by other forms of pleasure.

The drive model has no room for the distinction just described. In the drive theory, the shift from the original sexual object to the secondary social object is not meant in the weaker sense simply of the substitution of the one by the other, but is an actual displacement of the same libidinal energy now discharged in a new direction. The theory has no place for substitutions provoked by sensuality that are not themselves sexual in aim, the substitutive activity is a specifically sexual discharge, and this holds for all displacements, including those qualifying as sublimations.

Rapaport's Solution: Drive Without Libido

Caught in the dilemma, created by the libido drive theory, of how to attribute qualitative as well as quantitative attributes to sexual energy, some students of Freud, prominent among them Rapaport, resolved the problem by replacing the libido concept with a generalized conception of drive energy which is non-specific in aim. Between the aspect of the drive theory that tried to account for sexual aim (libido) and the aspect of it that chose to deal with force (the discharge model), Rapaport chose the latter. To him the libido concept was expendable but not the drive-discharge model. Consequently, his solution was on the side of believing that the most important aspect of sexuality—its motivational aspect—could be construed solely in terms of the mechanics of tension alleviation and of structures resulting from the control of tension level and of discharge.

Rapaport believed the main characteristic of drive to be its peremptoriness, interpreted as tension produced by an energic pressure—a purely quantitative matter—and he felt he could save this factor within the drive-discharge model. Hence, in Rapaport's model the critical terms were quantitative ones such as cathexis, tension, binding, and discharge, without invoking any assumption of a qualitatively different kind of energy that was specifically sexual. He thus rejected the dual theory of drives altogether.

However, in speaking of mounting drive tension in the abstract, Rapaport actually ignored Freud's account of the motivational properties of erotic experience. In effect, he ignored one of the greatest of Freud's contributions; one which distinguished his theories from all psychological theories of his time, namely, the unique conflict inducing potential of sexual experience compared with other motivational sources. It may be that the libido theory is expendable, but surely the clinical propositions regarding sexuality that it tried to embody are not.

The net effect has been that Rapaport's version of drive theory has no clear line to clinical data; it is not intimately tied to clinical observations which in Freud's theory took on new meaning as "sexual." Sexual phenomena have no more uniqueness for his model than the motivations of a nonsense syllable learning experiment, their identifying mark as drive being only peremptoriness, like an urgent bowel movement. Eliminating considerations of the human aspects of sexuality and emphasizing a wholly quantitative concept of motivation, Rapaport's model is no longer specifically psychoanalytic.

Different Assumptions of Physiological Substrate

The clinical and drive theories offer different perspectives to the physiological substrate of sexuality. Instead of viewing sexuality as a drive of relatively fixed quantity, small or large, the clinical theory considers sexuality as an appetite of variable quality, adjustable and malleable in different contexts. Its propositions imply a system conception of sexuality —an appetitive structure responsive to arousing and inhibiting activations including those which emanate from cognitive structures (schemata) in which concepts and memories of sensual experiences have been organized. If at one stage of development the child reacts sensually to a stimulus one way, and at another age exactly the opposite, one cannot help realizing that there is an internal structural change which decides each reaction.

A system conception seems more congenial as a framework for the clinical assumptions of an evolving and changing structure than a flow model of drive. Such a sensual system would be an open one in the sense that it is subject to differentiation and modification in the forms in which sensual pleasure is experienced. As such an open system, it would participate in the person's experiencing of the world and in the formation of his images of the world and of relationships. A system conception of sexuality also captures the proposition that the modes which are capable of yielding sensual pleasure are also the means of its control and inhibition. The functioning of the system would be organized around rules of operation, subject to developmental change, regarding sensuous mobilization and its inhibition—rules which specify, at each stage of development, the do's, cans, oughts, and must nots and express the conflicts of tendencies which hedge sexual experience.

The cognitive activity of such a system would seem also to be more congenially conveyed by the notion of a schema to which the sexual system is responsive. As we have seen, sensual pleasure is savored through activation of the record of previous arousals and reinforcement. The peremptoriness of sensual cravings has much to do with the persistent activation of this cognitive structure. It is capable of activating the *adient* tendencies of search, moving toward, embracing, merging, and so on which promise or afford and maintain sensual pleasure. According to the motivational context to which it is itself responsive, the schema is capable too of inducing *abient* responses and affects in relation to sensual arousal. It is through the schema that memories and accumulated conceptions of sensuality thus become capable of invoking or of inhibiting it. Whether or not sensuality will be aroused or sought, as well as the directions of search and avoidance, thus depends not simply on the energy involved in sensual arousal but its structured meanings as an experience to be accepted, rejected, or compromised with.

In its early stages of development, such a cognitive involvement of the sensual system could scarcely extend beyond the capability of experiencing sensual pleasure (that is, responsiveness to appropriate conditions of sensual stimulation). As sensual encounters occur and with the emergence of capacities for anticipating and expecting (structures capable of utilizing the record of sensual encounter), so does now the potential appear for experiencing sensual need. It would be foolish to say that the baby from the start seeks sensual pleasure. The experience of needing and therefore of seeking presumes a cognitive record, not simply a contentless build-up of tension.

In the structural imagery of a system and schema conception, force would refer, then, to the cognitively elaborated experience of sensual pleasure and to the extent of its pre-emption of thought and behavior. Certainly, the circumspections of which sexual expression is capable, its deflections and even disavowal, are among its most remarkable features, but we need not refer these to an implacable, not-to-be-denied linear force. What we actually observe, that is, the data behind references to a sexual force or delay of drive discharge, is a pleasure that is permitted to occur or not, activities that one is drawn toward for their promise of affording this experience, or that are averted for the same reason, and the capability of these tendencies of being stirred to repetitive arousal (peremptoriness) by a variety of motivational aims to which the system as a whole is responsive. If the term force is to be used at all within such a system approach, it would refer to the repetitiveness and pervasiveness of activation of the schema of sexual meanings—memories and concepts —in sensuous mobilization. It would lose its meaning of the drive model of an uncoded energic quantity from the soma which moves the organism toward sexual behavior.

Obviously, this is hardly an adequate account of the attributes that need to be assumed in a full scale system conception of sexuality. My purpose is to underscore the point that the drive-discharge model is essentially independent of the clinical theory and that the latter is capable of, indeed requires, another physiological interpretation. One of the important holds of the drive model on theorists has been the promise it seems to offer of a point of intersection between psychoanalysis and physiology, in spite of the fact that the physiological implausibility of the discharge model has been repeatedly and convincingly questioned (for example, Kaufman, 1960).[5]

It should be noted that there never was, of course, in Freud's work any data to directly support the idea of a drive quantity but only data about the cognitive matrix of erotic activity. Freud's earliest formulations of sexuality, which antedated the drive concept, involved an ideational structure which he called a "wish." Even later, Freud's drive theory implicitly assumed that drive always occurs in a cognitive matrix, in this fashion distinguishing *Trieb* from wish. But Freud never carried his thinking about this cognitive format beyond his formulations in Chapter VII of the *Interpretation of Dreams*.

This last point is especially important. In 1900, the theory of a developing sexual structure had not yet come into being, and Freud's notion of sexuality was still tied to the conventional one of referring only to genital sexuality. The cognitive aspect of sexuality was conceived solely in relation to how genital modes and aims are hemmed in by conflict, with the thwarted genital impulse being revealed in symbolic ways. Therefore, his model of the activity of the sexual wish, indeed the very notion of "wish," was framed within the terms of genital functions. The limitations of the wish concept reflect the narrow view of sexuality he still held.

It is easier to encompass the cognitive aspect of genital sensuality with the concept of wish than the sexual activity of early developmental stages and the correlative phenomena of fixation and regression. Nor is

[5]Kaufman concludes p. 324: ". . . it seems to me that we need no longer postulate that the panorama of sexuality as we know it in man is derived from an inborn biological urge of force pressing inexorably for discharge. Rather we may view the manifestations of sexuality in terms of an autogenetic development of inborn sensori-motor patterns, achieving a motivational, hierarchical structure by progressive synthesis of components through a series of transactional experiences, in the course of which goals and thereby drives are acquired."

it easy to provide for the variety of motive aims which include but can also take other forms than genital wishes and even than wishes altogether (for instance, erotization of functions).

For the later theory, the issue of immediate and remote aims of sensual gratification was very crucial, bringing into the foreground the possibility that sexuality can itself serve other motivational ends, that its motivational links extend beyond the immediate arousal and satisfaction of the appetite. Clinicians were alerted to the possibility that wishes themselves can have extended cognitive meaning, that a craving is the visible indication of converging facilitative arousals upon the sexual system. For instance, Jacobson (1967) describes a man struggling with a crisis of threatening dissolution of self, who experienced surges of sexuality and widespread erotization of behavior which she accounts for on the principle that sensual pleasure has various functional properties, in this instance, of serving a defensive or restitutional function.

Thus, the concept of sexual wish seems too narrow a structural unit with which to encompass the cognitive involvements of sexuality. Indeed, it was the anachronistic persistence of the early genital wish concept as the sole means of representing cognitively elaborated erotism, that contributed to the pan-sexual extremes to which psychoanalytic interpretations were often carried.

SUMMARY

In this chapter, I have tried to disentangle the psychoanalytic clinical propositions regarding sexuality from those of the drive-discharge model. In the clinical view, the critical identifying mark of sexuality at all ages is a distinctive class of pleasure experience different from both sensory experience and from other pleasurable affects. The word sensual rather than sexual underscores the central importance of the experiential aspect of sexuality in the theory, an experience directly arousable through a variety of forms of contact and principally involving human interaction. But the experience is also arousable through self-initiated stimulation and is associated with a variety of adient behaviors of contact, search, merging and joining. Anatomically, the equipment for its arousal is the same as the equipment for *doing*.

It is the potential for sensual experience that Freud proposed to be the critical invariant component of sexual development from infancy to adulthood. Sensual encounters and the maturing cognitive capacities give rise to an evolving structural record centering on this class of experience; this provides a governing schema of facilitative and inhibitive directives—canons or rules—affecting sensual sensibility in all its aspects. The subjective, pleasure aspect of sexuality, the forms of its direct arousal, and its symbolizations cover what is distinctive about human sexuality; they were for Freud the starting point of understanding the pervasive manifestation of sexuality in human motivation.

A crucial point of this radical reinterpretation of sexuality, which made it possible for Freud to conceive of stages of sexual development, was that the capability for sensual pleasure is not exclusively associated with the modes and behavior patterns of reproductive sexuality. This point led to the idea that sexuality can be manifested in a wide variety of ways accompanied by sensual pleasure and to the idea that preferences in these respects can be fixated or regressive. As an appetite of variable quality adjustable and malleable in different contexts, it lends itself to many options, not only of means of satisfaction but of facilitating or inhibiting it. Plastic in respect to the modes and objects of its arousal, sensuality acquires, moreover, a variety of motivational functions for the developing self-identity of a person, particularly as a means of dealing with unpleasure. Through its principle of plasticity, the clinical theory offers a profound, if also complex, view of the necessity for and possibilities of control of sensuality and of the inevitability of its provocation of developmental crises and conflicts.

From the standpoint of the clinical theory which emphasizes the meanings of sexuality, the drive-discharge model is a theory of a-meaning fundamentally. The critical difference of emphasis between the two viewpoints may be summarized in the statement that in the drive theory pleasure is derived not from the pursuit of drive but from the getting rid of it. Condensing the issues of sensual experience, modes, and sexual motivation to a process of release of tension and discharge, the language and grammar of the drive-discharge model fail to make contact with the qualitative propositions of the clinical theory, militating even against acknowledging such a subjective state as sensual experience.

The drive-discharge model served Freud as an interface concept to fill the gap in physiological understanding created by his revolutionary clinical conceptions which no physiological model of his time was able to encompass. For many analysts, this still seems to be the great virtue of the drive-discharge model. Indeed, it is usually to physiology rather than to clinical data that analysts look for confirmation of the drive model. But almost all such comparisons turn out not to involve actual tests of the model; rarely if ever have physiological studies been designed as tests of Freud's conception of drive. Attempts, therefore, to draw sustenance from physiological studies for the drive model amount to a tranquilizing potion, self-administered in the dosage necessary to dull sensibility to the clinical inadequacies of the model.

Actually, it is questionable whether the concepts of the drive model allow direct tests against clinical data. No method has been devised of constructing the appropriate intermediate terms that would reduce the distance between the drive concepts and clinical observation. As Rubinstein (1968) has aptly pointed out, the drive-discharge theory has not been developed on data appropriate to its concepts; it has drawn upon the same observational domain as the clinical propositions but by indeterminate steps of inference. The type of data that would be specifically suited to more direct tests of the drive model would have to be quite different from what is available through clinical observation. They would have to be data that lend themselves to the specification of an energic unit according to some specific standard of quantity (chemical or physical). Such chemical or physical data would in any case not be those of clinical psychoanalysis whose units are cognitive ones of meaning. In this sense, the drive model is irrelevant to clinical psychoanalytic efforts.

The consequence of the unchallenged pre-eminence of the drive model has been a notable failure to test the implications of the clinical propositions within the context of clinical observation. That is to say, there has been a failure to regard the clinical propositions as theory, as a means of deductive investigation, subject to revision. Psychoanalysis can grow only by pitting its theories against rival assertions and primarily through the use of its own clinical data. The clinical propositions of sexuality lend themselves to such confrontation, being more readily referable to clinical observation.

A situation exists, then, where a theory capable of exploration through clinical data lies more or less fallow, and a theory incapable of such development is constantly used to explain these self-same data. It cannot be denied that deductive exploration of the clinical propositions has not been extensively and rigorously attempted. Obviously, much remains to be done, too, in specifying the theory's propositions in empirically testable forms.

It is common for guardians of Freud's heritage to discount disavowals of the drive concept as only an effort to repress hard won insights about sexuality. And so stasis in the theory is solemnized. In the light of the wide gap that exists between the model used for explaining sexuality and the propositions of meaning by which analysts actually understand sexual phenomena in their consulting rooms, one may be permitted to wonder if a kind of prurient scientism does not intervene in the clinician's exposure of his clinical understanding to the glare of publication.

REFERENCES

Alexander, F. The logic of emotions and its dynamic background. *International Journal of Psycho-Analysis*, 1935, *16*, 399–413.

Bruner, J. Report at Colloquium on Affect and Cognition. Meeting of American Psychoanalytic Association, N. Y., May 5, 1968.

Buber, M. *Between man and man*. (Transl. R. G. Smith). London: Routledge & Kegan Paul Ltd., 1947.

Erikson, E. (1950) *Childhood and society*, rev. ed. New York: W. W. Norton & Co., Inc., 1963.

Erikson, E. *Identity: youth and crisis* (Chap. VII. Womanhood and the inner space, pp. 261–94). New York: W. W. Norton & Co., Inc., 1968.

Ford, C. S., and Beach, F. A. *Patterns of sexual behavior*. New York: Harper & Row, Publishers, 1951.

Freud, S. (1895), Project for a scientific psychology. *Standard Edition*, 1, 183–297. London: The Hogarth Press Ltd., 1966.

Freud, S. (1900), The interpretation of dreams. *Standard Edition*, Vols. 4 & 5. London: The Hogarth Press Ltd., 1953.

Freud, S. (1905a), Fragment of an analysis of a case of hysteria. *Standard Edition*, 7, 7–122. London: The Hogarth Press Ltd., 1953.

Freud, S. (1905b), Three essays on the theory of sexuality. *Standard Edition*, 7, 130–243. London: The Hogarth Press Ltd., 1953.

Freud, S. (1912–13), Totem and taboo. *Standard Edition*, 13, 1–161. London: The Hogarth Press Ltd., 1955.

Freud, S. (1924). The economic problem of masochism. *Standard Edition*, 19, 159–70). London: The Hogarth Press Ltd., 1961.

Gibson, J. J. The mouth as an organ for laying hold on the environment. In J. E. Bosma (ed.), *Symposium on oral sensation and perception*. Springfield Ill.: Charles C. Thomas, Publisher, 1967, 111–36.

Greenacre, P. Further considerations regarding fetishism. *The Psychoanalytic Study of the Child*. 1955, 10, 187–94.

Guntrip, H. *Personality structure and human interaction*. New York: International Universities Press, 1961.

Hardy, K. R. An appetitional theory of sexual motivation. *Psychological Review*, 1964, 71, 1–18.

Holt, R. R. A review of some of Freud's biological assumptions and their influence on his theories. In N. S. Greenfield and W. C. Lewis (eds.), *Psychoanalysis and Current Biological Thought*. Madison: University of Wisconsin Press, 1965, 93–124.

Holt, R. R. Beyond vitalism and mechanism: Freud's concept of psychic energy. *Science and Psychoanalysis*, 1967, 11, 1–41.

Jacobson, E. *Psychotic conflict and reality*. New York: International Universities Press, 1967.

Kaufman, I. C. Some theoretical implications from animal behavior studies for the psychoanalytic concepts of instinct, energy, and drive. *International Journal of Psycho-Analysis*, 1960, 41, 318–26.

Kenney, A. *Action, emotion and will*. London: Routledge & Kegan Paul Ltd., 1963.

Koch, S. Behavior as "intrinsically" regulated: Work notes toward a pre-theory of phenomena called "motivational." In M. R. Jones (ed.), *Current Theory and Research in Motivation*, Vol. 4. Lincoln: University of Nebraska Press, 1956, 42–87.

Kubie, L. S. The place of emotions in the feedback concept. In H. von Foerster (ed.), *Cybernetics: Circular, causal and feedback mechanisms in biological and social systems*. Transactions of the Ninth Conference, March 20–21, 1952. New York: Josiah Macy, Jr. Foundation.

Laing, R. D. *The divided self: An existential study in sanity and madness.* Baltimore: Penguin Books, Inc., 1965.

Lindzey, G. Some remarks concerning incest, the incest taboo, and psychoanalytic theory. *American Psychologist*, 1967, *22*, 1051-59.

Merleau-Ponty, M. *Phenomenology of perception* (transl. Colin Smith). London: Routledge & Kegan Paul Ltd.; New York: The Humanities Press, 1962.

Murray, H. A. *Explorations in Personality*. New York: Oxford University Press, Inc., 1938.

Pfaffman, C. The pleasures of sensation. *Psychological Review*, 1960, *67*, 253–68.

Rapaport, D. The structure of psychoanalytic theory: A systematizing attempt. *Psychological Issues*, Monograph 6. New York: International Universities Press, 1960.

Rapaport, D. (1960), Psychoanalysis as a developmental psychology. In *The Collected Papers of David Rapaport*. New York: Basic Books, Inc., 1967a, 820–52.

Rapaport, D. (1960), On the psychoanalytic theory of motivation. In *The Collected Papers of David Rapaport*. New York: Basic Books, Inc., 1967b, pp. 853–915.

Rubinstein, B. B. On the inference and confirmation of clinical interpretations. Unpublished manuscript, 1968.

Segal, M. M. Impulsive sexuality: Some clinical and theoretical observations. *International Journal of Psycho-Analysis*, 1963, *44*, 407–18.

Waelder, R. Adaptational view ignores "drive." *International Journal of Psychiatry*, 1966, *2*, 569–75.

White, R. W. Ego and reality in psychoanalytic theory: A proposal regarding independent ego energies. *Psychological Issues*, Monograph 11. New York: International Universities Press, 1963.

6. Dream Function:
An Information Processing Model

Louis Breger[1]

What is the function of dreams? What purpose, if any, is served by those often bizarre fantasies that occur every night in each of us? This chapter presents an information processing or cognitive model which attempts to shed light on these questions. In this model, dreams will be viewed as an output of memory systems operating under programs peculiar to sleep. The primary function of dreams will be hypothesized as the assimilation or integration of affect related information into existing memory systems. Before taking up this model in detail, several closely related issues will be considered. I will begin by discussing the functions of rapid eye movement (REM) sleep—the stage of sleep when dreaming typically takes place—and then consider the relation of REM sleep to dreaming. This will involve a brief review of developmental and evolutionary hypotheses concerning REM.

The most comprehensive and influential theory of the psychological function of dreams is, of course, that presented by Freud in *The Interpretation of Dreams* (1900). Freud's theory will be examined in some detail, leading to a critical re-working of the motivational hypotheses involved in his view of dreams as compromise formations which permit

[1]This chapter is a modified and expanded version from Breger, L., Function of dreams, *Journal of Abnormal Psychology Monograph*, 72, No. 5, Whole No. 641, 1967, 1–28 © 1967 by the American Psychological Association and reproduced by permission. I am indebted to James L. McGaugh, Les Davison and Kenneth M. Colby for critical comments and helpful suggestions.

Since the publication of that paper two others have come to my attention which present closely related models, one by Dewan (1967) and another by Shapiro (1967). The three of us seem to have independently arrived at very similar theories, from partially independent and partially overlapping sources of evidence: Dewan from an explicit computer model and consideration of the REM deprivation evidence; Shapiro from a wide array of evidence in the sleep, as well as dream, area; and myself primarily from a consideration of dreams.

drive discharge or impulse gratification. This re-working is essentially a cognitive formulation, closely related to the ideas developed in the chapters of the present volume by Loevinger, Klein and Wolff, as well as by Piaget (1962; see especially pp. 169–212). Having worked through these issues, we may then apply the cognitive model to a description of the dream process and to a consideration of dream function. Several hypotheses will be considered regarding the adaptive function of dreams, including their unique role in the integration of affectively aroused information.

REM SLEEP AND DREAMING

REM sleep has proven to be a biological state of cyclic regularity found in all humans and shared by all mammals. Early studies led to the belief that dreaming and REM were coterminous. However, subsequent work has forced a modification of this view. It now seems most reasonable to consider REM sleep as the typical and most convenient site for the psychological process of dreaming to occur. But this process may occur at other times (as in daydreaming, under certain drug states, and the like) and an interference with REM sleep may be the impetus for increasing dream-like activity at other times, at least in those individuals who are capable of engaging in such fantasies. Thus, I would agree with Cartwright (1967) that the essential features of the REM state are a high level of cerebral arousal together with a low level of sensory control. While these conditions may be present at various times, they characterize the REM stage of sleep par excellence. In terms of the present model, they greatly facilitate a concentrated processing of stored information at a time when no additional information input is occurring from the outside world. With these cautions in mind, we may now consider two hypotheses concerning the function of REM sleep.

Developmental Function

Roffwarg, Muzio and Dement (1966) discuss the role played by the endogenous stimulation of the REM state in early development. It has now been shown that the neonate spends 50 per cent of his sleep time (or one-third of his existence) in the REM state. Projections backward to uterine life, based on studies of premature infants, suggest that even higher percentages exist earlier. While the total sleep percentage declines from infancy to adulthood, the REM percentage shows a much greater proportional decline (total reduction in sleep involves a 25 per cent reduction in non-REM sleep and a 75 per cent reduction in REM sleep). This developmental pattern is consistent in all other mammals studied so far. These facts strongly suggest that the endogenous stimulation of the

REM state serves some important developmental function. Roffwarg *et al.* suggest that it functions to assist the maturation and differentiation of the central nervous system *in utero* and during earliest infancy when external stimulation is minimal. In support of this hypothesis, they cite evidence that functional stimulation does facilitate the structural development of nerve tissue. As they put it (p. 617):

We have hypothesized that the REM mechanism serves as an endogenous source of stimulation, furnishing great quantities of functional excitation to higher centers. Such stimulation would be particularly crucial during the periods *in utero* and shortly after birth, before appreciable exogenous stimulation is available to the central nervous system. It might assist in structural maturation and differentiation of the sensory and motor areas within the central nervous system, partially preparing them to handle the enormous rush of stimulation provided by the postnatal milieu, as well as contributing to their further growth after birth.

Evolutionary Function

In a very interesting paper, Snyder (1966) presents several hypotheses concerning the evolutionary function of the REM state together with the available phylogenetic evidence. As Snyder points out, mammals, following their initial evolution, lived for 100 million years or more in the shadow of ferocious reptiles, in comparison to which they were small and insignificant creatures. Their survival during this period was probably facilitated by long periods of sleep each day, which allowed them to hide and conserve their resources for brief, but active, periods of food gathering and related activities. (This pattern can be seen today in that "living fossil," the oppossum, which spends 75 to 85 per cent of each 24-hour period asleep.) What survival value would periodic REM periods serve during these long periods of sleep? Snyder suggests three. First, the increased metabolism likely to accompany REM sleep (particularly in lower forms) may serve to maintain temperature regulation during the long periods of sleep. Second, REM periods bring the animal to a state of near-waking readiness and, when terminated as they are by brief arousal, allow a sampling of the environment for danger. Third, if danger is detected, the REM state has prepared the organism for appropriate fight or flight. He further suggests that there is a sensitive adjustment of the REM cycle to perceived danger. When threat is high (presence of dangerous predators or scarcity of food), the REM state fails to preserve the continuity of sleep and there are more frequent and prolonged awakenings, leading to a "modest heightening of cerebral excitability, or drive oriented behavior," which could prove adaptive during waking life in coping with aroused threats, for instance, more vigorous food gathering.

The evolutionary and developmental considerations are not unrelated as the following quote from Roffwarg et al. (1966, p. 616) makes clear: ". . . the REM mechanism became necessary in phylogenetic evolution at the time that extensive telencephalization began because of the need for maintenance of large masses of neural tissue not directly involved in motor and sensory reactions taking place during the progressively longer period of sleep manifested by evolving species." Thus, it seems plausible that the REM state is intimately connected to the more lengthy development required by a more complex central nervous system, which eventually proved to be of tremendous survival value to mammals and man.

In a very general way, the central advantage of a more complex brain is that it allows the animal possessing it a greater independence from the immediate, stimulating environment. This is seen, in simple form, in Snyder's opossums whose fear (internalized anticipation of danger) when first brought into the laboratory causes them a greater number of REM period awakenings, just as their prehistoric brother probably awoke more frequently when there were predators about. In other words, the complex brain permits internal representations of the environment which gives long-term adaptive directions to behavior. The REM state in infancy (as well as in mammalian evolution) seems centrally related to the development of such cortical structures.

It should be noted that both the developmental and evolutionary hypotheses are concerned with the function of the REM state rather than with dreaming. If dreaming is defined as the complex, visual, symbolic dramas that we know from experience, it is hard to imagine that opossums or new-born infants dream, though it is clear that if dreaming is defined as the physiological process called the REM state, they do. Snyder (1966, p. 133) suggests a resolution to this problem:

While dreaming in the human sense would be confined to humans, dreaming as a state of perceptual activation would begin in the intrauterine life of each individual, just as it presumably began with the gradual emergence of the REM state in remote ages of early mammalian life. I am suggesting that although this condition of hallucinatory consciousness in the midst of sleep might be more or less complex and organized, and more or less integrated with other of the brain's functions at various developmental or phylogenetic states, perhaps the essence of dreaming as a biological phenomenon is simply endogenous perceptual activation.

This general view of the biological function of REM may be stated on the psychological level as follows: At birth the infant's mind is relatively undifferentiated and unstructured.[2] There are few established ways of processing input from the external environment. Differentiation and progressive structuring proceed rapidly, however, beginning with the development of the basic perceptual structures which enable the infant to perceive a relatively stable, recognizable world. It seems a most interesting hypothesis that the REM state, so prominent in infancy, may serve a crucial function in this regard, closely tied to its function in the differentiation and structuring of the central nervous system. It may be hypothesized that this early state of internal, perceptual activation (which might be called "proto-dreaming") serves to work over recent input from the external world—that it functions to consolidate[3] developing perceptual and memory structures. The fact that such structures are relatively undifferentiated at birth could necessitate the brief sampling of the environment and the longer periods of endogenous working-over consistent with the greater proportion of REM sleep found in the neonate.

An interesting study by McGinty (1968) lends support to this view. The percentage of REM sleep was measured in two groups of kittens, one raised in an isolated, restricted environment from age five to 23 weeks and the other in an enriched environment for the same period. REM sleep was markedly depressed in the isolated kittens. When this isolated group was placed in the enriched environment at 23 weeks of age, their REM sleep rebounded to a level 40 per cent above that of the group raised continuously in the enriched environment. This points to a close relationship between REM and the input of information that the organism cannot readily assimilate. In the isolated environment, there is little novel information to be assimilated and, consequently, REM percentage is low. When the isolation-reared kittens are placed in the enriched environment they, like the neonate, are faced with a large amount of new information to which they must adapt and, conse-

[2]Some provisional clarifications must be made with respect to the concept of structure which will play a central part in this paper. Let me suggest that we content ourselves with observations and theory that remain on a psychological level. Data, at this level, will consist of observations of thought, behavior, introspections, and the like. At the same time, the concepts we use in dealing with such data should be consistent with well validated aspects of neurophysiology, with what is generally known about the way the brain works. Thus, the concept of structure used in connection with the concept of memory systems (conceived as the way the mind has become differentiated or structured, or the innate structuring which directs "instinctual" behavior) is a theoretical term, inferred from psychological observations.

[3]Consolidation is a concept that has been primarily employed in experiments dealing with short-term memory (see McGaugh, 1965). It refers to the process, assumed to be necessary, by which input is stored as memory. Such storage processes are typically more rapid than the processes to be discussed in the present analysis. Here, where much longer periods of time are involved, the same term is used to suggest that the processes may be related. Pearlman and Greenberg (1968) provide experimental evidence on the role of REM in memory consolidation.

quently, REM percentage is much higher than that of the group which has already adapted to the enriched environment.

This consolidation or assimilation hypothesis suggests that the earliest psychological mode of functioning is one in which the environment is sampled briefly and then this input, which the infant has only crude ways of assimilating, is worked over for longer periods of time during the REM or proto-dream state. This hypothesis can then be extended, and the assumption made that this early pattern sets a framework which underlies the later functioning of dreams. *The early REM process is the anlage of the later process whereby dreaming serves to integrate recent perceived input into existing internal structures.* To be clear about this, these two processes are not identical; rather, the early REM state bears the same relationship to later dreaming as the infant's reflexive kicking movements do to later walking and running. It is an *anlage* and, as with other biological *anlage*, some understanding of the function of dreaming may be gained if an understanding of this much more complex, developed phenomena is coordinated with its simpler, early form.

The route from kicking to walking is relatively uncomplicated compared to the route from the infant REM state to the adult dream. What lies between these latter two is a tremendous amount of psychological development which includes the development of sensori-motor schemata, perceptual structures, the acquisition of language, and other symbolic processes. These processes allow for a number of internal transformations of perceived input as in thinking, planning, fantasy, and dreaming. Thus, to fill in the gap between the REM state of infancy and the adult dream, it is necessary to consider these processes which, of course, have their own functional importance. Nevertheless, it is worth keeping in mind that the earliest function of the REM state, the integration of perceived input, will bear an analogous relationship to the function of dreams.

Consideration must now be given to the theory which has contributed more to our understanding of dreams and their psychological function than any other.

FREUD'S DREAM THEORY

In *The Interpretation of Dreams* Freud gives, at different points, several answers to the question of dream function though his basic conception is presented in the theoretical discussion in Chapter VII. First, dreams are said to preserve sleep by protecting the sleeper from external stimulation. An example would be the case where an alarm clock bell is incorporated into a dream in such a way that the dreamer can continue sleeping. This function plays a relatively minor role in Freud's theory;

the more important sleep-protective function refers to protection from internal stimuli which are conceptualized as *both* somatic (bladder pressure, hunger pangs) and psychological (aroused memories). The treatment of these two types of "internal" stimulation as identical (which they are not), as well as the equation of internal with external stimulation, stems from the untenable assumptions concerning psychic energy and the nervous system that will be discussed shortly. At this point, it should be recognized that the major meaning that Freud assigns to the sleep-protective function of dreams refers to protection against threatening internal impulses (which are chiefly memories) arising from the unconscious. These are seen as pressing for discharge during sleep, as they are during waking life. During sleep, several factors conspire to facilitate the expression of these impulses, including the sleeper's relative immobility, which precludes discharge through motor activity, and the cessation of external stimulus input, which gives the stage over almost entirely to stimuli from within. These factors are involved in what Freud terms a regression within the mental apparatus in which the unconscious impulses are eventually represented as visual perceptions. The factors just cited permit a form of impulse gratification or drive discharge, insofar as visual perception is tied to the developmentally early form of drive-discharge, that is, hallucinatory wish fulfillment. It is in this sense that dreams may be termed "wish fulfillments"—that is, when "wish" is defined as an unconscious impulse, and *not* in the sense of gratifying a desire of the dreamer (though many psychoanalysts, including Freud, are inconsistent in their use of this concept). This should not be confused with the sort of reversals that may occur in dreams, as when a threatening person is represented as friendly. These may take the form of "wishes" but, in fact, are just one of the many forms that dreams take under the guidance of more primitive psychological organization.

While the function of dreams is to provide discharge for unconscious impulses, these impulses are not gratified directly. Rather the dream work (the processes of condensation, symbolization, and displacement) serves to disguise the dream content so that the final product is a *compromise formation*. Thus, while the dream functions to provide gratification for an unconscious impulse, it does so in an indirect, symbolized fashion that meets the demands of certain internalized standards (the dream censorship, later ego-defense mechanisms). In this sense, the basic paradigm for dream function is the same as that for a neurotic symptom, a joke, a slip of the tongue or, in some cases, character structure itself. All may function to provide indirect compromise gratification of unconscious impulses.

To complete this description, brief attention must be given to the concepts of day residues and manifest and latent dream content. Day residues are memories of recent events that may be incorporated into dream content, as when people whom one has recently encountered become the actors in the dream drama. Similarly, places, objects, recent thoughts or concerns, and the like may all be incorporated into the manifest content of the dream—the dream as it appears on the surface. The day residues may function as relatively peripheral aspects of the dream content or seem to make up its more central theme, as when an intense worry from the preceding day is represented as the dominant theme of the dream. But even in this latter case, Freud makes it clear that conscious concerns and preoccupations "have force" only insofar as they are connected with unconscious impulses and conflicts. Similarly with wishes. While the dreamer may have a dream which gratifies his wish to become a famous scientist, this wish reflects a more basic unconscious desire (for example, it may relate to the desire to outdo one's father). It is these more basic unconscious impulses that Freud calls the latent content of the dream and which, in his view, give it its motivational force.

In discussing the concept of regression during dreaming, Freud provides one of his earliest models of psychological functioning. He describes a model of the mental apparatus with the diagram represented in Figure 1 (adapted from Freud, 1900, pp. 538, 541).

Figure 1

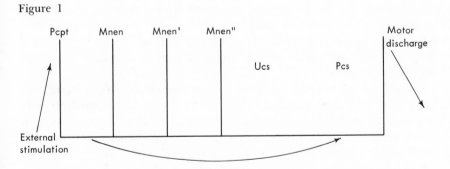

As can be seen, this is an input-output model with a particular direction characterizing its normal operation. That is, the basic guiding tendency of the apparatus is to rid itself of stimulation along the reflex path from sensory input to motor output. External stimuli are received by the perceptual apparatus (Pcpt) and lay down traces in the memory systems (Mnen). The earlier memories are more closely tied to perceptual processes since they come first developmentally. Input naturally moves toward discharge at the motor end of the apparatus, the simplest examples being the neurological reflexes. Stimulation may arise internally, however (here are the beginnings of one of the model's ambiguities), a simple example being hunger, and this, too, presses toward discharge in motor activity—initially seen in the movements and crying of the hungry baby. On the basis of the earliest experiences of pleasure and pain, the early memories are laid down, paving the way for the drive organization of memory characteristic of the primary process. Once this has happened, the next occasion of drive increase will lead to a hallucination of the previous memory of satisfaction. This is so because the apparatus tends toward immediate discharge, reality oriented functioning has not yet become possible, and, in fact, the infant probably cannot immediately distinguish between a perception based on external stimulation and one based on a memory. This hallucinatory wish fulfillment becames the earliest and one of the most important ways of attempting to deal with painful increases in stimulation that arise from within—that is, from the major drives. The basic tendency to rid oneself of stimulation, whether this impinges from the outside or arises from states of tissue deprivation, is termed the pleasure principle. The early mode of operation guided by the pleasure principle—the hallucination of a previous experience of satisfaction—is termed the primary process. While there is a tendency to conceive of psychological functioning during this early stage as completely without order, as a "seething cauldron of excitations all clamoring for discharge," in the terms with which Freud later described the id, it should be clear that even at the very early stage there is structure and organization. Holt (1967) points out a number of ways in which the conception of the primary process demands a certain amount of structure.

Freud uses the concept of regression in dreams in three interrelated ways. First, there is the regression within the psychic apparatus—referring to a reversal in the normal flow of excitations from perceptual input to motor output—so that stimulus excitations move "backward" through the memory systems toward the perceptual end, eventually resulting in a visual perception, that is, a dream. Second, this process represents a return to an earlier mode of functioning, the attempt to gratify impulses by hallucination, which is the second type of regression. Finally, regression refers to a return in time to earlier memories or older psychical structures.

These three are interrelated for, as Freud puts it: "All these three kinds of regression are, however, one at bottom and occur together as a rule, for what is older in time is more primitive in form and in psychical topography lies nearer to the perceptual end." (1900, p. 548)

Thus, regression to visual or perceptual representation and the presence of older memory material and structures are the *form* that dreams take in effecting a compromise between the ever-present force of uncon-scious instinctual impulses or drives which press for discharge and the necessity of these impulses being mediated through more recently ac-quired, reality oriented structures (censorship, defense mechanisms, the sleeping ego, and so on). Once again, according to Freud, the basic func-tion of dreams is to aid in the attempts of the psychical apparatus to rid itself of stimulation, to discharge drives. This view is clearly stated by Fisher, a leading contemporary psychoanalyst engaged in research on dreams. He states:

". . . the initiation and activation of the Stage 1 REM phase of sleep (that dur-ing which most dreaming occurs) is concomitant with instinctual drive discharge processes in the id and those energy shifts between ego and id leading to the hallucinatory dream." (Fisher and Dement, 1963, p. 1163)

The above has been, of necessity, a bare outline of the complex set of ideas presented in *The Interpretation of Dreams*, though it is probably a fair presentation of Freud's dominant view on dream function. The drive aspects have perhaps been overemphasized to the neglect of struc-tural components, since this drive emphasis is consistent with the direc-tion taken in Freud's subsequent works.

The difficult question now arises of what it means to "gratify an in-stinct" or to "discharge a drive." As shall be argued shortly, psycho-analytic drive theory, insofar as it utilizes a concept of psychic energy (libido) or a passive-reflex model or equates stimulus input and motor activity with quantitative energy shifts is unsupportable in the light of modern evidence from a variety of sources. A discussion of these issues will necessitate a detour in which the conception of energy in psycho-analytic theory is considered. This will suggest the sorts of modifications that must be made on the psychoanalytic model, following which the question of dream function may be taken up once again.

DRIVE, ENERGY AND MOTIVATION
IN PSYCHOANALYTIC THEORY

It was perhaps inevitable that a psychology growing out of nineteenth century science should formulate its theory in terms of forces and ener-gies. Bernfeld (1944) and Amacher (1965) demonstrate how Freud in-corporated into his work the basic ideas of the physicalistic physiology that he learned from Brücke and his other early teachers at the Uni-versity of Vienna. Brücke's laboratory, at the time Freud worked there, was a center of the Helmholtz school whose goal was to create a scien-tific physiology in the image of the successful physical sciences. Much of this effort centered on replacing concepts such as the "vital" or "life force" with concepts identical with, or equal in dignity to, those from the physical and chemical sciences. Scientific explanations, at this point in history, were in large part synonymous with physico-mechanical systems driven by force or energy. Thus, when Freud came to write a model of the mind (*The Project for a Scientific Psychology*, written in draft form in 1895 and subsequently abandoned), it took the form of a neuropsychological model that grew directly from his neurological training.

As is well known, Freud abandoned (or attempted to abandon) his efforts to formulate a neuropsychology. In his next major theoretical work, *The Interpretation of Dreams*, published in 1900, he presents the psychological model that has just been reviewed. While this model remains basic to psychoanalytic theory thereafter, Freud's training, and perhaps the whole *Zeitgeist* of nineteenth century scientific thought, prevented him from giving up the hope that some day his work would have a solid grounding in the physiology of the nervous system. For example, in the model presented in Chapter VII of *The Interpretation of Dreams*, he continues to refer to "excitations" and "innervations," neurological terms obviously carried over from *The Project*. In *The Ego and the Id* (published in 1923), in what is clearly a psychological model of the mind, he cannot resist the neurological aside: "We might add, perhaps, that the ego wears an auditory lobe—on one side only, as we learn from cerebral anatomy." (p. 29) In these and numerous other ways, he betrays this basic ambivalence about a purely psychological model. These small examples reveal an important strain that runs through much of Freud. For while his theoretical works from 1900 on are presumably on psychological ground, and he nowhere returns to the sort of large scale neuropsychology that he attempted in *The Project*, the background assumptions of his theorizing remain influenced by his early neurological training.

Robert R. Holt, in a series of excellent papers (1965, 1966, 1967), shows how Freud's early neurological assumptions, presumably abandoned after *The Project*, persist in more or less unchanging form throughout his later work. In brief summary, the main assumptions are:

(1) *The constancy principle*, originally formulated in *The Project* as the idea that neurons or the nervous system as a whole tends to keep itself "free from stimulus. This process of discharge is the primary function of neuronic systems." (p. 357) This idea occurs later as the pleasure principle and forms the basis for:

(2) *The passive-reflex model*. That the brain and nervous system (later mind or mental apparatus) have a natural or primary direction. That stimuli impinge on it, either from outside or from within the body, and

that it *reacts* by attempting to discharge them. This is related to the conception of the external world and internal drives as potentially pain-producing stimulation which the individual must protect himself against; which led to concepts such as "stimulus barriers," "ego defense," and the like. Finally, there is the assumption that:

(3) Quantitative increases and decreases in stimulation are directly reflected in quantitative changes in the nervous system, and that increases in stimulation or quantitative build-up is painful while discharge is pleasurable. It is this last assumption that gives the model its input-output character, later seen as libido and libido economy, as well as influencing other portions of the theory such as the concept of object relations, that is, the idea that there is a fixed quantity of energy in a more or less closed system, so that if libido is invested in one object it is unavailable for other purposes.[4]

Perhaps the most pervasive way in which these assumptions had their effect is in the general preference given to explanations in terms of force and energy. The drive discharge theory of dreams, just reviewed, is one example of this preference. As Holt (1965) points out, these assumptions exerted their influence from the background, as it were. Since they were primarily implicit rather than explicit, they were not readily changed when neurophysiology finally began the rapid progress which has proven them incorrect. Furthermore, much of this progress has taken place since Freud's death and political considerations within the official psychoanalytic movement have imposed additional barriers to changing these major aspects of the theory. Nevertheless, change we must because it is now clear that in almost every respect the assumptions are wrong. In brief summary, it is now known that:

(1) Far from being passively reactive, the brain and nervous system

[4]Energy was first defined by Freud as the physical energy of the environment which impinges on the receptors and is directly reflected in the energy state of the nervous system. A similar status was given to internal physical states, with hunger providing the chief example. (Even at this point, there are difficulties with this view, for it is not clear that there is necessarily any less stimulation arising from a full stomach than an empty one and there is certainly more stimulation arising from sexual gratification in orgasm than its absence). In any case, in the early model, the energy system was not closed—that is, the energy of the environment was thought to be conducted and discharged by the nervous system. Then, the shift was made to libido, a hypothetical psychic energy which seems to operate in a closed system. That is, there is only so much of it available for psychic work so that, for example, if most of it is used up in self-love (narcissistic libido) there isn't much left over to love others (object libido). On the other hand, libido remains connected in an inconsistent way to at least one source of physical stimulation, glandular sexual excitation. This is apparently directly convertible into psychic energy. These are the kinds of contradictions, among others, that urge the abandonment of the libido concept.

are spontaneously active. Even in deep sleep, cortical activity is great and is not directly dependent on stimulus input.

(2) It is misleading to think of the nervous system as simply transmitting energy. While the firing of receptor neurons is proportionally related to stimulus intensity (Miller, Ratliff and Hartline, 1967), this energy does not build up nor press for discharge. Rather, it is integrated as information in the active fields made up of reverberating neural networks. Thus, while there is electro-chemical energy involved in the transmission of nerve impulses, these impulses should be conceptualized as signals which convey information.

(3) In the light of the above, energy within the nervous system is quantitatively negligible. It bears no directly proportional relationship to pleasure nor to the motivational state of the person. (If it did, a bright sunny day with a lot of noise would be more motivating than the contemplation of an important decision in a quiet room.)

As Holt (1965, p. 109) puts it:

The electrical phenomena associated with the neuron are accessible to quantitative study today, but this work offers no basis for the economic point of view— the assumption that mental events might be meaningfully examined from the standpoint of the 'volumes of excitation' involved. Rather than this kind of 'power-engineering,' 'information engineering' seems to be the relevant discipline.

Brücke, Meynart and Exner (Freud's teachers) were wrong, therefore, as Fechner had been before them: The nervous system is not passive, does not take in and conduct out again the energies of the environment, and shows no tendency to 'divest itself of' its own impulses. The principle of constancy is quite without any biological basis.

It has been argued by a number of psychoanalytic writers that considerations stemming from neurophysiology have no force since Freud's theory may be treated as a purely psychological one for which biological facts are irrelevant. This position appears untenable for two reasons. First, as Holt (1965, 1966) and Amacher (1965) go to great pains to demonstrate, the model was never pure psychology in Freud's own thinking. The early neurological assumptions persisted in the form of an implicit model that guided the chief motivational explanations of the theory. Second, the pure psychology position seems unsupportable on the face of it. While no theorist is obliged to engage in explicit neurologizing when formulating propositions about psychological functioning, he *is* obligated to keep his propositions generally consistent with what is known about the way the brain works. There is no justification for clinging to a psychological theory that conceives of mental functioning in a way that is incompatible with our knowledge of brain function as, for example, traditional S-R theory has done. This is not an argument in favor of reductionism, of requiring that terms in a psychological theory be reduceable to neurophysiological terms. Psychological terms are frequently not translatable, particularly when they refer to the properties of a complex system. Nor should it be required that any psychological theory be consistent with the multiplicity of recent findings and theory in neurophysiology. After all, such theory may turn out to be wrong. Rather, what is being suggested is a general consistency between any psychological theory and well established aspects of neurophysiology. Such consistency, in addition to avoiding embarrassments for psychological theory, may lead to the formulation of new hypotheses in both disciplines.

From Energy to Motivation

Motivation is essentially the problem of defining what gives the dominant and persistent directions to thought and action. All living organisms are active; activity is one of the defining characteristics of life, hence it adds little when motivational concepts are put forth to explain activity itself. Rather, the problem is to account for the dominant directions of the activity, for how it is that one thing is done rather than another, or how one train of thought comes to preoccupy an individual in preference to others. This is the sort of problem that concepts such as drive or need are typically put forth to explain. As Klein (1967, p. 85) puts it:

Motivation is a matter of accounting for changes in direction of behavior, and the problem seems more manageable if we start out from the assumption, not that energy changes its quality, but that one and the same physical (neural) energy has changed its direction in traversing the structures that organize behavior. This consideration is true not only of sexuality but of any so-called drive.

How might such motivated activity be explained, once the energy doctrine is abandoned? A more acceptable account can be built utilizing two key ideas from Freud, ideas that have been typically relegated to secondary positions because of the primary emphasis on drive as stimulus or energy discharge. These are: (1) The centrality of emotion and affect to motivated activity and, (2) the idea that present motivated activity is a transformation of earlier patterns. It is possible to go through a great number of examples to which the traditional energy discharge idea is applied and show how they may more easily be dealt with in terms of dominant direction, a direction that may be understood as a transformation of an earlier direction, amplified by emotional or affective feedback. Such a view, however, requires some major modifications in the underlying psychological model. In what follows, some preliminary ideas concerning such modifications will be presented.

A Structural Theory of Motivation

The preceding considerations argue strongly for the abandonment of a conception of motivation based on energy, libido, conservation, or tension reduction. In addition to the reasons reviewed here, Colby (1955), Loevinger (1966), and White (1963) discuss a number of others. As is well known, no theory is abandoned because of a critical attack on its inadequacies. This is particularly true in the case of energy theory which is so central to the whole area of motivation. Rather, an alternative theory must be put forth that can deal more satisfactorily with the problems at hand.

We may begin by conceiving of the mind as an active system. The direction of an ongoing, active system is determined by the way it is structured; that is, the mind, as an information processing apparatus which interprets (perceives) input and guides output (behavior), functions according to the way it is organized. This organization or structure, in turn, is a result of innate factors that result from evolutionary selection, interacting with factors that result from specific experiences encountered during development.

Before elaborating this structural model further, brief consideration should be given to two ways in which the idea of structure is used in psychoanalytic theory. What is now most frequently referred to as "the structural theory" by psychoanalytic writers is the tri-partite division of the mind into id-ego-superego. While this model provides some conception of structure, it is of a rather general sort. Furthermore, the assumptions of a passive reflex apparatus and of motivation as arising outside of structure (in the form of external stimuli or internal impulses that must be warded off or dealt with in some way) create serious problems. All the assumptions of the tension-reduction model are retained in the concept of the id as a mass of excitations pressing for discharge. At the same time, the most interesting problems, those relating to the transformations of patterns (as in the development of interpersonal relationships, or changes in the way aggression is expressed) tend to be viewed as secondary to the flow of libido. This is one of the central paradoxes of psychoanalytic theory. Its observations and hypotheses deal with the meanings (conscious and unconscious) and symbolic transformations that characterize personality development. Yet the heart of the developmental theory, the psycho-sexual stages, is tied to untenable assumptions concerning progressive attempts to seek pleasure in certain somatic zones of the body. Tomkins (1962) presents an extensive analysis of this problem.

Thus, the id-ego-superego model is clearly in need of re-formulation. The concept of the id as an unstructured mass of excitations is simply unsupportable (see especially Holt, 1967). Along with the problems already noted, it overlooks the potential for specific organization that is built into the human brain as a result of evolutionary development. The concepts of ego and superego explain too much and not enough. By placing all of personality development under these rubrics, the impression is created that much more is known about the specifics of processes such as reality testing, delay of gratification, conscience development, and the like than is actually the case. One way these problems may be circumvented is by substituting a more general structural concept, the memory system, to deal with the same observations. This concept might best be approached by considering a second way in which the notion of structure has been employed in psychoanalytic theory.

Freud's early model contained a number of structural concepts similar to the idea of the memory system.[5] In fact, he uses this term in the model presented in Chapter VII of *The Interpretation of Dreams* (Freud, 1900). Here is the beginning of a structural theory with a non-anthropomorphic concept, the memory system, as the basic unit. Development can then be conceived as the progressive modification of such structures. For a number of reasons, in his subsequent writings Freud gave more and more preference to motivational explanations in terms of the discharge of psychic energy.

The difficulties stemming from the psychic energy theory may in large part be avoided by assuming that what is biologically basic ("instinctual" in Freud's terms) is *the direction given to thought and action by the structure or organization of the nervous system.* The ethologists (Tinbergen, 1951; Hess, 1962; Lorenz, 1966) take this approach when they posit structural mechanisms underlying the fixed action patterns that comprise the instinctual behavior of certain birds and fish. Such structures have evolved through the process of natural selection because of the adaptive advantages they confer on the species possessing them. That is to say, certain biological aims must be accomplished if an individual

---

[5]Freud, after all, did much of his early scientific work studying the histological structure of nerve tissue. The model he worked out in *The Project* contained at least as many structural as energy components. Holt points out that the model contains at least five feedback loops of the sort delineated by modern information theory, and Pribram's (1962) analysis of *The Project* indicates how the model can be coordinated with modern neuropsychology. For some examples in *The Project*, see the treatment of memory as change in structure of the "contact barriers" (synapses) on pp. 359–360 or the discussion of the effects of experience in determining the future course of neural activity, essentially a directional conception of motivation on p. 362. Similarly, the model presented in *The Interpretation of Dreams* contains a number of structural elements, as, for example, the concepts of memories laid down behind the "perceptual apparatus" (Freud refers to them alternately as "memory systems" and "psychical structures").

or a species is to survive. These include nourishment, escape from harm, reproduction, and others. In any species that one chooses to examine, adequate ways of achieving these aims have evolved. Those species which have not are the extinct rejects of evolution. These guiding structures are embodied in the brain and nervous system and have evolved to their present state of complexity over long periods of time, just as have the other biological systems of the body. These phenomena may be studied at the level of their behavioral manifestations which, in man, includes their psychological manifestations. A model can be constructed to do this consisting of the processes of *perception, internal processing* of perceived input, and *output*. The achievement of basic biological goals, even in simpler organisms, involves perception of stimuli in the environment, internal processing of perceived input (which becomes increasingly important as we ascend the phylogenetic scale to organisms with more complex nervous systems), and output. For example, the well adapted bird or fish or mammal has evolved neural structures which allow it to perceive certain cues associated with natural predators. These set in motion the internal processes leading to the output of flight. Similarly with nourishment and aggression. Animals must have evolved mechanisms which lead them to attack and eat their prey or to actively seek out those plants that sustain them.

If aggression is defined as intraspecific fighting, as Lorenz (1966) defines it, we can observe a mechanism which originally served to disperse members of the same species over an ecological domain which could support them. It is worth stressing that even in the case of the relatively fixed action patterns, it is typically goals or environmental achievements, and not rigid sequences of motor acts, that are built in. Conceptualizing instinctual structures in this way permits a unitary and consistent view in contrast to the duel life and death instinct doctrine that Freud was forced to formulate to deal with the problems of aggression. The basic mechanisms which give direction to nourishment, flight, reproduction, aggression, and exploration of the environment are all of the same form —all are evolved structures which insure that the biological aims necessary for survival will be met.

When these instinctual areas are examined in humans, it is apparent that a great deal of development and learning intervenes between birth and the achievement of biological aims such as reproduction. Motives are concepts that are employed to deal with this process. It is necessary to move from instinct as fixed action pattern in the simpler organism to motive in the complex organism. Motives, like fixed action patterns, however, are structures which give direction to behavior relevant to the major survival oriented functions. *But they are structures which have been shaped by the long period of development and learning that humans undergo.*

For the most part, psychoanalytic theory, like other theories of human motivation, is concerned with those motives that are most plastic, that involve the greatest amount of change during the course of development. This is particularly true for such plastic interpersonal motives as love, dependency, and aggression. The study of these motives is the study of the way the long period of development operates, of how cognitive structures mediate the eventual achievement of basic biological aims just as culture mediates man's relationship with his environment. Much of psychoanalysis may be seen as the study of such mediational processes (that is, the "vicissitudes of libido," the psychosexual stages of development, the development of the ego and ego-abilities which remain in the service of the id, and so on). In species like the human in which there is a prolonged period of development between infancy and adulthood, memory systems mediate between an original biological tendency and its eventual expression. In this way, the memory systems are intimately tied to culture which also serves these biological aims in complex, mediational ways. It is from this fact that the analogies between the function of cultural customs and those of biological functions arises. For example, when we examine the mating or fighting patterns of simpler organisms such as fish or reptiles, we see that certain responses are pre-programmed to appear, given minimal amounts of maturation and the appropriate releasing stimuli (for example, the ritualized movements of the female, coat color, odor, and so on). In the human, some 14 years or more of development must take place before successful reproduction can occur. A fixed pattern for reproduction does not exist in the more direct form found in simpler species. Rather, there is a basic direction, probably associated with the satisfaction of nourishment and dependency needs, that forms the pre-program for what will later, after a number of developmental transformations, become adult love and mating. On the basis of these transformations, which themselves interact and shape interchange with environment, memory systems are built up consisting of the stored material and programs guiding its various transformations—transformations that determine the individual's orientation toward males and females.[6] Through the childhood and adolescent years of development, further transformations occur, both as new content is added in the form of more memory material and as new programs are acquired, that is, advances in thinking, symbolizing, and so forth. When all goes well, the child emerges from adolescence with a normal sexual or reproduc-

[6]The use of the term program in this paper will not strictly follow its use by computer programmers. In their terms, there would be only one program running in the mind-computer at any one time, though this program might contain a number of ordered sub-routines or procedures. In the present paper, to remain at a less technical level, the term program will refer to both the overall program and to the sub-routines and procedures. These would represent, in terms of the present analogy, different ways of processing information, as in the programs guiding problem solving, those guiding language output, or those guiding dreaming.

tive orientation—that is, the *memory systems have functioned to mediate the aim of reproduction.* What they have used in this process is largely cultural material; the language, customs, fetishes, rites, rules, nuances, and so forth of the particular culture supply the material out of which the symbolic mediation is built.

Thus, it is the developmental socialization experiences that shape the motivational structures which guide the eventual sexual activities that lead to reproduction. It is in this sense that we may think of motives as mediational structures. Survival pressures operate with respect to cultures also, so that any given culture must have evolved adequate ways of mediating the eventual achievement of the basic survival functions. One might speculate that motivational structures relating to love and dependency, which insure the care of infants, have evolved in much the same way as those guiding fear and avoidance of harm. Similarly, structures relating to aggression, curiosity, and exploration are directly related to the unique selective advantage that humans attain by way of their intelligence. Again, this shows how a structural view is able to encompass a variety of basic biological tendencies without having to posit separate energies or attempting the cumbersome reduction of love, curiosity, and the like to the hunger-eating-pleasure paradigm.

The general model implied by the foregoing discussion may now be considered. The memory system refers to an organized or structured mass of stored information. This seems a good general term for what Piaget (Flavell, 1963) calls schemata, what Miller, Galanter, and Pribram (1960) call plans, what Klein (1967) terms ideomotor systems, or what other cognitive theorists have called cognitive maps, phase sequences, and the like. It would consist of stored information defined as differentiated structure. As such, it would not be separable from the perceptual apparatus since the process of perception always involves some form of matching of sensory or internal input with existing memory. On the other hand, it may be of value to think of two separate processes: (1) perception, which involves the coordination of input with memory, and (2) internal transformations, which involve various manipulations of stored information in relative independence from input (as in thinking, planning, the flow of associations, anticipations, fantasy, dreams, and the like). In addition, it is possible to think of two aspects of memory systems—the content or stored information and the programs for putting it together (analogous to vocabulary on the one hand and the rules or "grammar" governing language usage on the other). While there may be value in talking about content and program as if they were separate, in fact they are most probably intertwined with each other. Finally, it must be noted that, as Lashley (1950) has so convincingly shown, memory storage does not consist of the storage of specific memories in specific areas of the brain. Rather, memory material is coded in some neuro-chemical fashion. A key characteristic of this coded material is its generalizability or substitutibility, as demonstrated by the applications of old learning in novel situations, or by transposition, equipotentiality of response, displacement, the recognition and response to new symbols, language usage, and the like. Thus, content may be thought of as coded memory material which can be *translated by the operations of different programs.* Some of these would be programs involved in the processes of object recognition whereby a particular sensory input (for example, the infant sees his mother's face) is tried for fit against stored memories until a match is achieved and there results recognition and, perhaps, some form of output such as a smile. As the memory systems become progressively differentiated, a particular input may come to involve both more content and a greater variety of programs. Thus, for the older child, the sensory input of his mother's face leads to a relatively automatic recognition but also to the activation of other memories within the same system, such as anticipations of being fed (particularly if this input occurs simultaneously with input from hunger pangs). A number of related anticipations and outputs associated together in the same memory system may all be brought into play, such as magical, prelogical expectations and anticipations, hallucinatory wish fulfillments, and so forth.

Thus, it is necessary to think in terms of several levels of memory organization. On one level, coded material may exist in a state of greater fluidity permitting a freer associating of memory elements one with another. To put it another way, the programs guiding memory organization at this level permit a different means for the coupling of elements, as by association in time, physical appearance, common sound, connection with a common third element, psychological similarity, and other rules. These rules would be associated with the earliest functioning of the system. At another level, programs guiding memory organization might be more critical, that is, they might subject the material to a screening process which permits only certain types (for example, that which is more logical or socially acceptable) to pass on to an output system such as speech. These programs would be ordered so that information can be successively processed on its way toward output. See Colby (1965) for an attempt at an actual computer program for such a process. These two levels, as some may have noticed, bear a rough resemblance to the psychoanalytic notions of primary and secondary process. It was intended to conceptualize these processes in terms of the operations of different programs. This forms the core of a structural model of motivation, for it is these sorts of guiding structures that provide the direction of on-going activities that is motivation.

Structure and the Dominance of Motives

A chief difficulty with a formulation in terms of programs is that it does not necessarily provide any way of assigning predominance to one structure over another. In such a cognitive scheme, every activity seems equally possible. For each, a particular program is merely said to be in operation. In short, the model seems very unmotivational in this sense, since motives are typically thought of as dominant, as guiding the major directions of activity. As Holt (1967) points out, "pure psychology needs motivation if it is to move beyond a narrow range of cognitive problems." The solution utilized by Freud was to connect the mental to the body in some way, to bring in somatic sources of motivation such as hunger or physiological fright and flight reactions. This is seen most clearly in his earliest theories of anxiety where anxiety is viewed as damned up sexuality in the literal sense of blocked orgasm. The alternative solution just presented views the basic biological processes as built into brain structure. But in humans, where these drives are so plastic, all that exists initially is a tendency or general direction. It can be assumed, however, that this initial tendency sets the pattern for what comes later, and that the initial structuring (the differentiation of relatively undifferentiated structures, or what Piaget calls the accommodation of schemata) has lasting motivational consequences. The second idea that can be drawn on to make the cognitive model a motivational one is that certain structures have emotional-affective systems associated with them that feed-back and amplify or potentiate the activities guided by these structures. Tomkins (1962) develops such an affective theory of motivation in detail.

Let us first consider the role of emotion and then take up the issue of the importance of primary structure. It seems necessary to assume that a system of emotional responses has become attached to those structures which guide the basic survival oriented activities of the organism to insure that these activities will be pervasive and persistent. Thus, emotion and its psychological counterpart, affect, acts as an internal amplification system which, through a process of feedback, insures that the survival oriented activities will become dominant over all others. As an example, consider the role of fear in flight from danger.

Many species are pre-programmed, as it were, to recognize and react to certain stimuli associated with a natural enemy. This means that visual, olfactory, or other cues are perceived as dangerous and produce escape output—for example, they get the animal to start running or swimming or flying. Now we can ask, "Why doesn't the animal stop escaping as soon as he turns his head and no longer perceives the enemy?" After all, he is subject to new stimulus input as soon as he leaves the immediate stimulating situation. It is here that emotion plays its central part. The perception of danger causes the stimulation of an instinctual escape pattern. A part of this pattern involves output to emotional response systems, such as the activation of the sympa-thetic nervous system, the secretion of adrenalin with its accompanying changes, and the like. These internal changes are slower acting, and perseverate longer than cortical recognition. In addition, the animal reacts to them as signs of danger, so that the internal feedback they provide keeps the animal in the pattern of escape when the predator is not even in sight. This is an example of how a basic survival oriented motive has an emotional feedback system associated with it which poten-tiates its effects. The survival value of such potentiation should be obvi-ous—those animals possessing it have lived to reproduce another day while those without it have not. Furthermore, this hypothesis is consist-ent with the clinical observation that dominant motives are those with strong emotional components.

Consider now the second idea with which to make the cognitive model a motivational one. Recall that Freud's approach to the problem was to assign a primary tendency to the mental apparatus (the pleasure princi-ple, the tendency to divest itself of stimulation) and to explain later motivational states as transformations of this initial tendency. While he was wrong about the pleasure principle, the idea that *what comes early shapes what comes later* may be retained to make the structural account a motivational one, that is, to allow it to explain the major phenomena that the traditional energy model is applied to.

It can be assumed that the initial structuring of the memory systems takes place along primary process dimensions, that is, that the initial coding or representation of the environment is in terms of programs that are tied to motor acts (Piaget's sensori-motor intelligence). In addition to building up a sense of self identified with one's body, such programs might facilitate freer associations between stimuli and images. The fact that such programs become structured first would give them a more basic place as guiding structures. In other words, if mental development proceeds from undifferentiated to progressively more structured stages, it is reasonable to assume that the initial dimensions of differentiation become crucial in determining the later functioning of the system.

Initially, the mental apparatus is relatively undifferentiated, although certain reflexive structures and initial tendencies are present. Structure develops as these tendencies are modified and new ones created out of an interaction with the environment. Since this interaction is a function of the existing structures, the development of new ones must be based on those that already exist. Various analogies suggest themselves for de-scribing the way initial structure shapes subsequent organization. One would be the way the formation of the infant's skeleton determines what the adult skeleton will be, initial directions of growth or abnormalities being reflected in its final form. Another would be the idea of proto-programs, the initial programs that are involved in the development of later programs. Another analogy is suggested by what Harlow (1949) terms learning sets, essentially strategies that are acquired on the basis of past learning which cast subsequent learning in a new dimension. These analogies all convey the general point that initial structure provides a blueprint or framework for what develops later.

Since this early structuring is of the same form as that which develops from the interaction of initial tendencies with environmental experiences, it is reasonable to assume that its motivational consequences are just as basic. In other words, the form taken by these early precursors to thought and fantasy would provide blueprints such as a motor conception of the world or an identification of self with body (which is what Freud implies when he states that the original ego is "pure body ego"). These *anlage* of mental operation would be revealed during states favoring regression, that is, conditions where these early established programs guide psychological activity.

The structures associated with hunger, love, aggression, and flight have already been mentioned. Each may be thought of as a framework which shapes the direction of subsequent structures. These structures tend to involve systems of potentiating emotional response. For example, fear producing input sets into operation a number of physiological processes that prepare the organism for flight and assure, via internal feedback, that this reaction will be more than momentary. The fact that the basic biological goals involve these related emotional and affective systems is of the greatest importance, for it accounts, in large part, for their dominant character and persistence into adult life, even when they have become disconnected, as it were, from their original purpose.

Thus, the initial structuring along both basic biological lines and those stemming from the earliest forms of cognitive development provide the frameworks for the subsequent memory systems. Moreover, these lines of development are far from separate. They interact and exert various constraints one on the other. Thus, when the infant is extremely hungry or frightened, he is unable to engage in the sort of exploration of the environment that is necessary for the development of stable perceptual structures. On the other hand, under normal conditions of development, where intense hunger or fright are minimal or brief, activities in the service of cognitive and perceptual structures may take up a great deal of time.

In sum, it is the early structuring of the memory systems that is crucial for the development of motivation, that is, for specifying the basic directions that later activity will take. This early structuring takes place along several dimensions, including those defined by the major survival oriented functions and those defined in terms of the basic perceptual, sensorimotor, and cognitive areas. Thus, the explanation for the motivationally dominant effects of certain forms of early experience is in terms of their providing the framework or blueprint for later development within the memory systems. For example, the infant's earliest interactions with mother, father, and siblings lead to internalized memories and to certain primary programs guiding the organization of the memories. This initial structuring of the memory systems guides the output of interpersonal perception, emotional reactions to other people, the expectations of how others will react, actions taken on the basis of these expectations, and the like. This—rather than "the vicissitudes of the libido"—is the sort of underpinning needed to explain object relations and the importance of early family relationships.

Consider an overly simple example: a young man with a neurotic fear of sexually attractive women. This might traditionally be explained as due to the guilt and anxiety aroused by an unsuccessfully repressed Oedipal conflict (a truly cumbersome explanation if analyzed in terms of psychic energy). Now, consider this example in structural terms of: (1) perception, (2) internal organization and transformation of information, and (3) output. First, the woman is perceived in a particular way, which is a function of the organization and structuring of the perceptual apparatus. Perception is *organizing*, it is not the registering of stimuli upon a blank screen. In this example, the process of equating the input "woman" with "mother" already begins in the process of perception. Next, this perceived input is given further meaning in terms of the organized memory systems. In this case, part of the meaning given to the input brings into play a system having to do with "mother," "sexual attraction toward mother with accompanying emotional arousal," "fear of punishment," "the idea that the attraction is wrong," and so forth. These perceptions then lead to certain ways of dealing with the perceived input (such as defense mechanisms).

This process, whereby perceived input is given meaning in terms of memories related within certain systems, provides the possibility of a number of internal transformations, as by symbolism. This can then lead to certain output phenomena, such as panic; overt acts such as avoiding women, or seeking them out and establishing close, but intellectual relationships; particular thoughts and fantasies; dreams; and so forth.

In this example, it is assumed that anxiety plays a continuing role. It is worth stressing that while anxiety may frequently be involved in the origin of such a pattern it may not continue to be a part of the subsequent output. The passage of time, repetition, and other factors may cause the simplification and automatization of a particular pattern such as this. When this happens we may see, in the adult, a well established (characterological) way of dealing with women that runs relatively smoothly and shows little overt emotion or anxiety (that is, what is described as a well-defended person). What sense, then, has the traditional explanation of defenses as means to avoid anxiety when there is not necessarily any anxiety present? Again, it only makes sense if anxiety is conceptualized as an output phenomena of a process that involves perception, organization, transformation, and output. While anxiety, anger, sexual arousal, and the like may be involved at earlier periods in the development of particular perceptual-memory systems, it is the structuring of the systems that determines present output, and not the affect of anxiety.

This example implies a revision of the psychoanalytic theory of neurosis. Neurotic phenomena (such as symptoms, life-styles, choice of partners, forms of sexuality and of aggression) are essentially later symbolic transformations of early acquired patterns. We assume, for example, that a strong negative affect, such as anxiety or guilt, gets attached to the perception and internal representation of sexuality. This becomes represented in terms of early programs whereby parts of the body may stand for their function—which is what Freud refers to as the "attachment of anxiety to the sexual organs" (that is, attachment interpreted as symbolic representation). This representation then goes through a sequence of transformations, made possible by the development of defense mechanisms, the incorporation of cultural stereotypes and beliefs, all of which themselves involve symbolic substitute processes. Then, in the adult, we may see a neurotic disgust over sex, or the repetitive seeking out of partners who are rejecting, or the arousal of anxiety over some idea that represents the whole complicated system of memory transformations. A full accounting of an adult neurosis would entail an understanding of the series of internal transformations that the initial pattern has undergone. This is extremely difficult to carry out retrospectively, but it is what psychoanalytic case histories try to do from the relatively limited data of the patient's present memory material.

The present structural model is a most general one. For a more detailed model, the reader is referred to Klein's (1967) excellent paper which, among other things, deals explicitly with the motivating effects of repression. See also Klein's chapter in the present volume.

Before concluding this section, brief consideration must be given to some of the processes that occur in later development. To explicate fully the process whereby early structuring affects subsequent thought and action, consideration must be given to the transformations that can occur within the memory systems as a result of later experience and particularly the acquisition of language and other symbolic capabilities. Even the simplest forms of cognitive and perceptual development involve some form of internal representation of the environment. Human beings very rapidly move beyond such simple forms, however, and with the development of language and other symbolic modes, there develop more far-reaching modes of internal representation—that is, modes that enable one to code stored information according to different rules. The adaptive value of such processes should be obvious. Internal representation allows the child to break free from dependence on the immediate environment and it is just this ability that leads to those higher achievements made possible by man's intelligence. Progressive development of such internal representations may indeed become completely free from the environment, as in abstract mathematics.

But without jumping to this level, the type of process that develops after the first year of life (as exemplified by but not restricted to language development) may be noted. What is involved here is the ability to perform *transformations on internally stored representations of the environment*. Such transformations would, of necessity, work with existing stored symbolic material. For example, the infant develops a stored memory of a toy; this itself takes time and begins by the development of a simple object recognition schemata. He also develops a set of expectations having to do with mother doing things for him (feeding, making him comfortable, stimulating, playing, and the like). Then, at some point, given sufficient prior experience, he brings those two bits of stored information together to create the proto-fantasy of mother getting him the toy. This bringing together is a process whereby the symbols for the environment can be substituted one for the other. For example, the progression may be something like: (1) I want toy, (2) mother satisfies wants as when I want food, (3) mother satisfying one can substitute for mother satisfying another, to (4) mother gives me toy. Such a process assumes that the infant can equate wanting one thing with wanting another, as well as equating objects with each other—something that seems very simple to us because it is so readily facilitated by our language (that is, the concept "want" bridges the gap and we can assign toy and food to the class "objects of desire"). But for the infant, during a period before language or when only its crude beginnings are present, it is no easy task to develop such a fantasy. The symbolic tools available for such substitute activities are the earliest forms in which the environment is represented. Thus, receiving something from someone may be closely tied to the memory system dealing with feeding, while states of desire could be tied to the emotional reactions accompanying hunger. In a similar fashion, the relations between objects in the environment or between one's own actions and their effects would be symbolized in the form that characterizes Piaget's sensori-motor stages.

All of this points to a sort of primary process thinking as a necessary early way of performing transformations on stored, symbolic representations of the environment. In other words, certain programs develop to guide fantasy, expectations, and symbolic substitutions which make use of the symbolizing capabilities of the infant. These are the initial rules for performing internal, symbolic transformations on stored representations of input (from the environment and one's own body). Because of their primacy, they set the pattern for later, more complex transformations.

The possibility that the earliest forms of psychological operation could be facilitated by a primary-process-like combining of material has interesting consequences. That is, the free use of just those processes such as substitutions, displacements, and lack of a distinction between the internal and external environments that are viewed as maladaptive or even psychotic in the adult might be extremely useful in the early development of thinking, planning, and the like. It seems likely that so-called reality oriented thought is highly overrated, probably because it is more familiar to us from that aspect of conscious experience to which we attend.

Attempts to program computers to simulate complex psychological operations such as language sheds some interesting light on this. This work indicates that such complex processes require programs consisting of a variety of sub-routines or procedures, each with their own rules or special logic for processing information. Such procedures would bear an ordered, polyarchical relation to each other. What the present example suggests is that the primary process programs occupy an important, perhaps necessary, place in this order. Information might be processed according to primary process rules where, for example, elements could be combined on the basis of common sound or appearance or in terms of their personal import. The information so processed would then pass on for further processing of a critical nature to screen for social acceptability prior to output via a channel such as speech.

Later psychological development may be viewed as a series of stages in which these processes are progressively refined. The further development of language means the internalization of new programs for manipulating symbols. Concomitantly, there are a host of developments in thinking, fantasy, and so forth, all of which may be viewed as the development of new structures that are built on, or grow out of, the earlier structures. Whether the early structures continue to exist along with the later ones or are absorbed as the infant's skeleton is absorbed during growth is an interesting question. In any case, it seems likely that the earliest structuring exerts an influence that is central to later motivation.

A DESCRIPTION OF DREAM OPERATION

The previous analysis indicates that the view of dream function as discharging id impulses in compromise form should be abandoned. Having done so, we are now in a position to consider a structural formulation. This may be approached by describing dream operation in information processing terms. Briefly put, *dreams are one output of particular memory systems operating under the guidance of programs that are peculiar to sleep.* These programs stem from certain early modes of psychological operation and, hence, dreams may be said to be regressive, though not in exactly the sense that Freud used the term. Certain memory systems have been activated during the period prior to sleep and have set into operation emotional reactions that feed-back and keep these particular systems active or ready. Such activation may have been initially by a specific event—for example, a rejection by an important person—or by a train of thought or fantasy. But the involvement of emotional reactions serves to potentiate these systems as opposed to the many others that are in operation during the pre-sleep period.[7] It is important to note that the memory systems themselves are centrally involved in the process of perception so that the interpretation of input during the day is a function of the related material within the system, as well as stimulating the system to further internal activity.

Upon going to sleep, certain memory systems are more ready than others and, when the normal periods of nightly activation (the REM periods) occur in their cyclic fashion, it is these ready or primed systems that are brought into play. Dreams are one output of these memory systems, an output which includes images, thoughts and feelings, and a variety of psychophysiological reactions. The quality of dreams, their

[7]The fact that it is information associated with emotional arousal that determines subsequent dream content is confirmed by several lines of evidence. Studies which have attempted to influence dreams with relatively non-arousing pre-sleep material, such as the viewing of western movies (Foulkes and Rechtschaffen, 1964) or depriving subjects of water for a day (Dement and Wolpert, 1958), have shown little ability to effect the content of dreams. Being a subject in a dream experiment, which is a very personally arousing experience, has been shown to influence strongly dream content (Dement, 1965). Several recent studies have further confirmed this. In one (Collins, Davison and Breger, 1967) it was found that those subjects who were aroused by a threatening film incorporated elements of the film into their dreams while those who were not aroused did not. In a study of the effects of being at the focus of a psychotherapy group just prior to sleep, Breger, Hunter, and Lane (in press) found that this exceedingly arousing experience tended completely to dominate dream content. In a study of hospital patients prior to major surgery (Breger, Hunter, and Lane, in press) it was found that this threatening anticipation was centrally represented in dreams.

creative and sometimes bizarre nature, is due to the special programs guiding the internal transformations and output of the memory systems during sleep.

Sleep is a unique state; it is probably the single most "infantile" activity we engage in. That is, it persists from infancy with very little change (time spent sleeping declines as does percentage of REM sleep, but the pattern remains essentially constant) throughout life while other basic activities undergo tremendous modifications. Eating, for example, goes from a reflexive sucking at the breast to forms ranging as widely as the rigidly controlled diet or the gourmet dinner with exacting etiquette. Sexuality undergoes a number of transformations before adult mating can occur. Sleep, in contrast, manifests itself the same in the adult as in the infant. The comfortable warm bed, the relative lack of stimulus input, the lack of motor output or, indeed, any interchange with the external environment—all these factors recreate a state present in earliest infancy and contribute to regression. They facilitate the activation of those programs guiding psychological operation which characterized, in part, these early stages of life. It is for this reason that dreams can shed light on these early modes of psychological function.

What are the characteristics of these programs? They may be thought of as permitting a much freer combination of memory elements including association by shape, color, common sound or function, and so on as well as along ideosyncratic psychological dimensions. Other characteristics are indicated by the related dream work principles that Freud describes—displacement, condensation, and symbolization. The importance of emotional feedback is enhanced during this state, again due to its more direct influence and greater intensity in guiding activities during infancy and childhood. In Freud's terms, there are a number of manifestations of primary process operation.

Consider an example at this point. The dreamer was a young female graduate student who was serving as a voluntary S in our dream laboratory. She slept in one room while a male E monitored her sleep cycle (with the usual EEG and REM indicators) in an adjoining room and, at the appropriate times, awakened her to elicit reports of her dream experience. She served as an S for eight nights over a two-week period. During this time, she and her boyfriend of the past two years were in the midst of a crisis concerning marriage. Although she was conflicted, fearing that marriage might mean giving up graduate school and a possible career, she had made up her mind to go ahead with it. He, on the other hand, was vacillating and it was not until several weeks after her participation in the sleep laboratory that she heard, with great relief, that he would go through with the marriage. On the fourth night in the laboratory she reported the following dream:

My mother and I were living in the woods . . . we were walking down a highway and there were lots of deer running around. And the people on the highway kept stopping, ah, there were business stands along the highway like service station operators, and they kept asking us if we would like to buy one of the deer that was standing around. And so I went over to this jewelry store with one of these people following us. My mother kept trying to explain that we couldn't afford it and they never would understand. We went into this store and were looking for, I can't remember the article we were looking for. Anyway, we went into this place, and it was very, very small and ah . . . my mother would, this was pretty important, she slipped behind the counter along with the lady and I was sitting on a big stool on the other side of the counter. And I tried on several of whatever it was that I was looking for. And we all decided to go up, the three of us decided to go up, to a house to have some coffee and some cookies. And so, we, they were saying, I said "do you think I could get through this space to get behind the counter," because we were going to go out the back door, or, "do I have to go around the house?" They kept kidding me and said that I would probably have to go around the house. Apparently, I was fat or something, I don't know. Anyway, as a matter of fact, I couldn't get through the space. So I had to go around the house. The house was this very primitive looking wooden cabin. And for some reason or other we all sat down and started reading a paper. And we were also drinking tea or something . . . and some horrible tasting cookies. They were just totally tasteless and looked like honeycomb, apparently some specialty of the woods. And we were reading the paper, the paper was a New York City paper and it was talking about, I was reading about the advertisements for insurance companies and for undertakers and things like that. They were all just horrible. They were saying things like, ah, "so what if you die, ah, let's snap it up and get rid of them" and all these funny things. And you know, really strange peculiar things, like, "throw them in the ground real fast and they will forget tomorrow." And, ah, with smiling undertakers standing there. And then one kind of cute thing from a camera company saying something about, "for the kids who peeked away." And there was a picture of two little children who were skating, standing there looking, ah, ostensibly looking at the camera, both of them, when you examined them a little closer one was peeking to the right and one was peeking to the left just as the shutter was open. And ah, the next picture was, these same two kids and it's saying they are standing there on the street on an ice-skating rink, even though the subway down below is being renovated. So I thought for a while about the whole ice-skating rink falling into the subway station. I'm trying to remember some more advertisements, I don't think I can, I just know they were all pretty gruesome, except those pictures of the little kids.

On the next night the *S* reported the following dream:

I was walking down this street and I saw this booth and it said "help fat people" or something like this, and it was full of ugly fat people. This is nice repetition. I would be interested in finding out what this fatness is, ah, what it represents, ah, "help ugly fat people reduce," it said. "Pay here and we will give you the means" or something like this. So I went up and paid a lot of money and, ah, went away. I didn't refuse it. That was the end of the dream, I didn't get to use it or see any of the results or anything like that.

In this example we have a fairly good idea that the *S*'s general state of emotional arousal centers on marriage and its various implications for her life. The two dreams bear no obvious relation to this, however, and the *S* herself was at a loss to explain them. Following her last night in the laboratory, an extensive personality assessment was carried out. As a part of this, she was asked to associate to some of her dreams, including the first one, above. Initially, she had no associations to the "woods" nor to being "fat" (she is, in fact, a petite, attractive girl who has never had any problem with her weight). The unpleasant affect of the dream was quite prominent and when asked to associate to it she very rapidly went from the "undertakers" who smilingly deal in death to "abortionists" who do the same. Suddenly, some light was shed on the dreams. She reported having had an abortion a year previously when she had been pregnant by the same boyfriend. She connected the "gruesome" affect in the dream with the related fear of dying that she experienced at that time. She also spoke with some regret about having lost the child and expressed concern over what her mother would think if she found out about the incident. Interestingly, she reported that she had not thought about the abortion lately and purposefully told no one about it.

Without attempting a complete analysis of the two dreams, some suggested interpretations can be made drawing on her associations and the other data (the total sample of dreams from eight nights and the personality assessment material).

The pregnancy, abortion, and her feelings about it are portrayed in several ways. Her own fatness in both dreams probably symbolizes pregnancy. In the first, she is ridiculed by her mother and another woman, which related to her expectations of mother's reaction to her sexual transgressions. The ugly aspects of the fatness probably symbolize the guilt she experiences, both over being pregnant and of having had the abortion. Her nostalgic feeling about the lost child (in the interview she stated that she felt she could have had a baby that looked like the boyfriend, but now she does not) is alluded to as the kids who "peeked away" when the shutter was open. The abortion itself is kinetically represented as children falling through a hole in the context of death, that is, the undertakers who say, "throw them in the ground real fast and they will forget tomorrow."

The abortion is also symbolized in both dreams as something that costs a lot of money; reducing her ugly fatness in one and in the other the insistent salesman who wants a lot of money for the deer (perhaps a fusion of her lost "dear" and an innocent uncivilized creature). Her feelings toward the abortionist is more strongly conveyed in the frightening symbol of the smiling undertaker.

Finally, there is the contrast between the country (the "woods") and the big city (the newspaper from New York). This is a theme that runs through a number of other dreams of this S and that relates, in a complex way, to her feelings about her mother and her own role as a woman. At one level, she describes her mother as very unsophisticated—a simple country girl—while she has made a much more sophisticated life for herself, as an outstanding graduate student and fashion model. At the same time, several of her dreams portray her dissatisfaction with her sophisticated big-city way of life which is symbolized as a very complicated and difficult set of obstacles that she must negotiate. Here, she is drawn toward a simpler life which she equates with emotional security. Her decision in favor of marriage represents a partial resolution of this conflict in the latter direction. There remains, however, the possible barrenness of this life (the tasteless cookies, "a specialty of the woods") which relates to her view of her mother's life and the possibility that being a wife and mother herself would be very dull.

Several aspects of the theoretical ideas under discussion are illustrated by this example. Perhaps most prominent is the potentiating effect of emotion. In the previous theoretical analysis, emotion and affect are viewed as providing internal feedback which potentiates particular memory systems. Our S goes to sleep, we assume, with a great deal of affective arousal relating to marriage and to becoming a wife and possible mother. The memory systems that are activated all relate to this in some way. Thus, a highly charged memory, her pregnancy and abortion, is represented. Here was an occasion where she was almost a mother, a situation where she might have gotten married and didn't. We might assume that many of the same thoughts and feelings toward the boyfriend exist now as did then. Her guilt over the illegitimacy of her present relationship is also an affect that binds this past set of memories to her present concerns.

In addition, this example illustrates the organization and output of stored information under the guidance of different programs, programs that are associated with a developmentally early mode of function. Thus, a psychological concern—guilt over pregnancy—is expressed in body language, being fat and ugly. The general kinetic or motoric quality of the symbolism suggests a sensori-motor, as opposed to ideational, mode of functioning.

Finally, there are general themes, in this example the city vs. country theme, that seem to run through the dreams of different S's. These themes are indicative of certain basic dimensions of memory system organization. They typically relate to the major interpersonal concerns. Thus, for this S there is a theme concerned with the meaning, to her, of being a wife and mother which is complexly related to the feelings and memories concerning her own mother and the way she has lived her life as a woman to this point. This structure probably goes back to a basic organization within the system dealing with what might broadly be termed her feminine identification. Its earliest affects might have included a certain amount of rebelliousness against being like her mother, with concomitant guilt. During later development, a number of transformations take place—that is, the pattern becomes symbolized in a greater variety of ways—particularly as new modes of coping and more complex symbolic abilities are acquired. But certain aspects of the initial organization and particularly that involving emotional-affective feedback remain as an underlying framework. This is revealed in the ongoing life style and can be more directly inferred from states such as dreaming which favor regression—that is, the use of early programs.

In summary, particular memory systems are brought to the fore as they are involved in the *perception* (organization, interpretation, giving meaning to input) of events prior to sleep. Those systems which involve emotional affective arousal tend to become predominant due to potentiating feedback effects. During the REM periods of activation these memory systems guide output which takes the form of visual images, emotional arousal, affective experience, and various psychophysiological responses. The sleep state facilitates the use of early, more infantile or regressed programs which lead to the opening up of the system to memory material and ways of combining, symbolizing, and transforming it that stem from these earlier modes of operation. The dream, then, becomes a particularly rich source of data for getting at the way a particular individual's memory systems are organized and just what content, what memories, associations, or fantasies have come to symbolize the basic dimensions of the system.

The foregoing has essentially been a description of dream operation that has not, as yet, shed any light on the possible adaptive value of dreams in the adult. That is, if we accept this description as an accurate one, we are still left with the question of what purpose, if any, dreams serve. We have seen why an answer in terms of drive discharge won't do, so let us examine some other answers.

THE PSYCHOLOGICAL FUNCTION OF DREAMS

What are some of the functions that might be served by dreaming in the adult? Hypotheses will be considered, ranging along a continuum of adaptiveness. As should be clear, the probability that REM sleep served an important evolutionary function or that dreaming may be developmentally important does not necessarily mean that dreaming in the human adult remains a centrally adaptive function. Thus, as a first hypothesis, dreams might be conceptualized as essentially non-adaptive. Cortical activation occurs in accordance with the biologically given REM cycle, and this occasions the activation of those memory systems which, due to potentiating emotional effects, are in a state of readiness from the pre-sleep period. In this view, dreams may parallel and reflect the conflicts, affects, and experiences aroused during the day, displaying them in a different form due to the operation of different programs during sleep. But these would be essentially static representations; they would do nothing more with this information than display it.

The distinction must be maintained between dreams and what is done with recollected dream material. The laboratory work with EEG and REM monitoring techniques has established that, with a few very infrequent exceptions, all humans spend from 20 to 22 per cent of each night's sleep dreaming. They may recall none, a little, or a great deal of this the next day. Further, what is recalled may soon be forgotten or it may form the basis for several hours of psychoanalytic exploration in which a multitude of associations and meanings are examined. It should be clear that in this latter case, any adaptive changes that take place cannot be attributed to the dream alone but are due to the dream and what is done with it. In the present discussion, focus is on the adaptive value of dreams *per se*. What is done with remembered dreams remains a separate question, one concerning the value of working over fantasy or dream material during a waking, reality oriented state. The first hypothesis, then, is that dreams serve no particular adaptive function.

The question may be raised concerning the evidence from studies of dream deprivation (Dement, 1960; 1965). Do these studies not indicate that when Ss are prevented from dreaming, psychological disturbance results, indicating that dreams are necessary for maintaining some sort of adaptive balance? While a thorough discussion of these results cannot be presented here, it can be said that, to date, the findings from such experiments remain equivocal. For example, a recent study by Gulevitch *et al.* (1966) found no marked psychological disturbance in a young man deprived of all sleep for eleven days. For one thing, it is difficult to separate the effects of dream deprivation from the deprivation of REM sleep. The deprivation of REM sleep might indeed have certain disruptive effects in some people, but these might be psychologically nonspecific. Further research is needed to ascertain whether depriving Ss of the opportunity to dream about specific aroused material interferes with adaptation to such material (see Collins, Davison, and Breger, 1967, for a preliminary study bearing on this problem).

Another problem arises from the fact that the processes seen in dreams are by no means confined to REM periods. They may be seen in waking fantasy (daydreams), the hypnogogic imagery that occurs during sleep onset (see Foulkes and Vogel, 1965), and perhaps as an unconscious substrate during waking life. The fact that these and other activities, such as humor, may serve as forms of symbolic expression will certainly make it difficult to isolate the specific effects of dreams during sleep.

Some recent studies on the response of different subjects to REM or dream deprivation support the view that dream-like fantasy may appear at other times when REM sleep is interfered with. Early work with REM deprivation seemed to indicate that when a subject was deprived of REM sleep by being awakened at the outset of each REM period, two things occurred. The pressure for REM built up, as indicated by the greater frequency of REM periods and the greater difficulty awakening the subject. Second, when allowed to sleep without interruption on subsequent nights, subjects compensated for the amount of deprived REM; they showed a REM rebound effect. More recently, Cartwright and Monroe (1967) have shown that these findings hold only for a certain type of subject, the so-called "deep sleeper" who has probably been most frequently employed in sleep and dream experiments. Other subjects show different patterns; there seem to be some individuals who do not show the build up of REM pressure and lack REM compensation in response to REM deprivation. Some of these are subjects who report large amounts of dream content during the deprivation awakenings. Thus, whether a subject makes up for lost REM time or not seems to be a function of whether he is able to engage in dream-like activity during other phases of sleep. A further study by Cartwright and Monroe (in press) extends and confirms these findings. In both these studies, the need that the subject is deprived of seems to be the need to complete a certain amount of fantasy or dream experience. If he is able to do so outside of REM sleep as some subjects are, there is no need to engage in more REM on subsequent nights. A related conclusion is reached by Fiss and his coworkers (Fiss, 1969) in their studies of the effects of REM interruption on dream content.

Additional evidence is provided by Cartwright (1966). In this study, subjects were given a hallucinogenic drug during the day which induced dream-like experience in the waking state. This produced a marked reduction in REM sleep on post-drug nights, suggesting that if subjects get their dreaming done in advance, as it were, they have less need for REM sleep later.

Related evidence comes from another source—studies of the response to REM deprivation of different types of schizophrenics. Several studies (Gulevich, Dement, and Zarcone, 1967; Zarcone, Gulevich, Pivik, and Dement, in press; Zarcone, Pivik, Gulevich, Azumi, and Dement, 1968) have demonstrated different patterns of response to REM deprivation in acute and remitting schizophrenics. The acute schizophrenics fail to show any compensatory increase in REM sleep on post-deprivation nights. Schizophrenics in remission, on the other hand, show an exaggerated rebound (higher percentage of REM and shorter latency to first REM) in comparison to normal controls. I would interpret these findings as indicating that the acute schizophrenics, preoccupied with their own fantasies and perceiving reality in an idiosyncratic fashion, show no compensation for REM deprivation because they are, in a certain sense, dreaming all the time. They are in a state of high central arousal and low sensory control. Those in a state of remission, on the other hand, are engaging in a rather massive defensive effort which precludes free access to their fantasies during the waking state. This makes REM sleep a more likely site and accounts for their heightened sensitivity to REM deprivation.

These considerations suggest that the type of fantasy processes, seen most vividly in dreams, may serve important adaptive functions in all of the situations in which they are manifested. In addition to the work just reviewed, there are several lines of evidence that support this idea including catharsis (the finding, from different types of psychotherapy, that some benefit derives from an emotional release or simply talking things out), the work of mourning following the loss of loved ones and less severe but similar losses, and the repetitious reliving in fantasy that frequently follows a stressful experience, as seen most vividly in cases of combat neurosis (Grinker and Spiegle, 1945). To these examples may be added everyday experiences: when something upsetting happens, people worry about it and perhaps talk it over with friends, all of which seems helpful in coming to terms with the upsetting experience.

The conception of the dual role of memory systems in both perception and the internal processing of perceived input may be brought to bear at this point. What constitutes an upsetting experience is essentially a perceptual problem. Thus, while it is easy to think of extreme examples, such as combat, that are stressful or threatening to almost everyone, for less extreme examples it becomes nearly impossible to define psychological stress or threat independently of the individual's perception of it (Lazarus, 1966). To cite a few examples: An aggressive boss may arouse great anxiety in one employee in whom he stimulates murderous rage, while another employee may feel secure in the hands of an authority who provides direction and structure. A sexually attractive woman may arouse pleasurable excitement in one man, guilt over adulterous thoughts in a second, and anxiety that she will reject him, as mother did, in a third. The differing perceptions of a real stress experience, major surgery, are clearly revealed in a recent study (Breger, Hunter, and Lane, in press). Here, the surgery patients' perception of their impending operations ranged from the fear of a dependent ulcer patient that he would not be adequately cared for, to the hope of an isolated adolescent girl that a minor operation would solve her interpersonal problems by allowing her to lose weight. These examples, which could be multiplied a hundredfold from common experience, all show that it is the organizing, interpretive aspects of perceptual information processing that cause input to be differentially stressful for individuals whose histories have led to differentially structured memory systems.

Perceptual processes stem from the memory systems and are inseparable from the internal processing of perceived input. Thus, for every class of perceptual input, there are certain established modes of operation. These range from simple object recognition to the problem that causes a moment's thought before a solution is effected to those aspects of life that are most threatening and stressful and which involve prominent defense mechanisms over long periods of time. Stressful stimuli are those which the individual cannot "solve" immediately; those that cannot be adequately assimilated to some existing structure or system. We may then view catharsis, worrying, mourning, the repetition of terrifying experiences, and the like as attempts at solution, (assimilation, mastery, and so on).

From these considerations, a second hypothesis may be formulated concerning the adaptive function of dreams. This is: That dreams serve to integrate affectively aroused material into structures within the memory systems that have previously proved satisfactory in dealing with similar material. To illustrate: Suppose that a student is concerned and anxious about a pending examination and that this concern is related to a group of conflicting feelings about his overall adequacy. He goes to sleep after a night of anxious studying with these conflicts aroused. His dreams that night represent the current situation but also regress into the memory systems (that is, the aroused material is processed by earlier programs), allowing the presentation of other, related conflict situations *and their resolutions.* For example, he might dream of playing with a sibling to whom he felt inferior as a child but whom he eventually bested by withdrawing from active games into intellectual pursuits with accompanying fantasies of his superiority, rationalizations about the greater value of intellectual work over cloddish athletics, and so on. In effect, the present conflict is made potentially solvable, just as the similar situation was in the past. That is, the previous situation of inferiority is symbolically blended with the present one and solutions based on the old solutions are represented. These may be purely defensive solutions (all rationalization, no accomplishment), magical solutions, or solutions with a large reality component. Thus, during dreaming, the current conflict may be tested for fit with a variety of programs which are generally related to similar conflicts.

There are several reasons why mastery of this sort might be specially facilitated during dreaming. Since dreaming is a form of intense psychological activity that occurs in the relative absence or internal blocking off of stimulus input, it should be particularly suited to internal transformations of stored material. Such absence of attention to the external world is common to the other forms of attempted mastery—working over a problem in one's mind, worrying, and daydreaming. Dreaming represents an extreme case. (This might also be a carryover of one of the crucial functions served by the REM state during early development.) In addition to such concentration on internal transformations, there is the availability of a greater number of programs, including those primary process programs that guided mental activities during early development. Coincident with this, there is the availability of stored memory material that may not be available during the waking state. The fact that dreams are visual representations, as opposed to spoken or written ones, again means that the range of information processing methods is extended.

Finally, and this may be crucial, the processing of information during dreaming is not so constrained by the rules that critically process information for social acceptability of output during the waking state. This may be illustrated by comparing dream with waking thought. While a train of waking thought may wander a good deal, there is an automatic checking back and forth for something that can be crudely called making sense. That is, if one were to stop an individual and ask him, "What are you thinking?" he is expected to give an answer that is understandable to others. Such critical processing for social acceptability gets strongly built in during socialization and we regard people who lack it as autistic, psychotic, or bizarre. Dreams, apart from such unusual circumstances as the sleep laboratory or psychoanalytic treatment, are not the subject of social communication. Hence, they are in part free from the constraints of such critical processing. And it may be just this freedom that facilitates the mastery or integration of aroused information during dreaming.

All the foregoing factors make the dream a unique place for the integration or mastery of psychological material related to a state of affective arousal.[8] That is, dreams are uniquely adaptive insofar as they provide the conditions allowing for the integration of aroused material that is not so readily integrated during the waking state. These conditions would consist of the greater availability of memory material (stored information), the greater fluidity of associational processes, the freedom from critical processing for social acceptability, and in general, a greater variety of means of manipulating symbols or processing and transforming the stored information. The availability of these means would allow the integration of material; they would represent, in effect, the creative opening up of the memory systems.

A creative form of integration would be possible due to the special features of dreams just described. It is known that problem solving is facilitated by having a large number of psychological elements to draw upon and a greater freedom or more flexibility in combining them in new ways. These conditions certainly seem to characterize dreams, for example, the availability of different programs such as those drawn from the sensori-motor period or those permitting a greater range of symbolic transformation as illustrated by displacements, condensations, and so forth. In these respects, dreams are similar to works of art, jokes, and the like in which a creative solution arises from a state of emotional concentration.

Consider an example at this point. The dreamer, Al, was a sixty-four-year-old man serving in a study of the effect of pre-operative stress on dreams (Breger, Hunter, and Lane, in press). At the time of the study, he was in the hospital prior to an operation to correct a vascular blockage in his groin. He had suffered some loss of mobility and coldness in his feet and faced the prospect of reduced mobility after the operation. This was of some importance to him since he had always lived a very active, outdoor life. Al was a very outgoing, friendly individual who dealt with the stress of his impending surgery with repression, denial of any anxiety, and a good deal of talk concerning his past achievements and activities. This was consistent with a life style characterized by assertive activity. He tended to perceive the operation as a mechanical repair job akin to fixing a broken machine. For example, when asked

---

[8]This view of dream function is consistent with that put forth by French (1952) and French and Fromm (1964) when they speak of dreams as attempting solutions of "focal conflicts." As French puts it, "every dream is struggling to find a solution for an unsolved problem in the present, left over from the preceding day. As in waking life, memories . . . [of solutions] . . . from the past find their way into the dream thoughts to serve as guides for the solution of similar problems in the present." It is clear that to French and Fromm, problems refer to interpersonal difficulties and to that which arouses strong emotion. Thus, while the problem (or what they alternatively call the "focal conflict") may be current, it exists as a problem because of the way the memory systems are structured.

if he anticipated much pain in connection with the operation, he responded:

Oh hell no . . . I never have before, never known about that before in my life. I don't think about those things, just think that I've got something to fix and I'll go in there and get it repaired and then come out.

His perception of his vascular blockage is revealed in the following quotation:

. . . and my legs are cold . . . there's poor circulation . . . my feet are cold all the time . . . that thing is swoll up there so damned big . . . I think it's getting longer all the time . . . it's just like tying a string around a hose, you know . . . . . . you can't force it through there down to my feet . . . course I know what the penalty is if I, I don't happen to be around them [doctors] and that starts leaking and then it starts to drip, you know. Then pretty soon it bursts . . . course if it bursts you're dead.

Al's attempts at mastery (among other things, he was very active talking and helping the other patients) while awake were largely successful in keeping his fear at a low level. Nevertheless, the nature of the situation prevented him from actively doing anything about his problem; he was, in this sense, completely dependent on the doctors. In sum, the emotionally arousing aspects of his situation consisted of fear of the impending operation and its possible consequences, his discomfort over being in a dependent position, and the more general threat of his increasing loss of vigor with approaching old age, which would mean giving up his active way of life for a more passive, dependent one.

In terms of the present analysis, his approaching operation is perceived as threatening in terms of the structure of particular memory systems. Consistent with this, a much larger proportion of his pre-operation (as opposed to post-operation) dreams deal with symbolized versions of his aroused concerns, such as defective objects (a broken pocket knife, a plugged sewer, a clogged railroad switch), reduced mobility or blockage, water or fluid as a discomfort or threat, and cutting. Other situations in which he faced the threat of a passive-dependent role (for instance, with his former wife) were blended with these symbols.

Of central interest to the present hypothesis is the way in which the perceived threat is integrated into the solutions embodied in existing memory systems. In a number of these pre-operative dreams, Al is himself actively engaged in attempting to fix or repair something. In one, he and a "boy" are repairing a stove: ". . . you see, we had tore it down the year before and had the same trouble there." (He had, in fact, had a similar operation the previous year.) In another, he is discussing cutting up a "quarter of beef to preserve it"; and in a third he and some "young fellows" are trying to fix a septic tank that is clogged and flooding. The symbolism in these dreams seems closely related to his perception of his vascular problem. In addition to the "fixing" themes, the dreams deal with the discomfort he experienced as a result of his dependency on the doctors. They, or their symbolic stand-ins, tend to be depreciated for their relative youth—as the "boy" and "young fellows" above. In one vivid dream, a young boy knocks a crew of grown men "cold" by "kicking off their knee caps." While "half-scared," Al gets mad, grabs him, and is trying to kill him when awakened.

In sum, these few examples show how the current situation of impending surgery is perceived in terms of the structure of existing memory systems. The activation of these systems via the feedback of affective arousal leads to dreams which integrate the perceived input within the framework of old solutions, typically in a symbolized, creative fashion.

There are some suggestions in the literature (Trosman, et al., 1960; Rechtschaffen, Vogel, and Shaikun, 1963) and our own recent work (Breger, Hunter, and Lane, in press) that integration of information in dreams proceeds sequentially through the night. Whether this is always the case and exactly how the process operates remains open to investigation.

The hypothesis that dreams serve an integrative function seems a plausible one. It can be seen as an analog to the hypothetical function served by REM sleep during early development. It is consistent with the evidence from studies of dream deprivation, though by no means unequivocally confirmed by this evidence. According to this hypothesis, one would assume that on any given night an individual goes to sleep with certain memory systems in a state of readiness due to emotional arousal at some point preceding sleep. A representation of such aroused information that is part way between waking and dreaming may occur during the hypnogogic period that typically occurs during sleep onset. The dreams themselves represent transformations of stored information related to the arousal area and under the guidance of various programs, including those of a primary process nature. These transformations serve to integrate the aroused material into the solutions that are made available by the more variable operations of the systems during the dream state. Such integration might serve a variety of functions. It is possible that, like catharsis, mourning, and other such processes, dream integration actually allows one to awake psychologically "refreshed" in the morning.

The question may be raised as to whether integration of aroused material in dreams has any effects on the state of the dreamer the following day. If, for example, several symbolically satisfying and anxiety free solutions to an anxiety arousing experience are achieved during the course of a night's dreams, would the dreamer awake feeling less anxious than when such solutions are not achieved? Recall that the discussion centers on dreams *per se* and not on recalled dreams that are worked over during the waking state. Most dreams are not recalled (apart from such special conditions as the dream laboratory) or, if recalled in the morning, they are rapidly lost and or modified. Thus, such an adaptive function would entail some sort of unconscious mediation between the dream and waking life, something that can be assumed but which remains to be validated.

This last difficulty can be illustrated by consideration of the notion from ego psychology of "regression in the service of the ego" (Shafer, 1958). Psychoanalytic theorists, such as Kris and Shafer, who posit an adaptive function for regressive processes, at the same time stress the necessity for subsequent control of the material by the reality oriented ego. One would assume that the sort of integrative function being hypothesized for dreams would, in the view of these writers, require recall and some directed effort during the waking state. That is, the material made available by the dream would have to be worked over and integrated into the conscious, reality oriented aspects of the individual's life. This emphasis on the necessity for conscious, reality oriented control is consistent with the general depreciation of unconscious, primary process, infantile processes in psychoanalytic theory. Such depreciation stems, in part, from the fact that much of psychoanalytic theory derives from work with neurotic patients in which these processes are intimately implicated in pathology. But this may represent an overevaluation of conscious, reality oriented functioning. Rather, there is probably much more adaptive, fantasy-like, primary process activity in a whole variety of normal activities. Such processes may even be essential to a number of creative efforts.

Thus, while dreams may be utilized—as in regression in the service of the ego—to facilitate some direct adaptation to the environment, the possibility remains that even as private unrecalled events they may serve the important function of integrating aroused information into existing structures. This points back to the developmental and evolutionary functions of the REM state discussed at the beginning of this paper. The integrative function of dreams represents a much developed form of these early processes and ties the psychological function of dreams to its developmental and evolutionary predecessors.

REFERENCES

Amacher, M. P. Freud's neurological education and its influence on psychoanalytic theory. *Psychological Issues*, 1965, *4*, No. 4 (Monograph No. 16).

Bernfeld, S. Freud's earliest theories and the school of Helmholtz. *Psychoanalytic Quarterly*, 1944, *13*, 341–62.

Breger, L., Hunter, I., and Lane, R. W. Dreams under stress. *Psychological Issues*, in press.

Cartwright, Rosalind D. Dream and drug-induced fantasy behavior. *Archives of General Psychiatry*, 1966, *15*, 7–15.

Cartwright, Rosalind D. Dreams as compared to other forms of fantasy. Paper read at symposium on "Dream Psychology and the New Biology of Dreaming," Cincinnati, 1967.

Cartwright, Rosalind D., and Monroe, L. J. Individual differences in response to REM deprivation. *Archives of General Psychiatry*, 1967, *16*, 297–303.

Cartwright, Rosalind D., and Monroe, L. J. The relation of dreaming and REM sleep: the effects of REM deprivation under two conditions. Unpublished manuscript.

Collins, G., Davison, L. A., and Breger, L. The function of dreams in adaptation to threat: a preliminary study. Paper read at meetings of the Association for the Psychophysiological Study of Sleep, Santa Monica, 1967.

Colby, K. M. *Energy and structure in psychoanalytic theory.* New York: The Ronald Press Co., 1955.

Colby, K. M. Computer simulation of neurotic processes. In R. W. Stacey and B. Waxman (eds.), *Computers in biomedical research.* Vol. I. New York: Academic Press, Inc., 1965, 491–503.

Dement, W. C. The effect of dream deprivation. *Science*, 1960, *131*, 1705–7.

Dement, W. C. An essay on dreams: the role of physiology in understanding their nature. In *New directions in psychology II.* New York: Holt, Rinehart & Winston, Inc., 1965, 137–257.

Dement, W. C., and Wolpert, E. A. The relation of eye movements, body motility, and external stimuli to dream content. *Journal of Experimental Psychology*, 1958, *55*, 543–53.

Dewan, E. Sleep as a programming process and REM as a coding procedure. Paper read at meetings of the Association for the Psychophysiological Study of Sleep, Santa Monica, 1967.

Fisher, C., and Dement, W. Studies on the psychopathology of sleep and dreams. *American Journal of Psychiatry*, 1963, *119*, 1160–68.

Fiss, H. The need to complete one's dreams. In J. Fisher and L. Breger (eds.), *The meaning of dreams: recent insights from the laboratory.* California Mental Health Symposium, No. 3, 1969, 38–63.

Flavell, J. H. *The developmental psychology of Jean Piaget.* Princeton: D. Van Nostrand Co., Inc., 1963.

Foulkes, D., and Rechtschaffen, A. Presleep determinants of dream content: effects of two films. *Perceptual and Motor Skills,* 1964, *19,* 983–1005.

Foulkes, D., and Vogel, G. Mental activity at sleep onset. *Journal of Abnormal Psychology,* 1965, *70,* 231–43.

French, T. M. *The integration of behavior.* Chicago: University of Chicago Press, 1952.

French, T. M., and Fromm, Erika. *Dream interpretation.* New York: Basic Books, Inc., 1964.

Freud, S. The project for a scientific psychology. In M. Bonaparte, A. Freud, and E. Kris (eds.), *The origins of psychoanalysis: letters to Wilhelm Fliess, drafts and notes, 1887–1902.* New York: Basic Books, Inc., 1954, 352–445.

Freud, S. *The interpretation of dreams.* New York: Basic Books, Inc., 1955. (First printed in 1900.)

Freud, S. *The ego and the id.* Vol. XIX. (Standard ed.) London: The Hogarth Press Ltd., 1961. (First printed in 1923.)

Grinker, R. R., and Spiegel, J. P. *Men under stress.* Philadelphia: Blakiston, 1945.

Gulevich, G., Dement, W., and Johnson, Laverne. Psychiatric and EEG observations on a case of prolonged (264 hours) wakefulness, *Archives of General Psychiatry,* 1966, *15,* 29–35.

Gulevich, G. D., Dement, W. C., and Zarcone, V. P. All night sleep recordings in chronic schizophrenics in remission. *Comprehensive Psychiatry,* 1967, *8,* 141–49.

Harlow, H. F. The formation of learning sets. *Psychological Review,* 1949, *56,* 51–65.

Hess, E. H. Ethology: an approach toward the complete analysis of behavior. In *New directions in psychology.* New York: Holt, Rinehart & Winston, Inc., 1962, 157–266.

Holt, R. R. A review of some of Freud's biological assumptions and their influence on his theories. In N. S. Greenfield and W. C. Lewis (eds.), *Psychoanalysis and current biological thought.* Madison: University of Wisconsin Press, 1965, 93–124.

Holt, R. R. Beyond vitalism and mechanism: Freud's concept of psychic energy. In B. Wolman (ed.), *Historical roots of contemporary psychology.* New York: Harper and Row, Publishers, 1966.

Holt, R. R. The development of primary process, a structural view. In R. R. Holt (ed.), Motives and thought, psychoanalytic essays in memory of David Rapaport. *Psychological Issues,* 1967, *5,* No. 2–3, (Monograph No. 18–19), 345–83.

Klein, G. S. Peremptory ideation: structure and force in motivated ideas. In R. R. Holt (ed.), Motives and thought, psychoanalytic essays in memory of

David Rapaport, *Psychological Issues*, 1967, *5*, No. 2–3 (Monograph No. 18–19), 80–130.

Lashley, K. S. In search of the engram. *Symposium of the Society for Experimental Biology*, 1950, *4*, 451–82.

Lazarus, R. S. *Psychological stress and the coping process*. New York: McGraw-Hill Book Co., 1966.

Loevinger, Jane. Three principles for a psychoanalytic psychology. *Journal of Abnormal Psychology*, 1966, *71*, 432–43.

Lorenz, K. Z. *On aggression*. New York: Harcourt, Brace & World, Inc., 1966.

McGaugh, J. L. Facilitation and impairment of memory storage processes. In D. P. Kimble (ed.), *The anatomy of memory*. Palo Alto: Science and Behavior Books, Inc., 1965.

McGinty, D. J. Effects of prolonged isolation and subsequent enrichment on sleep patterns in kittens. Paper read at the meetings of the Association for the Psychophysiological Study of Sleep, Denver, 1968.

Miller, G. A., Galanter, E. H., and Pribram, K. H. *Plans and the structure of behavior*. New York: Holt, Rinehart & Winston, Inc., 1960.

Miller, W. H., Ratliff, F., and Hartline, H. A. How cells receive stimuli. In J. L. McGaugh, N. W. Weinberger, and R. E. Whalen (eds.), *Psychobiology: the biological bases of behavior*. San Francisco: W. H. Freeman, 1967, 201–14.

Pearlman, C., and Greenberg, R. Effect of REM deprivation on retention of avoidance learning in rats. Paper read at meetings of the Association for the Psychophysiological Study of Sleep, Denver, 1968.

Piaget, J. *Play, dreams and imitation in childhood*. New York: W. W. Norton & Co., Inc., 1951.

Pribram, K. H. The neuropsychology of Sigmund Freud. In A. J. Bachrach (ed.), *Experimental foundations of clinical psychology*. New York: Basic Books, Inc., 1962, 442–68.

Rechtschaffen, A., Vogel, G., and Shaikun, G. Interrelatedness of mental activity during sleep, *Archives of General Psychiatry*, 1963, *9*, 536–47.

Roffwarg, H. P., Muzio, J. N., and Dement, W. C. Ontogenetic development of the human sleep-dream cycle. *Science*, 1966, *152*, 604–19.

Schafer, R. Regression in the service of the ego: the relevance of a psychoanalytic concept for personality assessment. In G. Lindzey (ed.), *Assessment of human motives*. New York: Grove Press, 1958, 119–48.

Shapiro, A. Dreaming and the physiology of sleep. A critical review of some empirical data and a proposal for a theoretical model of sleep and dreaming. *Experimental Neurology*, 1967, Supplement 4, 56–81.

Snyder, F. Toward an evolutionary theory of dreaming. *The American Journal of Psychiatry*, 1966, *123*, 121–36

Tinbergen, N. *The study of instinct*. London: Oxford University Press, 1951.

Tomkins, S. S. *Affect, imagery, consciousness*. Vol. I. New York: Springer Publishing Co., Inc., 1962.

Trosman, H., Rechtschaffen, A., Offenkrantz, W., and Wolpert, E. Studies in psychophysiology of dreams: IV Relationship among dreams in sequence, *Archives of General Psychiatry*, 1960, *3*, 602–7.

White, R. W. Ego and reality in psychoanalytic theory, *Psychological Issues*, 1963, *3*, No. 3 (Monograph No. 11).

Zarcone, V., Gulevich, G., Pivik, T., and Dement, W. Partial REM phase deprivation and schizophrenia. *Archives of General Psychiatry*, in press.

Zarcone, V., Pivik, T., Gulevich, G., Azumi, K., and Dement, W. Partial deprivation of the REM state in schizophrenics with active symptomatology. Paper read at meetings of the Association for the Psychophysiological Study of Sleep, Denver, 1968.

7. Piaget's Sensorimotor Theory of Intelligence and General Developmental Psychology

Peter H. Wolff

Piaget's theory of cognitive development has modified the climate of American psychology to such an extent in the past ten years that it would be superfluous to review here his contributions to American scientific psychology. Yet this very impact and the popularization of his writings for English speaking readers have not been without their adverse effects. I am referring to the current view which regards Piaget's theories as synonymous with developmental psychology in general and which thereby obscures the theoretical questions Piaget sought to resolve. Equating Piaget's theory of cognitive development with general developmental psychology, before its applicability to other developing systems has been demonstrated, can be of service neither to the theory itself nor to the advancement of developmental psychology: It results in premature over-generalizations and distortions of concepts which were formulated to answer specific problems; and it encourages neglect of other comprehensive formulations about development, as well as of the phenomena for which those other theories were formulated. If the fate of psychoanalytic theory in the United States can provide us with any lessons, it should caution us that the zealous acceptance of a psychological theory and the subsequent uncritical popularization of its isolated segments will sooner or later pervert the theory's central intent (see Shakow Chapter 3).

   Without any pretense to completeness, I have therefore presumed to bring empirical data together which are incompatible with Piaget's views and to compare his formulations on sensori-motor development with divergent theoretical positions. My motive clearly has been not to render a critique for its own sake or to show how subsequent investigations may have proven that Piaget was wrong on this or that isolated point. I have hoped that a perspective gained in this way would encourage a re-examination of Piaget's major thesis and a more thorough reading of his theoretical works.

Piaget traced the logical thought of adult Western man back to the reflex stage of sensori-motor behavior so as to demonstrate the biological origins of abstract intelligence. In this endeavor, he observed young infants and proposed to show a functional continuity, for example, from the reflex behavior of the neonate to the first mental representations (in the sense of mental images) of permanent objects, physical space, physical causality, and temporal sequence. He selected five basic reflexes as his empirical point of departure—vision (or looking), hearing (or listening), prehension (or grasping), sucking, and crying (or vocalization in general); and he added general limb movements and postural reflexes of the head and trunk without, however, specifying their particular contribution to the ontogeny of sensori-motor intelligence.

Nowhere is it stated that these were assumed to be the only reflexes relevant to sensori-motor development; but from a description of their function and differentiation in the early months, we can infer something of the strategy by which Piaget demonstrated a continuity in development from the reflexes of the neonate to the first mental operations of the eighteen-month-old infant.

The changes in reflex behavior that occur during the first two months, although they are insignificant in magnitude, nevertheless bring into focus theoretical questions that are of direct interest to developmental psychology. How, for example, should one formulate the "transformation" of congenital reflex patterns (reflex schemata) into a first acquired adaptation or *primary circular reaction* of the two-month-old infant? Should one, together with classical neurology, assume that primitive reflexes are inhibited by maturation of the central nervous system and that new behavior patterns emerge in their place through "late maturing" mechanisms? Should one, instead, view the transformation as a physical alteration of form, by trial and error under the law of effect, or as a rearrangement of identical motor units into new temporal sequences through experience and adaptation? In what sense are reflexes and the action patterns derived from them identical, to what extent are they homologous, and to what extent are they simply analogies in form? Piaget proposed that developmental continuities be established by discovering "identities in function" (Piaget, 1936, p. 3); but he did not clarify by what criteria one could establish such identities without assuming that all of development, or at least all of cognitive development, is directed toward one unitary goal of logical-mathematical thought.

To the extent that developmental psychology on the one hand views behavior in terms of developmental sequences, on the other hand seeks to establish the part-whole or means-ends relations of independent totalities, it is committed to a dialectic of opposing views—the *organismic hypothesis* which stresses the self-contained autonomy of any system or any stage in development, regardless of its origins or future; and the *epigenetic conception* which stresses the stepwise differentiation of elements over time, partaking of the past and contributing to the future. These polarities in developmental analysis are not contradictory but alternative ways of regarding the same developmental process wherever it occurs; and although a theory must temporarily relax its holistic point of view when it emphasizes the directiveness in development, it may subsequently turn around on itself to examine the same processes in terms of the opposing tendency.

Piaget has, I believe, stressed the unilinearity and continuity in development and has left questions of individual difference and multiple forms in differentiation to be investigated another time. The goal which for Piaget defines the end point of this unilinear ontogenesis is an equilibration model that can be defined precisely in terms of logic and mathematics. As one of the intermediate goals which marks the end of sensori-motor development, he specified a thought process that paralleled the elaboration of a permanent object, physical space, and so on. When Piaget therefore traced the development of visual or grasping behavior from birth to the second month, he inferred their functional identity from the fact that the activities in question at both levels prolong material contact with an object and extend its permanence beyond the moment of accidental encounter.

For a *general* theory of development, a theory which conceives of multiple directions in developmental differentiation and judges each stage or system in its own terms, the criteria by which Piaget assigns functional identity are neither self-evident nor sufficient. The fact that the action of the eyes or the hands in both cases extend the object's permanence is an insufficient basis, in the broader perspective, for assigning functional identity, when one considers that by such a definition looking and grasping are also identical functions, whereas either the hands or the eyes can act on the object to "preserve" it in various ways which appear to be similar on the surface, but may have a different significance for the organism.

Visual pursuit by the neonate, for example, consists of saccadic movements; by these the infant maintains visual contact with the moving object even though he always focuses on that point where the moving object was just seen (Wolff and White, 1965; Dayton *et al.*, 1964). In contrast, the three-month-old infant pursues by conjugate movements of the eyes which *anticipate* the future position of the object and which are regulated in their smooth sweep by a feedback of visual data from the previous displacement (Fender, 1964). The changes in pursuit from birth to the second month represent a qualitative change in neural organization. What appears to be a gradual improvement of a single function through practice and repetition turns out to be a series of qualitative jumps whose identity of function is not self-evident but becomes more or less apparent only if viewed from the vantage point of object permanence.

The identity in function between the grasp reflex of the neonate and the prehension of a two-month-old infant is less self-evident than that of vision. In both cases, the infant holds the object and thereby extends the object's permanence beyond the momentary encounter. Studies by Twitchell (1965a,b), however, indicate that the palmar reflex of the neonate is not a grasp in the common meaning of that word but a traction response which can be elicited by applying the appropriate traction to the distal muscles of the upper limbs. Mere contact between palm and object does not elicit a grasping movement in the neonate, as it does in the two-month-old infant who grasps an object as soon as it is placed in his palm but who no longer closes his hand in response to traction. Should one infer from this that the primitive reflex is inhibited by progressive encephalization and that the true grasp reflex emerges in its place? Or should one assume that the traction response is converted into a grasp reflex? In part, our answer hinges on the definition of "conversion." More important, however, is the frame of reference within which one looks for continuities in development. The data on grasping are at least open to an interpretation which would state that functional identity of traction response and directed prehensions is not self-evident and that the two behavior patterns have different functions when each is analyzed in the context of its own stage.

The examples I have given may be trivial when viewed from the perspective of general intellectual development, but similar instances are reported for every stage of sensori-motor development. Among these are a number (for example, those related to the acquisition of practical groups of displacement) whose relevance for the ontogenesis of sensorimotor intelligence is more immediate.

Yet if one rejects Piaget's interpretation of an organic continuity of functions, does one then account for the observable changes in the use of the hands and the eyes, for example by assuming the spontaneous emergence of ready-made adaptive patterns? Piaget postulates that any developmental change is always the consequence of three interacting factors—*heredity, experience* (both social-cultural and physical), and *equilibration*. The last of these—equilibration—distinguishes his theoretical formulations most clearly from other developmental theories; it is also the one most often misunderstood, so that Piaget has taken the greatest pains to clarify its implications.

The ubiquitous interaction of maturation and experience has been stated so widely in biology and psychology that its limitations as a general principle are sometimes, perhaps, overlooked. Piaget maintains that any autogenous contribution to development by central nervous system maturation can never be isolated from the continuous flow of experience, be it experience through spontaneous repetition or in response to environmental stimulations. Similarly, he maintains that learning is always the assimilation of selected data by an organism which actively integrates new experiences with structures already at its disposal. "Conditionings which last are those which correspond to a need, and those which are confirmed. What is fundamental here is not the association itself but the association into a pattern [1956b, p. 105]." Piaget has answered his critics from learning theory often enough so that the theoretical conflict between assimilation and instrumental conditioning, habit training, and so on, need not be discussed in detail here.

That still leaves, however, the problem which was raised in the previous section about the emergence of late maturing behavior patterns. Investigators in experimental embryology, comparative zoology, and developmental physiology have devised techniques for altering radically, and in some instances eliminating completely, the influence of articulated experience. The results of their experiments constitute circumstantial evidence for the proposition that in selected instances, but by no means in all cases, maturation introduces developmental changes which are independent of experience, as this is usually defined.

It has been shown, for example, that whereas some perceptual functions and sensori-motor abilities will not develop unless the organism is exposed to the proper stimulus nutriment (Nissen et al., 1951; Riesen, 1958) or unless it is permitted to exercise its sensori-motor skills (Held, 1965; Held and Bossom, 1961), other motor functions mature without any opportunities for practice or when the central nervous system is effectively isolated from peripheral stimulation (Carmichael, 1926; Grohmann, 1939; von Holst, 1937). Experiments in which organ systems of non-mammalian species have been disarranged before birth demonstrate dramatically the exact pre-functional organization of the central nervous system in relation to its appropriate peripheral sensory and motor organs. The distortions of behavior resulting from such experimental disarrangements never correct themselves even after long practice and laboratory training (Weiss, 1941a, b; Sperry, 1951).

Controlled experiments on human subjects which would duplicate such animal studies are impossible to perform; but where ethical considerations preclude laboratory experiments, nature provides the relevant clinical instances from which one can infer partial answers.

Where nature has provided clinical experiments on humans that are analogous to the disarrangements of neuro-embryology, the results indicate that corrections for maladaptive behavior are achieved by a compensation through other motor means and a simultaneous suppression of

the disordered behavior but not by any direct modification of the pathological action through exercise (Weiss, 1950; Weiss and Brown, 1941;
Sperry, 1945).

A systematic comparison of behavior patterns in premature and full
term infants offers other opportunities for the experimental separation
of experience and autogenous maturation. Such comparisons have shown,
for example, that some patterns of behavior will appear at a particular
time after conception, regardless of opportunities for experience (Douglass, 1956; Wolff, 1966b), while the time of emergence of other functions
will depend on the exposure to an appropriate extra-uterine environment (Benjamin, 1961). Similar experimental conditions can be achieved
by comparing monozygous with dizygous twins (Freedman, 1965); or by
comparing normal infants to those with congenital sensory defects, (e.g.,
blindness, deafness).

The issue here is not to re-formulate the general laws of pre-formism
or radical behaviorism or to re-state the interaction of heredity and experience in another form. I have tried to indicate that each particular
function and each developmental sequence of the neonate must be
studied separately in order to assess the relative "contributions" of maturation and experience to its evolution. I suggested that certain behavior
patterns may be manifested in mature form at various intervals after
birth according to a maturational timetable, independent of experience,
and that new forms of behavior emerging after birth are not all necessarily derived from the hereditary structures present at birth.

The kind of "pre-formism" suggested here is more extensive than that
by which Piaget identifies hereditary reflex schemata of the neonate; it
is more limited than the *a priorism* which "appears only in the form of
essential structure at the end of the evolution of concepts [Piaget, 1936,
p. 3]."

Just as the reflex structures present in the neonate at birth do not always require the interaction of maturation and experience (in its specific
sense), so there may arise a variety of complex sensori-motor structures
in early development as if by emergent evolution. By confining his in-
ventory of hereditary structures to the reflexes at birth, Piaget may have
excluded the possibility of late maturing species specific sensori-motor
structures, late maturing capacities for more complex behavior, and late
maturing but nevertheless *a priori* anticipation patterns like those suggested by Thorpe (1956), which give to human development its uniquely
human qualities.

In general, it would appear that Piaget favors a formal or "empty"
interpretation of the infant's relation to the environment rather than
an interpretation in terms of species specific organism-*Umwelt* coordinations. He presupposes no inherent coordination between the infant's

perceptual motor organs and certain qualities of environmental stimulation or at least considers them to be of no more than peripheral interest. He rejects formulations which postulate inherent forces or instincts that direct the naïve organism to seek particular objects, since such formulations presuppose a foreknowledge on the part of the instinct of its goals and derivative goals. In place of such forces, Piaget postulates a need to function or *desirability*, which arises whenever the infant encounters a novelty to which he is not adapted. And Piaget analyzes the significance of objects according to their functional properties—that is, in terms of their capacity for arousing interest or need and for supporting the circular repetition of a schemata in the process of formation. The only dimensions of an object that have relevance for the neonate under such a conception are properties which can sustain the reflex circularities referred to earlier.

For the particular range of developmental questions that Piaget investigated, such a universal definition of the human organism's relation to the environment is justified. The concept of object permanence will be acquired by action on all concretely available objects, whether they are glossy or furry, red or green, large or small, provided they can be grasped, sucked, looked at, and so on. The same mental representation of physical space will be abstracted by a systematic displacement of a favorite toy animal as of an unfamiliar blue rattle. Even if some objects lend themselves better to experiments in physical causality (a ball rolling down an inclined plane might, for example, be preferable in this respect to a cube which will not roll), the ball is not essential for the acquisition of a concept of physical causality. The ordinary environment is populated with a sufficiently varied array of things and events so that no specific items are required for sensori-motor development, and different physical environments will not significantly alter the infant's representation of object permanence, abstract space, and causality.

Yet the case for a more nearly pre-formist interpretation of the newborn infant's relation to its environment has been strengthened in recent years by evidence from various directions—directly from precise observations of human infants and indirectly from animal studies and neurophysiological experiments.

The initially enthusiastic applications of ethological data on species specific parent-offspring relations to human behavior has not stood the test of time; it has not been possible to demonstrate anything resembling innate releaser mechanisms, specific action patterns, or imprinting (in its restricted sense) in human infants. While Lorenz (1943), Tinbergen (1951), Thorpe (1961), and others have suggested areas of possible convergence between the behavior of other vertebrates and humans, they have cautioned at the same time against any facile generalization from the study of one species.

Instinctive foreknowledge of the environment (such as hereditary "knowledge" of natural predators) seems not to be characteristic for the human species. Perceptual studies on human neonates suggest, however, that there may be built-in preferences for certain visual designs and that the infant is able to discriminate between geometric patterns at birth (Fantz, 1958, 1965). Neurophysiological investigations on mammals indicate that individual cells in the visual cortex respond selectively to the spatial relation between a stimulus and the receptor field of the retina. Kuffler (1953) has demonstrated that within limits the mammalian retina itself analyzes visual patterns; in other words, it "sees" shapes and responds selectively to them. In another direction, Harlow has shown that hand reared infant monkeys prefer contact with those surrogate mothers which are covered by a rough textured cloth to those which are bare wire constructions, even though the latter are the primary source of food (Harlow and Zimmerman, 1959). Perhaps a vestige of such preferences can be observed in the child's attachment to his favorite blanket or toy animal.[1]

Such evidence makes it reasonable to assume that the human infant is born with a practical foreknowledge of particular qualities of experience and particular rhythms of perception and activity. Some of these predilections will be characteristic for the species; as such they imply that the neonate is directed by heredity to repeat experiences of one quality in preference to others, therefore to achieve more refined differentiation of some action patterns than others. The organism's inherent interest in particular qualities is outside the range of "desirabilities" for functional aliment which are the significant motivation for sensori-motor differentiation. *A priori* coordinations with particular qualities may have little significance for sensori-motor theory since they probably do not figure largely in the elaboration of an autonomous logical intelligence. But for a general theory of development, which views symbolic thought in terms of aesthetic and affective schemata as well as in terms of cognitions, the quality of objects beyond their contribution to the elaboration of object permanence, physical causality, and so forth assumes greater importance.

[1]Wolff's postulation of hereditary preferences for particular patterns and stimulus qualities as well as particular rhythms is congruent with the hypotheses concerning autism presented in Chapter 8. There, it is assumed that the precursors of affective interpersonal bonds are the infant's initial preferences for patterns of stimuli resembling the human face and for tactile-kinesthetic stimulus qualities—including the building up and reduction of excitement—associated with close physical contact with other humans. (Editor)

Speculations about the organism's inherent sensitivity to, and preference for, certain qualities of experience direct our attention also to the more general questions of the organism's inherent motivational ties to its environment and whether it is possible to integrate all motivated behavior under a unitary concept of motivation.

Sensori-motor theory postulates the *need to function* or *desirability* as its exclusive motivation concept. In every particular instance of adaptation, the need to function is defined specifically by the behavior pattern in the process of formation; desirability does not imply a ubiquitous need for activity, competence, or mastery. In one instance, the motive is to suck the thumb again, once the thumb has encountered the mouth by chance; in another case, the motive is to see what the hand holds, once the hand has brought its contents into the visual field by chance. Through repetition, the behavior in question becomes more clearly adapted to the novel circumstance it has encountered, and at the same time the need to repeat the particular action diminishes. Since adaptation to any one novelty immediately exposes the infant to a host of other novelties, each of which in turn creates its own interest or desirability, no end point of activity is ever achieved in actuality. But with respect to a particular behavior, repetition ceases when the action is adapted and integrated into the ensemble of related action patterns. Thus, the infant stops opening and closing his hand for the sake of grasping alone and instead finds new ways of grasping different types of objects, of bringing them to his mouth or before his eyes.

Clinical observation indicates that perfection and stabilization of a behavior pattern does not necessarily interrupt the cycle of repetition. Some children will repeat preferred action patterns endlessly when repetition effects no further adaptive changes and when it serves no apparent "ludic" aim. Thumbsucking is the instance most frequently observed among normal infants; it would seem to be stretching a point to invoke a persistent need to function as the cause for such stereotypic behavior. Similar patterns are observed with much greater frequency and variation in pathological children.

Psychoanalytic theory accounts for these preferred action patterns under the concept of auto-erotism; but the assumption that such behaviors are caused by damned up drive energies is not sufficient to explain, for example, why all blind children at some time engage in stereotypic activities; why brain damaged, feeble-minded, and autistic children show more of such non-adaptive behavior than normal children; why the forms of stereotypy appear to be species specific, whereas their function varies from individual to individual. The most generally satisfactory assumption, which can encompass all special explanations, states that such rhythmical activity (auto-erotisms, blindisms, autisms, and so on) is the organism's response to a deficit of non-specific sensory input or stimulus nutriment and that it represents the organism's effort to establish or re-establish a balance with the environment through tactile, proprioceptive, and kinesthetic self-stimulation. With some important exceptions, it seems to be true that the more isolated an infant or child from its sensory environment, the more intense and frequent its stereotypic behavior will be.[2] The pathological response to loss of contact with the stimulus environment is also observed in adults, although their mode of responding will differ according to their level of developmental differentiation. Sensory isolation experiments are only one special instance of the more general phenomenon which can also be observed under special conditions of isolation as in the Antarctic, in concentration camps, and in institutions designed specifically for systematic "thought reform" (Rapaport, 1958).

The distribution of stereotypic behaviors among children with organic and functional diseases, as well as the bizarre behavior of adults living in aberrant sensory environments, suggests that the human organism has an inherent need for non-specific stimulus nutriment. Such nutriment is of little significance for intellectual adaptations as long as it is present; but even the most secure system of rational thoughts or the most well entrenched social morality seems to require constant concrete reaffirmation to maintain itself as a viable system. Environmental conditions which can induce mystical experiences, the psychotic reactions of apparently normal adults when they are denied a feedback of social and physical stimulations, and the environmental manipulations employed to bring about thought reform suggest that a more or less specific background of stimulations is not only required to maintain the balance of existing thought patterns but that it may also serve to inhibit the emergence of other (regressive) modes of thought which are thereby inhibited from flowering into qualitatively distinct systems of ideas.[3] The need for non-specific stimulation nutriment has no place either in the motivational scheme of sensori-motor theory or in classical psychoanalytic theory (see, however, Rapaport, 1958, for an integration of sensory isolation data with psychoanalytic ego psychology). Yet it seems to be a need which is already present in infancy and which persists throughout adult life.

[2]Wolff suggests here that stereotyped behaviors such as those observed in autistic children are an attempt on the child's part to re-establish a balance with the environment via self-stimulation. This is quite close to the view presented in Chapter 8 that much of the behavior of autistic children may be seen as attempts at supplying for themselves the sensori-motor stimulation that they are not receiving from their parents. (Editor)

[3]It is just such an absence of stimulus input during sleep which I hypothesize, in Chapter 6, as a causal factor in the emergence of more primitive forms of thought during dreaming. (Editor)

The concept of affect as a dimension in development has been implied at several places in the discussion so far. It came up when I discussed the naïve organism's preference for certain qualities of experience; it has come up again in connection with motive power for stereotypic behavior. While Piaget was not primarily concerned with the description of affective behavior, he has on several occasions discussed his view on affectivity, and these views are directly relevant to the question of sensori-motor theory as a general theory of development. It was therefore in keeping with the general purpose of this essay to compare his concept of affect, at least to compare his views on the relation between affects and structural differentiation, with other points of view.

Wherever Piaget defined the concept of affectivity, he spoke in terms that are similar to the following citations:

> I would say that affectivity is the regulation of values, everything which gives a value to the aim, everything which releases interest, effort, etc.; and then I would say that cognitive functions are the total of structural regulations. (Piaget, 1956c, p. 131)

> These ideals or values of every category are only totalities in process of formation, value only being the expression of desirability at all levels. Desirability is the indication of a system in disequilibrium or of an uncompleted totality to whose formation some element is lacking and which tends towards this element in order to realize its equilibrium. (Piaget, 1936, pp. 10–11)

Such a peaceful definition of affects will no doubt come as a surprise to the clinical observer who is accustomed to think of affects in association with the more passionate and peremptory dimensions of behavior— for example, with rage reactions, panic states, depression, and euphoria —and we may assume that Piaget did not intend to account for the quantitative aspect of affects when he equated affectivity with value, desirability, or interest.

Piaget's conception of affectivity is to be contrasted theoretically with formulations that consider affects as primary energies (Prince, 1921), or as quantities of charge attached to ideas (psychoanalysis), and that emphasize the peremptory character of affective behavior. Specifically it must be contrasted with formulations which consider affects to be structure building factors in their own right.

Sensori-motor theory assumes that "an affect is never the cause of a cognition, or the reverse, since both are built up in an indissociative manner (Piaget, 1965a, p. 25). In contrast, psychoanalytic theory speaks of affect as structure building in several senses: It assumes that defense mechanisms are elaborated specifically in response to, and as control structures for, affect discharge (anxiety attacks). It assumes that second-

ary affects may arise in response to, and as defenses against, the awareness of primary affects—as, for example, in the case of the compulsively
over-friendly individual who is nevertheless plagued by incessant aggressive wishes. Finally, the theory assumes that affects contribute significantly to character formation, both the pathological types encountered
in clinical practice (Reich, 1933), and non-pathological forms that distinguish rational adults according to their ways of being in and apper-
ceiving their environment.

In a more global sense, affect may also be considered as a determinant
of behavioral organization in the young infant, even though the evidence for such an assumption is fragmentary. In previous reports, I
have called attention to the *state of the organism* as a critical dimension
in behavior which modulates the infant's spontaneous activity and his
response to a particular environmental circumstance (Wolff, 1959, 1963,
1966a). Piaget refers briefly to the interdependence of state and behavior when he describes the first instances of recognitory assimilation that
occur when the infant is hungry (Piaget, 1936); but physiological causes
of behavior were considered to be of only peripheral interest since their
effect on intelligence was transient or "since the functioning of the
organs . . . engenders through its very existence, a psychic need *sui gen-
eris* . . . whose complexity transcends from the beginning, simpler organic satisfactions" (Piaget, 1936, p. 45).

In the reports referred to, I tried to show that changes in state were
accompanied by changes in the form as well as the quantity of a response to physically identical circumstances, and I proposed that the
significance of a particular event for the infant would change as a function of state. Further, I tried to show that psychological as well as physiological needs might alter the infant's general disposition to respond to
his immediate environment, and that psychological factors which at first
only participate, subsequently become the primary factors for alterations
of state. On the basis of such findings, I tentatively concluded that the
state of the organism must be viewed as one of the dimensions in behavior by which the organism assigns meaning to any encounter with its
environment, and that states which fluctuate rapidly during early infancy crystallize as semi-permanent sub-total organizations, such that one
state is distinguished from another according to the composition of state-
dependent behavior patterns.

In Piaget's terminology, one might say that the various meanings of
a novel event will be assimilated to one of several possible schemata
depending on the infant's affect state at the time of encounter. A paci-
fier, which is "something to suck on" on one occasion, will be something
to spit out in another state, and something to put into the mother's
mouth under still other conditions. What factor in the infant deter-

mines his choice when each of these action patterns is equally well practiced? Consonant with an organismic position one would propose that it is the total context or part-whole relation that will determine the choice. I am suggesting that the context of meaning will co-vary with the state of the organism, so that an affectively determined and more or less stable organization of behavior pattern (the affect state) will determine the infant's choice.[4]

This hypothetical relation of affects to psychological organization has relevance to a theory of cognitive development only if it can be shown that the affect states of the young infant become the semi-permanent dispositions or ways of being in the world which were discussed in terms of character formation above. If appropriate longitudinal studies of infants bring no evidence to support the fiction of qualitatively distinct and semi-permanent sub-total organizations of sensori-motor and thought patterns, "affect states" is no more than a description of the infant's general behavior during a momentary deviation from the optimal conditions for adaptation. But if "affect state" proves to be an adequate description for distinctive and stable form-functional relationships under different conditions in the same individual or between groups of individuals, and if these differences cannot be classified exhaustively by arranging them along a unilinear chronological sequence as earlier and later stages in intellectual development, then the question of affect states also becomes the question of a multiplicity of actual developmental forms.

This last issue brings me back to the initial question—whether the sensori-motor theory of intelligence is to be regarded as a specific theory applicable as an epistemology of logical thought or as a general psychology of comparative development. In various places, Piaget has explicitly stated that his "limited" goal is to formulate a genetic epistemology of logical thought: "I have not the slightest desire to generalize from the case of logic to all the rest of mental life; logic is the only field where equilibrium is fully achieved," (Piaget, 1956a; see also *op. cit.*, pp. 27, 81–82, 106). Although the equilibration factor was probably meant to be a general ordering principle which would define the direction of development wherever it occurs, Piaget did not propose to formulate general developmental laws or to write a comparative psychology of development. Throughout their programmatic studies, Piaget and his associates have assumed that intellectual development proceeds along a unitary path toward a self-regulating system of reversible and structured thought operations, and that that process could be described most precisely according to logical-mathematical models. Consonant with this

[4]The view of affects that Wolff develops here is quite close to that put forth by Klein (1967; also Chapter 5) and by myself in Chapter 6. (Editor)

assumption, the Geneva group locates the various manifestations of cognitive behavior on a chronological continuum and classifies each developmental form as being either closer to or further away from the operational structure of logical thought. Not only the thought patterns of normal infants, children, adolescents, and adults, but also intellectual processes of feeble-minded and senile individuals, psychotics, pre-literate adults, mystics, and artists can be classified in terms of this unitary scale. From a comparative study of feeble-minded children and regressed neurological patients, for example, Inhelder (1961) concluded:

> The imbecile remains fixed at the pre-operational level and is ignorant of the principals of conservation of matter . . . a retarded child attains in the course of his development the possibility of forming an integrated set of operations without, however, acquiring even the slightest notion of formal operation. . . . The senile patient may, again, show an admixture of concrete operations and pre-operational thought patterns, etc.

But the thought of an eighty-year-old patient with Alzheimer's disease, a normal nine-year-old child, a feeble-minded adolescent, and a psychotic adult are surely not the same. Nor would the Geneva group assert that they were except from a particular vantage point, with respect to particular forms of symbolic thought, and under particular conditions of "state."

A general or comparative theory of psychological development is as much concerned with the differences among individuals or groups of individuals as it is with similarities of certain part functions. It investigates the different modes of cognizing the world that are available to any individual, and it is concerned with the form-functional relations that characterize individuals directed toward different final goals (Werner, 1948). Levy-Bruehl calls attention to the fact that in some pre-literate societies an adult male will think in a characteristically mystical mode when he participates in social functions and public rituals, but when he is hunting, building, or trading, his symbolic mode is rational and, in some respects, "operational" (Levy-Bruehl, 1923). Is such intelligence to be characterized by its highest (that is, its most logical) expression alone or also by the individual's capacity to shift from one mode of symbolism to another according to the demands of the circumstance? (See Werner, 1957, for a discussion of the mobility of developmental levels.) The assumption made by many that the perspective of Western scientific thought is the proper vantage point from which to judge other developmental forms because it has made possible the greatest conquests of the physical world is not a valid one for a general psychology of development.

The intellectual development of the artist or the religious mystic who lives in the atmosphere of a modern technological society, but who has refined his symbolic expression in a direction which is contrary to the general ethos, can surely not be analyzed exhaustively by a study of his logical thought operations. Thus Werner writes (1967, pp. 137–38):

But the fact that in our culture physiognomic perception, developmentally, is superseded by logical, realistic and technical conceptualization poses some paradoxical problems such as: What genetic standing has adult aesthetic experience? Is it to be considered a "primitive" experience left behind in a continuous process of logification and allowed to emerge only in sporadic hours of regressive relaxation? Such an inference seems unsound; it probably errs in conceiving of human growth in terms of a simple developmental series rather than as a diversity of individual formations, all conforming to the abstract and general developmental conceptualization. Though physiognomic experience is a primordial manner of perceiving, it grows in certain individuals such as artists, to a level not below but on a par with that of "geometric-technical" perception and logical discourse.

It is when we try to integrate the different levels of symbolic function of one individual, or among groups of individuals, into a unitary theoretical framework that the limitations of sensori-motor theory as a general theory of development become most apparent. These limitations were imposed intentionally, and for a special genetic epistemology of logical thought they are irrelevant. But for a developmental theory that views logical thought as only one among many mature and equally adaptive expressions of the symbolic process, this limitation is a primary consideration.

REFERENCES

Benjamin, J. O. The innate and the experiential in child development. In H. W. Brosin (ed.), *Lectures in experimental psychiatry*. Pittsburgh: University of Pittsburgh Press, 1961, 19–42.

Carmichael, L. The development of behavior in vertebrates experimentally removed from the influences of external stimulations. *Psychological Review*, 1926, *33*, 51–58.

Dayton, G. O., Jones, M. H., Steele, B., and Rose, M. Developmental studies of coordinated eye movements in the human infant. Vol. II. *Archives of Opthalmology*, 1964, *71*, 871–75.

Douglas, J. W. The age at which premature children walk. *Medical Offerings*, 1956, *95*, 33–37.

Fantz, R. L. Pattern vision in young infants. *Psychological Reports*, 1958, *8*, 43–47.

Fantz, R. L. Visual perception from birth as shown by pattern selectivity. *Annals of the New York Academy of Science*, 1965, *118*, 793–814.

Fender, D. H. Control mechanisms of the eye. *Scientific American*, 1964, *211*, 2–11.

Freedman, D. B. Hereditary controls of early social behavior. In B. Foss (ed.), *Determinants of Infant Behavior*. Vol. III. London: Methuen & Co., Ltd., 1965.

Grohmann, J. Modifikation oder Funktionsreifung? *Zeitschrift für Tier-psychologie*, 1939, *2*, 132–44.

Harlow, H., and Zimmerman, R. Affectional responses in the infant monkey. *Science*, 1959, *130*, 421–32.

Held, R. Plasticity in sensory motor systems. *Scientific American*, 1965, *213*, 84–94.

Held, R., and Bossom, J. Neonatal deprivation and adult rearrangement: complementary techniques for analyzing plastic sensory motor coordinations. *Journal of Comparative and Physiological Psychology*, 1961, *54*, 33–37.

Hubel, D. H., and Wiesel, T. M. Receptive fields, binocular interacting and functional architecture in the cat's visual cortex. *Journal of Physiology*, 1962, *160*, 106–54.

Inhelder, B. A contribution of the genetic method of the study of various phenomena in the psychopathology of thinking. Lecture presented at the Center for Cognitive Studies, Harvard University, 1961. Translated by M. P. Nair and F. Bussgang.

Kuffler, S. W. Discharge patterns and functional organization of the mammalian retina. *Journal of Neurophysiology*, 1953, *16*, 37–68.

Levy-Bruehl, L. *Primitive Mentality*. London: George Allen and Unwin Ltd., 1923.

Lorenz, K. Die angeborenen Formen möglicher Erfahrung. *Zeitschrift für Tierpsychologie*, 1943, *5*, 235–409.

Nissen, H. W., Chow, K. L., and Semmes, J. Effects of restricted opportunity for tactual, kinesthetic and manipulative experience on the behavior of a chimpanzee. *American Journal of Psychology*, 1957, *64*, 485–507.

Piaget, J. *The origins of intelligence*. New York: International Universities Press, 1952.

Piaget, J. The general problems of the psychobiological development of the child. In J. M. Tanner and B. Inhelder (eds.), *Discussions on child development*. Vol. IV. New York: International Universities Press, 1956a, *83*, 3–27.

Piaget, J. Equilibration and the development of logical structures. In J. M. Tanner and B. Inhelder (eds.), *Discussions on child development*. Vol. IV. New York: International Universities Press, 1956b, 98–115.

Piaget, J. The definition of stages of development. In J. M. Tanner and B. Inhelder (eds.), *Discussions on child development*. Vol. IV. New York: International Universities Press, 1956c, 116–35.

Prince M. *The unconscious*. New York: The MacMillan Co., 1921.

Rapaport, D. The theory of ego autonomy: a generalization. *Bulletin of the Menninger Clinic*, 1958, *22*, 13–35.

Reich, W. *Character analysis,* 3rd ed. New York: The Noonday Press, 1949.

Riesen, A. H. Plasticity of behavior: psychological series. In H. Harlow and C. Woolsey (eds.), *Biological and biochemical bases of behavior.* Madison: University of Wisconsin Press, 1958, 425–50.

Shakow, D., and Rapaport, D. The influence of Freud on American psychology. *Psychological Issues,* 1964, *4,* No. 1, 243.

Sperry, R. W. The problem of central nervous reorganization after nerve regeneration and muscle transposition: a critical review. *Quarterly Review of Biology,* 1945, *20,* 311–69.

Sperry, R. W. Mechanisms of neural maturation. In S. S. Stevens (ed.), *Handbook of experimental psychology.* New York: John Wiley & Sons, Inc., 1951, 236–80.

Thorpe, W. H. *Learning and instinct in animals.* Cambridge: Harvard University Press, 1956.

Thorpe, W. H. Sensitive periods in the learning of animals and men. In W. H. Thorpe and O. L. Zangwill (eds.), *Current problems in animal behavior.* Cambridge: Harvard University Press, 1961.

Tinbergen, N. *The study of instincts.* Oxford: Oxford University Press, 1951.

Twitchell, T. E. The automatic grasping response of infants. *Neuropsychologia,* 1965, *3,* 247–59.

Twitchell, T. E. Normal motor development. *Journal of American Therapy Association,* 1965b, *45,* 419–23.

von Holst, E. Bausteine zu einer vergleichenden Physiologie der lokomotorischen Reflexe bei Fischen: II Mitteilungen. *Zeitschrift für vergleichende Physiologie,* 1937, *24,* 532–62.

Weiss, P. A. Autonomous versus reflexogenous activity of the central nervous system. *Proceedings,* American Philosophy Society, 1941a, *84,* 53–64.

Weiss, P. A. Further experiments with deplanted and deranged nerve centers in amphibians. *Proceedings,* American Philosophy Society, 1941b, *46,* 14–15.

Weiss, P. A. Nervous system (neurogenesis). In B. H. Willier, P. Weiss, and V. Hamburger (eds.), *Analysis of Development.* Philadelphia: W. B. Saunders Co., 1950.

Weiss, P. A., and Brown, P. F. Electromyographic studies on recoordination of leg movements in poliomyelitis patients with transposed tendons. *Proceedings,* Society for Experimental Biological Medicine, 1941, *48,* 284–87.

Werner, H. *Comparative psychology of mental development.* Chicago: Follett Publishing Co., 1948.

Werner, H. The concept of development from a comparative and organismic point of view. In D. B. Harris (ed.), *The concept of development.* Minneapolis: University of Minnesota Press, 1957, 125–47.

Wolff, P. H. Observations on newborn infants. *Psychosomatic Medicine,* 1959, *21,* 110–18.

Wolff, P. H. The early development of smiling. In B. Foss (ed.), *Determinants of infant behavior,* Vol. II. London: Methuen & Co. Ltd., 1963.

Wolff, P. H. The causes, controls and organization of behavior in the neonate. *Psychological Issues*, 1966, *5*, No. 1, (Monograph No. 17).

Wolff, P. H. The serial organization of sucking in the young infant. *Pediatrics*, 1968, *42*, 943–56.

Wolff, P. H., and White, B. L. Visual pursuit and attention in young infants. *Journal of the American Academy of Child Psychiatry*, 1965, *4*, 473–84.

8. A Theory and Treatment of Autism

Robert W. Zaslow and Louis Breger[1]

Man, more than any other animal, is intimately dependent on the other members of his species. Human beings are intrinsically social—from the newborn infant's complete dependence on his mother to the complex interdependencies of an industrialized society. A psychology relevant to human life must account for the fact of man's distinctive modes of relating to the members of his species.

Autism represents a disturbance in the basic human capacity to relate, a disturbance of early onset and profound degree. The human infant who cannot—or will not—relate to other humans is like an antelope that cannot run, a hairless polar bear or an anti-social bee; he shows disturbance in just that ability most central to his species' survival advantage. The study of the severely disturbed autistic child—seemingly indifferent to other people and maintaining his existence with a rigid control over his own narrow world—may shed light on this most human of all human capacities, the ability to relate to others.

In the present chapter, we wish to present a theoretical explanation of autism along with a treatment method that stems from this theory. Briefly stated, we see the autistic child as locked in a system in which humans are purposefully avoided while mastery of the non-human environment is attempted by a variety of self-initiated and self-maintained actions. The reflexive schemas of early infancy, along with later motor-

[1]The initial theoretical formulation and the description of the rage reduction method were presented in an earlier paper by Zaslow (1967). Both theory and treatment have subsequently been developed by Zaslow and a group of students and co-workers including: Marilyn Menta, Donald T. Saposnek, John Laver, Robert Lampee, Arthur Molho, and John Allan. The second author has contributed primarily to the development and extension of the theory. The critical comments of Peter H. Wolff, Jane Loevinger, and Del Morrison were helpful in the preparation of the final version of the chapter.

action patterns, predominate while effectively positive interpersonal schemas fail to develop due to specific deficiencies in the mother-infant relationship. In place of the affectively positive human relationship that develops in the normal mother-infant pair, the autistic child and his mother develop a "locked system" characterized by negative affective and orienting responses to people on the part of the child. This is most apparent in the "negative motor resistance" which develops during the earliest sensori-motor stages of infancy, for example, the child's refusal to look or smile at the human face in a socially meaningful way. This negative motor resistance shows itself in the autistic child's purposeful avoidance of human contact. For example, he may rely on primitive rage reactions (first seen as crying and protest reactions) or excessive passivity and related body tensional states to maintain his independence from human influence. These negative sensori-motor reactions are the precursors of negativistic perceptual and cognitive styles. This fixation or arrest of development tends to block or distort further socialization which is normally dependent on, and mediated through, the child's positive attachment to people.

The treatment stemming from these considerations—the "rage reduction" method—involves breaking up this locked system in order to reinstate affectively positive human relationships which are essential for socialization and further psychological development. The specific techniques involve physically handling the child to confront and work through his rage and motor resistance, leading to an affectively positive sensori-motor relationship not unlike that between normal mother and infant. This technique attempts to reproduce the mothering act that occurs when the infant is picked up and held because of crying, protest, and stress. Such holding leads to a condition of comfortable coupling centering around smiling and orienting reactions in which stress is transformed into positive affective responsiveness with the smiling response replacing the stress reaction.

In what follows, we will attempt to detail both theory and treatment method, beginning with a brief description of autism. Since autism, in our view, represents a severe disturbance in the child's relationships with people, it may prove helpful to understand how affective attachment develops in the normal mother-infant pair. To this end, a set of hypotheses concerning the development of attachment will be presented. This will be followed by a section in which these ideas are applied to the problem of autism. Next, the rage reduction method will be described along with a review of selected cases and some very exciting results achieved to date. We will conclude with a discussion of other theories and a consideration of the general implications of both theory and treatment method.

THE AUTISTIC SYNDROME

Kanner (1943) first described early infantile autism in a small number of children who showed a coherent clinical pattern. Since that time, a number of other workers have confirmed the picture of autism; see Rimland (1964) for a review. The central features of the syndrome are: (1) lack of positive contact with people beginning at birth or in early infancy, and (2) an apparent need for sameness in the physical environment.

Autistic children are typically healthy and attractive and many of them are described by their parents as having been "good babies." This may refer to their making few demands on the parents. At the same time, they show little or no positive affective response—the social smile fails to develop, and they show no anticipatory response to mother's approach and seem uninterested in the normal play and games of infancy. They usually do not "cuddle" and, in fact, may engage in vigorous movements and screaming to disengage from close human contact. They rarely imitate people and either fail completely to develop speech or make bizarre and idiosyncratic noises. Some develop a parrot-like speech (echolalia) in which they repeat the speech of others in a mechanical fashion.

Autistic children's interest in the non-human world of objects contrasts sharply with their response to people. They may show a good deal of skill with objects and can remain preoccupied with them for long periods of time. Some are very sensitive to small changes in the physical environment, being extremely upset if furniture is moved or if they are made to wear new clothing. Others become attached to particular objects which they repetitively manipulate. Kanner (1943, p. 245) speaks of their "anxiously obsessive desire for the maintenance of sameness."

It is also interesting to note some of the behavior that is not typical of autism. Thumb sucking and other auto-erotic activities are rarely if ever found. They manipulate their own bodies but rarely in a way that suggests enjoyment or pleasure.

The term autism may be used to describe a fairly narrow syndrome most frequently called "infantile autism" by Kanner (1943) and Rimland (1964). In the theory to be presented here, autism will be used in a somewhat broader fashion. In our view, it is a disturbance in affective and social attachment that takes its peculiar form from the early level at which developmental arrest occurs. Other forms of childhood disturbances such as "symbiotic psychosis" (Mahler, 1952) and childhood schizophrenia (Sarvis and Garcia, 1961; Bettelheim, 1967) represent related disorders stemming from arrest or disturbance at later developmental levels. These conditions may be classed together insofar as they all represent a disturbance of social-affective attachment stemming from the same set of factors and insofar as they are amenable to the same form of treatment. Hopefully, an understanding of the relatively rare syndrome of autism will shed light on other disturbances of childhood and perhaps on adult schizophrenia as well.

The theory to be presented requires an understanding of the development of affective and social relationships. With this end in view, we will now consider some ideas regarding the development of attachment and then attempt to show how the disruption of the normal attachment process leads to the specific symptoms of autism.

THE DEVELOPMENT OF HUMAN ATTACHMENT

The human infant, his brain and body, is the product of a lengthy and complex evolution. This evolution has produced a unique organism which is intrinsically active at birth (Wolff, 1966; Landreth, 1967). The earliest activity consists of simple reflex actions—the bases of the earliest sensori-motor schemas of Piaget—yet these are the precursors for specific forms of developing interchange with the environment and particularly the human environment. That is, the initial reflex schemas interact with the earliest experiences to produce schemas, plans, or cognitive maps which function to organize and direct behavior. Frank (1966) describes the infant as a purposive organism, operating in an open system with respect to mother and environment.

The earliest interactions between mother and infant may be thought of as central in establishing interpersonal schemas (see Loevinger, Chap. 4) which guide subsequent interactions with people.

The Primary Bond—Sensorimotor Experience

The bond of affective and social attachment between human infant and mother is initially and essentially developed through sensori-motor interactions, especially tactile-kinesthetic interplay. These interactions involve a range of pleasurable activities as well as those which stimulate the infant, arouse his interest, and control his stress reactions. The interaction of mother and infant around the hunger-feeding situation, so heavily emphasized in psychoanalytic thinking, is but one of the many sensori-motor interchanges and, for reasons that we will spell out shortly, probably not even the most important one. The earliest and most important interaction between mother and infant consists of holding. The human infant is less mature at birth than other primates and, whereas infant monkeys are capable of clinging to their mothers, the human mother must initiate, maintain, and control the holding interaction.

The infant is responsive to stimulation in several sensori-motor modalities including tactile-kinesthetic, auditory, and visual, with the tactile-kinesthetic mode assuming initial importance in the establishment of attachment. His initial security is that which derives from being securely held—first *in utero* (where pressure contact interaction occurs) and subsequently by the mother. Here the interactions consist of muscular pressures and counter pressures and kinesthetic sensations. A lack of secure holding produces stress reactions in the infant, the best example being the infant's reflex when he falls.

The sense of "basic trust" which Erikson (1950) cites as the favorable outcome of this earliest period stems, in our view, from the total sensorimotor experience of the infant in contact with the mother. Basic trust begins primarily in holding and not in oral gratification. Other psychoanalytic writers have expressed similar views, including Balint (1949), Erikson (1950), and Bowlby (1960). Bowlby postulates five species specific behaviors which combine to produce attachment: sucking, crying, clinging, following, and smiling. He emphasizes that clinging and, later, following are more important than sucking. The precursors of autonomy and aggressive assertiveness are seen in the infant's struggling in the mother's arms. Early initiative is seen when the infant initiates and terminates behavioral sequences, as when reflexive body movements effect adjustment reactions from the holding mother. It may be hypothesized that when the mother holds the infant in a sensitive but controlled fashion, reducing excessive activity or stimulating excessive passivity, an equilibrium of adequate but comfortable tension is achieved. The achievement of this equilibrium involves a number of response systems in both infant and mother including orienting reactions, total bodily movements, and the like. Hence, the traditional psychoanalytic focus on orality, on the importance of one zone of the body, is too narrow.[2] This does not mean that the pleasure derived from sucking and eating is without importance, only that it is one of many sources of pleasurable interactions that infants engage in. Harlow (1958) has shown that infant monkeys become attached to the mother surrogate who provides tactile-kinesthetic stimulation rather than the one who supplies oral gratification. Halverson (1940) has shown that one-third of a large group of infants between two and twelve months of age respond to stimulation of the body with a total bodily reaction which he sees as equivalent to orgasm in adults.

[2]Klein (Chapter 5) in a closely related issue shows how Freud's concept of infantile sexuality may most reasonably be interpreted as *sensuality* in which the total body surface is involved. We would add that certain sound and rhythmic qualities and visual patterns may also be involved in the infant's experience of pleasure. This again points up the unfortunate overemphasis on the oral zone stemming from the hunger-feeding model.

Stress Reduction in Human Contact

The infant reacts to stressful conditions with a range of reflexive actions. Garrison, Kingston, and Bernard (1967) state:

Generally the first response to distress and violent stimuli is the birth cry which starts the infant breathing. Many months pass in the infant's life before he substitutes other responses for this reaction to discomfort and tension and frustration. He also learns rapidly that crying brings relief through some other person who delivers an amazing array of pleasant sensations. Crying, then, becomes an effective way of gaining warmth, security, soothing motions, cuddling, and tactile stimulation as well as protection and lung exercise.

What is described above is the positive outcome of stress reduction in human contact in which the infant has acquired the purposeful use of crying. Such purposeful use comes about when the stress indicated by the crying response is reduced in the context of sensori-motor interaction between mother and infant. When such stress reduction does not take place in the context of human contact, the infant may internalize the beginning of a very different set of schemas; he begins to learn, in effect, that only non-human stimuli are associated with stress reduction. "Good babies" who do not experience much crying may lack the integrative experience of stress reduction.

The infant in a state of distress is receptive to attachment, but the reduction of stress must occur with some consistency in human contact for the attachment to occur. Some children are overly rigid or passive; others suffer from colic; in others, various physical problems, such as hernia or ear infections, make comfortable holding difficult. Mothers, too, vary in their skill, experience, comfortableness, or anxiety in holding infants, some of whom may be excessively vigorous or difficult to hold. Such holding to the end of the stress reaction is necessary, however, for the basic attachment to occur.

Cultural differences in mother-infant interaction seem to affect the rapidity with which early stress reactions drop out, permitting the development of more flexible sensori-motor interactions. For example, the Uganda infant (Landreth, 1967) receives a great deal of intense tactile-kinesthetic interaction from birth and primitive stress reactions drop out within an average of four days. Uganda infants raised according to European standards do not lose such reactions until approximately two or three months, a figure comparable with that observed in American children.

In autism, a lack of satisfying sensori-motor interaction, in which the infant passes from a startle-like state of arousal and stress to a comfortable state of relaxation in human contact, may lead to a failure in adequate attachment. The autistic child then continues to show an aroused, startle-like reaction to people and holding.

Blauvelt and McKenna (1961) have shown that in the typical infancy holding position the infant is positioned with the head on the mother's shoulder and mother's face close to the infant's head. Her mouth then moves in a line from the infant's cheek to the mouth, stimulating a smiling response. This is usually accompanied by walking, rocking, patting on the back, holding and touching the head, and speaking, singing or humming in a low, rhythmical manner. When the infant has shown rage or strenuous stress reactions for a period of time, he is apt to fall asleep in a very relaxed condition when mother holds him in the above manner. *This stress-to-relaxation cycle may be considered the basic unit of comforting. The greater and more intense the initial stress reactions, the greater the relaxation at the end of the sequence.* An insufficient number of such experiences may lay the foundation for weak or easily disrupted attachment which may, in time, prove a precursor to autism and other disturbances of childhood.

Disturbances in mother-infant attachment may begin in those instances when characteristics of the infant such as "non-cuddliness" (Shaffer and Emerson, 1964b, have shown that infants may be classified as "cuddlers" and "non-cuddlers" prior to specific experience with being held), excessively vigorous stress and rage reactions, or excessive passivity conspire with characteristics of the mother which seemingly make her incapable of handling the infant. In these instances, the relaxation at the end of the stress cycle does not occur in human contact; rather, the mother allows the child to disengage while still in a state of stress. The child then comes to associate contact with mother with bodily tension, discomfort, disengagement, and a non-human set of stimuli with relaxation and a state of comfort. One of the initial conditions for attachment—stress reduction in contact with mother—is not fulfilled, paving the way for an attachment to objects and the non-human environment, the extreme form of which is seen in autism.

The Smile and Attachment to the Human Face

The tactile-kinesthetic, auditory, and rhythmical stimulation stemming from holding and stress reduction in human contact forms the primary basis for positive attachment. The early holding and handling interactions form the basis for the mother-infant bond. From approximately six weeks of age onward, the infant begins to show selective responsiveness to the human face (Spitz, 1946; Franz, 1965; Gray, 1958; and Tomkins, 1962) which assumes increasing importance. As Tomkins stresses, facial expression is the primary means of affective communication between humans. The infant's smile at the human face may thus be considered the second earliest form of social-affective communication between infant and mother. Gray suggests that the smiling response of human infants, first occurring during the period of six weeks to six months of age, is the equivalent of the following response in lower animals so central in the critical period phenomena of imprinting on the mother figure.

While the smile initially appears as an almost reflexive response, it fairly rapidly develops into the meaningful social smile, elicited primarily by the sight of the human face in the context of pleasurable sensori-motor conditions. The social smile then becomes part of an *organized attentiveness* to the human face which is central to the development of social communication and permits a relaxed, flexible use of the facial muscles for speech development. With advancing development, sound stimulation becomes speech with the child's orientation to the face playing a central part in attending to the auditory stimulation necessary in the acquisition of language.

What we are suggesting, in brief, is that the uniquely human *meaningful social-affective attachment* is to the human face and not the breast, with the smile the primary mode of communicating positive affect. Negative affect, as in the child's anger over frustration or loss, is communicated by turning the head and refusing to look at the face (Brackbill, 1958), as well as by facial expressions characteristic of rage and anger. Humans seem to develop special mediating mechanisms that permit the prolonged face and eye contact characteristic of our species. Lower animals do not maintain face and eye contact as humans do. Apes under conditions of sustained face and eye contact typically show a build up of anger which leads to fighting. This is avoided when one of the pair breaks contact in accord with a dominance-submission hierarchy. The mechanisms that permit prolonged face-eye contact in humans are: (1) Infants are oriented cephalic-cephalic when held; (2) the tension of continued staring at the face and eyes is broken by smiling (thereby permitting a range of tensional and facial expressions in addition to the aggressive or avoidance reactions of lower animals) and by speaking (thereby providing auditory stimulation, intellectual-affective interest, and tension reduction through use of the vocal apparatus).

In sum, we are suggesting that sensori-motor interactions between mother and infant are the precursors to later, more complex, interpersonal interactions. This follows Piaget's emphasis on the sensori-motor basis of intelligence. In the present model, the anlage of love, affection, and approach consists of the pattern of pleasurable sensori-motor experiences centering around holding, smiling, and attachment to the mother's face. Early aggression and anger are seen in rage reactions, high intensity crying, and struggling when held.

Disturbance in Early Attachment—The Role of Aggression

There are various ways in which the infant's primary attachment may be disturbed. In some instances, the necessary interactions between mother and infant may be few, leading to weak or easily disrupted attachments. This may come about in different ways, some of which will be considered in the next section. Here we wish to focus on the general factors which are so frequently involved in early disturbances of attachment, factors which centrally involve the child's aggression.

The human capacity for aggression seems as basic as our capacity for love and attachment. Both begin as primitive sensori-motor activity and must be understood as such. That is to say, the response systems involved in aggression are primarily those involving the body, including cries, facial expressions of rage, kicking, and other gross body movements. While undergoing transformation during the course of development, there remains a continuity just as there does with the bodily or physical aspects of love. Unfortunately, fear of the destructive aspects of aggression, cultural de-emphasis or denial of the importance of the body, and other factors have led to a relative neglect of the primary sensori-motor components of human aggressiveness. Seen in this light, aggression has its adaptive aspects. Aggressive sensori-motor actions are those involved in the child's emerging autonomy—in pulling away from mother to try things for himself, in the well known negative stage occurring between one and three years of age, in curiosity and exploration of the environment, and in the many ways in which the world is actively encountered. The adaptive role of aggression in maintaining positive attachment will be discussed shortly.

Infants are human animals like the rest of us. They are endowed with the capacities to approach and avoid, to love and to hate, to form close positive affective ties with other people, and to aggress with the most violent emotions against those same people. Conceiving of infancy as intrinsically devoid of aggression is much like the pre-Freudian view of infancy as a period without sexuality. Both sexuality and aggression are present in infants but in forms consistent with the infant's relatively undeveloped state. Like the denial of sexuality, a denial of aggression may lead to difficulties. Aggression must be recognized and appropriately responded to so that it may develop in socially useful, adaptive directions. It requires socialization and control, but this cannot be accomplished by attempts at suppression nor by behavior that treats the child's aggressive behavior as if it did not exist or is something other than it is. Thus, when the infant displays vigorous aggressive activity while being held—say, during periods of stress—the mother must not allow these inevitably to lead to disengagement. If she does, as may happen with certain autistic children, the child may acquire a kind of premature, aggressive, or negativistic autonomy that interferes with subsequent socialization.

At later points in development, the parents must be able to tolerate the child's aggression, most naturally expressed in face-to-face contact, so that rage and stress may be worked through to positive interchange much like the stress-to-relaxation cycle described earlier. Failure to sustain such contact and to control the child's aggression within reasonable limits may result in a form of aggressive detachment. Such control and contact typically involve physical handling of the aggressive child and it is here that certain of our cultural taboos on touching cause trouble for some parents (and psychotherapists) who seem capable of relating only via intellectual or verbal modes.

Cultural stereotypes regarding the innocence of infancy and childhood lead to a related misunderstanding of crying. Crying tends to be stereotypically seen as due to pain or discomfort, as a signal that the infant requires nurturance and maternal protection. But infants also cry and scream in anger, or sometimes just for exercise. It may be that a confounding of these two forms of crying plays a part in the development of disturbances of attachment. That is, the cultural stereotype of infancy as a period free from aggression may lead certain parents to misperceive the infant's angry crying as a sign of pain or discomfort and to attempt to respond with nurturance. These crying reactions may be diagrammed on a continuum of total sensori-motor intensity.

	Low Intensity	Moderate Intensity	High Intensity
Type of Crying	Weeping, sobbing; tears present		Rage, screaming; tears frequently absent
Required reaction	Empathic, nurturance, protection		Firm control, maintenance of sensori-motor mastery

The unidimensional conception of crying over-emphasizes the low intensity end of the continuum which leads to an inability to adequately handle the reactions at the high intensity end. This, in turn, leads to disturbance in attachment and the difficulties encountered, in extreme form, in autism. What is required is a flexible response on the part of the mother that encompasses both ends of the continuum and leads to a stable midpoint. Failure to accomplish this may leave the child relying too heavily on passive dependency or angry manipulativeness as his primary interpersonal response modes. The rage reduction technique, to be described shortly, attempts to put the child through the entire range of intensity reactions with the goal of achieving a stable midpoint.

The child's development of a healthy balance of positive attachment and aggressive independence is a very complicated process that we will not presume to encompass here. We merely wish to point up the primary role of aggression and its socialization in those early human attachments which are so important for later affective and social development.

Early Separation and Reactions to Loss

Once the basic attachment to the mother has occurred at approximately six months, separation and experiences of loss of the mother or her care have very important disruptive effects on the child, effects which, if not adequately handled, may lead to disturbances in the mother-child affective bond. Bowlby (1960, 1961) and others have shown that after the initial positive bond is formed between mother and infant at about six months, the infant reacts to loss of his mother in three characteristic stages. First, there is "protest"—crying and rage which serve to bring mother back. If this is unsuccessful, a period of "despair" follows, characterized by withdrawal, depression, and decrease in activity. Finally, a stage of "detachment" appears in which the infant is relatively unresponsive to people. The child's anger toward the mother figure seems a central part of this pattern. The anger is expressed openly in the protest phase and indirectly in the detachment phase. For example, Bowlby (1960, p. 24) states, ". . . it is my belief that there is no experience to which a young child can be subjected more prone to elicit intense and violent hatred for the mother figure than that of separation. . . ."

Kaufman and Rosenblum (1967) note very similar reactions in infant monkeys when they are separated from their mothers in an experimental situation. Both Bowlby and Kaufman and Rosenblum point to the biological utility of the infant's reaction to loss. In species such as primates, where the infant's survival is dependent on continuous maternal care, any mechanism which promotes care is likely to be established by natural selection. Thus, the infant's crying and rage in the protest phase bring mother to him if she is able; the lack of activity during the despair phase conserves energy and the anger expressed in both protest and detachment "punishes" mother and makes it less likely that she will leave in the future. Bowlby sees the child's anger as stemming from the frustration caused by loss and as useful in overcoming obstacles and getting needs met—including reunion—as well as serving to discourage the mother figure from abandoning the child in the future. As he puts it (1961, p. 321) "Looked at as a means that in other circumstances aids the recovery of the lost object and the maintenance of union with it, the anger characteristic of mourning can be seen to be biologically useful."[3]

The intense reactions of the despair and detachment phases may, if not properly dealt with, have permanently disrupting effects on the mother-child bond. It is necessary for the mother to actively re-establish contact, which can be done most directly and meaningfully by holding the child and providing the appropriate sensori-motor stimulation. This is exactly what the monkey mothers do in the Kaufman and Rosenblum experiment. The mother must be able to do this in the face of the child's anger at her, whether this anger is expressed by a passive, negativistic detachment or by active protest. The mother must confront the anger, a confrontation which is facilitated when she realizes that the child is angry at her, allow the child to express it (which typically means moving from detachment to active protest), and still maintain contact and control. In a sense, she must communicate to the child that she loves him and will maintain her love in the face of his anger, that the anger will neither destroy her or the child, nor will she allow it to lead to detachment. The essential point is that this communication cannot be meaningully made to the child by verbal means; it is best communicated in the early sensori-motor modalities in which love is comfortable holding, eye contact, and smiling; anger is vigorous body activity and screaming; and control is literal, physical control of the child's body.

Research Evidence Relating to Attachment

Several studies have directly investigated attachment behavior and will be briefly summarized here.

Shaffer and Emerson (1964a) studied 60 infants via interview with their mothers every four weeks from age one to twelve months and again at eighteen months. Specific attachment to mother occurred between six and eight months being preceded by an indiscriminate attachment to people. This is precisely the time when, according to Piaget, object constancy develops, indicating that the infant must have the intellectual ability to conceive of mother as an independent object prior to forming a specific attachment. Shaffer and Emerson found considerable individual variability among the infants as to exact time and forms of

[3]Such a close biological link between aggression and attachment is consistent with the hypothesis advanced by Lorenz (1966) that the evolutionarily determined behavioral patterns involved in intraspecific fighting and "bonding" or attachments of love are closely related. Lorenz argues that this accounts for why those species which form permanent positive attachments, such as greylag geese, wolves, and humans, are also among the most aggressive.

the attachment. The intensity of attachment, which they assessed by the infant's response to separation, was *not* related to various demographic variables *nor* to feeding or toilet training practices *nor* to the amount of time mother spent with the infant. Strength of attachment was related to maternal responsiveness and amount of interaction initiated by the mother.

Ainsworth (1964) studied 28 infants by direct observation and interview with the mothers over the first fifteen months of life. She found that attachment developed in stages from initial contact (as in the grasp reflex) through use of visual and auditory apparatuses, clinging, following, and the like. In general, she confirms Bowlby's views on the presence of species specific behavior patterns related to attachment. Like Shaffer and Emerson, Ainsworth observed wide differences among infants; that is, attachments are mediated by different combinations of patterns, some infants relying more on crying and clinging whereas others smile and follow. She stresses that attachment consists of a complex of behaviors, as does mothering, and that the two interact in specific mother-infant pairs. As in the Shaffer and Emerson study, strength of attachment was not related to variables such as schedule *vs.* demand feeding or multiple *vs.* single caretakers. It was related to mother's involvement, the amount of care she directly gave the infant, and her pleasure in breast feeding. Ainsworth stresses the importance of frequent physical contact and soothing the infant's distress during the first six months of life.

Caldwell (1963) studied a large number of infants at six months and one year in terms of whether they had a mono- or polymatric environment. The infants with a single mother were less irritable, more active, more affective in interacting with mother, and more strongly attached. Interestingly, the mother's personalities were different in the two groups. Those in the monomatric group were more self-confident, more personal than intellectualizing, more stimulating and playful; they interacted more and were more dependent on their infant. Those in the multimatric group were more hostile, dominant, and insecure. The characteristics of the multimatric mothers, in more severe form, are seen in the mothers of autistic children.

Shaffer and Emerson (1964b), in a study of physical contact in the early development of 37 infants, found that they could be divided into cuddlers and non-cuddlers prior to specific experience with contact. The non-cuddlers resist close physical contact, are diverted by objects, and resist visual contact with mother. The restriction of physical activity central to cuddling seems to be extremely frustrating to these infants. They are very motorically active and also do not seem to seek soft toys nor engage in auto-erotic activities. In our clinical observations, we have noted that autistic children seem to prefer non-cuddly toys and rarely, if ever, suck their thumbs, preferring self-initiated motor activity.

Having less contact, the non-cuddler has less intense attachment by twelve months though the difference is not significant by eighteen months. Shaffer and Emerson did not observe autism, rather they describe the normal range of response on the dimension of cuddliness. We are suggesting that autism is likely to occur when infants at the extremely non-cuddly end of the continuum are raised by mothers who find it difficult to interact physically with their child. That is, the innate differences in activity levels and preferences for particular stimulus qualities may be precursors to disturbances in attachment, the extreme form of which is autism.

In sum, the studies reviewed in this section seem to support our general ideas regarding the development of attachment. Several points may be drawn in summary from theory, clinical observation, and research evidence. The concept of mother-child attachment may best be thought of as an active equilibrium, a sensori-motor-affective-cognitive balance between positive attachment, stimulation of passivity, the expression of emerging aggressive autonomy, and control of the child's aggression. These early interchanges are all necessary—the degree and type varying with the particular mother-child pair—for the establishment of the basic human relationship which leads to intrapersonal schemas and the sense of self. Disruptions in development occur when the positive attachment is not achieved and/or when the child's aggressive capacities are not controlled, leading to a premature "autonomy" external to positive human contact. Such autonomy is centrally involved in the mixture of anger and omnipotent grandiosity that plays a central part in psychoses both in children and adults. It is only by a socially directed control of the child's aggression that a meaningful autonomy may emerge, one based on the internalization and socialized use of human affective and symbolic capacities.

The Development of Autism

In this section, we will attempt to show how disruption in the normal development of the mother-infant bond produces the variety of features seen in the autistic child. Autistic children are described as isolated or indifferent to people and as manifesting an apparent need for sameness of environment (Kanner and Eisenberg, 1955; Rimland, 1964). The idea of indifference needs some clarification, since the young child or infant who was completely indifferent would probably perish. Rather, autistic children lack positive affective contact with people; they do not smile at people, nor look them in the face or eyes, nor are they responsive to social requests. They are, however, able to relate to achieve certain of their own desires, as by throwing prolonged temper tantrums which, while not positive contact, are neither indifference. In fact, they may show specific and definite negativism towards significant figures in their environment. Such behavior demonstrates the autistic child's capacity to relate to people *on the child's own terms*, as well as demonstrating the major affective component of his relationship—anger. Thus, we may hypothesize that the child's seeming indifference to people communicates his anger over loss of adequate care. In addition, the pattern of relating that autistic children have developed enables them to receive care in a way which is consistent with their anger.

The need for sameness in the environment, as well as the variety of bizarre actions they engage in—such as standing on the toes, twirling, twiddling of their hands, odd sounds and noises, and attachment to physical objects such as vacuum cleaners, phonographs, or TV sets—are all part of their attempts at self-initiated mastery resulting from blockage in development of the positive affective bond in which mastery of human relationships and the environment proceeds outward from the initially secure mother-infant relationship.

Before considering these features in detail, let us look at how this negative locked system between mother and autistic child may develop.

It is crucial to view autism as resulting from the *interaction* of a particular type of child with a particular mode of parental handling. Previous attempts at explaining the syndrome have tended to emphasize one or the other but have neglected this *interaction*. Keeping in mind the conditions outlined in the previous section as necessary components in normal development, we see autism resulting when characteristics of the child and of the mother conspire to block the development of normal attachment.

What are the characteristics of the child? Essentially, anything that leads to difficulty in holding, handling, and orienting. Some infants are less cuddly than others; others are clearly more active, aggressive, and motorically independent (as in the Shaffer and Emerson 1964b study just reviewed). In other infants, various diseases such as colic or ear infections may lead the infants to cry, stiffen and not mold to the mother's body when held. To these must be added the child's *characteristic* reaction to loss of the mother—protest, despair, detachment, and anger.

What are the characteristics of the parents? Essentially, anything that leads to their not persevering in holding, handling, and establishing a positive affective bond with children who, for reasons cited above, make this difficult.

The personality characteristics of intellectuality and lack of emotional responsiveness are cited by Kanner (1943) as typical of these parents.

Rimland (1964) confirms this picture while Bettelheim (1967) feels that this description is too restrictive and that other personality types are to be found in the parents. Singer and Wynne (1963), in a controlled study of 20 sets of parents of autistic children, describe them as "disaffiliating" themselves from their children in several ways, some by a cynical, almost sadistic outlook on interpersonal relations and emotional closeness, others by a passive or apathetic attitude towards human interactions, still others by a superficial attitude toward human relationships, and finally, those who, like Kanner's original group, maintain an obsessive, intellectualized distance from people. In our experience, we have found variability among the parents—some who clearly fit Kanner's original description, many who manifest other characteristics, such as those found by Singer and Wynne, and still others. Molho (1967), in a comparative study of the parents of autistic and normal children using objective tests, provides some confirmation for this picture. He found the mothers of autistic children to be less affiliative and more psychologically disturbed.

We must stress, however, that whatever the personality of the parents, it has an impact on the infant and young child only as it is involved in the specific ways in which the parent acts with him; and this, in turn, is a function of how easy or difficult the child is to handle.

In addition to the importance of interaction, we must stress the sequential nature of the development of the autistic pattern. Given a child who is difficult to hold and a mother who, for whatever reason, finds it difficult to establish affectively positive sensori-motor interactions, each failure by the mother leads to more difficulty with the child which leads to greater distance, or anxiety, or obsessiveness on the part of the mother—on up the spiral. Thus, as early as the child's first year the mother may find herelf in an interaction in which the child is unresponsive to her approach and displays anger that she does not know how to cope with. Such anger is a normal reaction of the child to loss, as we have seen in the previous discussion.

How does this pattern develop in autism? In some instances, there is an actual period of separation and loss due to factors such as the child's going to the hospital or the mother's absence when having another baby. Such separations produce the typical reactions described above—perhaps in intensified form since the initial affective bond is tenuous between these children and their mothers. That is, the child, on his reunion with his mother, expresses the intense anger or indifference (not looking, passivity, and so on), as well as attempts to seek closeness, typical of this phase. But it is here that the characteristic difficulties of the parents become a block; they are put off by the intense emotion, by the demand for close physical contact and, especially, by the child's anger. Hence, they tend not to provide the close sensori-motor stimulation that the child demands, and the indifference of the child is not overcome but becomes part of an established way of relating.

In other cases, there is no actual loss or separation, but the parents, because of their own difficulties and the characteristics of the children, do not provide the sensori-motor stimulation that the child needs. In a sense, this means loss to the child because his major mode of communication is sensori-motor and because little that is meaningful comes to him from mother in this mode. The child whose mother leaves him crying in his crib because she is too apathetic or cynical or unemotional to pick him up may just as well have lost her.

What we are suggesting is that failure to provide physical handling of the child, soothing human sounds, eye-contact, and establishment and reinforcement of the smiling response all amount to a form of loss of mother to which the child reacts with anger and, later, indifference. This forms the central component on the child's side of the locked system of autism. He develops patterns of behavior in which he tries to do for himself what mother is not doing for him and continues to express his anger, in the form of negativism, toward her. Since the child is at an early sensori-motor stage of development, both his anger and attempts at self-initiated mastery are expressed in developmentally early, sensori-motor terms.

Many of the behavior patterns of the autistic child are similar to the characteristic reflex behaviors that Piaget describes for the normal child in the first three sensori-motor stages. Here, the infant moves from simple grasping, touching, looking, and listening to swinging, rubbing and shaking objects, and intense interest in the sights and sounds elicited by such actions (see Flavell, 1963). The repetitive actions of the autistic child may be seen as a functional arrest of development at these early sensori-motor stages.

The Autistic Syndrome

In the following sub-sections we will consider some of the specific manifestations of autism in relation to the ideas previously presented.

Lack of Crying. While autistic children are sometimes described as good babies by their parents, their "goodness" seems to consist of not crying for attention when left alone. Because of uncomfortable or inadequate sensori-motor experience—with the crying response not being rewarded nor elicited—the autistic child does not develop the functionally useful cry. In this sense, they are like those infants who lose their mother; once the cry is extinguished in the protest phase they are more likely to show indifference. Like a lack of smiling, this represents a disruption at the primary level of mother-infant attachment.

Characteristics of both the child and mother may be involved in this process. Many of the mothers of these children, as the previously cited studies indicate, are uncomfortable with emotional expression, direct anger, and physical contact. Thus, they tend to avoid intense, emotional interactions with their infants. Their failure to make contact then prevents the functionally useful cry from developing. Since crying as vocal human communication is a precursor to babbling and speech, such a failure may be the precursor to the disturbance in language so prominent in autism. Mothers of normal children do not hesitate to handle and interact with their crying infants who may seem to protest; indeed, they may persevere in doing so when the infant appears to be protesting more vigorously. Such mothers are able to maintain contact until the stress associated with crying is transformed into a satisfactory end state of comfortable contact.

Motoric Rigidity. In the child who develops a secure affective bond to his mother, less and less of the world is novel and frightening. He progressively masters it in the context of this relationship. Where the bond is disrupted, as it is in autism, the child turns to self-initiated attempts at mastery. This is related to the heightened state of arousal and to such specific features as the autistic child's body stiffness, rigidity, and toe-walking. These behavioral patterns then become part of the negative reaction to people so that the child keeps himself in a state of more or less perpetual, self-induced arousal which interferes with the assimilation of unwanted stimulation from the outside world. This rigid sensori-motor pattern may lay the basis for the rigid cognitive style of autism.

Place security and attachment to objects. The autistic child's need for sameness of environment, his tremendous sensitivity to small changes in the arrangement of physical objects in his immediate world, and his propensity for intense rage and upset over such changes all attest to his great reliance on place security over person security. Lacking the positive affective bond to mother which forms the secure base from which exploration and eventual mastery of the environment normally proceed, the autistic child has become attached to his immediate and familiar environment and relies on this for security.

The autistic child's attachment to objects such as mechanical appliances is part of the same process. Observation shows that most normal infants and children become attached to certain physical objects such as a blanket, a special doll, or toy. Such objects are typically associated with the infant's experience of stress reduction and pleasant sensations, the objects themselves frequently being selected for their tactile quality. The attachment of Harlow's mother-surrogate reared monkeys to pieces of cloth is another example. In autism, we see an intensification of this process due to the lack of a satisfying human attachment, though the objects are likely to be uncuddly . . . wooden blocks, hairbrushes, and so on. It is as if the attachment to such non-human objects increases in proportion as the positive attachment to mother decreases.

In some cases, a process resembling imprinting seems to occur.[4] Evidence from a variety of studies (Scott, 1962) indicates that there are certain critical periods of development during which species specific bonds are formed. Imprinting is one such critical period phenomenon in which the young animal (geese in Lorenz's classic work) attaches itself to whatever moving object is present during a certain period of its development. While this is normally the mother, in her absence the young animal may imprint on a human or even a mechanical object. The autistic child's attachment to mechanical appliances and other objects may be understood as an analogous phenomenon. Like other young animals, the human infant possesses a readiness to form strong affective attachments. In the normal course of events, the mother, because of her many positive interactions with the infant, becomes the natural object of this attachment. In autism, when this is not the case, the infant may attach to non-human objects which are associated with stress reduction. For example, in one case an autistic child would follow mother and vacuum cleaner around the house and, when distressed, would stand crying outside the closet where the vacuum was stored rather than going to mother for comfort. In some instances, the objects seem to be selected, in part, for their symbolic value. In the case of Joey the Mechanical Boy (Bettelheim, 1967) his initial attachment to electric fans seems tied both to his having a small fan as a toy and to his recurring experience of seeing father leave in propeller driven airplanes. In one of our cases, mother continually carried her infant daughter over her shoulder, leading to an attachment to the hair on the back of mother's head. This then developed into an almost fanatical attachment to hairbrushes. These examples illustrate both the imprinting-like attachments to non-human objects that seem to take the place of the mother-infant attachment as well as their later elaboration by a form of crude symbolism where some object may serve as a symbol of what the child did receive from mother as well as an expression of his anger and turning away for what he did not receive. This use of symbolism indicates that the autistic child is not completely fixed on the sensori-motor level but is capable of certain symbolic attachments. Of course, some of them, such as Joey, have language and fairly complicated delusional systems.

What is central, however, is that the attachment to non-human objects,

---

[4]Wolff, in Chapter 7, discusses the necessary cautions in extending the concept of imprinting from animal studies to human infants. He also reviews some of the evidence favoring such an extension, a review which is consistent with the position outlined here.

like the reliance on place security, is part of the autistic child's attempt to master the world on his own terms, outside of positive human relationships. The attachment to specific objects, such as vacuum cleaners or TV sets, may become quite central to these children. They involve a turning away from mother and are a part of the indifference to her. The child may also imitate such objects, much as the normal child imitates people.

The Locked System and Negativism

So far, we have been focusing on the ways in which autism develops. After a certain point, which may occur as early as one to two years of age, the mother-child relationship becomes more or less locked around the child's negative response systems and the mother's inability to do anything about it. The child has essentially established a way of mastering his own life that excludes positive attachment to people. He maintains a condition of body tension and supplies his own "social" stimulation, as it were, by repetitive movements, twirling, self-directed sounds, and repetitive play with objects such as light switches and water faucets (which are some of the more complex objects in the physical environment). Approach by mother or others is met with motoric negativism; the child pulls away, becomes stiff when held, will not look in the face or eyes, holds his hands over his ears, and, if held long enough, goes into rage. Let us consider some of these reactions in more detail.

Standing on the toes. Stiffening the toes or standing on the toes occurs in the normal startle response. The strong influence of self-induced arousal on the autistic children's style of relating to people may be responsible for their toe standing and walking. In addition, body stiffness or rigidity is an important form of the general negative motor resistance exhibited by these children from infancy on. One autistic child was observed to rise stiffly on her toes whenever her mother entered the room.

Covering the ears. When disturbed or irritated, autistic children will frequently place their hands over their ears, even in the absence of sound. This may stem from several sources. Humming and whispering in the ear are typically associated with the infancy holding position which has become aversive to these children. They show a variety of responses which all serve the purpose of maintaining control over their own bodies. Thus, they resist holding, refuse to look at the human face and, in general orient themselves away from unwanted stimulation. Covering the ears is another aspect of this pattern in which they block out the auditory stimulation that they do not want to hear. As with the other components of their negativistic pattern, covering the ears represents a further attempt at the substitution of self-initiated mastery for the security that they do not receive from the mother-infant relationship.

Self-destructive behavior. Because autistic children do not aggress against others (partly because of their level of emotional fixation and partly because their parents, particularly the mother, do not demonstrate direct aggression), these children have little experience with direct aggression. The history of self-destructive behavior, frequently reported for autistic children, may relate to this. Autistic children frequently hit their faces or heads. It appears that they experience confusion and anger toward the human face which is, normally, the region of maximal socialization. It is possible that their self-destructive acts represent the substitution of themselves as the objects of their own aggression. This would be consistent with the many other ways in which their attempts at mastery turn inward on themselves due to the lack of the normal social and affective bonds.

Lack of social smiling and face contact. The autistic child does not smile at the human face because he has developed aversive motor and negative affective reactions when being held close to the human face. The parents of autistic children do not seem to have endured the infant's stress and rage reactions so as to bring about an acceptance of face-to-face orientation while the infant is held. Frequently, as case histories have shown, the smiling response has not been stimulated by the mother in the typical neonatal-infancy holding position. Autistic children show fleeting reflex-like smiling at objects, a characteristic seen in normal infants.

Case histories reveal that many of the parents are highly verbal and use speech in an intellectualized rather than an affectively communicative sense. This tends to produce an insensitivity to the rate and quality of speech required for adequate mother-infant interaction. The result is a sustained verbal flow that is either mechanical or overwhelming to the child, so that the social interaction and communicative value of speech is reduced. Also, many of these parents are humorless or express humor in a tense manner so that the infant does not receive adequate stimulation for smiling and relaxation.

In sum, the behavior of autistic children is characterized by an extreme form of negativism. The reflex behaviors of early infancy are utilized in their purposive opposition to human control. The height of this negativism is seen in their unwillingness to look at the human face or eyes, except on their own terms and then, only momentarily. Anthony (1958), attempting unsuccessfully to produce a startle response, has demonstrated that these children turn their backs on the sound made by dropping weights. Rubin (1964) describes Jordi, an autistic boy, as walking into a room *backward*. Lovaas (1965) reports on the negativism of these children which he attempts to treat with punishment (slapping and shocking). Morrison, Miller, and Mejia (1968) have demonstrated the negativism of these children in an experimental situation using operant conditioning procedures. Autistic children easily learn the word "no" but rarely say "yes."

Their subtle negativism toward tasks was experimentally demonstrated in an ingenious study by Cowen, Hoddinott, and Wright (1965). When given simple tasks, the autistic children would perform, systematically, any task except the one requested. It was clear that they understood all the tasks, yet avoided giving correct responses even when only the correct responses were "rewarded."

Lastly, the very stiffening of their bodies, their hyperactivity, or their excessive relaxation and limpness, their temper tantrums and rage reactions all indicate negativism, actively or passively. This again illustrates the way their rage and indifference to humans, stemming from the loss represented by the inadequate maternal-infant relationship, has become a core component of the locked system. Along with their essential isolation, it illustrates how they perpetually seek mastery through self-initiated actions in replacement for the missing social bonds. Such attempts at mastery, of course, are extremely limiting, and these children remain locked within these early systems.

Effects on Subsequent Development

Once his life becomes locked within a system of behavior in which early, reflexive sensori-motor schemata predominate, the subsequent psychological and social development of the autistic child is extremely limited. The normal child progresses from the early sensori-motor stages to increasingly complex and varied interchanges with the environment. Central to this process of development is the imitation of other people— primarily mother, father, and siblings—which, from about age one on, includes the acquisition of language, in which imitation plays a central role, and related symbolic processes. The acquisition of language and the symbolic capacity involved in such processes as the attainment of permanent objects and concepts allows the child to break free from the immediate stimulating environment and to apply memory and anticipations of the future in a much more complex fashion.

The autistic child's negativism leads to blocked performance of developmentally advanced, psychological activities. For example, the negativism toward people interferes with the normal imitative responses necessary for speech development. By not looking or attending to the human face, the autistic child is removed from the principle source of visual and auditory information necessary for the acquisition of language and the expression of affect. Thus, although his negativism is effective in preserving his self-initiated mastery, it leads to a profound developmental arrest. In this sense, the autistic child might as well be living in isolation from people, since his negative pattern of response functionally isolates him.

Although it seems fairly clear that the performance of higher symbolic activities is blocked, the question of symbolic capacity and symbolic learning remain open. Many workers feel that the developmental arrest is largely at the level of performance and that if the negativism and resistance can be worked through, a normal symbolic capacity will emerge. Such a view is consistent with the present theory but remains an unconfirmed hypothesis. There is, too, the question of stage specific learning and the possible irreversibility of arrested psychological development. Learning of particular symbolic activities may become increasingly difficult, if not impossible, as time increases beyond their normal developmental stage, until fixated performance becomes, essentially, fixated capacity.

Yarrow (1963) discusses the effects of various types of deprivation on infant attachment. While not specific to autism, the effects cited are consistent with the views presented here. For example, the principle long term effects of deprivation seem to be disturbance in social relatedness and language development while motor and perceptual functioning are much less impaired. In one of the best studies, Provance and Lipton (1962) compared 75 institutionalized with 75 home reared infants and found marked affective impoverishment, passivity, and little or poor attachment behavior in the institutionally reared children. Social and language development were, again, most markedly impaired. Although some of these disturbances seemed reversible when the children were placed in adequate foster homes, there remained impairment in impulse control, abstract thinking, language, and social relationships.

The question of the reversibility of the early disturbances in affect and social attachment seen in autistic as well as other deprived children remains an unanswered one. Using the treatment techniques to be described in the next section, we have observed some striking changes in the autistic pattern. But the long term effects remain to be evaluated.

TREATMENT: THE RAGE REDUCTION METHOD

The treatment techniques to be described have two main features: (1) Transactions between therapist and child are primarily sensori-motor as opposed to verbal and, (2) the negative motor resistance of the autistic child is directly confronted, even induced, in order that the locked system can be broken and an affectively positive relationship established. The initial goal is the establishment of satisfying tactile-kinesthetic, sound, and visual conditions, along with positive affective equilibrium, so that therapist and child form a relationship that resembles that between normal mother and infant. Once this relationship has been established, the affective reactions of love and hate and the behavioral reactions of passivity and aggression can all be expressed and resolved within the confines of this human contact.

After this relationship has been established, further socialization is made possible; it does not occur automatically, but the child, now freed from the locked system, can engage in the social learning, imitation, and language acquisition that have previously been blocked. That is to say, a working therapeutic relationship is established in which both further therapy (as in the working through of verbal and symbolic resistance) and social learning can take place. Just how far the child can progress (that is, the question of the reversibility of the early autistic syndrome) remains open. It probably relates to how early and effectively treatment is initiated as well as to other factors.

Procedure

Treatment ordinarily proceeds in two phases: a diagnostic evaluation and a treatment phase. In the diagnostic phase, the parents are interviewed concerning the history and present difficulties of the child. Particular attention is paid to difficulties in handling during infancy—too stiff, excessive passivity, hyperactive, orienting reactions (especially face and eye contact), general tempo of movement, response to verbal commands, and reaction to physical contact and restraint. The examiner observes the activity and orientation of the child as he moves freely about, including his response patterns with respect to parents, the physical environment, and particular posturing and movement characteristics. He then intervenes and makes contact with the child to determine what happens when free activity is interrupted. He may remove an object the child is holding or attempt to relate face-to-face and especially to make eye contact.

He then attempts a frontal attachment by holding the child's hands while facing him, thus testing the resistance to holding and the degree of rage or avoidance. He may attempt to position the child's head so that the child's face is turned toward his by placing both hands gently on the sides of the face and rotating the head appropriately as well as tilting it for full face and eye contact. The degree of hand pressure on the face is increased as the child's resistance increases to measure the strength of resistance. Lastly, the examiner smiles in an attempt to elicit a smiling response. These tests help to confirm the diagnosis as well as providing guidelines for how treatment may specifically be pursued.

The treatment itself is then begun, typically utilizing a horizontal holding position. The basic holding position begins with the child on the therapist's lap. The head is supported with one arm leaving the

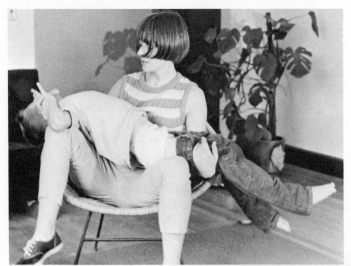

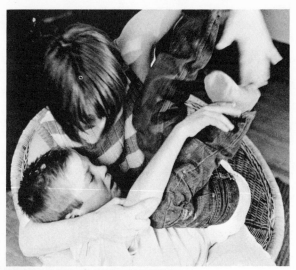

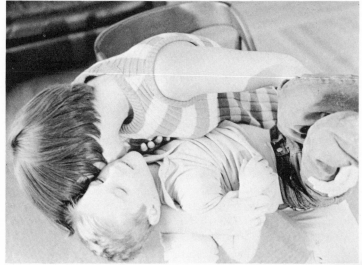

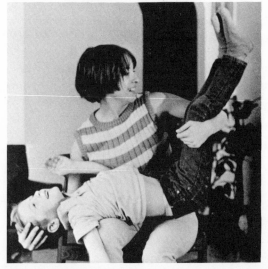

Various aspects of rage-reduction
holding procedures.

hand free to hold the child's hand or arm while the child's other arm is tucked away to the side of the therapist's body. The legs may be held by cradling them in the left arm, with the arm under the child's legs or over the child's legs as desired. The child's shoes should be removed so that the therapist can manipulate the feet or toes as they extend or contract. In the case of the larger child, a team of two therapists may work together, one controlling the upper part of the body and the other the lower. Many children, when held in such a position, will go into rage or demonstrate vigorous body movements to make holding difficult. Some children scream while they struggle. They usually twist their head away from the therapist, arch their back, or extend their feet and toes rigidly in a general stiffening of the body. They rarely attempt to hit the therapist even though they make aversive movements and try to wriggle out of the holding position. With the free hand, the therapist presses against the child's cheek to turn the head up and toward the therapist so that face contact will be established. The therapist gently talks to the child saying, "I love you," "It's all right if you want to be a baby." The therapist endeavors to establish eye contact and may have to push the skin above the child's eyelid upward in order to open the eyes. By maintaining this tension on the eyes, the therapist will eventually open them. The important point is that any sensori-motor resistance is overcome by superior pressure whether it be in the eyes, toes, rigidity of the hand or arm, rigidity of the legs, and even excessive abdominal tension.

If the physical condition of the child permits and if the child's teeth are clenched tightly, the therapist gently but firmly grips the cheeks with thumb and index finger at the point where the teeth meet so that they will eventually be forced open. The therapist must apply sufficient pressure only to open the mouth and maintain it open by pressing the cheeks in slightly. He should relax finger pressure as soon as the child relaxes and be careful to avoid any tissue damage. The therapist must always be aware of relaxing his counter pressure as soon as dominance has been established and resistance removed. In certain instances, the child's tongue may be held in stiff and rigid positions, thus impeding proper speech. This may be overcome by pressing the mouth open and pressing a finger against the tongue, firmly but gently, until the child is aware of a tactile dominance over his tongue. When the child's resistances subside and he becomes comfortable and relaxed in the holding position, he is then told to look at the therapist's eyes. When such contact can be made, the child may then be placed on his feet or in a chair.

At this point, the child is asked again to look at the therapist or to execute a task within his capacity or follow some request that the therapist may feel is necessary. For example, the therapist may request that the child walk toward him and put his arms around the therapist's neck in an embrace. If the child resists, he is returned to the horizontal holding position—usually for a shorter period of time—and is again requested to perform the task. The therapist should not undertake this procedure unless he has sufficient time. For the initial phase of the treatment, sometimes one, two, or even three hours may be required. As the course of treatment continues, the frequency and duration of holding encounters decrease. The task performance is gradually increased in a manner commensurate with the age and developmental level of the child. It is essential that the therapist understand that his task is to act as a socializing agent, mastering, controlling, dominating, and guiding the behavioral reactions of the child. This is necessary because, as our theoretical discussion attempted to make clear, these children suffer from a form of premature autonomy.

The hyperactive and very angry child will induce his own rage when held. However, the passive or inert child may have to be stimulated into rage reactions, for without rage, changes in equilibria and behavioral reactions would not occur. Rage may be induced by tickling or by moving the body or head in somewhat abrupt, jerky movements.[5]

It is important that the therapist not grasp the child too tensely or rigidly because such handling will increase the child's body rigidity. The holding and movements of the therapist must be fluid so that the required amount of tension and relaxation are produced to establish control over the child's motor behavior. The therapist must be motorically sensitive and flexible so as to reduce his muscular pressure in instantaneous response to the child's relaxation to a normal bodily posture and muscular tonus. In some respects, this process is similar to ballet dancing where a partner's body is held with seemingly effortless ease. In this manner, the child's excessive body tension, motoric aversion, or excessive relaxation are countered effectively by the therapist and a more normal motoric interaction is attained.

Much as with psychotherapy, the personality of the therapist is of great importance. He must feel comfortable in the close and prolonged physical contact as well as not be threatened by the expression of anger and love in intense forms. The therapist must be capable of readily shifting between the verbal and tactile-kinesthetic levels, using each sensi-

[5]Two additional modifications have been developed in more recent work, both of which facilitate the rage reactions. The first is a total envelopment procedure in which the therapist encases the child with his body, typically lying above him, pressing on his legs, and maintaining close eye and face contact. The second involves reducing the sensory input to the child by covering his eyes and/or ears, inhibiting vocalization by covering the mouth, and then stimulating the trunk region with random tickles and pokes. The unpredictable nature of the stimulation, together with the deprivation of accustomed patterned input, makes it difficult for the passively resistant child to assimilate the therapist's actions and is effective in breaking up resistance.

tivity as the situation demands. He may have to reinforce verbalization with tactile pressure or use a variety of movements that develop adequate intensity levels in the child. Control in the framework of confident, non-anxious loving produces different rhythms of therapeutic manipulation than does control with underlying hostility or anger. Such control is reflected in the way in which the therapist holds or grips the child. Loving and enjoyment of loving involves sensitive use of handling and hand pressure, ranging from very light touching to very firm gripping depending upon the resistance and feedback from the child's body. The therapist who is unconsciously angry or hostile will reflect his emotional state through his own bodily-hand tension or by inappropriate facial expressions. It is very difficult to conceal or mask hostility or anger that is present in the therapist when he implements the rage reduction method. Consequently, the therapist must be loving, confidently secure of his ability to master and dominate the resistances; he must be able to exhibit a range from sensitive acceptance to firm determination and be sufficiently aware of his own aggression and anger as they may be transmitted through his hands, facial expression, holding, or moving in the interaction system.

By achieving sensori-motor mastery in a manner that replicates the mother-infant holding position, the therapist gradually gains dominance over the child's bodily actions and re-directs behavior toward affectively positive contact between therapist and child. The effect of these procedures is to make the child more responsive to human interactions and socialization. We may hypothesize that the earliest resistances are those which utilize the motoric patterns of infancy, and these represent the basic core of resistance even when present on the verbal level. Anger, rage, negativism, and aggression are fundamentally expressed through the motor system, and the rage reduction technique is directed at this basic core of resistance.

Experience with this technique has shown that the resistance of the child, initially expressed in sensori-motor modes, may later appear in symbolic or cognitive modes. This represents therapeutic progress but indicates also that work remains to be done. That is to say, once the initial locked system of autism is broken up at the sensori-motor level, the child's conflicts and resistances may then be dealt with as they appear in the more usual verbal and play interactions.

A word of caution regarding the techniques just described: They may best be thought of as the sensori-motor counterparts of psychotherapy and, as is true for psychotherapy, they cannot be effected in a mechanical manner. The definition of the child's resistance and the invention of a particular means of dealing with it require therapeutic skill and flexibility. The therapist should view the technique as an attempt to counter the shifting foci of specific resistances embedded in the context of general negativistic purpose. Although it is our hope that this chapter will give a clear picture of the procedures, it should not, in any way, be taken as a rule book for rage reduction therapy. We find that demonstration and supervised participation are required for the acquisition of skill in this therapeutic method.

The rage reduction technique is a corrective for the over-emphasis on nurturance and excessive reliance on verbal and symbolic techniques that characterize much psychotherapy with children. It allows the therapist to deal with the total child including bodily processes, aggression, and his very real destructive capacities. The rage reduction method permits interaction at all developmental levels, including the most regressed. Holding procedures allow the therapist-child interaction to encompass affectively-positive, nurturant loving reactions as well as aggressive-hostile-destructive reactions in a context that is *secure for both child and therapist*. In traditional therapy, there is some real apprehension over the child's aggressive impulses getting out of control. And, insofar as the therapist feels he cannot touch the child or control him, such apprehension has a realistic foundation. By breaking free of the cultural taboo on touching and by recognizing that unsocialized or uncontrolled aggression is a central problem in most psychological disturbances of childhood (and adulthood, too), the rage reduction technique adds a dimension of great significance to therapy.

Finally, the expression of rage in the secure confines of the holding position permits a very important form of reality testing to take place. In a sense, the child experiences his full anger and finds that neither he nor the therapist is destroyed, that the therapist is not manipulated into letting the child have his way, and that a loving relationship is maintained. The rage reduction technique clarifies, in a basic sense, the relationship and actual dependency of the child upon the adult.

In this section, we have focused on the specific treatment of the child leaving aside, at least for the present, the very complex problems involved in working with the parents. We have found that when the parents become involved in the rage reduction therapy, participating during the sessions and carrying the work into the home, the procedures are much more effective. We have also found, as have many others who have worked with such children, that therapeutic progress in the child is frequently a threat to the parents and that they subvert it in various ways.

The rapidity of behavioral change produced in the child by the rage reduction method reveals parental resistances to change in clear form. These resistances may manifest themselves in a variety of ways, including an inability to "understand" what is happening or a refusal or inability to follow through on treatment in the home even when the parents seem convinced that it is producing desirable changes in the child. Some of the parents seem unable to encourage healthy growth and development in their children, a factor which may have been present in the initial development of the disturbance. In others, having a disturbed child may be necessary in maintaining the family structure in the same way that the schizophrenic family member functions to maintain family unity (see Bateson, *et al.* 1956). It is clear that for sustained therapeutic improvement the parents must be dealt with either by some combination of participation in treatment and therapeutic consultation for themselves or by treating the child in a residential setting.

SELECTED CASE REPORTS

The treatment techniques just described have been evolved over the past two years by the first author and his assistants.[6] Rather than attempting any systematic presentation of this experience, which is still evolving, we shall present selected cases which illustrate the theory and show how the techniques are implemented in specific ways.

The Case of "Diane"

Diane was the first child to be extensively treated with the rage reduction method. She had been diagnosed as autistic at a major medical center where treatment, including extensive drug treatment, had been attempted with little success. She would maintain periods of rage with intense screaming for up to six hours. Diane's behavior and case history fit the classic picture of autism as described by Kanner as well as confirming many aspects of the present theory. Her mother was an obese, obsessively talkative woman who had difficulty attending to Diane's needs, especially when they conflicted with her own. During infancy, Diane alternated between periods of passivity when she seemed content (according to mother) to lie in her crib staring at the ceiling and periods of irritable crying and colic when she would spit up her food. Eating disturbance persisted. Mother, who was herself neurotically preoccupied with food, reports that she would shove food into Diane at a rapid rate. She would frequently hold Diane on her shoulder, with Diane facing mother's hair or overlooking her back, while mother cooked large meals. She reports talking incessantly *at* Diane during this period due to her own loneliness. It seems that mother related to Diane in adult terms; picking her up when mother felt lonely, talking *at* her with words, sounds, and rhythms that were incomprehensible to an infant, and failing

---

[6]Marilyn Menta has been the principal therapist with a number of these children and the cases to be reported here are based on her original case summaries.

to establish face and eye contact, social smiling, the functionally useful cry, and other components of the positive mother-infant bond.

For her part, Diane began very early to develop attachments to objects rather than to mother, to turn inward in attempts at self-mastery, and to use angry and negativistic modes with mother and other people in lieu of positive affective interactions. She developed a fetish for hair and then hairbrushes (as if this stemmed from being "imprinted" on the back of mother's head) and one of her few early interests became playing with kitchen utensils. She would follow mother about while she was cleaning the house and crawl on top of the vacuum cleaner. Somewhat later, she would get excited and laugh when mother made sounds resembling the noise of the vacuum. Sometimes, when upset, she would go to the closet where the vacuum was stored, but she never approached her mother. Rage and temper tantrums also developed and were used to get favored objects, such as hairbrushes. Still later, she became very attached to a stiff-legged doll which she held in a particular way—the same way her parents held her (lifting her in the air by the ankles and swinging her with arms and legs stiff as if she were a doll).

The beginnings of positive attachment to mother seemed to be developing at age four to six months. However, when Diane was six months old, mother went into the hospital for a three-month period. When she returned, Diane would not look at her, smile, nor show any positive affection. Mother reports feeling hurt and rejected by her infant, but continued to attend to her physical needs. This illustrates the disruptive effect of loss that is so frequently found in these children. In this case, an actual loss of mother was added to the inadequate sensori-motor and affective care provided by mother. From this period on, attachment to objects and reliance on place security increased as did Diane's temper tantrums. Her behavioral pattern developed along classically autistic lines. She was preoccupied with water, spinning objects, and perfectly aligned blocks. Dressing her was an ordeal with frequent temper tantrums, particularly when new clothes were tried. Her life almost seemed to center around getting and devouring food, and the parents had to tie the refrigerator and hide food in high cupboards, though Diane would forage late at night and find most of it. A brother was born when Diane was one-and-a-half. She showed no jealousy and, in fact, did not relate to him in any way.

At the time treatment was begun, Diane, now four years, eight months old, and her mother were locked into this autistic system. Diane was attending a school for disturbed children but little progress was occurring. She related to no one, spent a good deal of time staring into space, repetitively filling jars of water, making bizarre sounds, or indulging in temper tantrums. Language consisted of about 200 single words—mostly

a

b

the names of food or people—which she uttered only when she wanted
something. For example, she would repeat "cookie" several times when
she wanted one, but if someone asked her to say "cookie," she would
ignore him or say "bye," as if telling them to "get lost." Bizarre noises
were more frequent and she would stimulate herself with these sounds
for hours during the day and when lying in bed at night.

Treatment. The initial goal of treatment was to break up the locked
system of autism and replace Diane's angry, negativistic, overly rigid or
passive sensori-motor modes with more flexible and affectively positive
ones. She was seen three to four times a week for sessions lasting two to
four hours. The first author conducted the initial session with Diane
and, at its conclusion, she approached him and gave a hug on his command. Miss Menta worked intensively with Diane during the following

c

Use of rage-reduction with "Diane." a) Patient displays minor rage in school setting; b) therapist controls and orients for face and eye contact; c) patient is calm, rage controlled; d) patient returns to school task.

d

sessions. Diane's rage was intense for the first month and a rage reduction was necessary at the onset of each visit. At the end of each rage reduction, Diane would reach up and explore the therapist's face with her hands and look directly in the therapist's eyes. Her frustration tolerance increased gradually as the therapist learned to anticipate and prevent her sudden darting movements and to control her running out of the room to the refrigerator or turning the water on full blast. At first, when such acts were bodily prevented, Diane would fall limp on the floor and scream in rage. A rage reduction was given on the spot until she was able to follow the directions of the therapist. Gradually, such behavior could be controlled by the therapist's hand guiding Diane's body in the proper direction, and finally verbal commands could prevent such movements, which were attempted less and less. Frequent bizarre noises interspersed with a few words such as "cookie" and "bye" and "hi" was the typical verbal pattern during the initial two months. She began to respond to simple commands such as "open the door" and "pile the blocks in a stack."

In the following two months, the length and intensity of Diane's rage was markedly reduced and she enjoyed the physical contact when not in rage and would smile and laugh when tossed in the air, swung around, or tickled. She began to show awareness of the therapist and became increasingly attached. She would frequently approach the therapist for physical play and would cry when the therapist left the room. She began to imitate the therapist's words and gestures, and eye contact was far more frequent as her glassy stares into space and darting glances diminished. At this time, the parents reported that Diane began to approach and sit on her mother's lap and say "whee," an expression meaning "let's play." For the first time, she spoke to her brother and played with him. When given a baby bottle, she drank from it and carried it with her. Her bizarre noises diminished as did her craving for food, and she appeared more relaxed and secure.

In the following two months of treatment, Diane appeared more retarded than autistic. She became very responsive to social situations and made frequent attempts to communicate at home, with other children, and in the therapy situation. Full sentences, such as "I want a candy" were emitted both clearly and spontaneously. Her primitive grunts and screams were being replaced by "no," "go away," and "I don't want to." She was quite willing to sit down with the therapist and put puzzles together, build with blocks, and fingerpaint; she also began to sit down with her brother and mother at home and play simple games with them.

Treatment progressed along these lines until a point a few months later when the resistance of the parents became disruptive. Mother went to work, leaving Diane in the care of others, and the family moved into a small apartment, the cramped quarters increasing the general stress. It became clear, retrospectively, that mother had herself become little involved in the treatment and was not carrying it into the home situation. More important, her own conflicts had not been adequately handled, and they led her to disrupt the therapeutic progress in the same way she had disrupted Diane's development initially. Subsequently. Diane has been admitted into a residential treatment setting where the rage reduction method is being continued and where her progress has been reinstated.

We have gone into some detail in this case to illustrate some of the specific ways in which autism develops from the mother-infant interaction, as well as to show how the rage reduction method can effect significant changes in the child. The following cases will be presented in briefer form chiefly to illustrate some of the specific variations which we believe stem from a common set of causal factors.

The Case of "John"

John was first seen at three years, ten months of age. He had previously been diagnosed as "emotionally disturbed with autistic tendencies." He was extremely active and would show intense rage reactions which his parents could not control. He had minimal eye contact, walked on his toes maintaining a tense, rigid muscular condition, and had contorted facial expressions. He had echolalic speech with little or no affect, and he showed little interest in blocks or toys though he was attached to several stuffed animals.

John was seen two to three times a week for sessions lasting one to two hours. Initially, he would go into rage before physical contact was made and could maintain an intense rage, with primitive arching responses, for as long as two hours. The therapist would maintain control via the holding techniques for as long as necessary until eventually John relaxed in contact. Frequently, he would fall asleep following a session.

As his rage reactions and avoidance of human contact were brought under control in the sessions, he very rapidly began to show increased control in social situations. His echolalic speech was reduced by requiring him to give "yes" and "no" answers to questions. During the second month of treatment, he was required to play with toys following the rage reduction. His ability to concentrate on the tasks increased, and he soon enjoyed and became involved with play objects. He began to prefer parallel play with children rather than solitary activity and, at a birthday party, he interacted, laughed, and played with other children for the first time. After six months of treatment, John entered a normal kindergarten and made an adequate adjustment to the class environment. He is now able to interact with other children, his facial expressions have softened, he smiles frequently, and his previously mechanical speech is more expressive. Treatment sessions have been reduced to once or twice a month.

Three factors seem related to his rapid improvement. First, he was relatively young at the time treatment was initiated; in effect, we were able to work with him before the autistic pattern became too firmly established. Second, both his parents entered into the treatment and were able to carry out rage reductions in the home situation as well as working with the therapist during the treatment sessions. And, finally, John seemed to improve markedly when placed in a peer environment, something that had been missing previously.

The Case of "Elaine"

Elaine represents an interesting variation in which the autistic pattern developed in a very different type of environment, a very large family which itself seemed to play a role in disrupting the normal development of the mother-infant bond.

Elaine is a six-year-old girl, youngest of thirteen children, seven of whom had serious emotional disorders. She came to treatment with the following symptoms: extreme hyperactivity, no speech (she pointed her fingers to communicate her needs), fleeting eye contact, and bizarre hand movements. She would seldom cry and would laugh when spanked. She appeared very alert. She was under medication to reduce hyperactivity, but this had only minimal effect in calming her down. She had just been removed from a normal kindergarten class with the recommendation of placement in a class for severely retarded children. The school psychologist reported her behavior in class as follows: (1) unable to remain seated with other children, (2) running, screaming, and throwing play materials around the room, (3) no response to commands, and (4) no eye contact to teacher or other children. While showing a number of autistic features, Elaine was also more friendly and approachable than is frequently the case.

At the time of treatment, medication was discontinued and she was being seen twice a week at a speech clinic. She was treated three times a week for a period of three months, with both parents cooperating in the rage reduction procedure both in the therapy sessions and two to three times a week at home.

The first five rage reduction sessions consisted of holding her and orienting her face gently but firmly toward the face of the therapist. During the first five minutes, she would laugh heartily while wriggling and squirming but would soon scream and cry and then go into intense primitive arching reactions which lasted up to two hours. During this time, her hyperactivity was reduced markedly at home. During the following sessions, she could look at the therapist's face and smile without going into rage.

Initially, the only sounds she would emit were "BaBa," but during the intensity of rage she would finally say "MaMa" and "DaDa." When the therapist calmed her down, she would again say "BaBa," so the intensity was increased several times in order to maintain a consistent "MaMa" and "DaDa." The therapy consisted of a series of sessions where Elaine was required to respond to a specific command which she resisted, such as described above, and a series of sessions where relating was reciprocal between therapist, mother, and Elaine. Elaine was encouraged to verbalize a request, such as to look at a book, and therapist and mother would request that she follow simple commands or respond verbally to a question within a pleasant context. This would be done both in and out of the holding position.

After two months of treatment, Elaine was again placed in kindergarten. Her school psychologist observed the following improvements: (1) she could sit quietly in a circle while listening to the teacher; (2) she made much better face and eye contact and orientation to the teacher's instructions; (3) she was cooperative in the classroom and in activities, and the teacher had better control over her behavior; (4) she would sing with the class. Her game activities required maintaining position in a group as well as harmonizing with the group's rhythmical activities. The school psychologist felt that Elaine's behavior had improved to the extent that she could remain in the normal kindergarten. Elaine is still cooperating in class, and her speech is continuing to increase and improve with respect to articulation and vocalization. The speech therapist reports considerable progress. Elaine presently initiates "I want up" in functionally appropriate ways. She says "My name is Elaine," "good girl," "hi," "bye," "MaMa," "DaDa," "I have a puppy," "thank you," "please," and so on.

We feel that her remarkable progress has been greatly facilitated by the parents' cooperative attitude in and out of treatment. The kindergarten teacher has also used a modified form of the holding technique which has contributed to progress.

These three cases are illustrative of the problems and successes that have been encountered with the twenty or so autistic/schizophrenic children treated so far with the rage reduction method. They are illustrative of the theory of autism, which is to be expected as the theory was largely developed out of the work with these children. Because they are clinical case studies, they lack control and must be viewed as illustrative examples consistent with the theory.

Controlled evidence is provided in a study carried out by Saposnek (1967) in which a one to two hour rage reduction session was compared with a comparable period of therapist contact on two matched samples of fifteen autistic children. Change on behavioral dimensions such as approach to therapist, eye contact, and so on, were rated before and after by independent judges. The two groups of autistic children did not differ on any of the variables before treatment and the group treated with the one to two hour rage reduction showed significant and positive changes which were not seen in the control group. This study, while limited to a single session, supplies some controlled data on the effects of the rage reduction method to supplement the data from the case reports.

DISCUSSION

Our purpose in this chapter has been to present a theory of attachment, show how this takes a particular course in the development of autism, describe a treatment method based on this theory, and illustrate both theory and method with selected evidence. We have made no attempt to survey other theories of autism or other treatment methods nor do we intend to do so in any systematic fashion. Rather, we will selectively discuss the relationship of the present work to other theories and treatment methods and its extension to other forms of psychological disturbance. Our purpose will be to indicate points of agreement as well as to clarify crucial differences, and to sketch out, in a general way, the broader implications of both theory and treatment.

Theories of Autism

Existing theories of autism range at all points on the continuum from organic to purely psychogenic. Rimland (1964) presents the most extensive organic theory, attempting to explain infantile autism on the basis of reticular system dysfunction. Others who favor an explanation in terms of organic factors are Bender (1947) and Kanner (1943), who speaks of "inborn disturbance." Such explanations suffer on several grounds. First, definite neurological evidence is minimal or non-existent. Rimland reviews the existing evidence relevant to autism which reveals, by his own account, a consistency of parental personality and no indication of organic disturbance and, paradoxically, argues for organic causation. Others who postulate non-specific organic factors seem to believe that a condition which develops as early as autism must be due to some inborn disturbance, a line of reasoning that begs the question. In an earlier paper, Zaslow (1967) presents a more extensive discussion of the evidence relevant to organic and psychological theories. He shows how the evidence—higher percentage of males and first borns, excellent physical condition, social class differences and the like—is consistent with the present theory.

The postulation of non-specific organic factors is frequently an escape from explanation rather than a meaningful approach toward one. As the present theory attempts to show, there are a variety of physical conditions —no doubt including the neurological factors that other writers stress— which may enter into the development of autism. But these are only operative insofar as they disrupt normal attachment. Certainly, non-cuddliness or hyperactivity in infancy is related to the state of the infant's nervous system, as are cuddliness and normal activity levels; but they are only causally implicated in autism when they are met with a certain type of sensori-motor response from the mother figure which leads to a disruption of attachment.

Bettelheim is perhaps the best known exponent of a psychoanalytic theory of autism. In his latest theoretical statement (1967), he attempts to utilize some aspects of Piaget's sensori-motor theory together with Erikson's ideas concerning the development of basic trust in a way that appears to partially overlap with the theory presented here. A full reading of his book, including the descriptions of what is done with the children in treatment, however, reveals that Bettelheim relies much more heavily on the traditional psychoanalytic concepts of orality and anality and that his references to Piaget and sensori-motor functions are peripheral. Thus, while he speaks of sensori-motor interactions between mother and infant, his examples return to the familiar breast-feeding paradigm.

The following quotation shows the congruence of the present theory with Piaget's ideas, as well as Bettelheim's misuse of sensori-motor theory.

Piaget (1950) is convinced that non-egocentric thought can develop only from repeated interpersonal interactions, especially those involving arguments and disagreements in which the child is actually forced, again and again, to take cognizance of the role of the other.

Here again the paradigm of breast feeding may illustrate. [Bettelheim, 1967, p. 458.]

Piaget recognizes the necessity of, in a sense, forcing socialization on the egocentric child. Such socialization occurs between total human beings who are arguing or disagreeing and not between "a breast" and a "mouth" or "oral zone." Bettelheim cites Piaget but misses the point. Bettelheim also has difficulty in conceptualizing the role of anger and aggression in autism—again due to his reliance on traditional psychoanalytic theory. The infant is not seen as fully purposeful, that is, as capable, at a sensori-motor level, of being purposefully angry or negativistic. Our differences with Bettelheim are most strongly reflected in treatment and will be discussed in the next section.

Other writers in the psychoanalytic tradition recognize the inadequacy of traditional psychosexual theory and propose various hypotheses, some of which overlap with the present theory (see Ruttenberg, 1968, for a review of these). These issues may best be clarified by discussing the concept of resistance as it has been employed in the present theory.

Resistance may be thought of as a purposeful attempt to maintain an existing pattern of behavior. Neuroses and psychoses, as well as normal defensive processes, all fit this definition. The individual utilizes a variety of behaviors, fantasies, and interpersonal modes in the service of preserving his self, of defending his ego.[7] Human aggression, when seen as a primary motive force, plays a central role in such resistances. In children, those behaviors used to resist are developmentally early ones and

[7] This is the same view that emerges from Loevinger's discussion of ego theories, that is, defense is essentially an attempt to preserve the consistency of the self or ego.

in autism we see such early motor resistances as refusing to look at the human face and various bodily rigidities (which have their adult counterpart in catatonia). Darwin (1965, originally published 1872) anticipated this concept in his discussion of negation—for example, shaking the head to indicate "no" originates in the child's turning his head to refuse food, an early interpersonal resistance. Tonic neck reflexes and primitive arching responses are still earlier motor patterns used as resistance in autism. Later, the child may use a variety of skills to resist social influence. For example, he may play dumb and either act as if he cannot understand what is being demanded of him or as if he is incapable of correct performance. These are revealed to be resistances during the rage reduction sessions when the child demonstrates his capacities to understand and perform quite clearly. Thus "stupidity" (or minimal brain damage, and so forth) is frequently revealed to be a resistant negativism on the part of the child, indicating the great dangers of employing such diagnostic labels.

Primitive motor resistances pervade conditions such as autism, and sensori-motor resistance, is, generally, the basis for later cognitive or symbolic resistances. As development proceeds, the child acquires symbolic capacities and can then use these for the same purposes. The later symbolic analogues of negativistic resistance are seen in the passivity and withdrawal into fantasy of psychotic patients. Fromm-Reichmann's (1950) remarks on psychotherapy with such patients are particularly illuminating and are consistent with the views developed here if one but transposes from the sensori-motor to the symbolic level.

Related Forms of Treatment

Components of the rage reduction method may be found in a variety of theories both old and new. Witmer, in 1919, described the treatment of what appears to be an autistic boy. Unencumbered by complex theory, Witmer tells how the child is held while he goes into intense rage, from which he eventually learns that the teacher, not he, is in control. Once this is established, the slow process of learning and socialization get under way.

The education of Helen Keller by Annie Sullivan, portrayed in the play and movie "The Miracle Worker," illustrates both our theory and the rage reduction method. Helen loses her sight and hearing in infancy and reacts to the loss of sensori-input much as the children who become autistic do. Prior to the work with Miss Sullivan, she is depicted as a wild and uncontrollable creature who only relates to people on her own terms and whose temper tantrums cannot be handled. Miss Sullivan's attempts to work with her meet with angry resistance from Helen and it is only by literally fighting it out and emerging the victor that Miss Sullivan is able to establish the relationship from which the miraculous education proceeds. In other words, she reduces Helen's rage, in human content, establishes the missing positive affective attachment, and reopens socialization and learning.

Both Witmer and Annie Sullivan were perhaps aided in their work by not having a complex theory which misled them; they could see a temper tantrum for what it was and control it in an appropriate way. Yet their methods were not generalized or carried on by others, indicating the need for an adequate theory which explains why treatment works and provides ideas to guide its generalization and development.

Bettelheim is an example at the other extreme; he has too much of the wrong kind of theory and the treatment seems, at least to us, to be more stifled than guided by it. Thus, his emphasis on the importance of oral gratification and the relative neglect of early aggression leads to an over-nurturant treatment approach in which the therapist patiently waits— sometimes for years—while the child gradually moves from psychotic non-relating to a positive relationship. This seems a general problem when psychoanalytic techniques, developed for work with motivated adults, are applied to children, particularly severely disturbed children.

Des Lauriers (1962), who also starts from a psychoanalytic position, develops a much different approach, one which converges in many ways with the rage reduction method. He sees the central problem in child-hood schizophrenia and psychosis as the break with reality. The principle task of the therapist is to re-establish contact with reality. Des Lauriers emphasizes the role of the body, the physical language of schizophrenia that must be responded to in physical terms. He speaks of the therapist intruding himself on the schizophrenic, of the need for structure and limits, and of its being a therapeutic error to accept the patient's delu-sional or autistic behavior. In each of these respects, his approach is congruent with ours and divergent with Bettelheim's.

We can mention only briefly the variety of other therapeutic methods which relate in one way or another to rage reduction. The importance of sensori-motor modes and of working with the body is stressed by Schopler (1962). He focuses on the role of sensori-motor interaction in the development of body image but fails, in our view, to deal adequately with resistance and anger. Luria (1966) and workers in the Russian tradition have long stressed the role of motor feedback, of the importance of action for perceptual and memory processes. They have also placed great importance on orienting reactions. Both of these emphases relate to the rage reduction method which forces the child to orient to the thera-pist and, via sensori-motor stimulation and manipulation, attempts to reshape cognitive processes. Asher (1966) presents a related view in which he stresses the importance of the total physical response in language learning.

Various treatment approaches with adult schizophrenics, such as those employed by Rosen (1953) or those using physical restraint (packs), may incorporate elements of the rage reduction technique. Rosen forcibly intrudes himself on the patient and clearly demonstrates that he is in control of the situation. The reduction of rage in physical restraint is described in Green's (1964) account in terms consistent with the present view of schizophrenia.

Lovaas (1967) has done the most work with autistic and schizophrenic children from a reinforcement learning point of view. This work utilizes some degree of physical contact with the children and Lovaas' recent writings indicate some recognition of the inadequacies of reinforcement theory in conceptualizing purposeful behavior.

In summary, there seem to be various methods which overlap with rage reduction in one respect or another. Our feeling is that it is most like psychotherapy of the Fromm-Reichmann (1950) style transposed from the verbal to the sensori-motor modality. While other forms of treatment may appear similar because of their emphasis on the body or sensori-motor interactions, their failure to deal with resistance either conceptually or practically makes them, in fact, quite different.

REFERENCES

Ainsworth, Mary D. Patterns of attachment behavior shown by the infant in interaction with his mother. *Merill-Palmer Quarterly*, 1964, *10*, 51–58.

Anthony, J. An experimental approach to the psychopathology of childhood: autism. *British Journal of Medical Psychology*, 1958, *31*, 211–25.

Asher, J. J. The learning strategy of the total physical response. *Modern Language Journal*, 1966, *50*, 79–84.

Balint, M. Early developmental states of the ego, primary object love. *International Journal of Psychoanalysis*, 1949, *30*, 265–73.

Bateson, G., Jackson, D. D., Haley, J., and Weakland, J. Towards a theory of schizophrenia. *Behavioral Science*, 1956, *1*, 251–64.

Bender, L. Childhood schizophrenia. *American Journal of Orthopsychiatry*, 1947, *17*, 68–79.

Bettelheim, B. *The empty fortress: infantile autism and the birth of the self.* New York: The Free Press, 1967.

Blauvelt, H. B., and McKenna, J. Mother-neonate interaction: capacity of the human newborn for orientation. In B. M. Foss (ed.), *Determinants of infant behavior.* New York: John Wiley & Sons, Inc., 1961, 3–35.

Bowlby, J. Separation anxiety. *International Journal of Psychoanalysis*, 1960, *41*, 89–113.

Bowlby, J. Processes of mourning. *International Journal of Psychoanalysis*, 1961, *42*, 317–34.

Brackbill, Yvonne. Extinction of the smiling response in infants as a function of reinforcement schedule. *Child Development*, 1958, *129*, 115–24.

Caldwell, B. Mother-infant interaction in monomatric and polymatric families. *American Journal of Orthopsychiatry*, 1963, *33*, 653–64.

Cowan, P. A., Hoddinott, B. A., and Wright, B. A. Compliance and resistance in the conditioning of autistic children: an exploratory study. *Child Development*, 1965, *36*, 382–90.

Darwin, C. *The expression of the emotions in man and animals.* Chicago: Phoenix Books, 1965. (First printed in 1872.)

Des Lauriers, A. M. *The experience of reality in childhood schizophrenia.* New York: International Universities Press, 1962.

Erikson, E. H. *Childhood and Society.* New York: W. W. Norton & Co., Inc., 1950.

Fantz, R. L. Visual perception from birth as shown by pattern selectivity. *Annals of the New York Academy of Sciences*, 1965, 793–814.

Flavell, J. *The developmental psychology of Jean Piaget.* Princeton: D. Van Nostrand Co., Inc., 1963.

Frank, L. K. *On the importance of infancy.* New York: Random House, Inc., 1966.

Fromm-Reichmann, Frieda. *Principles of intensive psychotherapy.* Chicago: Phoenix Books, 1950.

Garrison, K. C., Kingston, A. J., and Bernard, H. W. *The psychology of childhood.* New York: Charles Scribner's Sons, 1967.

Gray, P. H. Theory and evidence of imprinting in human infants. *Journal of Psychology*, 1958, *46*, 155–66.

Green, Hannah. *I never promised you a rose garden.* New York: Signet Books, 1964.

Halverson, H. M. Genital and sphincter behavior of male infants. *Journal of Genetic Psychology*, 1940, *56*, 95–136.

Harlow, H. F. The nature of love. *American Psychologist*, 1958, *12*, 673–85.

Kanner, L. Autistic disturbance of affective contact. *Nervous Child*, 1943, *2*, 217–50.

Kaufman, I. C., and Rosenblum, L. A. Depression in infant monkeys separated from their mothers. *Science*, 1967, *155*, 1030–31.

Landreth, Catherine. *Early childhood.* New York: Alfred A. Knopf, Inc., 1967.

Lorenz, K. Z. *On aggression.* New York: Harcourt, Brace and World, Inc., 1966.

Lovaas, O. I. A behavior therapy approach to the treatment of childhood schizophrenia. Minnesota Symposium on Child Psychology, 1967.

Luria, A. R. *Human brain and psychological processes.* New York: Harper and Row, Publishers, 1966.

Mahler, M. On child psychosis and schizophrenia: autistic and symbiotic psychosis. *Psychoanalytic Study of the Child*, 1952, *7*, 286–305.

Molho, A. I. Personality characteristics of parents of autistic children and parents of non-disturbed children. Unpublished Masters Thesis, San Jose State College, 1967.

Morrison, D., Miller, D., and Mejia, Berta. Compliance and negativism in child-hood autism. Paper presented at Langley Porter Institute, San Francisco, 1968.

Piaget, J. *The psychology of intelligence.* New York: Harcourt, Brace & World, Inc., 1950.

Provence, Sally, and Lipton, Rose C. *Infants in institutions.* New York: International Universities Press, 1962.

Rimland, B. *Infantile autism.* New York: Appleton-Century-Crofts, 1964.

Rosen, N. *Direct analysis: selected papers.* New York: Grune and Stratton, Inc., 1953.

Rubin, T. I. *Jordi.* New York: Ballentine Books, Inc., 1964.

Ruttenberg, B. A. A psychoanalytically based structural and developmental conceptualization of the origins and processes involved in the syndrome of infantile autism: and a consideration of the therapeutic principles inferred from this model. Paper presented at Indiana University Colloquium on Infantile Autism, Indianapolis, 1968.

Saposnek, D. T. An experimental study of rage-reduction treatment in autistic children. Unpublished Masters Thesis, San Jose State College, 1967.

Sarvis, M. S., and Garcia, P. Etiological variables in autism. *Psychiatry,* 1961, *24,* 307–17.

Schopler, E. The development of body image and symbol formation through bodily contact with an autistic child. *Journal of Child Psychology and Psychiatry,* 1962, *3,* 191–202.

Scott, J. P. Critical periods in behavioral development. *Science,* 1962, *138,* 949–58.

Shaffer, H. R., and Emerson, P. E. The development of social attachments in infancy. *Monographs in Social Research in Child Development,* 1964a, *29,* No. 3.

Shaffer, H. R., and Emerson, P. E. Patterns of response to physical contact in early human development. *Journal of Child Psychology and Psychiatry,* 1964b, *5,* 1–13.

Singer, Margaret T., and Wynne, L. Differentiating characteristics of parents of childhood schizophrenics, childhood neurotics, and young adult schizophrenics. *American Journal of Psychiatry,* 1963, *120,* 234–43.

Spitz, R. A. Smiling response in infants. *Genetic Psychology Monographs,* 1946, *34,* 57–125.

Tomkins, S. S. *Affect, imagery, consciousness.* New York: Springer Publishing Co., Inc., 1962.

Witmer, L. Orthogenic cases. Vol. XIV. Don: a curable case of arrested development due to a fear psychosis, the result of shock in a three-year-old infant. *Psychological Clinic,* 1919–1922, *13,* 97–111.

Wolff, P. H. Observations on the early development of smiling. In B. M. Foss (ed.), *Determinants of infant behavior.* New York: John Wiley & Sons, Inc., 1963, 113–34.

Wolff, P. H. The causes, controls and organization of behavior in the neonate. *Psychological Issues*, 1966, 5, No. 1 (Monograph No. 17).

Yarrow, L. J. Separation from parents during early childhood. In Hoffman, M. L., and Hoffman, L. W., *Review of child development research*. New York: Russell Sage Foundation, 1966.

Zaslow, R. W. A psychogenic theory of the etiology of infantile autism and implications for treatment. Paper read at meetings of the California State Psychological Association, San Diego, 1967.

INDEX OF NAMES

Ach, N., 69, 70
Adelson, J., 72, 77
Adler, A., 87, 94, 105, 115, 117, 131
Adorno, T. W., 89, 131
Adrian, E. D. 75, 77
Ainsworth, M. D., 258, 288
Alexander, F., 159, 179
Allan, J., 246
Allport, G., 84, 87, 92, 94, 98, 131
Amacher, M. P., 191, 194, 224
Angell, J. R., 57, 62
Angyal, A., 87, 131
Ansbacher, H. L., 87, 131
Anthony, J., 266, 288
Aristotle, 14, 97
Aserinsky, E., 47
Asher, J. J., 287, 288
Atkinson, J. W., 46, 53
Ausubel, D. P., 89, 99, 116, 117, 127, 131
Azumi, K., 217, 227

Bacon, F., 48
Baer, D. M., 49, 53
Bakan, D., 68, 69, 77
Baldwin, J. M., 89, 97, 100, 101, 103, 104, 106, 128, 131
Balint, M., 250, 288
Bandura, A., 41, 53
Bateson, G., 276, 288
Beach, F. A., 149, 180
Bender, L., 284, 288
Benjamin, J. O., 233, 242
Bentham, J., 83, 128, 134
Berkowitz, L., 41, 53
Bernard, C., 17, 71
Bernard, H. W., 251, 289
Bernfeld, S., 191, 224
Bernfield, S., 75, 77

Bernheim, H., 57
Bernoilli, 51
Bettelheim, B., 248, 261, 264, 285, 287, 288
Bijou, S. W., 49, 53
Bitterman, M. E., 41, 53
Black, M., 17
Blasi, A., 83
Blauvelt, H. B., 252, 288
Bohr, N., 26
Boring, E. G., 18, 24, 28, 36, 53, 66, 69, 75
Bossom, J., 232, 243
Bowlby, J., 250, 256, 258, 288
Brackbill, Y., 253, 289
Breger, L., 23, 25–55, 83, 182–227, 246–91
Brentano, F., 70
Breuer, J., 57
Bridgeman, P., 17, 35, 53
Bronowski, J., 2, 35, 48, 50, 53
Brown, P. F., 233, 244
Brücke, E., 57, 63, 64, 191, 194
Bruner, J. S., 3, 43, 49, 53, 144, 180
Buber, M., 136, 153, 180
Bühler, K., 69
Burtt, E. A., 18, 24
Butterfield, A., 18, 24

Caldwell, B., 258, 288
Carmichael, L., 232, 242
Carpenter, 57
Cartwright, R. D., 183, 216, 224
Cattell, R. B., 49, 53
Charcot, J. M., 57
Chein, I., 87, 98, 131
Chomsky, N., 3, 33, 36, 53
Chow, K. L., 243
Claparede, E., 70
Colby, K. M., 182, 196, 200, 224
Collins, G., 209, 216, 225

Columbus, C., 75
Conant, J., 35, 50, 53
Copernicus, N., 27
Cowen, P. A., 267, 289
Crane, S., 67
Cranefield, P. F., 60, 66, 77

Darwin, C., 28, 29, 62, 63, 75, 84, 286, 289
Davison, L. A., 25, 182, 209, 216, 224
Dayton, G. O., 230, 242
Debs, E. V., 67
Dell, F., 67
Dember, W. N., 117, 118, 131
Dement, W. C., 183, 191, 209, 215, 217, 224
Des Lauriers, A. M., 287, 289
Deutsch, J. A., 13, 24
Dewan, E., 182, 224
Dewey, J., 2, 57, 62, 69, 101, 103, 117, 118, 128, 131
Dodge, M., 67
Dollard, J., 38, 53, 71
Douglass, J. W., 233, 242
Dray, W., 20, 24
Dreiser, T., 67
du Bois-Reymond, E. H., 60, 64, 77

Eastman, M., 67
Ebbinghaus, H., 64
Einstein, A., 26, 75
Eisenberg, L., 259, 289
Ekman, P., 20
Emerson, P. E., 252, 257, 258, 259, 260, 290
Erikson, E. H., 49, 72, 84, 85, 88, 91, 92, 94, 96, 97, 111, 112, 115, 130, 131, 143, 144, 149, 156, 159, 160, 168, 171, 180, 250, 285, 289
Estes, W. K., 42, 53
Eysenck, H. J., 49, 53
Exner, S., 194

Fairbairn, W. R. D., 157
Fantz, R. L., 235, 242, 252, 289
Faraday, M., 50
Fechner, G. T., 28, 29, 50, 57, 194
Fender, D. H., 230, 243
Ferenczi, S., 105, 116, 131
Festinger, L., 46, 53, 95
Fingarette, H., 95, 99, 131
Fisher, A. L., 83, 99, 131
Fisher, C., 191, 224
Fiss, H., 216, 224
Flavell, J. H., 49, 53, 93, 132, 200, 262, 289
Fleming, A., 47
Flew, A., 98, 132
Ford, C. S., 149, 180
Foulkes, D., 209, 216, 225
Franck, J., 85

Frank, L. K., 249, 289
Freedman, D. B., 233, 243
French, T. M., 220, 225
Frenkel-Brunswik, E., 89, 131
Freud, A., 106, 132
Freud, S., 1, 4, 5, 12, 23, 26, 28, 49, 56–78, 84, 86–88, 94–96, 98, 99, 101, 103–9, 111–14, 116, 118–25, 127–30, 132, 136–46, 148–50, 152, 161, 162, 166–69, 172, 174, 176–80, 182, 187–95, 197, 198, 202–4, 206, 209, 210, 225, 250
Fromm, E., 220, 225
Fromm-Reichmann, F., 286, 288, 289

Galanter, E. H., 200, 226
Galileo, G., 14
Garcia, P., 248, 290
Gardiner, P., 20, 24
Garrison, K. C., 251, 289
Gergen, K., 96, 132
Gibson, J. J., 143, 180
Gill, M. M., 70, 72, 78, 97, 132
Goldman, E., 67
Goldstein, K., 87, 110, 111, 117, 132
Grant, J. D., 89, 92, 94, 99, 114, 134
Grant, M. Q., 89, 92, 94, 99, 114, 134
Gray, P. H., 252, 253, 289
Green, H., 288, 289
Greenacre, P., 154, 180
Greenberg, R., 186, 226
Grinker, R. R., 217, 225
Grohmann, J., 232, 243
Groos, 109
Gulevitch, G. D., 215, 217, 225, 227
Guntrip, H., 157, 180

Haley, J., 288
Hall, C. S., 39, 53
Hall, G. S., 69
Hallman, E., 60
Halverson, H. M., 250, 289
Hanson, N. R., 35, 45, 54
Hardy, K. R., 180
Harlow, H. F., 41, 46, 54, 204, 225, 235, 243, 250, 263, 289
Hartline, H. A., 194, 226
Hartmann, H., 85, 88, 97, 107, 108, 132
Hartshorne, H., 96, 132
Harvey, O. J., 89, 99, 132
Havighurst, R. J., 89, 92, 96, 134
Healy, W., 66
Hebb, D. O., 2, 23, 31, 41, 54, 84, 87, 100, 132
Hegel, G. W. F., 89, 121
Held, R., 232, 243
Helmholtz, H. L. F., 60, 61, 64, 191
Hendrick, I., 97, 109, 110, 111, 133

Herbart, J. F., 57, 70
Hering, E., 57
Herodotus, 14
Hess, E. H., 197, 225
Higgins, J. W., 83
Hilgard, E. R., 84, 132
Hoddinott, B. A., 267, 289
Hoffmann, F. J., 59, 78
Holt, E. B., 57, 99, 133
Holt, R. R., 58, 64, 78, 161, 180, 190, 192, 193, 194, 197, 202, 225
Home, H. J., 99, 133
Hook, S., 20, 24
Hubel, D. H., 243
Hull, C. L., 13, 15, 29, 30, 36, 46, 50, 54, 71
Hunt, D. E., 89, 99, 132
Hunter, I., 209, 218, 220, 222, 224

Inhelder, B., 93, 134, 241, 243
Isaacs, K. S., 89, 92, 95, 99, 133

Jackson, D. D., 288
Jacobson, E., 177, 181
James, W., 2, 3, 29, 57, 62, 63, 66, 69, 73
Janet, P., 57
Jaspers, K., 83, 133
Jesus, 75
Jones, M. H., 242
Jung, C. G., 65, 87, 133

Kanner, L., 248, 259, 260, 261, 276, 284, 289
Kant, I., 75
Kaplan, A., 20, 24, 35, 54
Kaufman, I. C., 176, 180, 256, 257, 289
Keller, H., 286
Kenney, A., 165, 181
Kessen, W., 109, 133
Kingston, A. J., 251, 289
Klein, G. S., 58, 64, 70, 72, 78, 91, 136–81, 183, 195, 200, 206, 225, 240, 250
Koch, S., 13, 24, 34–36, 39, 41, 54, 73, 74, 78, 153, 181
Kohlberg, L., 89, 92, 93, 95, 99, 133
Koyre, A. A., 18, 24
Krasner, L., 48, 54
Kris, E., 85, 108, 133, 223
Kubie, L. S., 159, 181
Kuffler, S. W., 235, 243
Kuhn, T. S., 2, 17, 26, 27, 34, 35, 44, 45, 54
Külpe, O., 68, 69
Kuo, Z. Y., 71, 104, 133

Laing, R. D., 149, 181
Lampee, R., 246

Landreth, C., 249, 251, 289
Lane, R. W., 209, 218, 220, 222, 224
Laplace, P. S. de., 52
Lashley, K. S., 2, 200, 226
Laver, J., 246
Lavoisier, 27
Lazarus, R. S., 217, 226
Lecky, P., 95, 96, 114–16, 133
Leonardo da Vinci, 75, 120, 121
Levinson, D., 89, 131
Levy-Bruehl, L., 241, 243
Lewin, K., 29, 71
Lindzey, G., 39, 53, 151, 152, 181
Lipps, T., 57
Lipton, R. C., 268, 290
Loevinger, J., 21, 22, 58, 64, 70, 72, 78, 83–135, 183, 196, 246, 249, 285
Loeward, H. W., 83, 88, 95, 97, 107, 109, 112, 113, 118, 122, 126, 127, 131, 133
Loewenstein, R., 85
London, J., 67
Lorenz, K. Z., 197, 198, 226, 234, 243, 257, 264, 289
Lovaas, O. I., 266, 288, 289
Lundin, R., 48, 54
Luria, A. R., 287, 289

McDougall, W., 69, 71, 89, 98, 100, 101, 104, 133
McGaugh, J. L., 25, 182, 186, 226
McGinty, D. J., 186, 226
McKenna, J., 252, 288
Magellan, 75
Mahler, M., 248, 289
Marx, K., 119
Maslow, A. H., 72, 78, 92, 96, 117, 133
May, M. A., 96, 132
Mead, G. H., 95, 97, 98, 101–3, 106, 128, 129, 133
Meehl, P., 20
Mejia, B., 266, 290
Menta, M., 246, 276, 278
Merleau-Ponty, M., 88, 95, 98, 114, 133, 156, 181
Messer, A., 67
Meyer, A., 87
Meynert, T., 57, 194
Michelangelo, 120
Mill, J. S., 83, 127, 128, 134
Miller, D., 266, 290
Miller, G. A., 200, 226
Miller, N. E., 31, 38, 41, 54, 71
Miller, W. H., 194, 226
Mills, C. W., 49, 54
Molho, A., 246, 261, 289
Monroe, L. J., 216, 224
Morrison, D., 246, 266, 290

Moses, 75
Mowrer, O. H., 71
Müller, G. E., 64
Murphy, G., 69
Murray, H. A., 164, 181
Muzio, J. N., 183, 226

Newton, I., 11, 12, 26, 27, 30, 51, 75
Nietzsche, F., 57, 119
Nissen, H. W., 232, 243
Norris, F., 67
Nunberg, H., 94, 134

Osgood, C., 31, 54

Pasteur, L., 50, 75
Paterson, D. G., 96, 134
Pavlov, I. P., 104
Pearlman, C., 186, 226
Peck, R. F., 89, 92, 96
Pfaffman, C., 143, 181
Piaget, J., 3, 46, 71, 85, 93, 95, 102, 116,
    129, 134, 183, 200, 202, 203, 208, 226,
    228-31, 233, 234, 238-40, 249, 253,
    262, 285, 290
Pivik, T., 217, 227
Plato, 97, 106
Polanyi, M., 2, 84, 87, 112, 134
Preyer, 109
Pribram, K. H., 197, 200, 226
Prince, M., 57, 238, 243
Provence, S., 268, 290

Rapaport, D., 22, 24, 72, 73, 78, 88, 97,
    104, 107-9, 134, 136, 138, 162, 173,
    174, 181, 237, 243, 244
Ratliff, F., 194, 226
Rechtschaffen, A., 209, 222, 225, 226
Reich, W., 239, 244
Richter, C. P., 41, 54
Ricoeur, P., 95, 99, 107, 109, 112, 113, 118,
    119, 122, 131, 134
Riesen, A. H., 232, 244
Rimland, B., 248, 259, 260, 284, 290
Roe, A., 75, 78
Roffwarg, H. P., 183, 184, 185, 226
Rogers, C. R., 49, 92, 99, 111, 117, 134
Roller, D., 34, 55
Roller, D. H., 34, 55
Rose, M., 242
Rosen, J., 288, 290
Rosenblum, L. A., 256, 257, 289
Rubin, T. I., 266, 290
Rubinstein, B. B., 179, 181
Ruttenberg, B. A., 285, 290
Ryle, G., 87, 134

Sanford, R. N., 25, 55, 89, 111, 112, 131,
    134
Saposnek, D. T., 246, 283, 290
Sartre, J. P., 98
Sarvis, M. S., 248, 290
Schachtel, E. G., 89, 134
Schafer, R., 223, 226
Schopenhauer, A., 57
Schopler, E., 287, 290
Schreiner, O., 67
Schroder, H. M., 89, 99, 132
Scott, J. P., 41, 46, 55, 264, 290
Scriven, M., 3, 4, 9-24, 16, 25, 35, 52, 64
Segel, M. M., 154, 181
Semmes, J., 243
Shaffer, H. R., 252, 257-60, 290
Shaikun, G., 222, 226
Shakow, D., 3, 5, 26, 28, 56-79, 228
Shand, A. F., 101
Shapiro, A., 182, 226
Sidis, B., 57
Sinclair, U., 67
Singer, M. T., 261, 290
Skinner, B. F., 3, 29, 42, 47, 48, 50, 55
Smith, M. B., 83, 118, 134
Smith, R. G., 136, 180
Snyder, F., 184, 185, 226
Socrates, 75, 97
Solomon, R. L., 42, 55
Sperry, R. W., 232, 233, 244
Spiegle, J. P., 217, 225
Spinoza, B. de, 121
Spitz, R. A., 252, 290
Steele, B., 242
Steffens, L., 67
Stern, W., 87
Strawson, P. F., 87, 134
Sullivan, A., 286, 287
Sullivan, C., 89, 92, 94, 99, 134
Sullivan, H. S., 88-92, 94, 95, 97, 99, 103,
    113, 114, 116, 127-29, 134

Tanner, J. M., 93, 134
Tansley, A. G., 68, 79
Tarbell, I., 67
Terman, L. M., 69
Thompson, W. R., 41, 54
Thorndike, E. L., 57, 71, 96, 104, 135
Thorpe, W. H., 233, 234, 244
Thurstone, L. L., 69
Tinbergen, N., 197, 226, 234, 244
Titchner, E. B., 29, 36, 61, 94
Tolman, E. C., 2, 25, 55, 71, 98, 104, 135
Tolman, R. C., 75, 79
Tomkins, S. S., 92, 135, 196, 202, 226, 252,
    290
Toulmin, S., 2

Trosman, H., 222, 226
Tufts, J. H., 104, 117, 118, 131
Twitchell, T. E., 231, 244

Vergote, 88, 135
Vogel, G., 216, 222, 225, 226
von Hartmann, 57
von Holst, 232, 244

Waelder, R., 86, 135, 138, 181
Walters, R. H., 41, 53
Wann, T., 9, 24
Watson, J. B., 3, 28, 30, 35, 36, 69, 71, 98, 104
Watt, J., 50
Weakland, J., 288
Weaver, W., 73, 79
Weiss, P. A., 232, 233, 244
Werner, H., 3, 93, 129, 135, 241, 242, 244

Wheeler, W. M., 68, 79
White, B. L., 230, 245
White, R. W., 93, 107, 109–12, 117, 135, 151, 181, 196, 227
Wiesel, T. M., 243
Witmer, L., 66, 286, 290
Wolff, P. H., 33, 55, 71, 183, 228–45, 246, 249, 264, 290, 291
Wolpert, E. A., 209, 224
Woodworth, R. J., 57, 66, 69, 71, 79, 104
Wright, B. A., 267, 289
Wundt, W., 28, 29, 30, 50, 64, 66
Wynne, L., 261, 290

Yarrow, L. J., 268, 291

Zarcone, V., 217, 227
Zaslow, R. W., 246–91
Zimmerman, R., 235, 243

INDEX OF SUBJECTS

Affect (see also Emotion)
  in autism, 251–57
  in motivation, 194–205
  in Piaget's theory, 238–40
  in psychoanalytic theory, 64, 65
Aggression, 254, 256
  as a drive, 38, 39
Anxiety, 10, 31
  as meaninglessness, 95
  in Sullivan's theory, 90, 113–14
Attachment, 249–59
The authoritarian personality, 92
Autism, 246–88
  cases of, 276, 283
  description of, 248, 249
  development of, 259, 262
  syndrome of, 262–65
  theories of, 284–86
  treatment of, 268–76

Behaviorism, 2, 3, 9, 12, 13, 25–55, 62, 65, 84
  behavior therapy, 17–18
Bentham (J. S. Mill), 83
Between man and man (Buber), 136
Beyond the pleasure principle (Freud), 128, 130

Cathexis, 98, 99, 107–9, 137–38, 157, 191–95
Civilization and its discontents (Freud), 106
Clinical method, 14, 15, 64
Computer models, 22, 23, 217–23
Control, in psychological research, 36–38, 50, 64, 65

Development
  of autism, 259–62
  dialectics of, 58, 89, 91
  of dreaming, 183–84
  of ego or self, 83–135
  of human attachment, 249–59
  sensorimotor and cognitive, 228–42
  of sexuality, 147–49
Discovery, in psychological research, 44–49
Displacement, 171–73
Dream deprivation, 215–17
Dreaming, 182–227
  developmental function, 183–84
  evolutionary function, 184
  Freud's theory, 187–91
  information processing model of, 23, 217–23
  psychological function, 214–23

Dreaming (cont.)
  and REM sleep, 183, 185–87
  symbolism in, 209–14, 220–21

Ego
  definition of, 84–86
  development, 83–135
  history of concept, 83–86
  and purpose, 98–100
  social aspect, 97–98, 101–3
  as structure, 94–97
  typologies of, 91–93
Ego development
  abstract models of, 93–94
  Ausubel's views, 116–17
  Baldwin's views, 100
  criticism of theories, 21–22
  Erikson's views, 91, 111–12
  Freud's views, 103–7
  Lecky's views, 114–16
  Loewald's views, 122–27
  McDougall's views, 100–101
  Mead's views, 101–3
  Merleau-Ponty's views, 114
  Motivation in, 104–5, 107–9, 117–18
  Ricoeur's views, 118–22
  Sullivan's views, 89–91, 113–14
The ego and the id (Freud), 105, 121
"Ego Psychology" (Hartmann, et al), 29, 107–9
Emotion, 195–96, 202–5, 238–40
Equilibration, 85, 231–32
Ethics (Dewey), 103–4
Ethology, 29, 197, 234–35
Evolution, theory of, 28–29
Experimental psychology, 28–30, 61, 64, 65, 73

Functional psychology, 26, 28, 29, 30, 34, 57, 62, 63, 65, 94

Generalization, 32–34, 38–39, 41
Gestalt psychology, 29, 32

Helmholtz program, 60–66, 76
Holism, 87–88

Identification, 106–7, 111–13, 125, 155–56, 177
Imprinting, 235–37, 252–53, 264–65
Infantile sexuality, 139–41, 168–69
Information processing model, 23, 207–8, 217–23
Inhibitions, symptoms and anxiety (Freud), 106
Instinct, 71, 100–101, 163, 234–36
Intelligence, 96, 228–42

Interpretation, 119–20
The interpretation of dreams (Freud) 85, 119, 128, 176, 182, 187, 191, 192, 197
Introspection, 9, 12, 15, 16, 24, 61–63, 68, 69

Logical positivism, 34–36

Macro-micro (molar-molecular) distinction, 10, 11
Mastery, 104–11, 126
Mind-body problem, 87
Motivation
  development of, 198–205
  drive discharge theory, 104–5, 138–39, 160–68, 170, 173–77, 192–95
  in ego development, 104–5, 107–9
  Freud's view re dreaming, 191–95
  Hull's theory of, 38–39, 71
  pacers, 117–18
  in Piaget's theory, 234–40
  in psychoanalytic theory, 22, 57, 58, 64, 70, 71, 98, 99, 107–9, 138–39, 160–68, 170, 173–77, 191–209
  role of emotion, 195–96, 202–5
  sexual, 152–60

On narcissism (Freud), 120
Negativism, 262–67
Neurophysiological psychology, 9, 10, 23
Neurophysiology in Freud's theory, 194–95
Neurosis, 38, 39, 124, 205–6
Newtonian theory, 11–14, 19, 20, 27, 51, 65

Oedipus complex, 116–17, 119–24, 151–52, 205
Operational definition, 20, 31, 34, 35, 38–40

Paradigm, 9, 17, 23, 26–30, 45–47
Phenomenological psychology, 9
Physics, 11–12, 14
Physiology, 60, 61, 65
Pleasure, 140–44
Prediction (in psychological research), 11, 12, 36–38, 51, 52
Primary circular reaction, 229
Project for a scientific psychology (Freud), 63, 77, 119, 192, 197
Proof, in psychological research, 44–47
Psychic energy, 22, 98, 99, 156, 192–95
Psychoanalysis, 1, 4, 9, 15
  method, 64–69
  as a model, 28–29
  relation to psychology, 56–78
  theory of ego development, 103–13

Psychoanalysis (*cont.*)
  theory of sexuality, 136–181
  training in, 72, 73
Psychotherapy, 10, 14
  and drug therapy, 10
  interpretation in, 119–21
  Lecky's technique, 115–16
  psychoanalytic, 64–69
  and rage reduction therapy, 273–76,
    286–88
  as a research method, 15–16
Punishment, 42, 43
Purpose
  in ego development, 98–100

Rage reduction, 247, 268–76
Regression in the service of the ego, 108,
    223
REM sleep, 47, 183, 185–87, 215–17
Repression, 86, 88, 124
Resistance, 68, 69, 88, 268–76

Schema, 145–47, 175–77, 201–9
Scientific method, 2, 4, 17, 26, 27
Self (see Ego)
Self-actualization, 110–11

Self-consistency, 94–96, 114–16
Self-system, 89–90
Sensorimotor theory, 228–42
Separation, 256–57
Sexuality
  conflict, 149–52, 169–70
  development of, 147–49
  Freud's theories, 136–81
  and motivation, 152–68, 170, 173–77
  role of schema, 145–47
Smile, in human attachment, 252–54
S-R theory, 18, 31–34, 195
The structure of scientific revolutions
    (Kuhn), 26
Sublimation, 171–73

Three essays on the theory of sexuality
    (Freud), 64
Transference, 51, 125–26

Unconscious
  concept of, 70, 85–86, 96–97
  in psychoanalytic theory, 57, 58, 70, 85

Wish fulfillment, 188–89
Würzburg school, 68